TOWARDS UNDERSTANDING THE QUR'ĀN

Towards Understanding the Qur'ān

Vol. X

SŪRAHS 38 – 46

English version of

Tafhīm al-Qur'ān

SAYYID ABUL A'LĀ MAWDŪDĪ

Translated and edited by
Zafar Ishaq Ansari

The Islamic Foundation

Towards Understanding the Qur'ān, Vol. X, SŪRAHS 38–46,
English version of *Tafhīm al-Qur'ān*

Published by
THE ISLAMIC FOUNDATION,
Markfield Conference Centre,
Ratby Lane, Markfield,
Leicester LE67 9SY, United Kingdom
E-mail: publications@islamic-foundation.com
Website: www.islamic-foundation.com

Quran House, PO Box 30611, Nairobi, Kenya

PMB 3193, Kano, Nigeria

Distributed by
KUBE PUBLISHING LTD.
Tel: +44(0)1530 249230, Fax: +44(0)1530 249656
E-mail: info@kubepublishing.com

Translated and edited by Zafar Ishaq Ansari

British Library Cataloguing in Publication Data is available from the British Library.

ISBN 978-0-86037-538-8 *casebound*
ISBN 978-0-86037-533-3 *paperback*

Typeset by: N.A. Qaddoura

Printed by: IMAK Ofset, Turkey

بسم الله الرحمن الرحيم

Contents

Transliteration Table vi

Editor's Preface – Zafar Ishaq Ansari viii

Sūrah 38: Ṣād (Madīnan Period)
Introduction 1
Text and Explanatory Notes 7

Sūrah 39: Al-Zumar (Makkan Period)
Introduction 49
Text and Explanatory Notes 51

Sūrah 40: Al-Mu'min (Makkan Period)
Introduction 91
Text and Explanatory Notes 95

Sūrah 41: Ḥā Mīm Al-Sajdah (Makkan Period)
Introduction 145
Text and Explanatory Notes 152

Sūrah 42: Al-Shūrā (Makkan Period)
Introduction 193
Text and Explanatory Notes 199

Sūrah 43: Al-Zukhruf (Makkan Period)
Introduction 245
Text and Explanatory Notes 249

Sūrah 44: Al-Dukhān (Makkan Period)
Introduction 287
Text and Explanatory Notes 292

Sūrah 45: Al-Jāthiyah (Makkan Period)
Introduction 311
Text and Explanatory Notes 315

Sūrah 46: Al-Aḥqāf (Makkan Period)
Introduction 333
Text and Explanatory Notes 338

Glossary of Terms 361
Biographical Notes 369
Bibliography 379
Subject Index 383
Name Index 393

Transliteration Table

Arabic Consonants

Initial, unexpressed medial and final: ء ʾ

ا	a	د	d	ض	ḍ	ك	k
ب	b	ذ	dh	ط	ṭ	ل	l
ت	t	ر	r	ظ	ẓ	م	m
ث	th	ز	z	ع	ʿ	ن	n
ج	j	س	s	غ	gh	هـ	h
ح	ḥ	ش	sh	ف	f	و	w
خ	kh	ص	ṣ	ق	q	ي	y

Vowels, diphthongs, etc.

Short:	ـَ	a	ـِ	i	ـُ	u
Long:	ـَا	ā	ـِي	ī	ـُو	ū
Diphthongs:			ـَوْ	aw		
			ـَيْ	ay		

Editor's Preface

The tenth volume of *Towards Understanding the Qur'ān*, comprising *sūrahs* 38-46 with their explanatory notes, is being sent to the press. To God are due both praise and thanks for enabling us to accomplish whatever we have been able to. From Him alone we seek succour to continue this work and Him alone we beseech to accept our effort as a contribution to a better understanding of His Book.

The present volume, as volumes III through IX, has been prepared with the able assistance of Dr. A.R. Kidwai. He translated into English *Tafhīm al-Qur'ān*'s explanatory notes to the *sūrahs* of which this volume is comprised. After a process of careful editing, that served as the basis out of which the explanatory notes of the present volume were given their final shape. While Dr. Kidwai's assistance is gratefully acknowledged, the responsibility for the present text, especially of its inadequacies, rests solely with the present writer. As for the English rendering of the text of the *sūrahs*, that is entirely mine.

In this volume, as in the previous ones, we have attempted to provide as adequate documentation as we possibly could. In documenting the *Ḥadīth* we have followed A.J. Wensinck's system in his *Concordance*. However, instead of referring to the number of the *Bābs* of traditions, as he did, we have mentioned the actual titles of the *Kitābs* and *Bābs* of those traditions. It may also be pointed out that, while referring to explanatory notes from various *Tafsīr* works, we have mentioned the relevant *sūrahs* and their verses rather than to the volumes and pages of those *tafsīrs*. This was done in view of the fact that, as in the case of *Ḥadīth* works, there exist numerous editions of *tafsīrs*, both old and new. Hence, had we referred to the page number of any specific edition of a *tafsīr*, it would possibly have been extremely difficult for our readers to check the references, because it is not certain that they would have access to the same edition to which we referred. Hopefully our method of referencing will facilitate for our readers the location of the cited materials. As for the Bible, all quotations are from its *Revised Standard Edition*.

In finalising the text, I have greatly benefitted from the excellent editorial suggestions of Dr. Susanne Thackray which, I am sure, have appreciably enhanced its readability. Mr. Naiem Qaddoura of The Islamic Foundation, Leicester, did a fine job of setting the English and Arabic material. Likewise, Dr. M. Manazir Ahsan of the Foundation merits ample thanks. His occasional reminders did not permit me to remain indolent for long. Professor Khurshid Ahmad, my very dear and lifelong friend, remains, as ever, a pillar of strength and an abiding source of inspiration.

The assistance and encouragement I received from these friends does not detract from the fact that my colleagues at the International Islamic University, Islamabad, assisted me in a variety of ways. As regards the present volume, Mr. Muhammad Islam of Islamic Research Institute worked extremely hard in ways just too many to be described. He assiduously culled out the information that has gone into Glossary of Terms and Biographical Notes. He remained occupied for months in extensive research, careful editing, painstaking identification and checking of relevant material and references, and myriad other sundry tasks. To him I am immensely beholden. I am also deeply thankful to Mr. Amjad Mahmood who, as ever before, tirelessly typed the text, time after time. My Personal Secretary, Mr. Muhammad Saleem, has also been constantly available for whatever assistance I needed.

Over the years my sons and sons-in-law, my daughters and daughters-in-law, and the steadily growing army of my grandchildren have been the sunshine of my life. I have no words to thank God enough for this benevolent provision to keep me happy and cheerful in the twilight of my life.

To all those mentioned above, and to many others who assisted, encouraged and inspired me in one way or another, I record my profound sense of gratitude. May Allah bless them all.

Islamabad **Zafar Ishaq Ansari**
Rabi' al-Awwal 1430 H
March 2013

N.B. ▸ *refers to the continuation of the paragraph adopted by Mawdūdī in the Urdu translation.*

Sūrah 38

Ṣād

(Makkan Period)

Title

The opening word *Ṣād* was made the *sūrah*'s title.

Period of Revelation

As we shall see later, according to some traditions this *sūrah* was revealed at the same time the Prophet (peace be on him) embarked on the public preaching of Islam in Makkah, an event which greatly unnerved the unbelieving Quraysh chiefs. (Ibn Sa'd, *al-Ṭabaqāt al-Kubrā, Dhikr Mamshā Quraysh ilā Abī Ṭālib fī Amrihi Ṣallā Allāh 'alayhi wa Sallam.*) Going by these traditions, the *sūrah* would have been revealed in the fourth year of the Prophet's mission.

There are, however, also other traditions which suggest that the *sūrah* was revealed after 'Umar's acceptance of Islam. (See Zamakhsharī, *al-Kashshāf*, comments on *Sūrah Ṣād* 38: 5; Rāzī, *al-Tafsīr al-Kabīr*, comments on *Sūrah Ṣād* 38: 5.) This, as we know, took place after the Muslims' migration to Abyssinia. (Ibn Sa'd, *al-Ṭabaqāt al-Kubrā, Dhikr Hijrat man Hājara min Aṣḥāb Rasūl Allāh… ilā Arḍ al-Ḥabashah; Islām 'Umar Raḥimahu Allāh.*) Still other traditions indicate that it was revealed during Abū Ṭālib's last illess. (Ṭabarī, *Tafsīr*, comments on *Sūrah Ṣād* 38: 5.) If this were to be accepted, the revelation of the *sūrah* should be considered to have occurred in the tenth or eleventh year of the Prophet's mission.

Historical Background

Aḥmad ibn Ḥanbal, Nasā'ī, Ṭirmidhī, Ṭabarī, Ibn Abī Shaybah, Ibn Abī Ḥātim and Muḥammad ibn Isḥāq suggest that when Abū Ṭālib fell ill and the Quraysh chiefs thought that he was on the verge of death, they decided to have a word with him about the Prophet (peace be on him). Since Abū Ṭālib was a respected and elderly figure, the Quraysh thought that he was in a better position to settle the dispute between them and the Prophet (peace be on him), his nephew. They were apprehensive lest Abū Ṭālib died before settling this dispute, which might leave them with no other option than to deal roughly with the Prophet (peace be on him). This in fact, would provoke people to taunt these diehard opponents of Islam for causing harm to the Prophet (peace be on him) after his uncle's death whereas during his life time they had remained pacific in deference to his uncle.

A broad consensus, therefore, emerged among the Quraysh chiefs that they should talk the matter over with Abū Ṭālib. As a result, something in the order of 25 Quraysh notables, including Abū Jahl, Abū Sufyān, Umayyah ibn Khalaf, 'Āṣ ibn Wā'il, Aswad ibn al-Muṭṭalib, 'Uqbah ibn Abī Mu'ayṭ, 'Utbah and Shaybah called on Abū Ṭālib. As was their wont, they first complained to Abū Ṭālib about the Prophet (peace be on him). They stressed that they had come to him with a fair proposal: that his nephew [to wit, the Prophet (peace be on him)] should let them practise their faith and that that they would allow him to profess his, providing he did not denounce their idols, nor dissuade people from idolatry. They were ready to draw up a pact with the Prophet (peace be on him) according to these conditions. (Aḥmad ibn Ḥanbal, *Musnad*, narrated by Ibn 'Abbās; Nasā'ī, *Kitāb al-Siyar, Bāb min man Tu'khadh al-Jizyah;* Tirmidhī, *Kitāb Tafsīr al-Qur'ān 'an Rasūl Allāh Ṣallā Allāh 'alayhi wa Sallam, Bāb wa min Sūrah Ṣād;* Ṭabarī, *Tafsīr*, comments on *Sūrah Ṣād* 38: 5; Ibn Abī Shaybah, *al-Muṣannaf, Kitāb al-Maghāzī, Bāb fī Adhā Quraysh li al-Nabī Ṣallā Allāh 'alayhi wa Sallama wa mā Laqiya minhum*; Ibn Abī Ḥātim, *Tafsīr*, comments on *Sūrah Ṣād* 38: 5; 'Abd al-Malik ibn Hishām, *al-Sīrah al-Nabawīyah*, Muṣṭafā al-Saqqā et al. eds., Beirut: Dār Iḥyā' al-Turāth al-'Arabī, n.d., vol. II, pp. 58-9.)

Abū Ṭālib sent for the Prophet (peace be on him) and apprised him of the Quraysh's proposal. To this he replied: 'O uncle! I am propounding before them a word. Were they to accept it, it would exalt them above the Arabs, and the non-Arabs would become their tributaries.' On hearing this they were first puzzled. They did not know how they could spurn this seemingly beneficial 'word.' However, after a while they enquired what this 'word' was that he had to offer. The Prophet (peace be on him) replied: 'There is none worthy of worship other than God.' On hearing this all of them suddenly got up and left, saying that which has been mentioned in the *sūrah*'s outset.[1]

---

1. *Ḥadīth* narrators differ as regards the precise wording used by the Prophet (peace be on him). According to one version, the Prophet (peace be on him) said: 'I want them to rally around a common word. Were they to affirm it the Arabs will become subservient to them and the non-Arabs will pay them *jizyah* (poll-tax).' (Ibn Abī Shaybah, *Musnad, Kitāb al-Maghāzī, Bāb Adhā Quraysh li al-Nabī Ṣallā Allāh 'alayhi wa Sallama wa mā Laqiya minhum.*) Others narrate the following version: 'I call upon them to utter a word. [If they do so] the Arabs will become subservient to them and by dint of it they will become masters of the non-Arabs.' (Ṭabarī, *Tafsīr*, comments on *Sūrah Ṣād* 38: 7.) Another tradition states that it was while addressing the Quraysh chiefs rather than Abū Ṭālib that the Prophet (peace be on him) said to them: 'There is just a word. Were you to give me that word, you will become masters of the Arabs and the non-Arabs too will become subservient to you.' (Ibn Kathīr, *al-Bidāyah wa al-Nihāyah, Bāb Hijrat man Hājara min Aṣḥāb Rasūl Allāh Ṣallā Allāh 'alayhi wa Sallama min Makkah ilā Arḍ al-Ḥabashah, Faṣl fī Wafāt Abī Ṭālib 'Amm Rasūl Allāh Ṣallā Allāh 'alayhi wa Sallam...*) According to still another tradition, the Prophet (peace be on him) said to them. 'How do you consider this proposition? I will suggest a word which, were you to affirm it, will make you masters of the Arabs and the non-Arabs too will become subservient to you'. (Ibn Jarīr, *Tafsīr*, comments on *Sūrah al-An'ām* 6: 108; Ibn Kathīr, *Tafsīr*, comments on *Sūrah al-An'ām* 6: 108, with slight variation.) Leaving aside the minor verbal variations in these traditions, their message is the same. The substance of what the Prophet (peace be on him) had pointedly asked them was essentially the following: 'What is better for you, the statement presented by me, one whose acceptance will enable you to gain ascendancy over the whole of Arabia and the rest of the world, or that which you are proffering, claiming it to be a fair proposition? Is your interest better served by your embracing my call or by letting you remain as you are while I devote myself to worshipping God?'

In his *al-Ṭabaqāt*, Ibn Sa'd narrates the above account but claims that it did not take place when Abū Ṭālib lay on his death-bed. Rather, he believes that the event took place when the Prophet (peace be on him) had embarked on public preaching and the news had begun to spread around Makkah that people were steadily joining his fold. It was then that several Quraysh chiefs successively called upon Abū Ṭālib, urging him to stop his nephew from preaching Islam. Ibn Sa'd believes that the above account reflects what transpired when one of these delegations met Abū Ṭālib. (Ibn Sa'd, *al-Ṭabaqāt al-Kubrā, Dhikr Mamshā Quraysh ilā Abī Ṭālib fī Amrihi Ṣallā Allāh 'alayhi wa Sallam.*)

Similarly, Zamakhsharī, Rāzī, Nīsāpūrī and other Qur'ān commentators also disagree with the version that the event took place when Abū Ṭālib was on the verge of death. They are, instead, of the opinion that the Quraysh delegation visited Abū Ṭālib after 'Umar's acceptance of Islam. In other words, it was 'Umar's conversion to Islam that caused them to panic. (Zamakhsharī, *al-Kashshāf*, comments on *Sūrah Ṣād* 38: 5; Rāzī, *al-Tafsīr al-Kabīr*, comments on *Sūrah Ṣād* 38: 5; Nīsāpūrī, *Tafsīr*, comments on *Sūrah Ṣād* 38: 5.) This, however, is not corroborated by any primary sources. Nor have these scholars referred to any source in support of their contention. However, it seems to make sense that this event took place as a sequel to 'Umar's conversion to Islam. The Quraysh chiefs were undoubtedly perturbed by the spread of the Prophet's mission. Here was someone, indeed one from their own ranks, who was widely acclaimed for his unblemished character and conduct, who was now engaged in the dissemination of Islam. Moreover, he was supported by Abū Bakr, known in and around Makkah for his utter uprightness, honesty and intelligence. When they saw 'Umar joining the Prophet's camp, they were all the more shaken. This because 'Umar was known to be a man of exceptional courage and determination. Therefore, when he accepted Islam, all alarm bells began to ring.

Subject Matter and Theme

The *sūrah* opens with comments on the meeting mentioned above. Referring to the deliberations in this meeting, God emphatically suggests that what had led the unbelievers to spurn Islam's message was not that it was in any way faulty. Instead, their rejection stemmed from their overweening arrogance, their entrenched spite, and their blind adherence to the ways of their forefathers. They simply preferred to cling to their ancestors' false beliefs which they had inherited from the past. As the Prophet (peace be on him) exposed the falsity of their beliefs, they were hugely uncomfortable about the truth being preached to them. They, thus, felt prompted to dismiss the Prophet (peace be on him) as an impostor. Rather than embrace his message, which required affirmation of monotheism and the Hereafter, they made these doctrines butts of their mockery and ridicule. Both in the *sūrah*'s opening and concluding parts, God clearly warns the unbelievers that notwithstanding their mockery of the Prophet (peace be on him), he would soon prevail. Indeed, before long they would find themselves subdued and vanquished in Makkah itself despite their fierce opposition and resistance.

This is followed by narratives of quite a few of God's Messengers. The stories of the Prophets David and Solomon (peace be on them) are especially recounted. The point brought home is that Divine justice is devoid of any undue bias, whether positive or negative. God loves those who do not insist on their error, who on realising their lapse are quite ready to repent and to live in the world with full consciousness of their accountability to Him.

This is followed by an account of the ultimate end that awaits both God's obedient and rebellious servants in the Hereafter. The unbelievers' attention is especially drawn to the following two points: (i) Their leaders, whom they follow along the path of error, will be the first to find themselves in Hell. Thereafter, they and their leaders will engage in mutual reproach regarding who was responsible for their sordid plight. (ii) To the utter surprise of the unbelievers, who dismiss believers with contempt, they will not find any trace of the believers in Hell while they themselves will be piteously groaning in it.

The story of Adam and Satan is related towards the end of the *sūrah*. The purpose is to impress upon the Quraysh unbelievers that the arrogance which had prompted them to reject the message of the Prophet (peace be on him) was no different from the arrogance of Iblīs that had prompted him not to prostrate himself before Adam. Essentially, he was jealous of Adam's exalted position and disobeyed God, as a result of which he stands accursed for ever. The Makkan unbelievers were afflicted with the same kind of spite for the exalted status that had been bestowed upon the Prophet Muḥammad (peace be on him). The unbelievers are not willing to obey him, though it is God Who appointed him His Messenger. They were thus bound to meet the same fate that befell Iblīs.

In the name of Allah, the Most Merciful, the Most Compassionate

(1) *Ṣād*[1], and by the Qur'ān full of exhortation![2] (2) Nay, but the unbelievers are steeped in arrogance and stubborn defiance.[3] (3) How many a nation did We destroy before them! (When they approached their doom) they cried out (for deliverance), but the time for deliverance was already past.

بِسْمِ ٱللَّهِ ٱلرَّحْمَٰنِ ٱلرَّحِيمِ

صٓ ۚ وَٱلْقُرْءَانِ ذِى ٱلذِّكْرِ ﴿١﴾ بَلِ
ٱلَّذِينَ كَفَرُوا۟ فِى عِزَّةٍ وَشِقَاقٍ ﴿٢﴾ كَمْ
أَهْلَكْنَا مِن قَبْلِهِم مِّن قَرْنٍ فَنَادَوا۟
وَّلَاتَ حِينَ مَنَاصٍ ﴿٣﴾

---

1. Like other abbreviated letters that feature in the Qur'ān, it is hard to ascertain the exact meaning of the letter *Ṣād* that occurs at the *sūrah*'s beginning. Nonetheless, the opinion of Ibn 'Abbās and Ḍaḥḥāk seems plausible that *Ṣād* here amounts to affirming the Prophet's truthfulness. (Baghawī, *Ma'ālim al-Tanzīl*, comments on *Sūrah Ṣād* 38: 1; see also Ibn 'Abbās, *Tanwīr al-Miqyās min Tafsīr Ibn 'Abbās*, comments on *Sūrah Ṣād* 38: 1.) Thus, ص here symbolises the following: Muḥammad is truthful in his statement or Muḥammad spoke the truth.

2. The Qur'ān has been described as *dhī al-Dhikr*. This admits the following two meanings: (i) That the Qur'ān is noble and majestic; and (ii) that the Qur'ān is full of exhortation insofar as it reminds man of the forgotten truth, and rouses him to wake from his heedlessness.

3. Were we to accept the meaning of *Ṣād* as given by Ibn 'Abbās and Daḥḥāk, it would mean swearing by the glorious Qur'ān, or the Qur'ān overflowing with judicious exhortation and good counsel, that it bears testimony that whatever the Prophet (peace be on him) was teaching was true. As for those who are adamant in rejecting it, they are 'steeped in arrogance and stubborn defiance'.

(4) They wondered that a warner had come to them from among themselves,[4] and the deniers of the Truth said: 'This is a sorcerer,[5] and a big liar. ▶	وَعَجِبُوٓاْ أَن جَآءَهُم مُّنذِرٌ مِّنْهُمْ وَقَالَ ٱلْكَـٰفِرُونَ هَـٰذَا سَـٰحِرٌ كَذَّابٌ ۝٤

On the other hand, should the letter *Ṣād* be taken as one of those abbreviated letters whose meaning cannot be determined, the opening statement would mean the following: The unbelievers do not reject Islam because it is marred by any flaw or because the Prophet Muḥammad (peace be on him) has failed to fully explain it. On the contrary, it is their foolish arrogance and obstinacy that accounts for their unbelief. This is borne out by the Qur'ān itself which, being full of exhortation, has left out nothing that is needed to direct people to the truth.

4. This was the height of the Makkan unbelievers' folly. When a person belonging to their own ethnic group, their nation and their community, one whom they knew perfectly well, was designated by God to warn them and direct them to the truth, they found it quite strange and bizarre. One simply wonders at their way of looking at things. One would think, on the contrary, that it would have been strange and bizarre if some alien belonging to an altogether different species or a total stranger began asking them to affirm his Prophethood. In such a scenario, these people would have been justified in branding this as strange. For how could a non-human serve as a guide to human beings when he has no appreciation of their situation, their emotional predilections and natural dispositions? Likewise, if a stranger suddenly appeared in their midst, how could they judge his veracity, how could they determine whether he was trustworthy or not?

5. The unbelievers branded the Prophet (peace be on him) a sorcerer in the sense that he had cast a spell over people so that they blindly followed him, and did so notwithstanding public criticism and social boycott. These believers were so convinced of the truth of their faith that for its sake they did not flinch from forsaking their near and dear ones, and even leaving their hearths and homes. In this respect, they willingly endured all manner of hardship ranging from loss of business to physical torment and ostracisation. (For further details, see *al-Anbīyā'* 21, n. 5, *Towards Understanding the Qur'ān*, vol. V, pp. 250-2.)

(5) Has he made the gods one single God? This is truly astounding. (6) And the elders among them went forth saying:[6] "Go ahead and be steadfast in adhering to your deities. What is being said[7] is with a design."[8] (7) We have not heard this in the religious community close to our time.[9] This is nothing but a fabrication. ▶

أَجَعَلَ ٱلۡأٓلِهَةَ إِلَٰهٗا وَٰحِدًاۖ إِنَّ هَٰذَا لَشَيۡءٌ
عُجَابٞ ﴿٥﴾ وَٱنطَلَقَ ٱلۡمَلَأُ مِنۡهُمۡ أَنِ
ٱمۡشُواْ وَٱصۡبِرُواْ عَلَىٰٓ ءَالِهَتِكُمۡۖ إِنَّ هَٰذَا
لَشَيۡءٞ يُرَادُ ﴿٦﴾ مَا سَمِعۡنَا بِهَٰذَا فِي ٱلۡمِلَّةِ
ٱلۡأٓخِرَةِ إِنۡ هَٰذَآ إِلَّا ٱخۡتِلَٰقٌ ﴿٧﴾

6. The allusion here is to the Quraysh chiefs who left Abū Ṭālib's assembly on hearing the Prophet's response.

7. Reference is made here to the Prophet's assertion that if the Makkans were to embrace Islam's basic creedal statement, 'There is none worthy of worship other than God', both Arabs and non-Arabs would follow them.

8. The unbelievers were excessively biased against Islam's basic message. Hence they suggested that the message ought not to be taken at its face value. Its true purpose, far from being altruistic, was simply to establish the Prophet's hegemony.

9. The Makkan unbelievers contended that neither their own ancestors, nor the Christians and Jews of Arabia and neighbouring countries, nor the Magians of Persia, Iraq and eastern Arabia ever preached that man should exclusively devote himself to the One True God as the sole Lord of the universe. Indeed, they found it hard to believe that man should confine his devotion to just one God to the exclusion of those that were held dear by the Supreme God. They drew attention to the rampant idolatry and polytheism in their own land: how men and women zealously invoked a host of gods and goddesses, visiting their shrines, making offerings at altars and addressing their prayers to idols. They visited the so-called sacred precincts expecting that they would be granted children and abundant wherewithal for these idols had the power to help them. Given

(8) Has this Exhortation been sent down among us only to him, to the exclusion of all others?' Nay, they are in doubt regarding My Exhortation,[10] and are saying all this because they have not yet had any taste of My chastisement. (9) Do they possess the treasures of your Lord, the Most Mighty, the Great Bestower? (10) Or do they possess the dominion of the heavens and the earth and of all that is in between them? If so, let them ascend the heights of the realm of causation and see![11]

أَءُنزِلَ عَلَيْهِ ٱلذِّكْرُ مِنۢ بَيْنِنَاۚ بَلْ هُمْ فِى
شَكٍّ مِّن ذِكْرِىۖ بَل لَّمَّا يَذُوقُوا۟ عَذَابِ ﴿٨﴾
أَمْ عِندَهُمْ خَزَآئِنُ رَحْمَةِ رَبِّكَ ٱلْعَزِيزِ
ٱلْوَهَّابِ ﴿٩﴾ أَمْ لَهُم مُّلْكُ ٱلسَّمَـٰوَٰتِ
وَٱلْأَرْضِ وَمَا بَيْنَهُمَاۖ فَلْيَرْتَقُوا۟ فِى
ٱلْأَسْبَـٰبِ ﴿١٠﴾

---

this, the Prophet's insistence on uncompromising monotheism sounded as totally outlandish to them. It was beyond them to believe that none of these gods and goddesses had any share in God's Godhead and that He alone was single-handedly the Lord of His entire realm.

10. In other words, God tells the Makkan unbelievers that they were in fact rejecting Him rather than rejecting the Prophet (peace be on him). As far as the Prophet (peace be on him) is concerned, they had never entertained any doubt about his veracity and integrity. It is stressed that the skepticism being expressed by the Makkan unbelievers was on account of the 'Exhortation' that God had revealed. It is only when the Prophet (peace be on him) began to teach the Book embodying Exhortation that they began to cast aspersions on one whose veracity was once held as absolutely beyond every doubt. The same observation was made in *Sūrah al-An'ām* 6: 33. (See *Towards Understanding the Qur'ān*, vol. II, 6: 33, n. 21, pp. 226-7.)

11. This is a rejoinder to the Makkan unbelievers' statement casting doubts about God's Messenger: 'Has this Exhortation been sent down

(11) This is only a small army out of the several armies that will suffer defeat here.[12] (12) Before them the people of Noah, 'Ād, and Pharaoh[13] of the tent-pegs gave the lie (to the Messengers) (13) and so did Thamūd and the people of Lot and the people of Aykah. These were all leagued together. ▶

جُندٌ مَّا هُنَالِكَ مَهْزُومٌ مِّنَ ٱلْأَحْزَابِ ﴿١١﴾
كَذَّبَتْ قَبْلَهُمْ قَوْمُ نُوحٍ وَعَادٌ وَفِرْعَوْنُ ذُو
ٱلْأَوْتَادِ ﴿١٢﴾ وَثَمُودُ وَقَوْمُ لُوطٍ وَأَصْحَٰبُ
لْـَٔيْكَةِ ۚ أُو۟لَٰٓئِكَ ٱلْأَحْزَابُ ﴿١٣﴾

---

among us only to him, to the exclusion of all others?' In response to this God makes it plain that it is for Him and for none else to choose whomsoever He wants to appoint as His Prophet. Others can only make such decisions if they can scale to the heights of God's Throne and thereby determine who should and who should not receive the revelation. This point is made at several places in the Qur'ān in response to the Quraysh unbelievers' query: why was Muḥammad (peace be on him) rather than one from among the noted chiefs of the Quraysh designated as God's Prophet? (See *Banī Isrā'īl* 17: 100 and *al-Zukhruf* 43: 31-2 below.)

12. The word 'here' in the verse refers to Makkah. It is being said that right in Makkah, where Islam's opponents delivered such hostile nonsense, they will be worsted and will eat dust. The time is not far off when they will stand as sorry figures before the man whom they dismissed as too humble for Prophetic office.

13. Pharaoh has been called as one of the 'tent-pegs'. This expression is being used either to denote that Pharaoh's empire was firmly established as though its pegs were deeply rooted into the earth, or to denote that he had a very large army and wherever that army was stationed the area became full of tents secured by pegs. It is also possible that the allusion here is to the fact that Pharaoh also used to punish those who angered him and did so by having pegs hammered into their bodies. Moreover, it is also possible that the pegs might allude to the pyramids that were deeply rooted in the earth, as are pegs.

(14) Each of them gave the lie to Messengers and My decree of chastisement came upon them. (15) They are waiting for nothing except a single Cry, after which there will be no second Cry.[14] (16) They say: 'Our Lord, hasten to us our share (of chastisement) before the Day of Reckoning.'[15]

(17) (O Prophet), bear with patience what they say[16], and call to mind Our servant David,[17] ▶

إِن كُلٌّ إِلَّا كَذَّبَ ٱلرُّسُلَ فَحَقَّ
عِقَابِ ﴿١٤﴾ وَمَا يَنظُرُ هَٰٓؤُلَآءِ إِلَّا صَيْحَةً
وَٰحِدَةً مَّا لَهَا مِن فَوَاقٍ ﴿١٥﴾ وَقَالُوا۟ رَبَّنَا
عَجِّل لَّنَا قِطَّنَا قَبْلَ يَوْمِ ٱلْحِسَابِ ﴿١٦﴾
ٱصْبِرْ عَلَىٰ مَا يَقُولُونَ وَٱذْكُرْ عَبْدَنَا دَاوُۥدَ

14. A single blast will suffice to obliterate them and there will be no need for the second. This might also mean that once God's chastisement suddenly strikes them, there will be no occasion for any further respite, not even the time that is needed for a she-camel's udders to be filled with milk after milk has been drained from them.

15. On the one hand is the graveness of God's punishment as depicted in the preceding verse. On the other hand is the utter folly of those who asked the Prophet (peace be on him) to have their punishment hastened!

16. This alludes to the foolish utterance of the Makkan unbelievers about the Prophet (peace be on him): that he was a magician and a liar; their sarcastic statement that God had none other than Muḥammad to endow with Prophethood, assuring that the Prophet had an axe to grind by calling people to monotheism.

17. This can be translated either as: 'Recall [the story of] Our servant, David,' or 'Call to mind Our servant David.' Taken in the former sense, the point brought home is that there is a lesson for people in this story. Were we, however, to follow the latter meaning, it implies that the recounting of this story will help them persevere. Both aspects are intended in the

who was endowed with great strength[18] and who constantly turned (to Allah). (18) With him We had subjected the mountains that they join him in celebrating Allah's glory, evening and morning, (19) and the birds, too, in their flocks, and turn again and again to ▶

ذَا ٱلۡأَيۡدِۖ إِنَّهُۥٓ أَوَّابٌ ١٧ إِنَّا سَخَّرۡنَا ٱلۡجِبَالَ
مَعَهُۥ يُسَبِّحۡنَ بِٱلۡعَشِيِّ وَٱلۡإِشۡرَاقِ ١٨
وَٱلطَّيۡرَ مَحۡشُورَةٗۖ

narration. Accordingly, the words used here lend themselves to both meanings. (For a detailed account of the Prophet David's story see *al-Baqarah* 2, n. 273, *Towards Understanding the Qur'ān*, vol. I, p. 193; *Banī Isrā'īl* 17, nn. 7 and 63; and *al-Anbiyā'* 21, nn. 70-2, vol. V, pp. 53 and 282-5; *al-Naml* 27, nn. 18-20, vol. VII, pp. 144-5; and *Saba'* 34, nn. 14-16, vol. IX, p. 158).

18. *Dhā al-aydi* is a metaphor of authority. Used with reference to the Prophet David (peace be on him), it stresses his power and authority. Indeed, it might refer to many aspects of his power. One aspect of this was that he had been endowed with exceptional physical prowess, which was demonstrated in the violent encounter between him and Goliath. It might also refer to his military and political might, which enabled him to inflict defeat upon the polytheistic communities of neighbouring countries, and as a result of which a vast Islamic state was established. This statement might also be an allusion to David's moral strength, which lay in his simple ascetic ways notwithstanding his kingship. For David was a devout and God-fearing person and despite his preoccupation with the affairs of a huge state he spent most of his time worshipping God. According to Bukhārī and Muslim, he fasted every alternate day and devoted one-third of the night to Prayer. (Muslim, *Kitāb al-Ṣawm, Bāb al-Nahy 'an Ṣawm al-Dahr...*; Bukhārī, *Kitāb al-Ṣawm, Bāb Ṣawm al-Dahr.*) Bukhārī narrates on the authority of Abū al-Dardā' that whenever the Prophet David (peace be on him) was mentioned, the Prophet (peace be on him) used to remark: 'He was God's most devout servant' (verse 17). (Bukhārī, *Kitāb al-Ta'rīkh al-Kabīr, Bāb al-Alif min Tarājim Baqiyyat Muḥammadīyīn, Bāb Sīn.*)

celebrating Allah's glory.[19] (20) And We strengthened his kingdom and endowed him with wisdom and decisive judgement.[20] (21) Has the story of the litigants reached you – of those who entered his private chambers by climbing over the wall?[21] (22) As they came upon David – and he was frightened of them[22] – they said: 'Be not afraid. We are just two litigants: one of us has committed excess against the other. So judge rightly between us, and be not unjust; and guide us to the Right Way. ▶

كُلٌّ لَّهُۥٓ أَوَّابٌ ﴿١٩﴾ وَشَدَدْنَا مُلْكَهُۥ
وَءَاتَيْنَٰهُ ٱلْحِكْمَةَ وَفَصْلَ ٱلْخِطَابِ ﴿٢٠﴾
۞ وَهَلْ أَتَىٰكَ نَبَؤُا۟ ٱلْخَصْمِ إِذْ تَسَوَّرُوا۟
ٱلْمِحْرَابَ ﴿٢١﴾ إِذْ دَخَلُوا۟ عَلَىٰ دَاوُۥدَ فَفَزِعَ
مِنْهُمْ ۖ قَالُوا۟ لَا تَخَفْ ۖ خَصْمَانِ بَغَىٰ بَعْضُنَا
عَلَىٰ بَعْضٍ فَٱحْكُم بَيْنَنَا بِٱلْحَقِّ وَلَا تُشْطِطْ
وَٱهْدِنَآ إِلَىٰ سَوَآءِ ٱلصِّرَٰطِ ﴿٢٢﴾

---

19. For further details see *al-Anbiyā'* 21, n. 71, *Towards Understanding the Qur'ān*, vol. V, pp. 282-5.

20. David's speech was not marred by ambiguity or equivocation that might cause people to feel confused about what he meant. He was exceptionally articulate so that whenever he spoke about something it became absolutely clear to his audience. He had the ability to bring to the fore all such questions that called for decision and solution. This ability requires an abundance of intelligence, understanding and eloquence.

21. The main objective of mentioning the Prophet David (peace be on him) is to narrate this aspect of his story, which commences here. The narrative is prefaced with an account of his excellent attributes in order to underscore his exalted rank.

22. What frightened David (peace be on him) was that two people suddenly barged into his private apartment despite his being the ruler of the realm. Furthermore, they did so by scaling the wall.

(23) Behold, this is my brother;[23] he has ninety-nine ewes and I have only one ewe. And yet he said: "Give her into my charge," and he got the better of me in argument.'[24] (24) David said: 'He has certainly wronged you in seeking to add your ewe to his ewes;[25] and indeed many who live together commit excesses, one to the other, except those that believe and act righteously; and they are but few.' (While so saying) David realised that it is We Who have put him to test; therefore, he sought the forgiveness of ▶

إِنَّ هَٰذَآ أَخِى لَهُۥ تِسۡعٌ وَتِسۡعُونَ نَعۡجَةً
وَلِىَ نَعۡجَةٌ وَٰحِدَةٌ فَقَالَ أَكۡفِلۡنِيهَا
وَعَزَّنِى فِى ٱلۡخِطَابِ ﴿٢٣﴾ قَالَ لَقَدۡ ظَلَمَكَ
بِسُؤَالِ نَعۡجَتِكَ إِلَىٰ نِعَاجِهِۦۖ وَإِنَّ كَثِيرًا
مِّنَ ٱلۡخُلَطَآءِ لَيَبۡغِى بَعۡضُهُمۡ عَلَىٰ بَعۡضٍ
إِلَّا ٱلَّذِينَ ءَامَنُواْ وَعَمِلُواْ ٱلصَّٰلِحَٰتِ
وَقَلِيلٌ مَّا هُمۡۗ وَظَنَّ دَاوُۥدُ أَنَّمَا فَتَنَّٰهُ فَٱسۡتَغۡفَرَ

---

23. The expression 'my brother' here does not signify a blood relationship; it rather signifies the tie of brotherhood in faith or nationhood.

24. It is noteworthy that the plaintiff did not contend that the person had forcibly appropriated his ewe from him and had mixed it up with his own lot. Rather, he claimed that the other party asked him to hand over that ewe to him and that he had overwhelmed him in argument. While the other party was influential and powerful, the plaintiff was poor and resourceless and thus unable to refuse his demand.

25. This should not give rise to the misunderstanding that the Prophet David (peace be on him) pronounced his judgement after giving hearing to only one party. However, since the defendant did not say a single word to clear his position, this amounted to an admission of guilt. David, therefore, took the other party's version as true.

his Lord, and fell down, bowing and penitently turning (to Him).[26] ▶	رَبَّهُۥ وَخَرَّ رَاكِعًا وَأَنَابَ ۩ ﴿٢٤﴾

26. There is some disagreement as to whether one is required to prostrate oneself when one recites these words. Imām Shāfiʿī does not consider it *wājib* (obligatory) to do so as there is reference here to the repentance of a Prophet. (Rāzī, *al-Tafsīr al-Kabīr*, comments on *Sūrah Ṣād* 38: 24.) However, Imām Abū Ḥanīfah is of the opinion that it is obligatory to prostrate. (Khaṭṭābī, *Maʿālim al-Sunan, Kitāb al-Ṣalāh, Wa min Bāb al-Sujūd fī Ṣād.*) Three reports on this issue are on record on the authority of Ibn ʿAbbās. ʿIkrimah states that Ibn ʿAbbās said: 'It is not one of those Qurʾānic verses whose recitation entails *sajdah* (prostration). However, I saw the Prophet (peace be on him) performing *sajdah* (prostration) while reciting it.' (Bukhārī, *Kitāb al-Jumuʿah, Bāb Sajdat Ṣād;* Abū Dāʾūd, *Kitāb al-Ṣalāh, Bāb al-Sujūd fī Ṣād;* Tirmidhī, *Kitāb al-Jumuʿah ʿan Rasūl Allāh Ṣallā Allāh ʿalayhi wa Sallam; Bāb mā Jāʾa fī al-Sajdah fī Ṣād;* Nasāʾī, *al-Sunan al-Kubrā, Kitāb al-Tafsīr, Bāb Qawlihi Taʿālā: Ulāʾik al-Ladhīna Hadā Allāh...;* and Aḥmad ibn Ḥanbal, *Musnad,* narrated by Ibn ʿAbbās.) Saʿīd ibn Jubayr also quotes Ibn ʿAbbās as follows: 'Insofar as this verse of *Sūrah Ṣād* is concerned, the Prophet (peace be on him) performed *sajdah,* saying: "The Prophet David (peace be on him) prostrated as part of his seeking repentance. We, however, perform *sajdah* while reciting this verse as a token of our gratitude to God that He graciously accepted his [to wit, David's] repentance,"' (Nasāʾī, *Kitāb al-Iftitāḥ, Bāb Sujūd al-Qurʾān, al-Sujūd fī Ṣād.*) Mujāhid recounts that Ibn ʿAbbās said: 'God commands the Prophet (peace be on him): "(O Muḥammad), those are the ones God guided to the Right Way. Follow, then, their way," (*al-Anʿām* 6: 90.) Since David (peace be on him), who was a Prophet, had performed *sajdah,* the Prophet Muḥammad (peace be on him) also performed it in emulation of his example,' (Bukhārī, *Kitāb Tafsīr al-Qurʾān, Sūrah Ṣād.*)

These three traditions have come down from Ibn ʿAbbās. We also have the following tradition from Abū Saʿīd al-Khudrī: 'Once, while delivering a sermon, the Prophet (peace be on him) recited this particular verse, then he got down from the pulpit and performed prostration and all those present did the same. On another occasion when he recited the same verse, those present got ready to perform prostration. On noting this the Prophet (peace be on him) said to them: "This is a Prophet's repentance and I see you ready to perform *sajdah*". After so saying the Prophet (peace be on him) came down from the pulpit and prostrated, and all those present did the same' (Abū Dāʾūd, *Kitāb al-Ṣalāh, Bāb al-Sujūd fī al-Ṣalāh.)*

(25) Thereupon We forgave him his shortcoming and indeed (an exalted position of) nearness awaits him, and an excellent resort.[27] ▶	فَغَفَرْنَا لَهُۥ ذَٰلِكَ ۖ وَإِنَّ لَهُۥ عِندَنَا لَزُلْفَىٰ وَحُسْنَ مَـَٔابٍ ﴿٢٥﴾

True, these traditions do not conclusively establish the obligation for prostration while reciting this verse. They do, however, establish that when the Prophet (peace be on him) recited it, he often prostrated and that prostrating while reciting this verse is therefore better than not doing so. In point of fact the above-cited narration from 'Abd Allāh ibn 'Abbās in Bukhārī turns the scale in favour of its obligatoriness.

Another point that emerges from the verse under discussion is that the Qur'ān speaks of the Prophet David (peace be on him) in the following words: 'He fell down, bowing' (verse 24). All Qur'ānic commentators unanimously take this to mean David's falling into prostration. Accordingly, Imām Abū Ḥanīfah and his disciples are of the opinion that, as regards those Qur'ānic verses whose recitation or hearing requires *sajdah,* that obligation is fulfilled either by prostrating or even by bowing. (Muḥammad 'Alā' al-Dīn al-Ḥaṣkafī, *al-Durr al-Mukhtār, Kitāb al-Ṣalāh, Bāb Sujūd al-Tilāwah.*) In other words, *rukū'* (bowing) may be taken as a substitute for *sajdah,* as is implicit in this verse. Among Shāfi'ī jurists, Imām Khaṭṭābī holds the same opinion. While this opinion is doubtlessly sound and plausible, we do not find any record that the Prophet (peace be on him) or his Companions ever performed *rukū'* in place of *sajdah.* Therefore, one should have recourse to *rukū'* only in situations when there is some constraint in performing *sajdah.* Even Imām Abū Ḥanīfah and his disciples did not prescribe *rukū'* as the normal practice. At most, they regarded this practice as valid but not that one should follow it routinely.

27. One thus learns that the Prophet David (peace be on him) had committed some lapse. However, it was a lapse that resembled in certain respects the case above in which one of the litigants laid claim to the other party's ewes. Therefore, while pronouncing his judgement, it suddenly struck David that he was being tested. His lapse, however, was not of a serious nature. God clarifies that as he fell down bowing and penitently turned to Him he was forgiven. Thus, this lapse did not have any bearing on his exalted status either in this world or the Next.

(26) (We said to him): 'O David, We have appointed you vicegerent on earth. Therefore, rule among people with justice and do not follow (your) desire lest it should lead you astray from Allah's Path. Allah's severe chastisement awaits those who stray away from Allah's Path, for they had forgotten the Day of Reckoning.'[28]

(27) We did not create this heaven and earth and ▶

يَـٰدَاوُۥدُ إِنَّا جَعَلْنَـٰكَ خَلِيفَةً فِى ٱلْأَرْضِ
فَٱحْكُم بَيْنَ ٱلنَّاسِ بِٱلْحَقِّ وَلَا تَتَّبِعِ ٱلْهَوَىٰ
فَيُضِلَّكَ عَن سَبِيلِ ٱللَّهِ ۚ إِنَّ ٱلَّذِينَ يَضِلُّونَ
عَن سَبِيلِ ٱللَّهِ لَهُمْ عَذَابٌ شَدِيدٌۢ بِمَا نَسُوا۟
يَوْمَ ٱلْحِسَابِ ﴿٢٦﴾ وَمَا خَلَقْنَا ٱلسَّمَآءَ
وَٱلْأَرْضَ

---

28. This represents the warning God delivered to the Prophet David (peace be on him) at the time when He accepted the latter's repentance and gave him the glad tiding of granting him the exalted position of vicegerency. This implies that David was prompted by his base self to commit a lapse, that it was linked to an inappropriate exercise of his political authority. It was essentially an act involving the use of his authority in a manner that did not behove a just ruler.

Thus, one is faced here with three questions: (i) What lapse was committed by David? (ii) Why did God make an oblique reference to it, instead of clearly spelling it out? (iii) Why has this lapse been referred to in this particular context?

Those who have studied the Bible know that it squarely charges the Prophet David with committing illicit sex with the wife of Uriah the Hittite and with having her husband deliberately killed in a war so that he could then take his wife in marriage. The Bible even states that the same woman gave birth to the Prophet Solomon (peace be on him). This account appears in detail in *2 Samuel*, 11-12. Being part of the Bible, this account was known to the Jews and Christians. Indeed it was the Bible that circulated this outrageous story. Even to this day, all works on the history of the Israelites and Judaism resonate the same charge against the Prophet David (peace be on him). Just consider the following Biblical passage which is illustrative:

And the Lord sent Nathan to David. He came to him, and said to him, 'There were two men in a certain city, the one rich and the other poor. The rich man had very many flocks and herds; but the poor man had nothing but one little ewe lamb, which he had bought. And he brought it up, and it grew up with him and with his children; it used to eat of his morsel, and drink from his cup, and lie in his bosom, and it was like a daughter to him. Now there came a traveller to the rich man, and he was unwilling to take one of his own flock or herd to prepare for the wayfarer who had come to him, but he took the poor man's lamb, and prepared it for the man who had come to him.' Then David's anger was greatly kindled against the man; and he said to Nathan, 'As the Lord lives, the man who has done this deserves to die; and he shall restore the lamb fourfold, because he did this thing, and because he had no pity.'

Nathan said to David, 'You are the man... You have smitten Uriah the Hittite with the sword, and have taken his wife to be your wife, and have slain him with the sword of the Ammonites.' (2 *Samuel* 12: 1-7 and 9.)

Since the story was commonly known, there was hardly any need to repeat it in detail in the Qur'ān. Even otherwise God does not expatiate on such matters in His Book. Accordingly, only a few oblique references have been made to the story, pointing out what actually happened and how it was altogether misrepresented and distorted by the People of the Book.

The actual event as it emerges from the Qur'ānic account is that the Prophet David (peace be on him) had asked Uriah (or whatever that person's name was) to divorce his wife. Now since this desire had been expressed to a commoner by a great ruler and a person of immense religious stature, the person concerned found it hard to refuse the request though no coercion was exercised to obtain his consent. However, before that person could actually carry out David's wish, two righteous people from the Prophet David's community suddenly barged into his presence and presented a hypothetical case to him for judgement. David considered it to be an actual case of litigation and gave his judgement. However, no sooner had David pronounced his verdict than he realised the parallel between this case and the other case involving him and the person whom he had asked to divorce his wife. David's conscience alerted him that what he had branded as an act of injustice in this case was equally applicable to him with regard to the earlier case. Upon realising this, David fell into prostration, repented profusely to God and refrained from proceeding any further in that particular matter.

Even a little reflection over this Biblical narrative reveals that the Prophet David (peace be on him) had somehow come to know the exceptional qualities of this woman and it occurred to him that such a gifted woman should better be a queen rather than the wife of a petty official. Swayed by this thought, David simply asked Uriah (or whatever his name was) to divorce his wife. In so doing, he did not feel any qualm of conscience because this kind of divorce and remarriage was fairly common among the Israelites at the time. None was offended by such requests for divorce, which would enable another man to remarry the divorced woman. Indeed, close friends often divorced their wives in order to facilitate their friends' marriage to them. However, in making this request the Prophet David (peace be on him) had become oblivious of his high position. For a word from him to this effect could be taken as a command. When the same point was pressed home through the parable of the ewes, he immediately gave up the idea of taking this woman as his wife, for it would have amounted to coercion. This, then, is how the matter ended. However, at a later date, Uriah was slain in battle. The Prophet David (peace be on him) had no part in his death. It was only after Uriah's death that he married his widow. However, all this led perverse Jewish minds to fabricate the heinous charge against David as described above.

This fabrication grew in malice when a group of Jews took to opposing the Prophet Solomon (peace be on him). They circulated this outrageous story, adding further odious material by their own accord to increase its outrageousness. (For further details see *al-Naml* 16, n. 56, *Towards Understanding the Qur'ān*, vol. VII, p. 164.) Prompted by ulterior motives, they fabricated the story that the Prophet David (peace be on him) had caught a glimpse of Uriah's wife from the roof of his palace when she was naked, taking a bath. Thereupon he summoned her and had illicit sex with her, as a result of which she became pregnant. Then, he deputed Uriah to fight against the Ammonites, directing his commander, Joab, to post him to a position that would ultimately cause his death in battle. Once he had been so slain, David then married his widow. It was she who bore him Solomon.

These wicked people interpolated all this scandalous material into their Scripture in order to misguide their coming generations. They are guilty of calumniating against their two greatest benefactors, the Prophets David and Solomon (peace be on them) even though they were next only to the Prophet Moses (peace be on him) in their beneficence to the Israelites.

Some Qur'ānic commentators have almost unquestioningly accepted these reports of Israelite origin. Indeed, they have discounted only that part of the narrative which charges the Prophet David (peace be on him) with indulgence in illicit sex and making Uriah's wife pregnant. Another group of commentators, however, rejects such reports out of hand. They deny the occurrence of any such incident involving the Prophet David (peace be on him) which has any resemblance with the parable of the 99 ewes. While so doing, they offer far-fetched interpretations. Indeed, it is not only that the version of the incident offered by them does not fit in with the Qur'ānic context but is also not corroborated by any authentic source.

Nevertheless, some scholars have duly grasped the true import of the parable as presented in the verse and have taken the right cues from the Qur'ānic account. Consider the following which is illustrative. Both Masrūq and Sa'īd ibn Jubayr cite Ibn 'Abbās as follows: 'The Prophet David (peace be on him) had only asked Uriah to divorce his wife so that he could marry her.' (Ṭabarī, *Tafsīr*, comments on *Sūrah Ṣād* 38: 23.) Zamakhsharī maintains in *al-Kashshāf*: 'It clearly emerges from the Qur'ānic account that the Prophet David (peace be on him) had suggested to Uriah that he divorce his wife for him.' (Zamakhsharī, *al-Kashshāf*, comments on *Sūrah Ṣād* 38: 21.) Abū Bakr al-Jaṣṣās, however, is of the view that this woman was not Uriah's wife, but rather his fiancé. The Prophet David (peace be on him) also proposed to her, something which incurred God's displeasure for he had thus tried to supercede the marriage proposal of a brother in faith at a time when he already had several wives in wedlock. (Jaṣṣās, *Aḥkām al-Qur'ān*, comments on *Sūrah Ṣād* 38: 23.) Some other *Tafsīr* scholars also subscribe to the same view, (See Qurṭubī, *al-Jāmi' li Aḥkām al-Qur'ān*, comments on *Sūrah Ṣād* 38: 24.) Nonetheless, this version is not fully in line with the Qur'ānic narrative. For the plaintiff in the Qur'ānic narrative contends: 'I have only one ewe. And yet he said: "Give her into my charge"' (verse 23.) In his judgement, too, the Prophet David (peace be on him) pressed home the same point: 'He has certainly wronged you in seeking to add your ewe to his ewes,' (verse 24.) This parable is applicable to David and Uriah only if that woman was Uriah's wife. Had the situation only involved a marriage proposal with Uriah's fiancé, the wording would have been different.

While discussing this issue at length in his *Aḥkām al-Qur'ān*, Abū Bakr ibn al-'Arabī writes: 'This is the main point of the story: that the Prophet David (peace be on him) had asked one of his men to divorce his wife for him, and had asked for this seriously... The Qur'ān does not mention that the person concerned parted with his wife, or that David (peace be on him) actually married that woman, or that Solomon was born of her womb. What brought God's censure upon him was that he had asked Uriah to divorce his wife for him... This act may, in itself, be all right as such but it was unbecoming of a Prophet to do so. Hence he was reminded about it and was censured and admonished,' (Abū Bakr ibn al-'Arabī, *Aḥkām al-Qur'ān*, comments on *Sūrah Ṣād* 38: 23, 26.)

This interpretation seems consistent with the context in which the story has been narrated in the Qur'ān. Were we to carefully consider the discourse in connection with which this story has been narrated, it will become absolutely clear that the narration aims to emphasise two points. One, it aims at urging the Prophet Muḥammad (peace be on him) to remain patient in the face of offensive statements people were making about him. He is, therefore, told: '(O Prophet), bear with patience what they say, and call to mind Our servant David…' (verse 17). That is, while the Prophet Muḥammad's detractors charged him with sorcery and lying, David was charged with something even more outrageous – adultery and killing by guile. In view of what befell David the Prophet Muḥammad (peace be on him) is asked to endure with equanimity and patience the storm of false accusations made against him.

The other purpose of this narration was to impress upon the unbelievers that they were strutting around committing all kinds of excesses without the least fear of being called to account. They were told that God, in Whose dominion they were committing those iniquities, spares none from holding them to account, not even those whom He particularly likes and favours with the grant of His proximity. Whenever a slight lapse occurs, God rigorously takes such favoured ones to task. It is in this regard that the Prophet Muḥammad (peace be on him) was asked to narrate the story of David. David was full of excellent qualities, but when he did something that did not befit him, God did not spare admonishing him.

It is also be pertinent at this point to clarify a misgiving. In the parable the plaintiff claimed that while the other party had 99 ewes, he still wanted him to hand over the only one ewe he had. This apparently gives rise to the suspicion that what it hints at is that although David (peace be on him) had 99 wives, he wanted to add another wife to reach the figure 100. However, there is no reason to believe that every little detail of the parable should be literally applicable to David or Uriah the Hittite.

The number mentioned in the parable should be seen in the context of the known linguistic practice of mentioning figures mainly to stress numerousness rather than to indicate an exact number. The plaintiff sought to draw the Prophet David's attention to the fact that he already had quite a few wives yet he wanted to have someone else's wife as well. This insightful observation was made by al-Ḥasan al-Baṣrī, as cited by Nīsāpūrī in his *Tafsīr*, 'David did not have 99 wives. This statement is figurative.' (Nīsāpūrī, *Tafsīr*, comments on *Sūrah Ṣād* 38: 24.) (We have also discussed this issue at length in another work of ours. Those interested in a detailed discussion of the matter should see Sayyid Abul A'lā Mawdūdī, *Tafhīmāt* (Urdu), 17th ed., Lahore: Islamic Publications Ltd., 1995, vol. II, pp. 39-58.)

all that lies between them in vain.[29] That is the fancy of those who denied the Truth. So woe from the Fire to all who deny the Truth. (28) Shall We then treat alike those that believe and act righteously and those that create mischief on earth? Or treat alike the God-fearing and the wicked?[30] ▶

وَمَا بَيْنَهُمَا بَـٰطِلًا ۚ ذَٰلِكَ ظَنُّ ٱلَّذِينَ كَفَرُوا۟ ۚ
فَوَيْلٌ لِّلَّذِينَ كَفَرُوا۟ مِنَ ٱلنَّارِ ﴿٢٧﴾ أَمْ نَجْعَلُ
ٱلَّذِينَ ءَامَنُوا۟ وَعَمِلُوا۟ ٱلصَّـٰلِحَـٰتِ
كَٱلْمُفْسِدِينَ فِى ٱلْأَرْضِ أَمْ نَجْعَلُ
ٱلْمُتَّقِينَ كَٱلْفُجَّارِ ﴿٢٨﴾

---

29. God did not create the heavens and the earth in sport so that His creation would be devoid of wisdom and purpose, justice and fairness. Nor is His creation an act of futility so that regardless of whether one's acts are good or bad, they would lead to no consequence.

This statement represents the core of the previous discourse and is a prelude to the forthcoming one. The present statement aims to drive home to the audience that man has not been left in the world as an unbridled animal to wander around at will nor is this world a realm of chaos and arbitrariness wherein a person may go about with impunity, free from any thought of accountability.

As a prelude to the discourse that follows, it is stressed that whoever does not believe in ultimate reward and punishment suffers from the illusion that the end of everyone, whether good or bad, is the same: all will be reduced to dust after death without facing any consequence of their deeds. Such people think that the Creator has indulged in an act of utter futility by creating man in the first place. The same point is made at several other places in the Qur'ān. Some instances in point are the following:

Did you imagine that We created you without any purpose, and that you will not be brought back to Us? (*al-Mu'minūn* 23: 115).

It was not in idle sport that We created the heavens and the earth and all that is between them. We did not create them except in Truth. But most of them do not know. The Day of Final Decision is the appointed time for all (*al-Dukhān* 44: 38-40).

30. The unbelievers are asked whether they find it reasonable that both good and evil should ultimately come to the same end. How can

(29) This is the Blessed Book[31] that We have revealed to you, (O Muḥammad), that people with understanding may reflect over its verses and those with understanding derive a lesson.

(30) We bestowed upon David (an illustrious son), Solomon.[32] How excellent a servant (of Ours he was)! ▶

كِتَـٰبٌ أَنزَلْنَـٰهُ إِلَيْكَ مُبَـٰرَكٌ لِّيَدَّبَّرُوٓا۟
ءَايَـٰتِهِۦ وَلِيَتَذَكَّرَ أُو۟لُوا۟ ٱلْأَلْبَـٰبِ ﴿٢٩﴾
وَوَهَبْنَا لِدَاوُۥدَ سُلَيْمَـٰنَ ۚ نِعْمَ ٱلْعَبْدُ ۖ

it possibly satisfy them, for example, that a pious person should be left unrewarded for his righteousness and a wicked person be left unpunished for his evil? Denial of the Hereafter, of Divine recompense, of Hell and Paradise amounts to denying the Divine attributes of wisdom and justice. Furthermore, this denial also divests the entire system underlying the universe of all meaning. Should the line of thinking which underlies the denial of the Hereafter be taken seriously, there remains no incentive to do good or to refrain from evil. If God's realm is indeed so arbitrary and chaotic, then whoever lives righteously and endures pain for the sake of righteousness and seeks to bring about reform in the lives of God's creatures is no better than a fool. By the same token, whoever accumulates all possible advantages, legitimate or otherwise, and thereby enjoys a life of illicit pleasures is indeed a smart fellow!

31. *Barakah* signifies the growth of goodness and felicity. That the Qur'ān is a blessed Book underscores that it is of immense benefit to man. Contained in it are the best directives to mend and improve his life. One's adherence to the Qur'ān ensures nothing but goodness, discounting all possibility of loss or harm.

32. An account of the Prophet Solomon (peace be on him) also features in *al-Baqarah* 2, n. 104, *Towards Understanding the Qur'ān,* vol. I, p. 96; *Sūrah Banī Isrā'īl* 17, n. 7, vol. V, pp. 12-16; *Sūrah al-Anbiyā'* 21, nn. 70-5, vol. V, pp. 282-7; *Sūrah al-Naml* 27, nn. 18-56, vol. VII, pp. 144-64; and *Sūrah Saba'* 34: 12-14, nn. 17-24, vol. IX, pp. 159-72.

Indeed he constantly turned to Us in devotion. (31) And when one evening well-trained and running horses of noble breed were brought to him[33] (32) he said: 'Lo! I have come to love this wealth[34] on account of the remembrance of my Lord.' And when the horses disappeared, (33) (he ordered): 'Bring these horses back to me,' and then he began to gently stroke their shanks and necks.[35] ▶

إِنَّهُۥٓ أَوَّابٌ ﴿٣٠﴾ إِذْ عُرِضَ عَلَيْهِ بِٱلْعَشِىِّ
ٱلصَّـٰفِنَـٰتُ ٱلْجِيَادُ ﴿٣١﴾ فَقَالَ إِنِّىٓ أَحْبَبْتُ
حُبَّ ٱلْخَيْرِ عَن ذِكْرِ رَبِّى حَتَّىٰ تَوَارَتْ
بِٱلْحِجَابِ ﴿٣٢﴾ رُدُّوهَا عَلَىَّ ۖ فَطَفِقَ مَسْحًۢا
بِٱلسُّوقِ وَٱلْأَعْنَاقِ ﴿٣٣﴾

33. The actual words are الصَّافِنَاتُ الجِيَادُ which refer to the horses that maintain poise while standing and that are also known for their speedy gallop.

34. The word used is *khayr*. It denotes abundant wealth and is also used figuratively for horses. Since the Prophet Solomon (peace be on him) had consecrated these horses for *jihād* in God's cause, they are here described as *khayr*.

35. The Qur'ānic commentators disagree in their understanding and interpretation of these verses. According to some scholars, the Prophet Solomon (peace be on him) was so absorbed in watching the horses and observing their gallop that he either missed the *'Aṣr* Prayer or forgot to recite the supplications he used to recite between *'Aṣr* and *Maghrib* Prayers. He remained so occupied with watching the horses until the sun set. It was then that Solomon (peace be on him) ordered that the horses be brought back to him. When they came, he began to cut them into pieces; or to put it differently, he began to sacrifice them as an offering to God. He did so because they had made him oblivious of God's remembrance, (Qurṭubī, *al-Jāmi' li Aḥkām al-Qur'ān*, comments on *Sūrah Ṣād* 38: 33.) Taken in this sense, some scholars translate the above verses thus: 'He said: "I was so overcome by the love of these horses that I missed my Lord's

remembrance [*'Aṣr* Prayer or recitation of the usual supplications]." After the sunset, he recalled these horses and slashed their necks and shanks (with sword).'

Although this interpretation has been offered by some leading Qur'ānic scholars, it is nonetheless not persuasive. This because in order to make this interpretation acceptable, these scholars have had to add three points of their own accord, none of which has any basis in any of the relevant sources. The points they have added are the following: (i) It is assumed that the Prophet Solomon (peace be on him) missed his *'Aṣr* Prayer, or the supplications which he used to recite at that hour, because of his preoccupation with the horses. In this regard, it is pertinent to point out that the Qur'ānic words are no more than the following إِنِّي أَحْبَبْتُ حُبَّ الْخَيْرِ عَن ذِكْرِ رَبِّي, 'Lo! I have come to love this wealth to the extent of becoming headless to the remembrance of my Lord' (verse 32.)

These words, at most, can be construed to mean that so intense was Solmon's love of the wealth [to wit, the horses] that it made him negligent of God's remembrance. However, the Qur'ānic narrative does not mention that Solomon missed the *'Aṣr* Prayer or some particular supplications that he used to recite. Moreover, these scholars tend to suppose that the sun set. However, when one reads the words حَتَّىٰ تَوَارَتْ بِالْحِجَابِ one is instantly reminded of الصَّـٰفِنَاتُ الْجِيَادُ (well-trained and running horses) in the preceding verse. Hence the words حَتَّىٰ تَوَارَتْ بِالْحِجَابِ simply mean that the horses disappeared from sight.

(ii) These scholars further assume that the Prophet Solomon (peace be on him) did not simply pat the horses' shanks and necks; they rather think that he began to slash them with his sword or, to put it differently, he began to sacrifice them in God's cause because the love of these horses had made him heedless to the Prayer. (iii) These scholars also assume that Solomon struck the horses with the sword although there is no mention of a sword; what is mentioned is that Solomon 'struck their shanks and necks.' Not only there is no explicit mention of striking with the sword, but the context too does not lend itself to believing that Solomon would have struck these horses with a sword.

We are, in principle, opposed to this kind of interpretation of the Qur'ān. In our opinion, any addition to the content of a Qur'ānic statement is valid in no more than the following four cases: (a) either there should be some contextual indication in the text of the Qur'ān itself to support that addition; (b) or there should be some reference or allusion to that addition somewhere else in the Qur'ān; (c) or that it is an explanation of a *mujmal* (unexplained) statement of the Qur'ān by a *ḥadīth*; or (d) that there is some other reliable source to support the addition: if it is a historical matter, then a historical source should explain it; and if it relates to the natural phenomena, then it should be explained by reliable scientific data; and if the matter relates to *fiqh*, then it should be explained by any of the recognised works of *fiqh*.

In the absence of any of the above, it is altogether unjustified for people to weave a story out of their imagination and then pass it off as a plausible explanation of a Qur'ānic narrative.

Another group of scholars offers a slightly different explanation. For them, the word حَتَّىٰ تَوَارَتْ بِالْحِجَابِ as well as رُدُّوهَا عَلَيَّ refer to the sun. In other words, the Prophet Solomon (peace be on him) prayed that the sun be sent back in time so that he might offer *'Aṣr* Prayer. Accordingly, the sun reappeared and he performed the Prayer, (Qurṭubī, *al-Jāmi' li Aḥkām al-Qur'ān*, comments on *Sūrah Ṣād* 38: 33.) However, this explanation is even less acceptable than the one above, for the Qur'ānic verse in question does not say a word about the sun or its return. We do not say so on the grounds that God does not have the power to send the sun back in time if He so wills. We rather say so because had that happened, it would have been an event of such dazzling importance that it would necessarily have found a place in the historical sources.

These scholars also refer to some *aḥādīth* to show that the sun's reappearance occurred not simply once but on several occasions. It is mentioned that this took place on the occasion of the Prophet's Ascension. (Al-Qāḍī Abū al-Faḍl 'Iyāḍ al-Yaḥṣubī, *al-Shifā bi Ta'rīf Ḥuqūq al-Muṣṭafā, al-Bāb al-Rābī' fīmā Aẓharahu Allāh 'alā Yadayhi min al-Mu'jizāt, Faṣl Inshiqāq al-Qamar wa Ḥabs al-Shams*.) The same was also caused to happen on the occasion of the Battle of the Trench. It is also reported to have happened when 'Alī lay asleep in the Prophet's lap, as a result of which he missed *'Aṣr* Prayer. The Prophet (peace be on him) is said to have prayed that the sun be made to reappear and this prayer of his was granted. (Al-Qāḍī Abū al-Faḍl 'Iyāḍ al-Yaḥṣubī, *al-Shifā bi Ta'rīf Ḥuqūq al-Muṣṭafā, al-Bāb al-Rābī' fīmā Aẓharahu Allāh 'alā Yadayhi min al-Mu'jizāt, Faṣl Inshiqāq al-Qamar wa Ḥabs al-Shams*.) However, these reports are even less plausible than the explanation itself. Ibn Taymīyah has examined all the versions and chains of narrators in the tradition about the reappearance of the sun wherein 'Alī has been mentioned and has shown the tradition to be spurious. (Taqī al-Dīn Aḥmad ibn 'Abd al-Ḥalīm ibn Taymīyah al-Ḥarrānī, *Kitāb Minhāj al-Sunnah al-Nabawīyah fī Naqd Kalām al-Shī'ah wa al-Qadarīyah*, Būlāq: al-Maṭba'ah al-Kubrā al-Amīrīyah, 1322 AH, vol. IV, pp. 185-95.) Aḥmad ibn Ḥanbal believes that these reports have no basis. (Muḥammad Ṭāhir ibn 'Alī al-Hindī al-Fatnī, *Tadhkirat al-Mawḍū'āt, Bāb Faḍl Ṣaḥābatih wa Ahl Baytih wa Uways wa Radd al-Shams 'alā 'Alī wa 'Adhāb Qātil al-Ḥusayn wa Ta'rīkh Qatlih*.) Ibn al-Jawzī, too, dismisses them as false and fabricated reports, (Ibn Taymīyah, *Kitāb Minhāj al-Sunnah*, vol. IV, p. 186.) Some scholars brand the reports about the reappearance of the sun during the Battle of Trench as weak and others as fabricated.

As to the traditions about the Prophet's Ascension, it is worth clarifying that when the Prophet (peace be on him) recounted the details of his Ascension before the unbelievers, the latter asked him to produce some proof. In reply, he told them of an incident that took place on his way to Jerusalem. On being asked as to when that caravan would arrive in Makkah, he indicated the day of its arrival. On the appointed day, the Makkans waited for the caravan to arrive. As evening was about to fall, the Prophet (peace be on him) prayed to God that the sun may not set until the caravan's arrival and the caravan did indeed arrive before sunset. (Al-Qāḍī Abū al-Faḍl 'Iyāḍ al-Yaḥṣubī, *al-Shifā bi Ta'rīf Ḥuqūq al-Muṣṭafā, al-Bāb al-Rābī' fīmā Aẓharahu Allāh 'alā Yadayhi min al-Mu'jizāt, Faṣl Inshiqāq al-Qamar wa Ḥabs al-Shams.*) Some narrators, however, have recounted the same in a manner that leaves the impression that on that day the sun set an hour later than its appointed time. For them, the sun too waited until the caravan had arrived. Such reports do not constitute sufficient proof for an extraordinary event such as an hour's long delay in the setting of the sun. Had this really happened, it would have been very widely reported and would not have been confined to some stray reports by a few individuals.

Another group of Qur'ānic scholars, however, interprets these verses in a way that conforms to the understanding of those who read this verse without any pre-conceived notions. According to these scholars, what happened was the following: As some high quality horses were presented before the Prophet Solomon (peace be on him) he remarked that he did not love them out of any personal motive, but rather because of their effectiveness in exalting the Word of God. He directed that a race between these horses be held. As a result, the horses galloped and disappeared from his sight. According to 'Abd Allāh ibn 'Abbās, when they returned to Solmon (peace be on him), he affectionately patted their necks and shanks.

This version of the incident appears to us as the most plausible one. Furthermore, it not only fits in with the wording of the Qur'ānic text but is also not marred by any addition to the meaning of the relevant verses not endorsed by the Qur'ān, authentic *Ḥadīth* or Israelite history.

It is also pertinent to point out that at the conclusion of this narrative, God pays the following tributes to the Prophet Solomon (peace be on him): 'How excellent a servant (of Ours he was)! Indeed he constantly turned to Us in devotion' (verse 30.) These remarks make it quite clear that notwithstanding the abundant resources available to Solomon, he valued them only insofar as they were instrumental in serving God's

(34) Surely We put Solomon to the test and cast upon his throne a mere body. Thereupon he penitently turned (to Us). (35) He said: 'My Lord, forgive me and bestow upon me a kingdom such as none other after me will deserve. Surely You are the Bounteous Giver.'[36] (36) We subjected the wind to him, so that it blew gently at his bidding, ▶

وَلَقَدْ فَتَنَّا سُلَيْمَـٰنَ وَأَلْقَيْنَا عَلَىٰ كُرْسِيِّهِۦ
جَسَدًا ثُمَّ أَنَابَ ﴿٣٤﴾ قَالَ رَبِّ ٱغْفِرْ لِى
وَهَبْ لِى مُلْكًا لَّا يَنۢبَغِى لِأَحَدٍ مِّنۢ
بَعْدِىٓ ۖ إِنَّكَ أَنتَ ٱلْوَهَّابُ ﴿٣٥﴾ فَسَخَّرْنَا لَهُ
ٱلرِّيحَ تَجْرِى بِأَمْرِهِۦ رُخَآءً

---

cause. Hence, when he inspected a splendid parade of high quality horses he remembered God and God's favours instead of engaging in arrogant self-boasting.

36. In the sequence of the discourse, the real purpose of the narrative is to recount this very incident for which the preceding verse serves as a prelude. We have seen in the case of the Prophet David (peace be on him) that he was first praised and then a mention was made of his being subjected to a test which shows that God does not spare even His beloved servants from putting them to test. It was also shown that once David (peace be on him) was informed of his lapse, he repented, submitting himself fully to God. In like manner, it is first mentioned in the context of the Prophet Solomon (peace be on him) that his was an exalted position as a sincere and devoted servant of God. He too was tested as was David. When a body was cast upon his throne, Solomon instantly realised his lapse, sought forgiveness from God and recanted from what had necessitated that test. In other words, God brings home the following two truths through this story: (i) Even such distinguished and beloved Messengers of God such as the Prophets David and Solomon (peace be on them) were not spared being put to test. (ii) As soon as one realises one's lapse, one should humbly turn to the Lord. As the same attitude was displayed by both the Prophets, David and Solomon, God not only pardoned them, but showered further bounties upon them. However, this also raises questions about the nature and details of the

Prophet Solomon's test and the significance of casting a body upon his throne. So let us ascertain the nature of the warning directed at Solomon upon which he was prompted to seek God's forgiveness.

The Qur'ānic commentators offer four varying answers. One group relates an elaborate version of the story, some of the details of which are mutually divergent. Common to this version is the assertion that the Prophet Solomon (peace be on him) had committed some lapse. Either one of his wives indulged in idolatry in his palace for forty days, something that he remained unaware of, or it is said that he stayed indoors for a few days, neglecting the petitions of his people. As punishment, his ring was taken away by a devil. This was the ring through which Solomon governed the *jinn* and men and established control over the winds. With its loss, Solomon (peace be on him) became deprived of his power and for 40 days ran from pillar to post looking for his lost ring. During this time, it was the devil who had stolen the ring, rather than he, who ruled over his kingdom, impersonating himself as Solomon. The reference here is to the same devil that had been cast upon his throne. Some reports go to the extent of stating that during this period even the king's wives were not safe from that devil's amorous encroachments.

Eventually, noticing the unusual conduct of the devil, Solomon's ministers and courtiers became suspicious and concluded that he could not be Solomon. Hence, they opened, in his presence, a copy of the Torah and subsequently the devil took to his heels. While fleeing, the ring fell into water and was swallowed by a fish. By sheer coincidence, the Prophet Solomon (peace be on him) happened to catch that fish. When he cut open its belly to cook it, he recovered his lost ring. No sooner than this had happened, did all *jinn* and humans appear before him, renewing their pledge of service. (Qurṭubī, *al-Jāmi' li Aḥkām al-Qur'ān*, comments on verse 34, *Sūrah Ṣād* 38: 34.)

This whole story is full of superstitious tales, which some early converts to Islam uncritically took over from Judaic and Christian sources and spread among the larger body of Muslims. They had accepted this stuff from the Talmud and some other unauthentic popular Israelite sources. What is intriguing is that some Muslims bought this story, mistaking it to be a part of the Qur'ānic account. Unsuspectingly and uncritically they further transmitted this bizarre story. There is, however, no truth about the miraculous qualities of this ring. Nor did the Prophet Solomon (peace be on him) owe his extraordinary power to that ring. Moreover, devils are not capable of impersonating a Messenger and thus of misguiding people. It is unthinkable that God would punish a Messenger of His in such a way as would let a devil go about under his identity, wreaking havoc within a whole nation.

It should be noted, first of all, that the Qur'ānic account refutes this story outright. Furthermore, verses 36 and 37 of the *sūrah* declare that the Prophet Solomon (peace be on him) was subjected to this test and sought God's forgiveness and God once again yoked the winds and the devils to Solomon's service. In this respect, then, we observe how this story reverses the chronology of events by stating that, thanks to the magical ring, the devils had already been under Solomon's control. Qur'ānic commentators who narrate this story did not take note of the subsequent verses which are at odds with the content of this narration.

The second group of Qur'ānic commentators expounds the following version: After 20 years of waiting, a son was born to the Prophet Solomon (peace be on him). This made the devils all the more apprehensive that even after Solomon's death, they would still be subservient to his son. They, therefore, resolved to kill his son. On learning about their evil design, the Prophet Solomon (peace be on him) hid his son in the clouds. This betrayed a serious lapse on Solomon's part, for instead of reposing his trust in God, he had placed his faith in the clouds. As a punishment, his son died and his corpse fell on his own throne. (Zamakhsharī, *al-Kashshāf*, comments on verse 34, *Sūrah Ṣād* 38: 34.)

This story is equally baseless and totally at variance with the Qur'ānic account. It presupposes that the devils and winds had been subservient to the Prophet Solomon (peace be on him) from the very outset of his designation as God's Messenger. In contrast, the Qur'ān clearly states that their subservience was ordered by God after the Prophet Solomon (peace be on him) had successfully stood the test to which he was put.

The third group of Qur'ānic commentators adds the following details to the Qur'ānic account. The Prophet Solomon (peace be on him) once vowed that he would have sex with his 70 wives in one night and that each one of them would give birth to a son who would strive in God's cause. However, he did not add to this assertion the customary formula, 'if God so wills.' Consequently, only one of his wives conceived and she had a still birth and the body of that child was cast upon Solomon's throne. (Rāzī, *al-Tafsīr al-Kabīr*, comments on verse 34, *Sūrah Ṣād* 38: 34.) This version occurs in a *ḥadīth* narrated by Abū Hurayrah on the Prophet's authority. It has been recorded by Bukhārī, Muslim and other *Ḥadīth* scholars with several chains of narration. (Bukhārī, *Kitāb al-Jihād, Bāb man Ṭalab al-Walad li al-Jihād*; Muslim, *Kitāb al-Aymān, Bāb al-Istithnā' fī al-Yamīn wa ghayrihā*.) The number of Solomon's wives variously appears in these reports as 60, 70, 90 or 100. (Bukhārī, *Kitāb al-Jihād, Bāb man Ṭalab al-Walad li al-Jihād; Kitāb Aḥādīth al-Anbiyā', [Bāb] Qawl Allāh Ta'ālā: 'wa Wahabnā li Dāwūd Sulaymān Ni'm al-'Abd Innahū Awwāb'; Kitāb al-Nikāḥ, Bāb Qawl al-Rajul: 'La'aṭūfann al-Laylah 'alā Nisā' ī'; Kitāb al-Aymān wa al-Nudhūr, Bāb kayfa*

Kānat Yamīn al-Nabī Ṣallā Allāh 'alayhi wa Sallam; Kitāb al-Tawḥīd, Bāb al-Mashī'ah wa al-Irādah.) As far as the chain of narrators is concerned, in case of most reports they are not flawed. Technically speaking, therefore, the report cannot be brushed aside. Nevertheless, the content of these reports altogether defies reason. One therefore has the distinct impression that this particular version could not have come from the Prophet (peace be on him); rather, he may have cited it as an instance of the weird reports circulated by the Jews. Any attempt to force people to believe these reports on the grounds of a sound chain of narrators amounts to reducing Islam to a laughing stock.

Let us now consider the content of the report: that Solomon had sex with all his wives in one night. The number of these wives was at least sixty. Supposing the reference here is to a night in winter at the time between *'Ishā'* and *Fajr* when even, the longest night is not more than ten or eleven hours. Now anyone can see whether it is at all possible for a person to have sex with all of his 60 wives. This means that he would have had uninterrupted sex throughout an eleven hour-long night, that he would be disposing of six wives in an hour. Is that credible stuff? How can we believe that the Prophet Muḥammad (peace be on him) would relate such a fantastic report as an actual fact?

The *ḥadīth* under discussion makes no reference to 'a mere body that was cast upon the Prophet Solomon's throne,' (verse 34.) It is understandable that Solomon might have prayed to God for forgiveness on the occasion of this child's birth. However, it is far from clear in the light of the above version, as to why Solomon prayed as follows: 'Bestow upon me a kingdom such as none other after me will deserve,' (verse 35.)

We also encounter another interpretation, one preferred by Imām Rāzī. According to this interpretation, the incident was as follows: Once the Prophet Solomon (peace be on him) was afflicted with some grave disease, or with anxiety on account of some serious danger he faced. So absorbing was this anxiety that Solomon (peace be on him) became thoroughly emaciated. (Rāzī, *al-Tafsīr al-Kabīr*, comments on *Sūrah Ṣād* 38: 34.) The Qur'ān says only this much: 'Surely We put Solomon to the test and cast upon his throne a mere body. Thereupon he penitently turned (to Us),' (verse 34.) Evidently, the body does not allude to that of the Prophet Solomon himself. What emerges from the reading of the verse is that the Prophet Solomon (peace be on him) had committed some lapse and, in order to warn him, a body was cast upon his throne. When he realised his lapse, he penitently turned to God.

There is no doubt that this is one of the most difficult passages in the Qur'ān, one for whose definitive explanation no textual material is

wherever he directed it,[37] (37) and We also subjected the devils to him – all kinds of builders and divers; (38) and others that were bound with chains.[38] ▶

حَيْثُ أَصَابَ ﴿٣٦﴾ وَٱلشَّيَـٰطِينَ كُلَّ
بَنَّآءٍ وَغَوَّاصٍ ﴿٣٧﴾ وَءَاخَرِينَ مُقَرَّنِينَ فِى
ٱلْأَصْفَادِ ﴿٣٨﴾

available. However, the Prophet Solomon's own supplication: 'My Lord, forgive me and bestow upon me a kingdom such as none other after me will deserve', seems to provide a clue. Studying the above verse in the light of Israelite history, it seems that perhaps the Prophet Solomon (peace be on him) had desired that his son should succeed him and that kingship should remain in his line. God, however, considered this a test for Solomon. Solomon too realised that this was a test for him. When his son, Rehoboam, grew into a youth his ways betrayed his utter incapacity to succeed his grandfather and father, the Prophets David and Solomon (peace be on them). That a dead body was placed upon Solomon's throne indicates that the son whom he had wanted to succeed him was altogether unsuited for the task. He, therefore, recanted his wish, sought God's pardon and prayed that his kingdom may end with his demise. In other words, he abandoned the idea of kingship continuing in his line. It is also evident from Israelite history that the Prophet Solomon (peace be on him) did not name anyone as his successor. In just a short span of time after his death his ministers and the notables of the kingdom placed Rehoboam, Solomon's son, on the throne. Within a short period, ten Israelite tribes broke away and set up their own kingdom in northern Palestine, leaving only the tribe of Judah loyal to the kingdom of Jerusalem.

37. This point is elucidated elsewhere (see *al-Anbiyā'* 21, n. 74 *Towards Understanding the Qur'ān*, vol. V, p. 285.) It is, nonetheless, pertinent to clarify that in *Sūrah al-Anbiyā'* it is stated that the winds were made subservient to Solomon (peace be on him). In the present verse, however, it is pointedly said that the wind blew smoothly at his command. What this signifies is that the wind – forceful though it is and essential for the sailing of ships – was made subservient to the Prophet Solomon (peace be on him) so that it facilitated the movement of his navy.

38. For further details see *al-Anbiyā'* 21, n. 75, *Towards Understanding the Qur'ān*, vol. V, pp. 286-7; and *al-Naml* 27: 23, 28 and 45, vol. VII, pp. 146, 149-51 and 158-9. The devils here refer to the *jinn*. As to the devils

(39) 'This is Our bestowal. So give or withhold as you wish without account.'[39] (40) Indeed an exalted position of nearness awaits him and an excellent resort.[40]

(41) And remember Our servant Job:[41] when he cried to his Lord: ▶

هَٰذَا عَطَآؤُنَا فَٱمۡنُنۡ أَوۡ أَمۡسِكۡ بِغَيۡرِ حِسَابٖ ﴿٣٩﴾ وَإِنَّ لَهُۥ عِندَنَا لَزُلۡفَىٰ وَحُسۡنَ مَـَٔابٖ ﴿٤٠﴾ وَٱذۡكُرۡ عَبۡدَنَآ أَيُّوبَ إِذۡ نَادَىٰ رَبَّهُۥٓ

in fetters, the reference is to those devils who had been imprisoned for their misconduct. It rendered them incapable of fleeing or committing any other mischief.

39. This verse admits three meanings: (i) God's bestowal of bounties is without measure. The Prophet Solomon (peace be on him) was authorised to grant out of these bounties to whomsoever he wished and deny them to whomsoever he wished. (ii) Solomon was not taken to task for granting or withholding bounties. (iii) The devils were placed under Solomon's authority. He was free to release or detain them and was not subject to any accountability in this regard. (Rāzī, *al-Tafsīr al-Kabīr*, comments on *Sūrah Ṣād* 38: 39.)

40. The truth enunciated in this verse is that God detests pride and arrogance on man's part and loves his humility. Both the Prophets David and Solomon (peace and be on them) were showered with His bounties as reward for their humility. The Prophet Solomon's supplication following his prayer for God's forgiveness was accepted and he was accordingly granted a kingdom unprecedented in the annals of history. Likewise, the bestowal of control over the wind and the *jinn* also makes Solomon (peace be on him) unique and distinctively more powerful than any ruler in history.

41. This is the fourth instance in the Qur'ān where the Prophet Job (peace be on him) is mentioned. (For a detailed account about him see *al-Anbiyā'* 21, nn. 76-9, *Towards Understanding the Qur'ān*, vol. V, pp. 287-90.)

'Behold, Satan has afflicted me with much hardship and suffering.'[42] (42) (We commanded him): 'Stamp your foot on earth, and here is cool water to wash with and to drink.'[43] (43) And We granted to him his family and also the like of them,[44] ▶

أَنِّي مَسَّنِيَ ٱلشَّيْطَٰنُ بِنُصْبٍ وَعَذَابٍ ﴿٤١﴾
ٱرْكُضْ بِرِجْلِكَ ۖ هَٰذَا مُغْتَسَلٌۢ بَارِدٌ
وَشَرَابٌ ﴿٤٢﴾ وَوَهَبْنَا لَهُۥٓ أَهْلَهُۥ وَمِثْلَهُم مَّعَهُمْ

42. This does not mean that Job's complaint was that Satan had actually subjected him to hardship and suffering. Rather, his real complaint was about Satan's evil promptings which hurt him more than his serious illness, his loss of wealth and the desertion of his family members. Satan tried his level best to make Job (peace be on him) lose all hope in God and prompted him to become an ungrateful servant of His. Satan thereby wanted that Job (peace be on him) should forego his perseverance.

The above interpretation of Job's supplication is preferable to others on the following grounds: (i) According to the Qur'ān, God has granted Satan only the ability to infuse some promptings; he does not have the power to afflict anyone with disease or physical pain. (ii) In *Sūrah al-Anbiyā'* (*Sūrah* 21) the Prophet Job (peace be on him) prays to God in which he simply says: 'Behold, disease has struck me and you are the Most Merciful of those that are merciful' (21: 83.) It is noted that here it has not been said that Satan caused him that disease.

43. As Job (peace be on him) stamped his foot on the ground, there gushed forth a spring by God's command. Its water cured the Prophet Job (peace be on him) as he drank and bathed in it. Presumably what Job (peace be on him) suffered from was some kind of severe skin disease. The Bible states that his body, from the crown of his head to his soles, was afflicted with sores. According to the Bible: 'So Satan went forth from the presence of the Lord, and afflicted Job with loathsome sores from the sole of his feet to the crown of his head.' (*Job* 2: 7.)

44. Reports suggest that all, except Job's wife, deserted him during this sickness. God alludes to this by saying here that [after Job was cured], 'We granted to him his family and also the like of them as a mercy from Us…'

as a mercy from Us, and as a reminder to people of understanding,[45] (44) (and We said to him): 'Take in your hand a bundle of rushes and strike with it, and do not break your oath.'[46] ▶

رَحْمَةً مِّنَّا وَذِكْرَىٰ لِأُو۟لِى ٱلْأَلْبَٰبِ ﴿٤٣﴾
وَخُذْ بِيَدِكَ ضِغْثًا فَٱضْرِب بِّهِۦ وَلَا تَحْنَثْ ۗ

45. There is a lesson in this for all people endowed with reason. The lesson is that neither one should forget God and become disobedient and rebellious to Him in a state of prosperity nor succumb to despair in adversity. Man's prosperity and adversity lie entirely with God and none has any share in His power and authority. Were God to so will, He can transform a person's adversity into prosperity and vice versa. Hence in all circumstances a wise person should repose His trust in God and pin all hopes and expectations in Him alone.

46. Reflection over these words makes it evident that during his illness the Prophet Job (peace be on him) had vowed to beat someone by striking them with a certain number of lashes. (There are reports which indicate that he had vowed to beat his own wife). (Jaṣṣās, *Aḥkām al-Qur'ān*, comments on *Sūrah Ṣād* 38: 44.) When God restored his health and he was able to overcome the anger which had caused him to take this vow he felt disconcerted. For, if he were to fulfil the vow, he would be hurting an altogether innocent person without any justifiable reason. On the other hand, if he were not to fulfil the vow, he would still be a sinner. Then God showed him a way out of the dilemma by directing him to take a bundle of rushes, and strike with it, the volume of rushes equating to the number of times he had vowed to strike. This would fulfil his vow without causing any pain to the person concerned.

Some jurists consider this to be a concession exclusively meant for the Prophet Job (peace be on him). Other jurists, however, believe that the directive is of a general nature and is meant for all. The former view is held, according to Ibn 'Asākir, by 'Abd Allāh ibn 'Abbās and according to al-Jaṣṣās, by Mujāhid. As for the latter view, it is held by Abū Ḥanīfah, Abū Yūsuf, Muḥammad ibn al-Ḥasan, Zufar and Shāfi'ī. For them, if someone had vowed to punish a person, say his servant, with ten lashes, his vow will be deemed to have been fulfilled if he joined the whips together and struck the servant just once. (Jaṣṣās, *Aḥkām al-Qur'ān*, comments on *Sūrah Ṣād* 38: 44.)

Several *aḥādīth* stress that the Prophet (peace be on him) followed the same principle in punishing a sick or age-stricken culprit charged with illicit sex, who would not have survived had he been lashed a hundred times. Abū Bakr al-Jaṣṣās narrates, on the authority of Sa'īd ibn Sa'd ibn 'Ubādah, that a member of the Banū Sā'id had committed illicit sex. This person, however, was extremely frail and sick and had virtually been reduced to a skeleton. The Prophet (peace be on him), therefore, directed that he be lashed with a date trunk with a hundred branches. Thereby this would constitute the punishment of one hundred lashes for him. (Jaṣṣās, *Aḥkām al-Qur'ān*, comments on *Sūrah Ṣād* 38: 44.)

There are traditions in the *Musnad* of Aḥmad ibn Ḥanbal, in Abū Dā'ūd, Nasā'ī, Ibn Mājah and al-Ṭabarānī and the *Muṣannaf* of 'Abd al-Razzāq and in other *Ḥadīth* collections which support this. It is well established that the Prophet (peace be on him) prescribed this method for punishing sick and infirm culprits. (Aḥmad ibn Ḥanbal, *Musnad*, narrated by Sa'īd ibn Sa'd ibn 'Ubādah; Abū Dā'ūd, *Kitāb al-Ḥudūd, Bāb fī Iqāmat al-Ḥadd 'alā al-Marīḍ*; Nasā'ī, *al-Sunan al-Kubrā, Kitāb al-Rajm, Bāb al-Ḍarīr fī al-Khilqah Yuṣīb al-Ḥadd*; Ibn Mājah, *Kitāb al-Ḥudūd, Bāb al-Kabīr wa al-Marīḍ; Yajib 'alayhi al-Ḥadd*; Ṭabarānī, *al-Mu'jam al-Kabīr*, narrated by Sa'īd ibn Sa'd ibn 'Ubādah; 'Abd al-Razzāq, *Muṣannaf, Kitāb al-Aymān wa al-Nudhūr, Bāb Taḥlīl al-Ḍarb*.) Jurists, however, insist that every branch or rush should touch the culprit's body, even if it be once, and that it should also cause him some pain. The point is that lash should not simply touch or brush the culprit's body but should strike it. (Jaṣṣāṣ, *Aḥkām al-Qur'ān*, comments on *Sūrah Ṣād* 38: 44.)

Another question arising from this discussion is: what course of action should one take if one later realises that one's vow was inappropriate. A tradition states the Prophet's directive that in such an instance one should do only what is proper and this, in itself, constitutes the expiation for the unfulfilled vow. There is also another tradition which mentions that the Prophet (peace be on him) asked such a person to act fairly and that at the same time they should expiate for their vow as well. The verse under discussion seems to support this position. Had the avoidance of an inappropriate vow by acting fairly alone been its expiation, God would not have asked the Prophet Job (peace be on him) to 'Take in your hand a bundle of rushes and strike with it' (verse 44), in order to fulfil the vow he had made. It is evident that God did not thereby direct him not to fulfil his inappropriate vow. (For further details see *al-Nūr* 24, n. 20, *Towards Understanding the Qur'ān*, vol. VI, pp. 214-15.)

Some scholars, however, consider this verse to provide proof in support of legitimate legal devices (*ḥiyal*). This because the Prophet Job (peace

Indeed We found him steadfast. How excellent a servant (of Ours) he was. Indeed he constantly turned (to his Lord).[47] (45) And remember Our servants – Abraham, ▶	إِنَّا وَجَدْنَٰهُ صَابِرًا ۚ نِّعْمَ ٱلْعَبْدُ ۖ إِنَّهُۥٓ أَوَّابٌ ﴿٤٤﴾ وَٱذْكُرْ عِبَٰدَنَآ إِبْرَٰهِيمَ

be on him) was obviously informed of a way out of his legal obligation. However, this was not designed to enable him to avoid or evade a duty; rather, it was a means to avoid a wrong. Thus legitimate devices are only those to which one might resort to avoid a wrong, injustice, evil or sin. If that is not the case, and one resorts to a legal device (*ḥīlah*) to render something unlawful into lawful or to evade a religious duty or to avoid doing something good, this borders on sheer unbelief because through such devices one virtually tries to deceive God. For example, if one were to transfer one's assets before the expiry of the mandatory one year period in order to evade the payment of *zakāh*, one would be guilty not only of non-observance of a religious duty, but also of deluding oneself that the trick would deceive God and that He will absolve one of the duty to pay *zakāh*. Jurists who have laid down legal devices in their works have done so not in order to encourage people to resort to them with the aim of substantively evading legal commands. The purpose of so doing is to indicate that judges and rulers need not object to those legal devices to which people might resort, providing they do so to avoid a sinful act. What is crucial in such matters is a person's intention, and judges and magistrates are hardly in a position to reproach people on the grounds that they had acted with bad intent. It is better that judgement regarding intention should be left to God.

47. The story of the Prophet Job (peace be on him) is narrated here to highlight the truth that when God's pious servants are faced with hardships, they do not complain to their Lord. On the contrary, they patiently withstand the test to which they have been put by Him, while they invoke His help and look forward to His mercy and grace. Eventually, they are rewarded with God's favours and beneficence as is evident from the Prophet Job's story. Even when under stress such people are caught in a moral dilemma, God Himself suggests a way out. This is again best illustrated by the Prophet Job's story.

Isaac and Jacob – they were endowed with great strength and vision.[48] (46) Verily We exalted them in consideration of a sterling quality: their remembrance of the Abode of the Hereafter.[49] (47) In Our sight they are among the chosen and excellent ones. ▶	وَإِسْحَـٰقَ وَيَعْقُوبَ أُو۟لِى ٱلْأَيْدِى وَٱلْأَبْصَـٰرِ ﴿٤٥﴾ إِنَّآ أَخْلَصْنَـٰهُم بِخَالِصَةٍ ذِكْرَى ٱلدَّارِ ﴿٤٦﴾ وَإِنَّهُمْ عِندَنَا لَمِنَ ٱلْمُصْطَفَيْنَ ٱلْأَخْيَارِ ﴿٤٧﴾

48. The sense of the words (ذُوْ الأَيْدِي وَالأَبْصَارِ) is '[those] endowed with great strength and vision'. To describe the Prophets as people of great strength means that they were pre-eminently men of action who had been granted tremendous strength and fortitude to carry out God's command and to eschew sin and evil, and who strove vigorously to exalt the Word of God. Their additional characterisation is that they are endowed with 'vision'. This vision obviously refers to their ability to discern and perceive the truth; the vision here meaning the vision of the heart and the mind rather than of the eyes. The Prophets were so described for they had the ability to perceive truth and reality. Such people do not go around stumbling like the blind. Instead, they move along the Straight Way, with open eyes, in the light of knowledge and understanding.

Implicit in this is the subtle point that the wicked and the disobedient are devoid of power and insight. The really powerful are those who work for God's cause. Likewise, the people of vision are those who can distinguish between the light of truth and the darkness of falsehood.

49. The Prophets attained great heights of success and achievement but did not hanker after the world, let alone worship it; instead, their thoughts and efforts were focused on the Hereafter. Hence God speaks of the Hereafter here as 'the real abode' which underlines the truth that the world is not man's true abode. It is only a passing resort, one from which man has to depart soon, man's true abode, then, is the Hereafter. Those endowed with insight therefore work to improve their prospects in the Hereafter. God loves such people. As for those who indulge in such acts as to embellish their worldly lives, they will find that they destroy their prospects in the Hereafter; such people are naturally not of His liking.

(48) And remember Ishmael, Elisha,[50] and Dhū al-Kifl.[51] All were of the best.

(49) This was a remembrance. An excellent retreat awaits the God-fearing (50) – everlasting Gardens with gates wide open for them[52] ▶

وَٱذْكُرْ إِسْمَٰعِيلَ وَٱلْيَسَعَ وَذَا ٱلْكِفْلِ ۖ
وَكُلٌّ مِّنَ ٱلْأَخْيَارِ ﴿٤٨﴾ هَٰذَا ذِكْرٌ ۚ وَإِنَّ
لِلْمُتَّقِينَ لَحُسْنَ مَـَٔابٍ ﴿٤٩﴾ جَنَّٰتِ عَدْنٍ
مُّفَتَّحَةً لَّهُمُ ٱلْأَبْوَٰبُ ﴿٥٠﴾

---

50. Al-Yasa' is mentioned twice in the Qur'ān. (See also *al-An'ām* 6: 86.) At both places no further details are provided about him. He is simply mentioned along with other Prophets. What we do know, however, is that he was a distinguished Israelite Prophet. He came from Abel Meholah, which is situated on the bank of the River Jordan. Jews and Christians speak of him as Elisha. When the Prophet Elijah (peace be on him) was stationed at the Sinai Peninsula, he was directed to return to Syria and Palestine to accomplish some important task. One of these was to prepare and train Elisha as his successor. When Elijah met him, he saw him ploughing his field with a yoke of twelve oxen before him. Later on, he abandoned farming, (*1 Kings* 19: 15-21.) For more than a decade Elisha was under the care of the Prophet Elijah (peace be on him) and succeeded him after his demise (*2 Kings*: 2.) A detailed account of him features in the Bible (see *2 Kings*: 2-13.) One learns from it that it was he who inspired a prince to stand against the polytheism, idolatry and moral degeneracy that had overtaken the Israelite kingdom. It was he who put an end to Baal worship. He also put to death all members of such degenerate families. However, this reform movement could not extirpate all the evils that had made deep inroads in the society. After Elisha's demise, these evils reached their zenith and were followed by the Assyrian incursions against Samaria. (For further details see *al-Ṣāffāt* 37, nn. 70-71, *Towards Understanding the Qur'ān*, vol. IX, pp. 310-11.)

51. The Prophet Dhū al-Kifl is mentioned twice in the Qur'ān; in this verse and in *Sūrah al-Anbiyā'* 21: 85. (For details about him, see *al-Anbiyā'* 21, n. 81, *Towards Understanding the Qur'ān*, vol. V, pp. 291-2.)

52. The statement that 'everlasting Gardens with gates wide open' admits several meanings. One, that when the God-fearing enter Paradise they will find its gates wide open merely by their desiring to enter

(51) wherein they shall recline, wherein they shall ask for abundant fruit and drinks, (52) and wherein there shall be with them well-matched, bashful mates.[53] (53) All this is what you are promised for the Day of Judgement. (54) This is Our provision for you, never to end.

(55) All this (is for the God-fearing). But for the transgressors, an evil resort awaits them – (56) Hell, where they will be roasted. An evil place to dwell! (57) All this (is for them); so let them taste boiling water and pus,[54] ▸

مُتَّكِـِٔينَ فِيهَا يَدۡعُونَ فِيهَا بِفَـٰكِهَةٖ
كَثِيرَةٖ وَشَرَابٖ ﴿٥١﴾ ۞ وَعِندَهُمۡ قَـٰصِرَٰتُ
ٱلطَّرۡفِ أَتۡرَابٌ ﴿٥٢﴾ هَـٰذَا مَا تُوعَدُونَ
لِيَوۡمِ ٱلۡحِسَابِ ﴿٥٣﴾ إِنَّ هَـٰذَا لَرِزۡقُنَا
مَا لَهُۥ مِن نَّفَادٍ ﴿٥٤﴾ هَـٰذَاۚ وَإِنَّ لِلطَّـٰغِينَ
لَشَرَّ مَـَٔابٖ ﴿٥٥﴾ جَهَنَّمَ يَصۡلَوۡنَهَا
فَبِئۡسَ ٱلۡمِهَادُ ﴿٥٦﴾ هَـٰذَا فَلۡيَذُوقُوهُ
حَمِيمٞ وَغَسَّاقٞ ﴿٥٧﴾

Paradise. Two, that those whom God chooses for Paradise will have to make no effort to enter it; no sooner than they want to, its gates will be flung open. Three, that the angels appointed as keepers of Paradise will open its gates as soon as they observe any of the people of Paradise. This last aspect is mentioned more clearly in the following verse of the Qur'ān: 'Its gates will have already been thrown open when they arrive there. Its keepers will tell them: "Peace be upon you! You have done well. Herein you shall abide"', (*al-Zumar* 39: 73.)

53. This possibly means that the mates of the people of Paradise will be of one and the same age. It can also mean, however, that the age of the mates will match the age of their spouses.

54. Lexicographers consider the word *ghassāq* to mean the following: (i) fluids of the body such as pus, blood and tears; (ii) intensely cold objects;

(58) and other sufferings of the kind. (59) (Observing their followers advancing to Hell they will say, among themselves:) 'This is a troop rushing in to you. There is no welcome for them. They are destined to roast in the Fire.' (60) They will reply: 'Rather, no welcome to you. (You will roast in Hell.) It is you who led us to this end. What an evil resort!' (61) They will say: 'Our Lord, give twofold punishment in the Fire to him who has led us to this.' (62) They will say to one another: 'But why do not we see those whom we considered among the wicked?[55] (63) Is it that we mistakenly made fun of them; or have they disappeared from our sight?' ▶

وَءَاخَرُ مِن شَكْلِهِۦٓ أَزْوَٰجٌ ﴿٥٨﴾ هَٰذَا فَوْجٌ
مُّقْتَحِمٌ مَّعَكُمْ ۖ لَا مَرْحَبًۢا بِهِمْ ۚ إِنَّهُمْ صَالُوا۟
ٱلنَّارِ ﴿٥٩﴾ قَالُوا۟ بَلْ أَنتُمْ لَا مَرْحَبًۢا بِكُمْ ۖ أَنتُمْ
قَدَّمْتُمُوهُ لَنَا ۖ فَبِئْسَ ٱلْقَرَارُ ﴿٦٠﴾ قَالُوا۟ رَبَّنَا
مَن قَدَّمَ لَنَا هَٰذَا فَزِدْهُ عَذَابًا ضِعْفًا فِى
ٱلنَّارِ ﴿٦١﴾ وَقَالُوا۟ مَا لَنَا لَا نَرَىٰ رِجَالًا كُنَّا
نَعُدُّهُم مِّنَ ٱلْأَشْرَارِ ﴿٦٢﴾ أَتَّخَذْنَٰهُمْ سِخْرِيًّا
أَمْ زَاغَتْ عَنْهُمُ ٱلْأَبْصَٰرُ ﴿٦٣﴾

(iii) objects with a foul, rotten smell. While it is correct to use the word to mean all of these, it is generally used to denote pus and blood.

55. In other words, the true believers, whom the unbelievers had treated with contempt and scorn in the world, will not be found in Hell. To their astonishment, the unbelievers will find their own leaders in Hell. However, they will not see there any of those they had condemned in the world and had mocked for talking about God, His Messenger, and the Hereafter.

(64) Verily all this is true. This is how the inmates of the Fire will dispute among themselves.

(65) Tell them,[56] (O Prophet): 'I am nothing but a warner.[57] There is no deity but Allah, the One, the Supreme, (66) the Lord of the heavens and the earth and all that is in between them, the Most Mighty, the Most Forgiving.' (67) Say: 'This is a tiding of tremendous import (68) from which you are turning away.'[58]

إِنَّ ذَٰلِكَ لَحَقٌّ تَخَاصُمُ أَهْلِ ٱلنَّارِ ﴿٦٤﴾ قُلْ
إِنَّمَآ أَنَا۠ مُنذِرٌ ۖ وَمَا مِنْ إِلَٰهٍ إِلَّا ٱللَّهُ ٱلْوَٰحِدُ
ٱلْقَهَّارُ ﴿٦٥﴾ رَبُّ ٱلسَّمَٰوَٰتِ وَٱلْأَرْضِ
وَمَا بَيْنَهُمَا ٱلْعَزِيزُ ٱلْغَفَّٰرُ ﴿٦٦﴾ قُلْ هُوَ نَبَؤٌا۟
عَظِيمٌ ﴿٦٧﴾ أَنتُمْ عَنْهُ مُعْرِضُونَ ﴿٦٨﴾

---

56. From here on the theme that was broached in the opening part of the *sūrah* is resumed. For a better understanding of the part that follows it is useful to read it in comparison with the opening verses of the *sūrah*.

57. In verse 4, it was stated that the Makkan unbelievers were amazed at the fact that 'a warner had come to them from among themselves…' Here the Prophet (peace be on him) is apprising them that he is 'a clear' warner to them. In other words, his vocation was to preach and to admonish rather than to coerce people to believe. If they refuse to pay heed to him, they will have only themselves to blame. If they persist in heedlessness and error, they themselves will face its dire consequences.

58. This is a response to the unbelievers' statement in verse 5 of this *sūrah*: 'Has he made the gods into one single God? This is truly astonishing.' The unbelievers took serious exception to the monotheism propounded by the Prophet (peace be on him). He made it plain to them that he was informing them about something that is utterly true, to wit, monotheism.

(69) (Tell them): 'I had no knowledge of the High Council when they were disputing. (70) I am told (about matters) by means of revelation only because I am a clear warner.' (71) When your Lord said to the angels:[59] 'Verily I am creating a human being from clay.[60] ▶

مَا كَانَ لِيَ مِنْ عِلْمٍۭ بِٱلْمَلَإِ ٱلْأَعْلَىٰٓ
إِذْ يَخْتَصِمُونَ ﴿٦٩﴾ إِن يُوحَىٰٓ إِلَيَّ
إِلَّآ أَنَّمَآ أَنَا۠ نَذِيرٌ مُّبِينٌ ﴿٧٠﴾ إِذْ قَالَ رَبُّكَ
لِلْمَلَٰٓئِكَةِ إِنِّى خَٰلِقٌۢ بَشَرًا مِّن طِينٍ ﴿٧١﴾

The unbelievers greeted this with frown and scorn. However, their frown and scorn could not change reality. The unbelievers thought that God was simply one of several gods. Accordingly, they resented the Prophet's insistence on monotheism. It is being asserted that God is the Only True God. He is Almighty, He is the Lord of the heavens and the earth, the Lord of all that exists. On the other hand, none of the unbelievers' idols has any power or authority. These are simply created beings who are under God's control. How can such objects that are utterly powerless and are owned in fact by God be regarded as partners in God's Divinity? Also, by what logic can they be considered deities?

59. This indicates some details of the dispute mentioned in verse 69. The dispute consists of Satan's contention against God. Let us also clarify that the verse additionally speaks of the angels insofar as this exchange between God and Satan took place through the agency of some angel. The event discussed here also features at other places in the Qur'ān. (See, for example, *al-Baqarah* 2: 30-39; *al-A'rāf* 7: 11-24; *al-Ḥijr* 15: 28-43; *Banī Isrā'īl* 17: 61-5; *al-Kahf* 18: 47-50 and *Ṭā Hā* 20: 115-24; *Towards Understanding the Qur'ān,* vol. I, pp. 58-66; vol. II, pp. 7-16; vol. IV, pp. 288-90; vol. V, pp. 56-60, 112 and 231-40.)

60. Lexically, *bashar* denotes a dense body whose exterior is covered by something. It is used specifically for man when reference is made to him after his creation. In this pre-creation context, it means one who will be made of clay and will be devoid of feather and wings. In other words, unlike other creatures, man's skin will not be covered with wool, fur or feathers.

(72) After I have created him and breathed into him of My spirit,[61] fall you down, prostrating yourselves to him.'[62] (73) Then the angels, all of them, prostrated themselves before Adam (74) except *Iblīs*. He waxed proud and became one of the unbelievers.[63] (75) The Lord said: 'O *Iblīs*, what prevented you from prostrating yourself before him whom I created of My Two Hands.[64] Are you waxing proud, or fancy yourself to be too exalted?' (76) He replied: 'I am nobler than he. You created me from fire and created him from clay.' ▶

فَإِذَا سَوَّيْتُهُۥ وَنَفَخْتُ فِيهِ مِن رُّوحِى فَقَعُوا۟
لَهُۥ سَٰجِدِينَ ﴿٧٢﴾ فَسَجَدَ ٱلْمَلَٰٓئِكَةُ كُلُّهُمْ
أَجْمَعُونَ ﴿٧٣﴾ إِلَّآ إِبْلِيسَ ٱسْتَكْبَرَ وَكَانَ
مِنَ ٱلْكَٰفِرِينَ ﴿٧٤﴾ قَالَ يَٰٓإِبْلِيسُ
مَا مَنَعَكَ أَن تَسْجُدَ لِمَا خَلَقْتُ بِيَدَىَّ ۖ
أَسْتَكْبَرْتَ أَمْ كُنتَ مِنَ ٱلْعَالِينَ ﴿٧٥﴾
قَالَ أَنَا۠ خَيْرٌ مِّنْهُ ۖ خَلَقْتَنِى مِن نَّارٍ وَخَلَقْتَهُۥ
مِن طِينٍ ﴿٧٦﴾

---

61. For further details see *al-Ḥijr* 15, n. 19, *Towards Understanding the Qur'ān*, vol. IV, pp. 289-90 and *al-Sajdah* 32, n. 16, vol. VIII, pp. 164-5.

62. For further details see *al-Baqarah* 2, n. 45, *Towards Understanding the Qur'ān*, vol. I, p. 62 and *al-A'rāf* 7, n. 10, vol. III, pp. 7-10.

63. For further details see *al-Baqarah* 2, n. 47, *Towards Understanding the Qur'ān*, vol. I, p. 63 and *al-Kahf* 18, n. 48, vol. V, p. 112.

64. This brings out man's exalted status. That the Lord Himself accomplished man's creation signifies the major importance of the task. Had the task been of an ordinary nature, the Sovereign would have assigned it to His servants. On the contrary, when the Sovereign carries out a task himself, it shows that the task is of extraordinary importance. Now, since God Himself created man, nothing should deter man from submitting to Him.

(77) He said: 'Get out
of here;[65] surely you are
accursed,[66] (78) and My curse
shall remain upon you till
the Day of Resurrection.'[67]
(79) Satan said: 'My Lord,
then grant me respite till
the Day that they are raised
up.' (80) He said: 'You are
of those who have been
granted respite (81) till the
Day whose Hour I know.'
(82) (*Iblīs*) said: 'By Your
glory, I shall mislead them
all (83) except those of Your
servants, the chosen ones
from amongst them.'[68] ▶

قَالَ فَٱخۡرُجۡ مِنۡهَا فَإِنَّكَ رَجِيمٞ ٧٧ وَإِنَّ
عَلَيۡكَ لَعۡنَتِيٓ إِلَىٰ يَوۡمِ ٱلدِّينِ ٧٨ قَالَ رَبِّ
فَأَنظِرۡنِيٓ إِلَىٰ يَوۡمِ يُبۡعَثُونَ ٧٩ قَالَ فَإِنَّكَ
مِنَ ٱلۡمُنظَرِينَ ٨٠ إِلَىٰ يَوۡمِ ٱلۡوَقۡتِ ٱلۡمَعۡلُومِ ٨١
قَالَ فَبِعِزَّتِكَ لَأُغۡوِيَنَّهُمۡ أَجۡمَعِينَ ٨٢
إِلَّا عِبَادَكَ مِنۡهُمُ ٱلۡمُخۡلَصِينَ ٨٣

As to the expression 'My Two Hands', this probably underscores two important aspects of God's creative power: one, that man was endowed with a body that links him to animals, and two, that the spirit was breathed into him, making him superior to all creatures on earth.

65. The reference is to Adam's creation and the directive to the angels to prostrate themselves before him. Satan, however, disobeyed God.

66. *Rajīm* denotes the one who is accursed or expelled. It is used for a person who falls from favour and stands humiliated and disgraced. Almost the same point is made in *Sūrah al-A'rāf* 7: 13 in which Satan is spoken of as follows: 'Be gone. You will be among the humiliated'.

67. This does not mean that Satan will not be cursed after the Day of Resurrection. What is rather stressed is that he will be cursed till the Day of Judgement. At a later stage, he will face the punishment for the misdeeds he had committed since Adam's creation till the Last Day.

68. The point being made is not that Satan will not try to mislead 'the chosen ones'. The purpose of the statement is to stress that Satan will not be able to mislead them.

(84) He (i.e. Allah) said: 'This is the Truth – and I only speak the Truth – (85) I will certainly fill the Gehenna[69] with you and with all those among them who follow you.'[70]

(86) (O Prophet), tell them: 'I do not ask you for any recompense for ▶

قَالَ فَٱلۡحَقُّ وَٱلۡحَقَّ أَقُولُ ۝٨٤ لَأَمۡلَأَنَّ
جَهَنَّمَ مِنكَ وَمِمَّن تَبِعَكَ مِنۡهُمۡ أَجۡمَعِينَ ۝٨٥
قُلۡ مَآ أَسۡـَٔلُكُمۡ عَلَيۡهِ مِنۡ أَجۡرٍ

69. The address is directed to all devils, i.e. Satan as well as his accomplices who are engaged in misleading mankind.

70. This story is narrated in response to the Quraysh chiefs' sarcastic query: 'Has this Exhortation been sent down among us only to him, to the exclusion of all others?' This was partly addressed in verses 9-10 above: 'Do they possess the treasures of your Lord, the Most Mighty, the Great Bestower? Or do they possess the dominion of the heavens and the earth and all that is in between them? If so, let them ascend to the heights of the realm of causation and see!' In other words, they were told that they had no right to question who should be designated a Prophet and who should not.

The second response is articulated here. The Quraysh notables are being told that their jealousy towards the Prophet Muḥammad (peace be on him) and their self-conceit and arrogance resemble Iblīs's jealousy and arrogance. Iblīs had refused to recognise God's right to appoint Adam as His vicegerent. Following in his footsteps, the unbelieving Quraysh denied God His right to appoint anyone whom He pleases as His Messenger. Iblīs had declined to prostrate himself before Adam and the Quraysh are guilty of refusing to obey the Prophet Muḥammad (peace be on him). The resemblance of the Quraysh with Iblīs, does not end with being alike in iniquity. In fact, their ultimate end will also be the same. Like Iblīs, they will remain accursed in this life and face Hellfire in the Next.

وَمَآ أَنَا۠ مِنَ ٱلْمُتَكَلِّفِينَ ۝٨٦ إِنْ هُوَ إِلَّا ذِكْرٌ لِّلْعَٰلَمِينَ ۝٨٧ وَلَتَعْلَمُنَّ نَبَأَهُۥ بَعْدَ حِينٍۭ ۝٨٨

the performance of this task;[71] nor am I given to affectation.[72] (87) This is nothing but an Admonition for all people the world over. (88) You will know the truth of the matter after a while.'[73]

71. The Prophet (peace be on him) points out that he is a selfless person who has no axe to grind by preaching the truth.

72. The Prophet (peace be on him) is not one of those who make false claims in order to achieve eminence and glory. This was not merely a verbal assertion but the Prophet's entire life bore testimony to its truth. He had lived for full 40 years in the midst of his people and every Makkan knew that he was not a fake. The entire body of Makkans was aware that the Prophet (peace be on him) had never uttered as much as a word that would give rise to the suspicion that he was hankering after power and glory.

73. What this meant is that those who will remain alive will see in a few years that what the Prophet (peace be on him) said will come to pass. As for those who die, no sooner than they enter the portal of death they too will realise that what the Prophet (peace be on him) had said was true.

Sūrah 39

Al-Zumar

(Companies)

(Makkan Period)

Title

The title is taken from the word *al-zumar* (companies), which occurs in verses 71 and 73 of this *sūrah*.

Period of Revelation

Verse 10, which states that 'Allah's earth is spacious' contains the clue that the *sūrah* was revealed before the Muslims' migration to Abysinnia. Some traditions indicate that this verse was revealed with regard to Ja'far ibn Abī Ṭālib and his companions after they made up their minds to migrate. (See al-Ālūsī, *Rūḥ al-Ma'ānī*, comments on *Sūrah al-Zumar* 39: 10.)

Subject Matter and Theme

The entire *sūrah* stands out as an inspiring discourse delivered in Makkah on the eve of the migration to Abyssinia, in an atmosphere charged with violence and oppression. Essentially, it is addressed to the Makkan unbelievers, though at times Muslims are also addressed. On the whole, the *sūrah* brings into sharp relief the real objective of the Prophet's call to Islam, which consists in worshipping the One True God without tainting it with any form of polytheism. This fundamental principle is expressed in a variety of ways. The purpose is to stress the truth of monotheism and the excellent consequences of embracing it as well as to emphasise the error of polytheism and its dire consequences. People are asked to give up their erroneous attitude and turn to their Lord's mercy and compassion. It is in this context that believers are told that if they find it hard to worship God at any particular place because of persecution they should move to somewhere where they can keep their faith. For God's earth is vast and He will reward them for their patience and fortitude. The Prophet (peace be on him) is directed to let the Makkan unbelievers realise that their persecution will, in no way, lead to the reversion of Muslims to their ancestral faith. Furthermore, no matter what the unbelievers do to dissuade the Prophet (peace be on him) to give up his mission, he will never do so.

In the name of Allah, the Most Merciful, the Most Compassionate.

بِسۡمِ ٱللَّهِ ٱلرَّحۡمَٰنِ ٱلرَّحِيمِ

(1) The revelation of this Book is from Allah, the Most Mighty, the Most Wise.[1]

(2) (O Prophet), it is We Who have revealed this Book to you with Truth.[2] So serve only Allah, consecrating your devotion to Him.[3] ▶

تَنزِيلُ ٱلۡكِتَٰبِ مِنَ ٱللَّهِ ٱلۡعَزِيزِ ٱلۡحَكِيمِ ۝١ إِنَّآ أَنزَلۡنَآ إِلَيۡكَ ٱلۡكِتَٰبَ بِٱلۡحَقِّ فَٱعۡبُدِ ٱللَّهَ مُخۡلِصٗا لَّهُ ٱلدِّينَ ۝٢

1. This constitutes a short introduction to the *sūrah*. It emphasises that, contrary to the contention of his opponents, the Prophet (peace be on him) had no hand in the authorship of the Qur'ān. Far from that, it is God's Own Word that He Himself revealed. It is forcefully stressed that people should not treat the Qur'ān lightly; instead, they should take its contents with utter seriousness.

In this connection two attributes of God have been mentioned in order to highlight two realities pertaining to the Qur'ān. One, that God Who has revealed the Qur'ān, is 'Most Mighty'; hence, no power can prevent His will from being done or His decrees from coming into effect. Two, that God is 'Most Wise'; hence, the Qur'ān's guidance is steeped in wisdom. So it is only those who are ignorant or foolish that turn away from it. (For further details see *al-Sajdah* 32, n. 1, *Towards Understanding the Qur'ān*, vol. VIII, pp. 156-7.)

2. That is, the Qur'ān is all truth and veracity, altogether unblemished by falsehood.

3. This is a very important verse which enunciates the objective of Islam's mission. One should, therefore, pay due attention rather than cursorily pass over it. It comprises two basic points which need to be grasped in order to understand this verse: (i) Man is asked to worship God. (ii) The worship that he is required to render is characterised by exclusive and total devotion and obedience to God.

'Abd is the root word of *'ibādah*. The word *'abd* is used in Arabic as an antonym of the one who is free, hence denoting a slave, one who is in someone else's ownership. Hence *'ibādah* has two meanings: (i) worship and devotion as mentioned in the renowned standard dictionary of Arabic *Lisān al-'Arab*. To say about someone: *'abada Allāh* (he worshipped God) means *ta'allaha lahu* (he held him to be God). As for the word *ta'abbud*, it means *tanassuk* (to be pious, devout and otherworldly); (ii) to render service with utter humility, to obey someone cheerfully. According to *Lisān al-'Arab, 'ibādah* is obedience. The linguistic meaning of *'ibādah* is obedience with submissiveness and humility. He who obeyed (*dāna*) a king is his *'ābid* (*wa qawmuhumā lanā 'ābidūn!*). An *'ābid* is he who humbles himself before his Lord, surrendering himself and obeying His command. A person is said to have worshipped *Ṭāghūt* (Satan) if he obeys Satan by following his commands and doing whatever he entices and misleads him to do. To say *iyyāka na'budu* (we worship You alone) means that we obey You with humility. *U'budū rabbakum* means 'obey Your Lord.' Thus according to these authoritative lexical explanations, what is required of man is not only to worship God and be devoted to Him but also to obey Him unquestioningly and willingly and to adhere to His law and carry out His commands with all his heart and soul.

As for the word *dīn*, it carries several meanings in Arabic: for example, dominance, authority, overlordship and the power to enforce one's decisions over others. *Lisāan al-'Arab* says *dāna al-nāsa*, meaning that 'he overpowered people to obedience.' Likewise, to say *dintuhum* means that 'I overpowered them.' To say *dintuhum* also means that 'I subjugated them and became their master and possessed them.' It is said in a *ḥadīth*: *'al-kayyis man dāna nafsahu,'* meaning 'the clever one is he who subdued his self,' that is, 'humbles it and enslaves it.' The word *al-dayyān* means judge, arbitrator or ruler. To say: *'wa lā anta dayyānī'* means: 'You are not someone who has overpowered me so that you would rule over my affairs.' To say: *'mā kāna liya'khudhu akhāhu fī dīn al-malik'* means that 'his brother did not have the authority to bring him to be judged by the law of the king.' The other connotation of *dīn* is that of obedience, servitude and slavery. According to *Lisān al-'Arab, dīn* means obedience. To say *dintuhu* or *dintu lahu* means: 'I obeyed him.' *Al-dīn li Allāh* means that obedience and worship are consecrated for God. In a *ḥadīth* it is said: *'urīdu min Quraysh kalimatan: tadīnu lahum bihā al-'Arab.'* This means: 'I want from Quraysh the affirmation of a word that would lead the Arabs to become subservient to them.' To say: *thumma dānat ba'd al-rabāb* means: 'then the *rabāb* became subservient to him and obeyed him.' The expression *'yamraqūna min al-dīn'* means 'they went out of the [fold of] religion,' meaning that 'they went out of the obedience of the *imām* whose obedience is obligatory.'

(3) Lo, religion is exclusively devoted to Allah.[4] Your religion is entirely consecrated to Him. As for those who have taken others than Allah for their guardians, (they say): 'We worship them only that they may bring us nearer to Allah.'[5] ▶

أَلَا لِلَّهِ ٱلدِّينُ ٱلْخَالِصُ ۚ وَٱلَّذِينَ ٱتَّخَذُوا۟
مِن دُونِهِۦٓ أَوْلِيَآءَ مَا نَعْبُدُهُمْ إِلَّا لِيُقَرِّبُونَآ
إِلَى ٱللَّهِ زُلْفَىٰٓ

The word *al-madīn* means slave. In the statement: *'fa law lā in kuntum ghayr madīnīn'* the word *madīnīn* means slaves. The third meaning of *dīn* is the way or custom which men generally follow.

In view of these three meanings of the word *dīn*, in this verse it signifies the attitude and way of life one adopts in recognition of someone's supremacy. The words, 'So serve only Allah, consecrating your devotion to Him' means that one should not mix service to any others with service to God. Man is required to serve and worship God alone, to follow only His Guidance and to obey only His injunctions and commands.

4. Man is directed to exclusively worship God for He alone deserves this. No one has any share in the worship and obedience that are due to Him. None other than God is entitled to be served and he who serves any others besides God is guilty of a serious wrong. The same holds true with regard to him who adulterates service to God with service to others. This verse is best explained by the following *ḥadīth* cited by Ibn Marduwayah on the authority of Yazīd al-Raqqāshī: 'Someone asked the Prophet (peace be on him) whether he would receive any reward for the money he donates in order to attain renown. To this he replied in the negative. When the same person asked about his act of charity which was motivated by earning God's reward as well as fame in this world, the Prophet (peace be on him) clarified: "God accepts only what one does exclusively for His sake." After making this observation the Prophet (peace be on him) recited the verse under discussion'. (See al-Suyūṭī, *al-Durr al-Manthūr*, comments on *Sūrah al-Zumar* 39: 2-3.)

5. Although the polytheists of Makkah, (and the polytheists of the world over for that matter), recognised God as the Creator and looked upon Him as their Lord, they claimed that they did not worship any

Allah will judge between them concerning what they differ about.[6] Verily Allah does not guide anyone who is given to sheer lying, is an utter unbeliever.[7]	إِنَّ ٱللَّهَ يَحْكُمُ بَيْنَهُمْ فِى مَا هُمْ فِيهِ يَخْتَلِفُونَ ۗ إِنَّ ٱللَّهَ لَا يَهْدِى مَنْ هُوَ كَـٰذِبٌ كَفَّارٌ ﴿٣﴾

objects or beings other than God as their Creator, and that the purpose of their worship of their deities was simply to have access to the Creator through them.

6. It should be clearly understood that monotheism alone can lead to unity and concord among human beings. As for polytheism, it cannot bring about any consensus. Polytheists can never agree as to who has the power to grant them access to God. Although some credit their gods and goddesses with this ability, they differ as regards the exact identity of those gods and goddesses. Some look upon the moon, the sun, or Mars and Venus as their intercessors with God. Nevertheless, they cannot fully decide which one of these occupies the highest position in the hierarchy. Some believe that the saints of the past can draw them close to God, although there are fierce differences among them on this matter. Some believe in one saint and others in another. These disagreements are quite understandable for the assumptions about these holy people are not based on any authentic knowledge, nor did God provide them with a list of those holy people who are highly stationed with Him and who could therefore serve as intermediaries for access to Him. In fact, notions such as the ones mentioned above gained currency among people merely because of superstitiousness, blind adoration and uncritical following of eminent people of the past. This being the case, serious disagreements were bound to occur in determining who were the true intermediaries between God's creatures and their Lord.

7. God brands polytheists as liars and utter unbelievers. They are also called *kuffār*. This word has two meanings: (i) that they are diehard unbelievers, for even after monotheism has been expounded to them, they still cling to their false polytheistic notions. (ii) They are an ungrateful lot. This because while they receive all possible bounties from God they do not give thanks to Him. They rather give thanks to those deities whom they have come to believe to be the means for these bounties.

(4) If Allah had wanted to take to Himself a son, He could have chosen anyone He wanted out of those whom He creates.[8] Glory be to Him (that He should have a son). He is Allah: the One, the Overpowering.[9] ▶

لَّوۡ أَرَادَ ٱللَّهُ أَن يَتَّخِذَ وَلَدٗا لَّٱصۡطَفَىٰ مِمَّا يَخۡلُقُ مَا يَشَآءُۚ سُبۡحَٰنَهُۥۖ هُوَ ٱللَّهُ ٱلۡوَٰحِدُ ٱلۡقَهَّارُ ٤

8. That God betook a son is simply out of the question. At most, God might elevate some creature's rank with Him. However, no exalted person, howsoever high his station, can be God's issue, for there is a world of difference between the Creator and the creature. Having a child necessarily implies that the two belong to the same species, which is impossible in this case.

The present verse makes it quite clear that God never intended to take anyone as His son: 'If Allah had wanted to take to Himself a son, He could have chosen anyone He wanted out of those whom He creates.' It is clear, therefore, that God never wanted to take to Himself anyone as His son. Far from taking anyone as His son, He never even entertained such an idea.

9. These arguments totally repudiate the notion of God's sonship. The first and foremost argument is that God is free from every imperfection, flaw or weakness. It is obvious that the person who needs a son does so because of his weakness and dependence on another. Since he himself is bound to die he wants a son so as to ensure the perpetuity of his family and lineage. The same holds true of those who adopt someone because there is none to inherit them or some do so out of their overflowing love and affection for a particular child. To ascribe these weaknesses to God and make the notion of sonship an article of faith simply betrays rank ignorance and intellectual short-sightedness.

The second argument is that God is unique. He does not belong to any particular species, while children are born to members of the same species. Moreover, a child is simply inconceivable without marriage with a spouse who should also belong to the same species. Therefore, only an ignorant and foolish person can ascribe children to God.

The third argument is that God is Overpowering. He exercises total control over everything in the universe. No one, whether high or low,

(5) He created the heavens and the earth with Truth,[10] and He folds up the day over the night and folds up the night over the day. He has subjected the sun and the moon, each is running its course until an appointed time. Lo, He is the Most Mighty, the Most Forgiving.[11] (6) He it is Who created you from a single being, and He it is Who made from it its mate.[12] He it is Who created for you eight heads of cattle ▶

خَلَقَ ٱلسَّمَٰوَٰتِ وَٱلْأَرْضَ بِٱلْحَقِّ ۖ يُكَوِّرُ
ٱلَّيْلَ عَلَى ٱلنَّهَارِ وَيُكَوِّرُ ٱلنَّهَارَ عَلَى ٱلَّيْلِ ۖ
وَسَخَّرَ ٱلشَّمْسَ وَٱلْقَمَرَ ۖ كُلٌّ يَجْرِى لِأَجَلٍ
مُّسَمًّى ۗ أَلَا هُوَ ٱلْعَزِيزُ ٱلْغَفَّٰرُ ﴿٥﴾ خَلَقَكُم
مِّن نَّفْسٍ وَٰحِدَةٍ ثُمَّ جَعَلَ مِنْهَا زَوْجَهَا
وَأَنزَلَ لَكُم مِّنَ ٱلْأَنْعَٰمِ ثَمَٰنِيَةَ أَزْوَٰجٍ ۚ

---

has even the slightest resemblance to Him that might be suggestive of any kinship with God.

10. For further details see *Ibrāhīm* 14, n. 26 and *al-Naḥl* 16, n. 6, *Towards Understanding the Qur'ān,* vol. IV, pp. 263 and 313, and *al-'Ankabūt* 29, n. 75, vol. VIII, p. 40.

11. God is so powerful that were He to decide to punish someone, no one can prevent Him from doing so. He is nonetheless so gracious and kind that despite a person's blasphemy, He does not instantly seize him for punishment; instead, He continues to grant him respite. (The grant of respite rather than immediate punishment is mentioned here as a manifestation of God's attribute of forgiveness.)

12. This does not mean that God first created human beings from Adam and then created Eve. Instead of a temporal sequence what we find here is a certain sequence of propositions. Examples of this are found in all languages. We shall illustrate this by the following sentence: 'Your deeds of today are known to me and so are your deeds of yesterday.' This does not mean that the deeds of yesterday followed the deeds of today though that happens to be the sequence in the sentence.

in pairs.[13] He creates you in your mothers' wombs, giving you one form after another in threefold depths of darkness.[14] That, then, is Allah, your Lord.[15] His is the kingdom.[16] There is no god but He.[17] So, whence are you being turned astray?[18]

يَخْلُقُكُمْ فِي بُطُونِ أُمَّهَٰتِكُمْ خَلْقًا مِّنۢ
بَعْدِ خَلْقٍ فِي ظُلُمَٰتٍ ثَلَٰثٍ ۚ ذَٰلِكُمُ
ٱللَّهُ رَبُّكُمْ لَهُ ٱلْمُلْكُ ۖ لَآ إِلَٰهَ إِلَّا هُوَ ۖ فَأَنَّىٰ
تُصْرَفُونَ ﴿٦﴾

---

13. The reference here is to the camel, cow, sheep and goat. Four males and four females of each species make a total of eight heads of cattle.

14. The reference here is to the belly, the womb and the membrane enveloping the foetus.

15. God is the Lord, the Sovereign and the Sustainer.

16. God alone has all authority. His command is in force throughout the universe.

17. In other words, the reasoning is that since God alone is the Lord and the Sovereign, He alone should be worshipped. Others have no share in Godhead since they have no share in His lordship and dominion. The unbelievers should know that God alone created the heavens and the earth, that He alone made the sun and the moon of service to man, that He alone alternates day and night, and that He alone brought all men, women and animals into being. In view of the above, none else but He deserves to be served and worshipped.

18. The point is made in the passive voice as the unbelievers are asked: 'whence are you being turned astray?' What the statement implies is that someone is misguiding them. Hence, they fail to grasp something that is quite simple and straightforward, something that pertains to common sense. It is clear, nevertheless, that this Qur'ānic discourse is addressed not to the evil ones who are misguiding people but to those who, under the spell and overwhelming influence of evil ones, are going astray. It would have been futile to address those who were actively engaged in misguiding people. This because their pursuit was informed by their

(7) If you disbelieve, know well that Allah has no need of you.[19] Yet He does not like unbelief in His servants.[20] But if you are ▶

إِن تَكْفُرُوا۟ فَإِنَّ ٱللَّهَ غَنِىٌّ عَنكُمْ ۖ وَلَا يَرْضَىٰ لِعِبَادِهِ ٱلْكُفْرَ ۖ وَإِن

vested interests which required that they should try to turn people away from service to the One True God and entice them to serve and keep serving others than Him. It is obvious that such people were not amenable to reason, for their interests lay in not seeing reason. In fact, even if such people had seen any reason in what they were told, it would be most unlikely for them to sacrifice their interests for the sake of truth. Those who really deserved sympathy, however, are the common people who had fallen prey to the enchanting delusions of those who were out to mislead.

19. Their unbelief has no bearing on God's dominion. God continues to be the Supreme Lord, whether they accept this or not. God's overlordship needs no external support; it remains unaffected by its affirmation or denial by anyone. According to a *ḥadīth* [*qudsī*], the Prophet (peace be on him) narrated that God said: 'O My servants, if those of you of the earlier times and those of you of later times, the humans among you and the *jinn* among you become like the heart of the most wicked person among you, nothing will diminish of My Kingdom,' (Muslim, *Kitāb al-Birr wa al-Ṣilah wa al-Ādāb, Bāb Taḥrīm al-Ẓulm.*)

20. It is not out of consideration for any interest of God's but rather in consideration of man's own interest that God does not desire that humans succumb to unbelief, for unbelief is detrimental to the latter's own interest.

It should be noted that there is a difference between God's will and His pleasure. Nothing can take place without God's will. Man can, however, do what does not please God. Indeed, this happens quite often. There are tyrants, wrongdoers, thieves, highway robbers, murderers as well as people guilty of illicit sex. All this is because God has made it possible for people to commit evil in the natural scheme of things that He has created. By the same token, He makes it possible for the righteous to perform good deeds. Had He not provided opportunities for this, there would have been no good and evil in this world. The existence of good and evil is an integral part of God's design. However, all that happens

thankful, your thankfulness will please Him.[21] No one shall bear another's burden.[22] You are destined to return to your Lord and He will tell you what you used to do. He is well aware even of what lies hidden in your breasts.

(8) When any affliction befalls man,[23] he cries out ▶

تَشْكُرُواْ يَرْضَهُ لَكُمْ وَلَا تَزِرُ وَازِرَةٌ وِزْرَ أُخْرَىٰ ثُمَّ إِلَىٰ رَبِّكُم مَّرْجِعُكُمْ فَيُنَبِّئُكُم بِمَا كُنتُمْ تَعْمَلُونَ إِنَّهُۥ عَلِيمٌۢ بِذَاتِ ٱلصُّدُورِ ۝٧

۞ وَإِذَا مَسَّ ٱلْإِنسَٰنَ ضُرٌّ دَعَا

does not necessarily enjoy God's pleasure. For example, if one resolves to earn one's bread by unlawful means, God lets one do so. This is part of His dispensation. However, the person who draws his sustenance through robbery or bribery should not think that God approves of such means of earning. Likewise, He has granted man the freedom to disbelieve insofar as He does not force man to become a believer. However, God disapproves of His creatures refusing to believe in their Creator and Sustainer. Whilst this is ruinous for them it will not cause the least damage to God's dominion.

21. The word used here as the opposite of *kufr* is *shukr* (thankfulness), rather than *īmān* (faith, belief). This automatically shows that unbelief basically consists of denying God's favours whereas faith is an expression of one's gratefulness to God for His bounties. Thankfulness to God and faith in Him complement each other. In contrast, an unbeliever is devoid of gratefulness, and disbelief makes gratitude meaningless.

22. Every man bears responsibility for his own deeds. If someone chooses to disbelieve in order to please others or to avoid their displeasure, others will not be taken to task for that person's unbelief. Rather, they will ultimately leave that person to face the consequences of his unbelief. Anyone who recognises the distinction between belief and unbelief should instantly give up unbelief and join the camp of belief. Furthermore, the person who chooses belief should not incur eternal perdition out of deference to one's family, community or nation.

23. Reference here is to the unbelieving person who is thankless to God despite His bounties.

to his Lord, penitently turning to Him.[24] But when his Lord bestows His favour upon him, he forgets the affliction regarding which he had cried out[25] and sets up compeers to Allah[26] that they may lead others astray from His Path.[27] Say, (O Prophet): 'Enjoy your unbelief for a while. Surely you will be among the inmates of the Fire.' (9) Is such a person (preferable or he) who is obedient, and prostrates himself in the watches of the night, stands (in Prayer), ▶

رَبَّهُۥ مُنِيبًا إِلَيۡهِ ثُمَّ إِذَا خَوَّلَهُۥ نِعۡمَةً مِّنۡهُ نَسِيَ
مَا كَانَ يَدۡعُوٓاْ إِلَيۡهِ مِن قَبۡلُ وَجَعَلَ لِلَّهِ
أَندَادًا لِّيُضِلَّ عَن سَبِيلِهِۦۚ قُلۡ تَمَتَّعۡ بِكُفۡرِكَ
قَلِيلًاۖ إِنَّكَ مِنۡ أَصۡحَٰبِ ٱلنَّارِ ۝٨ أَمَّنۡ
هُوَ قَٰنِتٌ ءَانَآءَ ٱلَّيۡلِ سَاجِدًا وَقَآئِمًا

24. In times of crisis, even the polytheist abandons his false gods and turns in desperation to the One True God, the Lord of the universe. This highlights the fact that in the depths of his heart even the polytheist realises that his deities are powerless. Within him too there is the realisation that God alone has all power and authority.

25. Once man tides over his straits, he tends to forget that in utter desperation he had eschewed all false gods and turned to the One True God in prayer.

26. He subsequently resumes worshipping and obeying and praying to beings other than God and making offerings to them.

27. Such a person's error is not confined to himself. He also misleads others by telling them that some saint or idol had rescued him from his distress. This, in turn, leads others to adore those deities besides God. This, then, is how ignorant people continually contribute to the growth of error by narrating their so-called experiences.

is fearful of the Hereafter, and looks forward to the mercy of His Lord? Ask them: 'Are those who know equal to those who do not know?'[28] Only those endowed with understanding take heed.

(10) Tell them (O Prophet): 'O you servants of Mine who believe, have fear of your Lord.[29] A good end awaits those who did good in this world.[30] ▶

يَحۡذَرُ ٱلۡأٓخِرَةَ وَيَرۡجُواْ رَحۡمَةَ رَبِّهِۦۗ قُلۡ هَلۡ
يَسۡتَوِي ٱلَّذِينَ يَعۡلَمُونَ وَٱلَّذِينَ لَا يَعۡلَمُونَۗ
إِنَّمَا يَتَذَكَّرُ أُوْلُواْ ٱلۡأَلۡبَٰبِ ٩ قُلۡ
يَٰعِبَادِ ٱلَّذِينَ ءَامَنُواْ ٱتَّقُواْ رَبَّكُمۡۚ
لِلَّذِينَ أَحۡسَنُواْ فِي هَٰذِهِ ٱلدُّنۡيَا حَسَنَةٞۗ

---

28. Let it be clear that here two types of people are being compared. There is one who turns fervently to God in crisis, though he serves others than the One True God at other times. The other type of person is committed fully to obeying, worshipping and glorifying God alone. That he worships Him in the privacy of night underscores his sincere devotion to God. God brands the former kind as ignorant, as 'those who do not know', even if he might have devoured whole libraries. On the other hand, He characterises the latter as 'those who know' even though they might be illiterate. For, true knowledge consists in grasping the truth and acting according to it. This is what man's success and well-being depend on. In the sight of God, these two different types of people cannot be considered alike. Since they follow different ways in this life, they will not and cannot have the same end in the Next.

29. That is, it is not enough merely to believe but it is also required that one should be God-fearing; do what one is commanded to do by God and refrain from what He has forbidden and live in the world in constant and unremitting fear of accountability to Him.

30. This signifies success in both worlds. Those who do good prosper both in this life and in the Next.

Allah's earth is spacious.[31] Verily those who persevere shall be granted their reward beyond all reckoning.'[32]

(11) Tell them, (O Prophet): 'I am bidden to serve Allah, consecrating my devotion to Him, (12) and I am bidden to be the first of those who surrender to Him.'[33] (13) Say: 'If I disobey my Lord, I fear the chastisement of an Awesome Day.' (14) Say: 'Allah alone shall I serve, consecrating my devotion to Him. (15) So serve, apart from Him, whomsoever you please.' Say: 'Behold, the real losers shall be those who will have lost their own selves and their kith and kin on the Day of Resurrection. ▶

وَأَرْضُ ٱللَّهِ وَٰسِعَةٌ ۗ إِنَّمَا يُوَفَّى ٱلصَّٰبِرُونَ
أَجْرَهُم بِغَيْرِ حِسَابٍ ﴿١٠﴾ قُلْ إِنِّىٓ أُمِرْتُ
أَنْ أَعْبُدَ ٱللَّهَ مُخْلِصًا لَّهُ ٱلدِّينَ ﴿١١﴾ وَأُمِرْتُ
لِأَنْ أَكُونَ أَوَّلَ ٱلْمُسْلِمِينَ ﴿١٢﴾ قُلْ إِنِّىٓ
أَخَافُ إِنْ عَصَيْتُ رَبِّى عَذَابَ يَوْمٍ
عَظِيمٍ ﴿١٣﴾ قُلِ ٱللَّهَ أَعْبُدُ مُخْلِصًا لَّهُۥ دِينِى ﴿١٤﴾
فَٱعْبُدُوا۟ مَا شِئْتُم مِّن دُونِهِۦ ۗ قُلْ إِنَّ
ٱلْخَٰسِرِينَ ٱلَّذِينَ خَسِرُوٓا۟ أَنفُسَهُمْ وَأَهْلِيهِمْ
يَوْمَ ٱلْقِيَٰمَةِ ۗ

31. If believers find it hard to profess and practise faith in a particular town, region or country, they should migrate to wherever it should not be hard to do so.

32. Those who endure hardship and persecution in God's cause and yet persevere will be granted immeasurable rewards. These rewards will also embrace those who migrate from their homeland and face the hardships of banishment as well as those who continue to stay in their homeland, bearing the afflictions that might befall them.

33. The Prophet's task is not merely to preach righteousness to others but also to put it into practice in his own life. In fact, his own practice precedes inviting others to live righteously.

Behold, that is the obvious loss.[34] (16) There shall be sheets of fire above them and beneath them. This is the end against which Allah warns His servants. So dread My wrath, O you servants of Mine!' (17) (On the other hand), good tidings await those who eschew serving false gods[35] and penitently return to Allah. (O Prophet), give good tidings to My servants, ▶

أَلَا ذَٰلِكَ هُوَ ٱلْخُسْرَانُ ٱلْمُبِينُ ﴿١٥﴾ لَهُم
مِّن فَوْقِهِمْ ظُلَلٌ مِّنَ ٱلنَّارِ وَمِن تَحْتِهِمْ
ظُلَلٌ ۚ ذَٰلِكَ يُخَوِّفُ ٱللَّهُ بِهِۦ عِبَادَهُۥ ۚ يَٰعِبَادِ
فَٱتَّقُونِ ﴿١٦﴾ وَٱلَّذِينَ ٱجْتَنَبُوا۟ ٱلطَّٰغُوتَ أَن
يَعْبُدُوهَا وَأَنَابُوٓا۟ إِلَى ٱللَّهِ لَهُمُ ٱلْبُشْرَىٰ ۚ
فَبَشِّرْ عِبَادِ ﴿١٧﴾

34. Generally speaking, an insolvent person is he who loses all his invested capital and is, thus, unable to pay off his liabilities. God employs this metaphor with regard to all unbelievers and polytheists. The reason is that they are granted life, a certain term of existence, intellect, physical body, various potentialities, faculties, and a variety of resources and opportunities. These constitute their capital. If people waste or misuse their capital in the erroneous belief that God does not exist, or that there are many gods, or that they will not be held accountable for their deeds, or that someone will come to their rescue in the Hereafter, they will end up as utter losers. Another loss they might suffer is because they might have wronged themselves and their fellow beings as well as generations of people still to come. Since they will not have anything left to their credit, they will not be able to meet the demands of reparation made against them. They will suffer losses and will be held responsible for ruining the lives of their children, of their kith and kin and friends because of the false ideas they espoused and the wrong examples they set. The present verse refers to all these losses that the unbelievers will incur.

35. *Ṭāghūt*, which is derived from *ṭughyān*, denotes rebellion and transgression. If someone is called *ṭāghūt* rather than *ṭāghī* (the rebellious), this amounts to calling them extremely rebellious, to holding them to be the epitome of rebelliousness. This can be understood by considering an example. If someone is beautiful – *ḥasīn* in Arabic – and one calls him/

(18) to those who pay heed to what is said and follow the best of it.[36] They are the ones whom Allah has guided to the Right Way; they are the ones endowed with understanding.

(19) (O Prophet), can you save him (from chastisement) against whom the sentence of chastisement has become due;[37] him who has, (as it were), already fallen into the Fire?' (20) But those who fear their Lord shall have lofty mansions built over one another ▶

ٱلَّذِينَ يَسْتَمِعُونَ ٱلْقَوْلَ فَيَتَّبِعُونَ أَحْسَنَهُۥٓ ۚ
أُو۟لَٰٓئِكَ ٱلَّذِينَ هَدَىٰهُمُ ٱللَّهُ ۖ وَأُو۟لَٰٓئِكَ هُمْ
أُو۟لُوا۟ ٱلْأَلْبَٰبِ ﴿١٨﴾ أَفَمَنْ حَقَّ عَلَيْهِ
كَلِمَةُ ٱلْعَذَابِ أَفَأَنتَ تُنقِذُ مَن فِى ٱلنَّارِ ﴿١٩﴾
لَٰكِنِ ٱلَّذِينَ ٱتَّقَوْا۟ رَبَّهُمْ لَهُمْ غُرَفٌ مِّن
فَوْقِهَا غُرَفٌ مَّبْنِيَّةٌ

---

her *ḥusn* (beauty), it means that his/her beauty has reached the point of perfection.

Deities other than the One True God have been called *ṭāghūt* because while worshipping others than God amounts to rebellion, those who cause others to worship them have reached the climax of rebelliousness. (For further details, see *al-Baqarah* 2, nn. 286 and 288, *Towards Understanding the Qur'ān*, vol. I, pp. 199 and 200, *al-Nisā'* 4, nn. 91 and 105, vol. II, pp. 53 and 59-60.) In this verse the word *ṭāghūt* has been employed in the plural sense. This is evident from the usage أَنْ يَعْبُدُوهَا rather than أَنْ يَعْبُدُوهُ which would have been employed if the object were singular.

36. This verse is open to two meanings: (i) That these servants of God do not indiscriminately follow everyone; instead, they carefully consider what people say, accepting only what they find to be true. (ii) That when they hear something, they are not inclined to distort its meaning; instead, they follow 'the best of it'.

37. The reference here is to the person who makes himself merit God's punishment and who God has decided to punish.

beneath which rivers flow. This is Allah's promise and never does Allah fail to fulfil His promise.

(21) Do you not see that Allah sent down water from the sky, then made it flow on earth as springs and streams and rivers[38] and then with it He brings forth vegetation of various hues; then this vegetation ripens and dries up, turning yellow, whereafter He reduces it to broken straw? Surely there is a lesson in this for those endowed with understanding.[39] ▶

تَجْرِى مِن تَحْتِهَا ٱلْأَنْهَٰرُ ۖ وَعْدَ ٱللَّهِ ۖ
لَا يُخْلِفُ ٱللَّهُ ٱلْمِيعَادَ ﴿٢٠﴾ أَلَمْ تَرَ أَنَّ
ٱللَّهَ أَنزَلَ مِنَ ٱلسَّمَآءِ مَآءً فَسَلَكَهُۥ
يَنَٰبِيعَ فِى ٱلْأَرْضِ ثُمَّ يُخْرِجُ بِهِۦ زَرْعًا
مُّخْتَلِفًا أَلْوَٰنُهُۥ ثُمَّ يَهِيجُ فَتَرَىٰهُ مُصْفَرًّا ثُمَّ
يَجْعَلُهُۥ حُطَٰمًا ۚ إِنَّ فِى ذَٰلِكَ لَذِكْرَىٰ
لِأُو۟لِى ٱلْأَلْبَٰبِ ﴿٢١﴾

38. The word *yanābī'* refers to all these three forms of water – [springs, streams and rivers].

39. The common phenomenon of crops and their decay imparts an important lesson to a person endowed with a good common sense: a lesson whereby one knows that worldly life and its allurements are ephemeral. Every spring that blossoms ends up in an autumn. The age of youth is destined to give way to old age and death. All that rises ultimately witnesses fall. Hence this world should not infatuate one to the point of making one heedless of God and the Hereafter. Likewise, the passion to pounce upon the fleeting pleasures of this world should not make one negligent of the abiding good of the Life to Come. When an intelligent person looks at the changing spectacle of spring and autumn he instantly knows that both prosperity and adversity are in God's Hand. It is He Who lets someone prosper and flourish and lets others face decay and destruction. None can prevent Him from granting prosperity to whomsoever He wills or prevent Him from wreaking destruction upon whomsoever He wills.

(22) Can he whose breast Allah has opened up for Islam[40] and who is thus (moving along a Path) illumined by a light from Allah[41] (be likened to him who derives no lesson from what he observes)? Woe, then, to those whose hearts were further hardened ▶	أَفَمَن شَرَحَ ٱللَّهُ صَدْرَهُۥ لِلْإِسْلَٰمِ فَهُوَ عَلَىٰ نُورٍ مِّن رَّبِّهِۦ ۚ فَوَيْلٌ لِّلْقَٰسِيَةِ قُلُوبُهُم

40. The reference here is to the person whom God enables to grasp these facts in depth and become firmly persuaded of Islam's truth. This inner state has been described by saying that God opened up that person's breast for Islam. The *sūrah* thus makes a pointed reference to such a person's state of conviction which drives away every doubt and reservation. Neither the fear of any risk nor of any possible loss prevents him from the resolve to recognise and embrace the truth. Therefore, he follows what he regards as truth irrespective of the difficulties he may have to face in so doing. A person with such resolve willingly and cheerfully obeys the commands of God and His Messenger. He readily embraces the beliefs, ideas, principles and rules that he finds in the Qur'ān and the *Sunnah*. He does not grieve at any loss that might have afflicted him as a result of his decision to embrace the truth. For such a person no unlawful gain holds any attraction. On the contrary, he celebrates his ability to eschew unlawful gains for that would undermine his prospects in the Hereafter. By the same token, he does not regret any loss that may accrue to him as a result of following the Straight Way. He cheerfully endures all such loss and prefers it to disobeying God. Likewise, he is not fearful of any danger that might confront him for the sake of this cause. For there is only one Straight Way leading to God and he is likely to encounter dangers in traversing that way. Since there is no other way, one should be ready to greet all dangers that might confront him.

41. A true believer is enlightened by the Qur'ān and the *Sunnah*. It is in their light that he finds the Straight Way in the midst of a multitude of false paths.

after Allah's admonition.[42] Such are indeed in obvious error.

(23) Allah has revealed the best teaching, a self-consistent Book which repeats its contents in manifold forms[43] whereat shiver the skins of those that hold their Lord in awe, and then their skins and their hearts soften for Allah's remembrance. That is Allah's Guidance ▶

مِّن ذِكْرِ ٱللَّهِ ۚ أُو۟لَـٰٓئِكَ فِى ضَلَـٰلٍ مُّبِينٍ ﴿٢٢﴾
ٱللَّهُ نَزَّلَ أَحْسَنَ ٱلْحَدِيثِ كِتَـٰبًا مُّتَشَـٰبِهًا
مَّثَانِىَ تَقْشَعِرُّ مِنْهُ جُلُودُ ٱلَّذِينَ يَخْشَوْنَ
رَبَّهُمْ ثُمَّ تَلِينُ جُلُودُهُمْ وَقُلُوبُهُمْ إِلَىٰ ذِكْرِ
ٱللَّهِ ۚ ذَٰلِكَ هُدَى ٱللَّهِ

42. As opposed to the 'opening up of one's breast', one may be faced with its constriction. In this state, there remains some possibility, however meagre, that the truth might penetrate unto one's heart. Alternatively, it is also possible that one's heart may become utterly hardened as though it were a piece of rock, becoming altogether devoid of the ability to embrace the truth. Such people are doomed to sheer destruction. What this suggests is that it is possible that the person who has some inclination to embrace the truth may attain deliverance. This, however, is implicit in the verse rather than stated explicitly. This is because the main objective of the verse is to warn those who were immersed in opposing the Prophet (peace be on him) to the point of becoming utterly obdurate. Such people had simply made up their minds not to accept any part of the Prophet's message. They are plainly warned against their zealous unbelief of which they were proud. They are told that it is the height of a person's misfortune that God's Exhortation is delivered to them and then their hearts should become even more hardened.

43. The Qur'ān is free from every kind of self-contradiction and discrepancy. The Book in its entirety is coherent; all along it gives the same message and expounds the same worldview. Each part of the Qur'ān reinforces, complements and supplements its other parts. The Book as a whole stands out for its cohesiveness, harmony and consistency.

wherewith He guides whosoever He pleases. And he whom Allah does not guide to the Right Path has none to guide him. (24) How woeful is the plight of him who has nothing except his face to shield him from severe chastisement on the Day of Resurrection?[44] Such evil-doers shall be told: 'Taste now the consequence of your deeds.'[45] (25) Their predecessors gave the lie to the Truth and then chastisement came upon them from whence they could not imagine. (26) So Allah made them taste degradation in the life of this world, and certainly the chastisement of the Hereafter will be much more grievous. Would that they knew!

يَهۡدِي بِهِۦ مَن يَشَآءُۚ وَمَن يُضۡلِلِ ٱللَّهُ فَمَا لَهُۥ
مِنۡ هَادٍ ﴿٢٣﴾ أَفَمَن يَتَّقِي بِوَجۡهِهِۦ سُوٓءَ
ٱلۡعَذَابِ يَوۡمَ ٱلۡقِيَٰمَةِۚ وَقِيلَ لِلظَّٰلِمِينَ
ذُوقُواْ مَا كُنتُمۡ تَكۡسِبُونَ ﴿٢٤﴾ كَذَّبَ ٱلَّذِينَ
مِن قَبۡلِهِمۡ فَأَتَىٰهُمُ ٱلۡعَذَابُ مِنۡ حَيۡثُ
لَا يَشۡعُرُونَ ﴿٢٥﴾ فَأَذَاقَهُمُ ٱللَّهُ ٱلۡخِزۡيَ فِي
ٱلۡحَيَوٰةِ ٱلدُّنۡيَاۖ وَلَعَذَابُ ٱلۡأٓخِرَةِ أَكۡبَرُۚ
لَوۡ كَانُواْ يَعۡلَمُونَ ﴿٢٦﴾

---

44. To have nothing but one's face to shield one from chastisement reveals the state of one's utter helplessness. In such a situation, everyone tries their level best to protect their face with their hands. In this context, then, those destined for God's chastisement will receive blows on their faces on the Day of Judgement.

45. *Kasb* in its Qur'ānic usage refers to one's earnings in terms of one's deeds. Anyone who performs good deeds makes himself deserving of reward from God. By the same token, those given to error and wickedness make themselves deserving of punishment in the Hereafter.

(27) We have indeed propounded for mankind all kinds of parables in this Qur'ān that they may take heed. (28) It is an Arabic Qur'ān[46] free of all crookedness[47] that they may guard against their evil end. (29) Allah propounds a parable: there is a man whose ownership is shared by several quarrelsome masters, each pulling him to himself; and there is another who is exclusively owned by one man. Can the two be alike?[48] ▶

وَلَقَدْ ضَرَبْنَا لِلنَّاسِ فِي هَٰذَا الْقُرْءَانِ
مِن كُلِّ مَثَلٍ لَّعَلَّهُمْ يَتَذَكَّرُونَ ﴿٢٧﴾
قُرْءَانًا عَرَبِيًّا غَيْرَ ذِي عِوَجٍ لَّعَلَّهُمْ يَتَّقُونَ ﴿٢٨﴾
ضَرَبَ اللَّهُ مَثَلًا رَّجُلًا فِيهِ شُرَكَاءُ
مُتَشَاكِسُونَ وَرَجُلًا سَلَمًا لِّرَجُلٍ هَلْ
يَسْتَوِيَانِ مَثَلًا

46. The Qur'ān was not imparted in some foreign tongue. Had it been so the services of a translator or interpreter would have been required to communicate its message to the Makkans or the Arabs as a whole. But since the Qur'ān was delivered in their own tongue, they were well-placed to directly comprehend it.

47. There is no confounding complexity in the Qur'ān that makes it difficult for the average person to comprehend its message. The Qur'ān states in clear, lucid terms whatever it condemns as wrong and evil. Likewise, it states in clear terms whatever it extols as good and the reason why it extols it. Essentially, then, the Qur'ānic belief system can be comprehended easily and adequately. There is no difficulty in ascertaining what it commands and what it forbids.

48. This parable brings out the difference between polytheism and monotheism and the varying impacts each makes on human life. In a few words, the moral of the parable is effectively articulated. It stands to reason that if a person is under several lords and masters his is likely to be a most miserable lot, especially if his masters happen to be selfish and ill-tempered. These masters may put the person to various and difficult

tasks at one and the same time and none of them might have the patience and sensitivity to appreciate that he might also be required to carry out tasks given to him by other masters. Such a person is likely to be rebuked and even punished by one of his masters for performing the task given by another master. On the contrary, his lot is likely to be much better if he is not required to serve several masters at the same time. This obvious truth can be readily grasped by the average person. Given this, it is not hard for a person to realise that he cannot enjoy any peace of mind if he serves more than one god.

It is pertinent to point out that this parable does not bring out its full thrust if we consider it only in the context of stone idols. It is even more applicable to those masters who are living beings and who issue divergent commands to their devotees. It is only in this sense that each of them vigorously pulls a man towards himself. Idols of stone are unable to do this. It is only living human lords and masters who are able to do so. There is, first of all, man's own self that comes forth with a series of desires, each urgently calling for satisfaction. This compels him first to seek one thing and then another. Masters other than one's self are one's family, one's community and one's country. Besides, there are also innumerable other lords and masters in the form of holy men, rulers, law-makers, businessmen and others who occupy the socio-cultural landscape. The divergent demands of each of them bring their pressures to bear on the individual. They expect a person to follow him and they do not mind brutally jostling him if he neglects their due. These masters inflict various types of punishment, ranging from expression of displeasure to stigmatisation and social boycott, insolvency, expulsion and imprisonment. Man's only way out from this impasse is to embrace monotheism and serve only the One True God. This enables him to free himself from bondage to all others.

There are two ways of practising monotheism. Obviously, each of these leads to different results. According to one of these ways, someone can decide to become God's servant in his individual capacity while the world around him lends him no support in his effort to serve God. In this case, external pressures might increase, subjecting him to ever greater constraint and hardship. However, if he sincerely follows the course he has chosen, he is bound to enjoy mental peace and tranquillity. He will be able to reject all that runs counter to God's commands or the requirements of godliness and piety. He will not oblige his family, community, government, clergy or economic oligarchy in ways that entail any violation of God's commands. This may, indeed it will, entail severe hardships for him. His heart, however, remains satisfied as he is his Lord's born servant and he has been faithful to Him. As for any others than the One True God, since he was not the born servant of any of them, he did not owe obedience to any of them. This will further prompt him to reject others' demands to act against God's commands. No power on earth can deprive such a person of peace and tranquillity of mind, so much so that he will not care even if he has to lay down his life in God's cause. Such a person will not grieve at the thought that rather than bow before false gods he was making the supreme sacrifice of his own life for God's sake.

The second option is that the whole of society be founded on the principle of monotheism. All aspects of life – morality, culture, civilisation, education, law, customs and mores and the political and economic systems, in short, all principles prescribed by God through His Book and His Messenger – are intellectually endorsed and practically put into effect in all walks of life. The government would seek to eradicate all that is evil and sinful; the educational system would endeavour to mould the minds of the young in such a manner that they refrain from what the Qur'ān brands as evil and sinful. Not only that, whatever is evil and sinful would also be berated from the pulpit, society would be opposed to it, and every form of business involving it would be disallowed by the economy. By the same token, what God's chosen religion declares to be good and wholesome would enjoy the support of law, the administrative apparatus would promote it, the entire educational system would inculcate it in people's minds, trying to make it an integral part of the people's character and personality; the pulpit would urge people to imbibe it; society would exalt it and make the current customs and usages conform to it, and economic transactions would proceed in harmony with it. This is a state of affairs wherein a person will enjoy full peace and tranquility, both internal and external. In such a state the avenues of material and spiritual growth would be flung wide open. Society would thereby be purged of all conflict between obligations to God and to anyone else.

Islam requires everyone to practise monotheism as his/her faith and to serve God whether the second possibility – founding the whole of life on monotheism – becomes a reality or not. In all circumstances a man is required to follow the monotheistic way and to patiently face the dangers and hardships that might come his way in his effort to serve the One True God. It cannot be denied, however, that Islam's ideal remains that man's entire life should be governed wholly by Islam. All Messengers of God strove to create a community of believers that would follow the way of life prescribed by God, free from the dominance of unbelief and unbelievers. Only he who is ignorant of the Qur'ān and the *Sunnah* and who lacks common sense will argue that the objective of the mission of God's Messengers was simply to enable individuals to practise their faith and to obey God, disregarding the need to put faith into effect in the believers' collective and social lives.

ٱلْحَمْدُ لِلَّهِ ۚ بَلْ أَكْثَرُهُمْ لَا يَعْلَمُونَ ﴿٢٩﴾
إِنَّكَ مَيِّتٌ وَإِنَّهُم مَّيِّتُونَ ﴿٣٠﴾ ثُمَّ إِنَّكُمْ
يَوْمَ ٱلْقِيَٰمَةِ عِندَ رَبِّكُمْ تَخْتَصِمُونَ ﴿٣١﴾
۞ فَمَنْ أَظْلَمُ مِمَّن كَذَبَ عَلَى ٱللَّهِ وَكَذَّبَ
بِٱلصِّدْقِ إِذْ جَآءَهُۥٓ ۚ أَلَيْسَ

All praise and thanks be to Allah.[49] But most of them are unaware.[50] (30) (O Prophet), you are destined to die[51] and they too are destined to die. (31) Then eventually all of you will contend before your Lord on the Day of Resurrection. (32) Who, then, can be more unjust than he who lied against Allah and denied the Truth when it came to him, calling it a lie? Is there no room ▶

49. The real import of *al-ḥamdu li Allāh* ('All praise and thanks be to Allah') can be appreciated in the context in which it occurs here. A question was posed to the Qur'ān's addressees, followed by a pause. Since the opponents of monotheism failed to come forth with any answer, the pause was followed by the expression *al-ḥamdu li Allāh*. The silence of the unbelievers in response to the query meant that even they could not dare say that devotion to several gods was equal to or better than devotion to the One True God.

50. The unbelievers do somehow recognise the distinction between serving one and several masters in ordinary life. However, when the difference between serving the One True God and several false gods is pointed out to them, they act as though they are idiots.

51. There is a subtle gap between the two statements, the previous and the present. This gap, however, can readily be filled by the common sense of an intelligent person who takes cognisance of the context. The Prophet (peace be on him) is told that even though he was preaching his message in a clear and straightforward manner, the unbelievers rejected that message out of sheer intransigence. Not only that, they were even bent upon harming the Prophet (peace be on him) so as to suppress the evident truth of his message. However, all mortals are bound to die and a day will come when everyone's *finale* will become known to all.

for such unbelievers in Hell? (33) But he who brought the Truth, and those who confirmed it as true, such are the ones who shall be guarded against the chastisement.[52] (34) They shall have from their Lord all that they wish for.[53] That is the reward of those that do good, (35) so that Allah may remit their worst deeds and reward them according to the best of their deeds.[54]

فِى جَهَنَّمَ مَثْوًى لِّلْكَـٰفِرِينَ ﴿٣٢﴾ وَٱلَّذِى
جَآءَ بِٱلصِّدْقِ وَصَدَّقَ بِهِۦٓ ۙ أُو۟لَـٰٓئِكَ هُمُ
ٱلْمُتَّقُونَ ﴿٣٣﴾ لَهُم مَّا يَشَآءُونَ عِندَ رَبِّهِمْ ۚ
ذَٰلِكَ جَزَآءُ ٱلْمُحْسِنِينَ ﴿٣٤﴾ لِيُكَفِّرَ ٱللَّهُ
عَنْهُمْ أَسْوَأَ ٱلَّذِى عَمِلُوا۟ وَيَجْزِيَهُمْ أَجْرَهُم
بِأَحْسَنِ ٱلَّذِى كَانُوا۟ يَعْمَلُونَ ﴿٣٥﴾

52. They are told as to who will be punished after being tried on the Day of Judgement. It is the wrongdoers who invent false beliefs, associate others with God in His essence, attributes, powers and rights, and who reject the truth who are destined for the worst punishment in the Next Life. An even more outrageous iniquity of theirs is that they decried for lying the person who presented the truth to them. As for the person who brought the truth (peace be on him) to them and those who affirmed the veracity of his message, it is simply out of the question that they will be condemned to punishment.

53. Note that this verse does not make any reference to Paradise. Rather, it is stated that the pious will receive all that they desire from their Lord. Obviously, each person will return to his Lord immediately after death. It seems, therefore, that the pious will be treated kindly from the moment of their death through their entry into Paradise. The pious will naturally desire to be spared torment in *barzakh*, the rigours on the Day of Judgement, stringent interrogation, and humiliation in the Grand Assembly and punishment for their lapses. They will desire all this and God will fulfil all these desires.

54. Those who embraced faith at the hands of the Prophet (peace be on him) had committed serious sins in matters of belief and practice in pre-Islamic days. After accepting Islam, they not only gave up all their false

(36) (O Prophet), does Allah not suffice for His servant? They frighten you with others apart from Him,[55] although he whom Allah lets go astray, none can guide him to the Right Way. (37) And he whom Allah guides to the Right Way, none can lead him astray. Is not Allah the Most Mighty, the Lord of Retribution?[56] (38) If you ask them: 'Who created the heavens and the earth?' they will surely answer: 'Allah.' Tell them: 'What do you think, then, of the deities whom you call upon instead of Allah? ▶

أَلَيْسَ ٱللَّهُ بِكَافٍ عَبْدَهُۥ ۖ وَيُخَوِّفُونَكَ
بِٱلَّذِينَ مِن دُونِهِۦ ۚ وَمَن يُضْلِلِ ٱللَّهُ فَمَا لَهُۥ
مِنْ هَادٍ ﴿٣٦﴾ وَمَن يَهْدِ ٱللَّهُ فَمَا لَهُۥ مِن مُّضِلٍّ ۗ
أَلَيْسَ ٱللَّهُ بِعَزِيزٍ ذِى ٱنتِقَامٍ ﴿٣٧﴾ وَلَئِن سَأَلْتَهُم
مَّنْ خَلَقَ ٱلسَّمَٰوَٰتِ وَٱلْأَرْضَ لَيَقُولُنَّ
ٱللَّهُ ۚ قُلْ أَفَرَءَيْتُم مَّا تَدْعُونَ مِن دُونِ ٱللَّهِ

beliefs but also faithfully followed the truth propounded by the Prophet (peace be on him). With regard to morality, worship and relationship with others, their conduct was excellent. God, therefore, promises that the sins committed by them in pre-Islamic time (*Jāhilīyah*) will be removed from their Record and they will be rewarded in accordance with the very best of their deeds in their Record of conduct.

55. The Makkan unbelievers threatened the Prophet (peace be on him) with dire consequences as a sequel to his opposition to their idols. Indeed, they thought that their idols were so immensely powerful that anyone who insulted them would simply be devastated.

56. The unbelievers are devoid of God's guidance. Therefore, they place great premium on the power and glory of their gods. So doing, they fail to recognise that God is supreme and that their blasphemous attitude to Him as evident from their polytheism amounts to inviting His wrath upon them.

إِنْ أَرَادَنِيَ ٱللَّهُ بِضُرٍّ هَلْ هُنَّ
كَٰشِفَٰتُ ضُرِّهِۦٓ أَوْ أَرَادَنِى بِرَحْمَةٍ هَلْ
هُنَّ مُمْسِكَٰتُ رَحْمَتِهِۦ ۚ قُلْ حَسْبِىَ
ٱللَّهُ ۖ عَلَيْهِ يَتَوَكَّلُ ٱلْمُتَوَكِّلُونَ ﴿٣٨﴾ قُلْ يَٰقَوْمِ
ٱعْمَلُوا۟ عَلَىٰ مَكَانَتِكُمْ إِنِّى عَٰمِلٌ ۖ فَسَوْفَ
تَعْلَمُونَ ﴿٣٩﴾ مَن يَأْتِيهِ عَذَابٌ يُخْزِيهِ وَيَحِلُّ
عَلَيْهِ عَذَابٌ مُّقِيمٌ ﴿٤٠﴾ إِنَّآ أَنزَلْنَا عَلَيْكَ
ٱلْكِتَٰبَ لِلنَّاسِ بِٱلْحَقِّ ۖ فَمَنِ ٱهْتَدَىٰ

If Allah should will that an affliction befall me, will those deities remove the harm inflicted by Him? Or if Allah should will that I receive (His) Mercy, will they be able to withhold His Mercy from me?' Say: 'Allah is sufficient for me; those who have to put their trust, let them put their trust in Him.'[57] (39) Tell them: 'My people, continue to work in your position as you will,[58] I too will continue with my work. Soon you shall know (40) whom the degrading chastisement will visit and upon whom the everlasting chastisement will alight.' (41) (O Prophet), We revealed to you the Book with the Truth for all mankind. So he who follows the Right Way ▸

57. Ibn Abī Ḥātim has narrated on the authority of Ibn 'Abbās that the Prophet (peace be on him) said: 'He who desires to be the most powerful among men should repose his trust in God. He who desires to be the richest should have greater trust in what is in God's possession than in what he himself possesses. Likewise, he who desires to be the most respected man, should fear Almighty God.' (Ibn Abī Ḥātim, *Tafsīr* on *Sūrah al-Zumar* 39: 38 and comments on *Sūrah al-Ṭalāq* 65: 2.)

58. The unbelievers are being sarcastically asked to persist in their bid to harm the Prophet (peace be on him) and to spare no effort in that regard.

does so to his own benefit, and he who goes astray, shall hurt only himself by straying. You are not accountable on their behalf.[59]

(42) It is Allah Who takes away the souls of people at the hour of their death, and takes away at the time of sleep the souls of those that have not died.[60] Then He retains the souls of those against whom He had decreed death and returns the souls of others till an appointed time. Surely there are Signs in this for a people who reflect.[61] ▶

فَلِنَفْسِهِۦ ۖ وَمَن ضَلَّ فَإِنَّمَا يَضِلُّ عَلَيْهَا ۖ
وَمَآ أَنتَ عَلَيْهِم بِوَكِيلٍ ﴿٤١﴾ ٱللَّهُ
يَتَوَفَّى ٱلْأَنفُسَ حِينَ مَوْتِهَا وَٱلَّتِى لَمْ تَمُتْ
فِى مَنَامِهَا ۖ فَيُمْسِكُ ٱلَّتِى قَضَىٰ عَلَيْهَا ٱلْمَوْتَ
وَيُرْسِلُ ٱلْأُخْرَىٰٓ إِلَىٰٓ أَجَلٍ مُّسَمًّى ۚ إِنَّ فِى
ذَٰلِكَ لَءَايَٰتٍ لِّقَوْمٍ يَتَفَكَّرُونَ ﴿٤٢﴾

---

59. The Prophet (peace be on him) has not been mandated to compel people to follow the Straight Way. All he is required to do is to clearly expound that Straight Way. However, if people still prefer error, it is they who will be held accountable for it while the Prophet (peace be on him) will be absolved of his responsibility if they continue to wallow in error after he has fulfilled his part of the duty.

60. To take away the souls of people at the time of sleep means that one's consciousness, perception, understanding and volition remain suspended while one is asleep.

61. By so saying, God stresses that He exercises total control over man's life and death. No one can say with certainty that the next day he will rise from his bed alive. Nor does anyone know whether after a moment he will be dead or alive. While one is awake or asleep, sitting in one's home or moving around, it is not at all certain that some calamity

(43) Or have they taken others instead of Allah as intercessors?[62] Say: 'Will they intercede though they may have no power and though they may not even understand?' (44) Say: 'All intercession lies with Allah.[63] His is the dominion of the heavens and the earth. And to Him will all of you be sent back.'

أَمِ ٱتَّخَذُواْ مِن دُونِ ٱللَّهِ شُفَعَآءَۚ قُلۡ أَوَلَوۡ
كَانُواْ لَا يَمۡلِكُونَ شَيۡـًٔا وَلَا يَعۡقِلُونَ ﴿٤٣﴾ قُل
لِّلَّهِ ٱلشَّفَٰعَةُ جَمِيعًاۖ لَّهُۥ مُلۡكُ ٱلسَّمَٰوَٰتِ
وَٱلۡأَرۡضِۖ ثُمَّ إِلَيۡهِ تُرۡجَعُونَ ﴿٤٤﴾

or any untoward affliction from outside might not cause one's sudden death. Thus, it would be sheer foolishness for man, whose life is always in God's Hand, to become heedless or defiant of God.

62. The unbelievers are guilty of gratuitously imagining that there are sacred beings who enjoy a very high degree of influence with God. Such is their influence that were they to intercede on behalf of any of their devotees their intercession will never be turned down. There is no basis, however, for any such belief. God has not sent down any sanction on the basis of which anyone can claim to have such an authority with God. More importantly, even those beings whose names are mentioned in this regard never claimed that they could effectively help others. The unbelievers are utterly foolish insofar as they fail to directly approach Him Who is the Lord of all, and instead direct their devotional feelings and entreaties to these so-called intercessors.

63. No one can even approach God with a request to intercede on anyone's behalf, let alone that he should believe that anyone has the power to have his intercession inexorably accepted. It is God's prerogative alone to allow or disallow requests for intercession. (For a detailed discussion of the Islamic concept of intercession and its comparison with the polytheistic concept, see *al-Baqarah* 2, n. 281, *Towards Understanding the Qur'ān,* vol. I, p. 196; *al-An'ām* 6, n. 33, vol. II, p. 235; *Yūnus* 10, nn. 5 and 24 and *Hūd* 11, n. 84, vol. IV, pp. 7, 24 and 120-1; *Ṭā Hā* 20, nn. 85-6 and *al-Anbiyā'* 21, n. 27, vol. V, pp. 227-9 and p. 262; *al-Ḥajj* 22, n. 125, vol. VI, p. 68; and *Saba'* 34, n. 40, vol. IX, p. 184.)

(45) When Allah alone is mentioned, the hearts of those who do not believe in the Hereafter contract with bitterness, but when deities apart from Allah are mentioned, they are filled with joy.[64] (46) Say: 'O Allah, the Originator of the heavens and the earth, the Knower of the unseen and the seen, You it is Who will judge among Your servants concerning what they differed.' (47) If the wrong-doers ▶

وَإِذَا ذُكِرَ ٱللَّهُ وَحْدَهُ ٱشْمَأَزَّتْ قُلُوبُ
ٱلَّذِينَ لَا يُؤْمِنُونَ بِٱلْءَاخِرَةِ وَإِذَا ذُكِرَ
ٱلَّذِينَ مِن دُونِهِۦٓ إِذَا هُمْ يَسْتَبْشِرُونَ ۝٤٥ قُلِ
ٱللَّهُمَّ فَاطِرَ ٱلسَّمَٰوَٰتِ وَٱلْأَرْضِ عَٰلِمَ
ٱلْغَيْبِ وَٱلشَّهَٰدَةِ أَنتَ تَحْكُمُ بَيْنَ عِبَادِكَ
فِى مَا كَانُوا۟ فِيهِ يَخْتَلِفُونَ ۝٤٦ وَلَوْ أَنَّ
لِلَّذِينَ ظَلَمُوا۟

64. 'When Allah alone is mentioned, the hearts of those who do not believe in the Hereafter contract with bitterness, but when deities apart from Allah are mentioned, they are filled with joy'. This characteristic is common to all those who have a polytheistic disposition, so much so that unfortunately even those Muslims who share this disposition are not devoid of it. While they say that they believe in God, whenever God alone is remembered one notices a kind of discomfiture on their faces. Such people do not fail to denounce those who fail to make mention of saints while remembering God. They protest that such people have no reverence for saints or else they would not simply talk of God alone. On the other hand, when the names of others are mentioned besides God they instantly react with gratification, their faces beaming with joy. This shows whom they truly love and care for. While commenting on this verse Ālūsī narrates a personal experience of his. He mentions that once he saw a person calling upon a deceased saint to deliver him from distress. Ālūsī counselled him to call upon God Who Himself says: 'When My servants ask you about Me, tell them I indeed am quite near; I hear and answer the call of the caller when he calls Me', (*al-Baqarah* 2: 186.) When that person heard this he was enraged. Later on, Ālūsī came to know from others that he accused him of disbelieving in saints. Some even heard him say that saints are quicker in responding [to prayers] than God." (Al-Ālūsī, *Rūḥ al-Ma'ānī*, comments on *Sūrah al-Zumar* 39: 45.)

possessed the treasures of the earth in their entirety and as much besides, they would gladly offer it on the Day of Resurrection to redeem themselves from the harrowing chastisement. This because there will appear to them from Allah something (exceedingly dismal which) they had never even imagined. (48) The evil consequences of their deeds will become fully apparent to them, and what they had scoffed at will encompass them.

(49) When an affliction befalls man,[65] he cries out to Us; but when We grant him a favour from Us, he says: 'I have been granted this on account of my knowledge.'[66] Nay; this (favour) is a test; ▶

مَا فِى ٱلْأَرْضِ جَمِيعًا وَمِثْلَهُۥ مَعَهُۥ لَٱفْتَدَوْا۟
بِهِۦ مِن سُوٓءِ ٱلْعَذَابِ يَوْمَ ٱلْقِيَٰمَةِ ۚ وَبَدَا
لَهُم مِّنَ ٱللَّهِ مَا لَمْ يَكُونُوا۟ يَحْتَسِبُونَ ﴿٤٧﴾ وَبَدَا
لَهُمْ سَيِّـَٔاتُ مَا كَسَبُوا۟ وَحَاقَ بِهِم مَّا كَانُوا۟
بِهِۦ يَسْتَهْزِءُونَ ﴿٤٨﴾ فَإِذَا مَسَّ ٱلْإِنسَٰنَ ضُرٌّ
دَعَانَا ثُمَّ إِذَا خَوَّلْنَٰهُ نِعْمَةً مِّنَّا قَالَ
إِنَّمَآ أُوتِيتُهُۥ عَلَىٰ عِلْمٍۭ ۚ بَلْ هِىَ فِتْنَةٌ

65. This refers to the person who feels ill at ease when he hears someone remembering God alone.

66. This statement can mean any of the following: First, that God knows that someone is worthy of a particular favour and He accordingly grants it to him. Had he been unworthy of that favour in God's sight because his beliefs are faulty or his behaviour is wicked, God would have denied him that favour in the first place. Second, it can also mean that the bounties that he enjoys were bestowed upon him because he was worthy of them.

but most of them do not know.[67] (50) Their predecessors also said the same, but their earnings proved of no avail to them,[68] (51) and the evil consequences of their deeds overtook them. The wrong-doers among these will also be overtaken by the evil consequences of their deeds. They will be utterly unable to frustrate (Us). (52) Do they not know that Allah enlarges and straitens the provision of whomsoever He pleases?[69] ▶

وَلَٰكِنَّ أَكْثَرَهُمْ لَا يَعْلَمُونَ ﴿٤٩﴾ قَدْ قَالَهَا
الَّذِينَ مِن قَبْلِهِمْ فَمَا أَغْنَىٰ عَنْهُم مَّا كَانُوا
يَكْسِبُونَ ﴿٥٠﴾ فَأَصَابَهُمْ سَيِّئَاتُ مَا كَسَبُوا ۚ
وَالَّذِينَ ظَلَمُوا مِنْ هَٰؤُلَاءِ سَيُصِيبُهُمْ
سَيِّئَاتُ مَا كَسَبُوا وَمَا هُم بِمُعْجِزِينَ ﴿٥١﴾
أَوَلَمْ يَعْلَمُوا أَنَّ اللَّهَ يَبْسُطُ الرِّزْقَ لِمَن
يَشَاءُ وَيَقْدِرُ ۚ

67. People mistakenly think that the one who is granted bounties is really worthy of them and that those bounties indicate that person's position of nearness to God. The truth is that God's bestowal of bounties on a person amounts to putting him to a test. This explains why we see many righteous people leading miserable lives, whereas wicked people are rolling in affluence and prosperity. Quite evidently, worldly bounties do not necessarily indicate how close a person is with God. All of us know that a great many people have been afflicted with misery although they were undeniably people of sterling character. In contrast, many people enjoy abundant luxuries of life although their wickedness is unmistakable. Doubtlessly, this cannot be taken to mean that God loves the wicked or that He is annoyed with the pious.

68. When God's chastisement seized such people, the exceptional ability of which they had boasted proved of no avail. Moreover, the misfortune that overtook them also demonstrated the hollowness of their claim that they enjoyed a position of special closeness with God. Had that been true, they would not have been confronted with the calamity that beset them.

69. It is being explained that the bestowal of wherewithal is governed by an altogether different law of God, one which is based on a different

Therein are Signs for those that believe.

إِنَّ فِي ذَٰلِكَ لَآيَٰتٍ لِّقَوْمٍ يُؤْمِنُونَ ﴿٥٢﴾

(53) Tell them, (O Prophet): 'My servants[70] who have committed excesses against themselves, do not despair of Allah's Mercy. ▶

۞ قُلْ يَٰعِبَادِيَ ٱلَّذِينَ أَسْرَفُوا۟ عَلَىٰٓ أَنفُسِهِمْ لَا تَقْنَطُوا۟ مِن رَّحْمَةِ ٱللَّهِ ۚ

---

set of considerations. The measure of sustenance granted to someone does not necessarily correspond to his worth in God's sight nor do his earnings necessarily indicate that person's nearness to God. (For a detailed discussion, see *al-Tawbah* 9, nn. 54, 75 and 89, *Towards Understanding the Qur'ān,* vol. III, pp. 217-18, 228-9 and 239; *Yūnus* 10, n. 23, *Hūd* 11, n. 3, *al-Ra'd* 13, n. 42, vol. IV, pp. 21-4, 80, and 238; *al-Kahf* 18, nn. 37-8, *Maryam* 19, n. 45, *Ṭā Hā* 20, nn. 113-14 and *al-Anbiyā'* 21, n. 99, vol. V, pp. 107, 169-70 and 299-302; *al-Mu'minūn* 23, nn. 1 and 50, vol. VI, pp. 77-8 and 105-7; *al-Qaṣaṣ*: 28, nn. 97-8 and 101, vol. VII, pp. 245 and 247; and *Saba'* 34, nn. 54-60, vol. IX, pp. 193-6.)

70. Some people offer a queer explanation of the opening words of this verse. They point out that here God Himself directs the Prophet (peace be on him) to address people as 'my servants'. Hence all men are the servants of the Prophet (peace be on him).

This is not an explanatory comment but the worst possible distortion of the meaning and message of the Qur'ān. In fact, this amounts to making the Qur'ān an object of jestful play and sport. It is possible that a section of ignorant and gullible devotees might be swayed by such contentions. But if this line of thinking is seriously pursued, it will undermine the whole message of the Qur'ān. This because the Qur'ān proclaims here, there and everywhere that humans are servants of none other than the One True God. The quintessence of the Qur'ānic message is: serve none except the One True God. According to the Qur'ān, the Prophet Muḥammad (peace be on him) too was God's servant. He was raised not as man's lord and deity but as God's Messenger and the purpose of his advent was to serve God and urge others to serve Him alone. In view of the above, how can any rational being believe that one fine day Muḥammad (peace be on him) will stand up in Makkah and begin to proclaim: 'O people you are not servants of deities such as 'Uzzā and Sun; in fact you are the servants of Muḥammad.' May God protect us from such blasphemy!

إِنَّ ٱللَّهَ يَغۡفِرُ ٱلذُّنُوبَ جَمِيعًاۚ إِنَّهُۥ هُوَ ٱلۡغَفُورُ
ٱلرَّحِيمُ ۝٥٣ وَأَنِيبُوٓاْ إِلَىٰ رَبِّكُمۡ وَأَسۡلِمُواْ لَهُۥ
مِن قَبۡلِ أَن يَأۡتِيَكُمُ ٱلۡعَذَابُ ثُمَّ
لَا تُنصَرُونَ ۝٥٤ وَٱتَّبِعُوٓاْ أَحۡسَنَ
مَآ أُنزِلَ إِلَيۡكُم

Surely Allah forgives all sins. He is Most Forgiving, Most Merciful.[71] (54) Turn to your Lord and surrender yourselves to Him before the chastisement overtakes you; for then you will receive no help. (55) Follow the best of what has been revealed[72] ▶

71. This discourse is addressed to all beings. There is no weighty basis to believe that it is addressed only to believers. As Ibn Kathīr has pointed out, this universal directive does not mean at all that God forgives the sins of people without their repentance and their turning to Him. God's pardon is contingent upon people's servitude, obedience and their following the message revealed by God, (Ibn Kathīr, *Tafsīr*, comments on *Sūrah al-Zumar* 39: 53.) This verse holds out a ray of hope to those who had been guilty of murder, illicit sex, stealing, highway robbery and such other major sins in the time of *Jāhilīyah*. Such people had given up the hope of ever being forgiven by God. Here they are directed not to despair. They are assured that if they become God's obedient servants, their past sins will be forgiven. This interpretation is endorsed by Ibn 'Abbās, Qatādah, Mujāhid, Ibn Zayd, Ibn Jarīr al-Ṭabarī, Bukhārī, Muslim, Abū Dā'ūd and Tirmidhī. (Ṭabarī, *Tafsīr*, comments on *Sūrah al-Zumar* 39: 53; Bukhārī, *Kitāb al-Tafsīr, Bāb Qawlihi: 'Yā 'Ibādiya al-Ladhīna Asrafū 'alā Anfusihim lā Taqnaṭū min Raḥmat Allāh...'*; Muslim, *Kitāb al-Īmān, Bāb Kawn al-Islām Yahdim mā qablahu wa kadhā al-Hijrah wa al-Ḥajj*; Abū Dā' ūd, *Kitāb al-Fitan wa al-Malāḥim, Bāb fī Ta'ẓīm Qatl al-Mu'min*; Tirmidhī, *Kitāb Tafsīr al-Qur'ān 'an Rasūl Allāh Ṣallā Allāh 'alayhi wa sallam, Bāb wa min Sūrah al-Zumar*.) (For further examples see *al-Furqān* 25, n. 86, *Towards Understanding the Qur'ān*, vol. VII, pp. 42-43.)

72. 'Follow the best of what has been revealed' means the following: to carry out God's commands, to abstain from what He forbids, and to derive wholesome lessons from the stories and parables He narrates. On the contrary, he who turns away from God's commands, who commits forbidden acts and pays no heed to God's counsel and admonition is guilty of following the Qur'ān in the worst possible manner.

to you from your Lord before the chastisement suddenly comes upon you without you even being aware of it.' (56) Lest a person should say: 'Alas for me for neglecting my duty towards Allah and for being among those that scoffed'; (57) and lest a person should say: 'If only Allah had guided me, I should have been one of the God-fearing'; (58) or lest he should say, when he sees the chastisement: 'O that I might return again, and be among those who do good.' (59) Yes indeed! But My Signs came to you and you rejected them as lies, and waxed arrogant and were among those who disbelieved. (60) On the Day of Resurrection you shall see that the faces of those who had lied against Allah have turned dark. Is Hell not vast enough to provide a room to the vainglorious? (61) But as for the God-fearing, Allah will deliver them on account of their achievements: no harm shall visit them nor shall they grieve.

مِّن رَّبِّكُم مِّن قَبۡلِ أَن يَأۡتِيَكُمُ ٱلۡعَذَابُ
بَغۡتَةٗ وَأَنتُمۡ لَا تَشۡعُرُونَ ﴿٥٥﴾ أَن تَقُولَ نَفۡسٞ
يَٰحَسۡرَتَىٰ عَلَىٰ مَا فَرَّطتُ فِي جَنۢبِ ٱللَّهِ
وَإِن كُنتُ لَمِنَ ٱلسَّٰخِرِينَ ﴿٥٦﴾ أَوۡ تَقُولَ
لَوۡ أَنَّ ٱللَّهَ هَدَىٰنِي لَكُنتُ مِنَ ٱلۡمُتَّقِينَ ﴿٥٧﴾
أَوۡ تَقُولَ حِينَ تَرَى ٱلۡعَذَابَ لَوۡ أَنَّ لِي كَرَّةٗ
فَأَكُونَ مِنَ ٱلۡمُحۡسِنِينَ ﴿٥٨﴾ بَلَىٰ قَدۡ
جَآءَتۡكَ ءَايَٰتِي فَكَذَّبۡتَ بِهَا وَٱسۡتَكۡبَرۡتَ
وَكُنتَ مِنَ ٱلۡكَٰفِرِينَ ﴿٥٩﴾ وَيَوۡمَ ٱلۡقِيَٰمَةِ
تَرَى ٱلَّذِينَ كَذَبُواْ عَلَى ٱللَّهِ وُجُوهُهُم
مُّسۡوَدَّةٌۚ أَلَيۡسَ فِي جَهَنَّمَ مَثۡوٗى
لِّلۡمُتَكَبِّرِينَ ﴿٦٠﴾ وَيُنَجِّي ٱللَّهُ ٱلَّذِينَ ٱتَّقَوۡاْ
بِمَفَازَتِهِمۡ لَا يَمَسُّهُمُ ٱلسُّوٓءُ وَلَا هُمۡ يَحۡزَنُونَ ﴿٦١﴾

(62) Allah is the Creator of everything; He is the Guardian over everything.[73] (63) To Him belong the keys of the heavens and the earth. It is those who disbelieve in Allah's Signs who will be the losers. (64) (O Prophet), say: 'Ignorant people! Do you bid me to serve any other beside Allah?' (65) (Tell them clearly that) it was revealed to you and to all Prophets before you: 'If you associate any others with Allah in His Divinity, your works will surely come to naught[74] and you will certainly be among the losers.' (66) Therefore, serve Allah alone and be among those who give thanks.

(67) They did not recognise the true worth ▶

ٱللَّهُ خَٰلِقُ كُلِّ شَيْءٍۖ وَهُوَ عَلَىٰ كُلِّ شَيْءٍ
وَكِيلٌ ٦٢ لَّهُۥ مَقَالِيدُ ٱلسَّمَٰوَٰتِ وَٱلْأَرْضِۗ
وَٱلَّذِينَ كَفَرُواْ بِـَٔايَٰتِ ٱللَّهِ أُوْلَٰٓئِكَ هُمُ
ٱلْخَٰسِرُونَ ٦٣ قُلْ أَفَغَيْرَ ٱللَّهِ تَأْمُرُوٓنِّيٓ
أَعْبُدُ أَيُّهَا ٱلْجَٰهِلُونَ ٦٤ وَلَقَدْ أُوحِيَ
إِلَيْكَ وَإِلَى ٱلَّذِينَ مِن قَبْلِكَ لَئِنْ
أَشْرَكْتَ لَيَحْبَطَنَّ عَمَلُكَ وَلَتَكُونَنَّ مِنَ
ٱلْخَٰسِرِينَ ٦٥ بَلِ ٱللَّهَ فَٱعْبُدْ وَكُن مِّنَ
ٱلشَّٰكِرِينَ ٦٦ وَمَا قَدَرُواْ ٱللَّهَ حَقَّ قَدْرِهِۦ

73. God did not simply create the universe and then withdraw from the scene; instead, He continues to look after and superintend everything. He not only created everything but everything continues to exist because of His will. It is He Who sustains them and causes them to thrive.

74. If someone engages in polytheism, none of his deeds will be accepted as good deeds. He will not be rewarded for any of the deeds that he performs as good deeds because of his polytheism. In view of this basic error, his own life will simply be one of utter loss and futility.

of Allah.[75] (Such is Allah's power that) on the Day of Resurrection the whole earth will be in His grasp, and the heavens shall be folded up in His Right Hand.[76] Glory be to Him! ▶

وَٱلْأَرْضُ جَمِيعًا قَبْضَتُهُۥ يَوْمَ ٱلْقِيَٰمَةِ
وَٱلسَّمَٰوَٰتُ مَطْوِيَّٰتٌۢ بِيَمِينِهِۦ ۚ سُبْحَٰنَهُۥ

75. The unbelievers are unaware of God's glory and greatness. They have never fully appreciated His exalted status that makes the deities they worship pale into absolute insignificance. Astonishingly, however, such people look upon the objects which they themselves have made into God's associates and partners and then consider them to be worthy objects of worship.

76. In order to emphasise God's absolute control over the heavens and the earth, the Qur'ān has recourse to the metaphor 'and the heavens shall be folded up in His Right Hand'. Just as it is easy for someone to hold a ball in his palm, and doing so does not weary him, so it will be on the Day of Judgement when the heavens and the earth will be rolled up in God's Hand. This image is especially presented to the unbelievers who are ignorant of God's greatness and glory so as to impress on them that for God the universe is no greater than a ball or a handkerchief. We find traditions in Aḥmad ibn Ḥanbal, Bukhārī, Muslim, Nasā'ī, Ibn Mājah and Ibn Jarīr al-Ṭabarī on the authority of 'Abd Allāh ibn 'Umar and Abū Hurayrah to the effect that once when the Prophet (peace be on him) was delivering a sermon from the pulpit he recited this particular verse, adding:

> God will rotate the heavens and the earths [that is, planets] in His palm, as a child rotates a ball. He will pronounce: 'I am the One God. I am the King. I am the Irresistible. All greatness belongs to Me. Where are the earthly kings? Where are the tyrants? Where are the mighty ones?'

While recounting these words, the Prophet (peace be on him) shook so violently that the Companions feared that he would collapse on the pulpit. (Bukhārī, *Kitāb Tafsīr al-Qur'ān, Bāb Qawlihi: 'Wa al-arḍ jamī'an qabḍatuhu'*; Muslim, *Kitāb Ṣifat al-Qiyāmah wa al-Jannah wa al-Nār*; Aḥmad ibn Ḥanbal, *Musnad*, narrated by 'Abd Allāh ibn 'Umar; Ṭabarī, *Tafsīr*, comments on *Sūrah al-Zumar* 39: 67.)

Exalted be He from all that they associate with Him.[77] (68) And the Trumpet shall be blown[78] and all who are in the heavens and the earth shall fall down dead save those whom Allah wills. Then the Trumpet shall be blown again, and lo! all of them will be standing and looking on.[79] (69) The earth shall shine with the light of its Lord, and the Scroll (of deeds) shall be set in place, and the Prophets and all witnesses[80] Shall be brought, ▶

وَتَعَٰلَىٰ عَمَّا يُشۡرِكُونَ ٦٧ وَنُفِخَ فِي ٱلصُّورِ
فَصَعِقَ مَن فِي ٱلسَّمَٰوَٰتِ وَمَن فِي
ٱلۡأَرۡضِ إِلَّا مَن شَآءَ ٱللَّهُۖ ثُمَّ نُفِخَ فِيهِ
أُخۡرَىٰ فَإِذَا هُمۡ قِيَامٞ يَنظُرُونَ ٦٨ وَأَشۡرَقَتِ
ٱلۡأَرۡضُ بِنُورِ رَبِّهَا وَوُضِعَ ٱلۡكِتَٰبُ
وَجِاْيٓءَ بِٱلنَّبِيِّـۧنَ وَٱلشُّهَدَآءِ

77. On the one hand is God's infinite glory. Just bear that in mind and then bring to mind the pettiness of holding other objects as associates with Him in His Godhead.

78. For an elaboration of the Trumpet, see *al-An'ām* 6, n. 48, *Towards Understanding the Qur'ān*, vol. II, p. 244; *Ibrāhīm* 14, n. 57, vol. IV, pp. 276-7; *Ṭā Hā* 20, n. 78, vol. V, pp. 223-4; and *al-Ḥajj* 22, n. 1, vol. VI, pp. 5-6.

79. The present verse states that the Trumpet will be blown twice. In *Sūrah al-Naml* 27: 58, however, there is reference to a blowing of the Trumpet preceding which all creatures will fall dead with dread and awe. *Aḥādīth,* therefore, speak of the blowing of the Trumpet thrice: (i) The first such occasion will fill everyone with awe and dread. (ii) The second will cause everyone's death. (iii) The third will bring about resurrection. All the dead will rise from their graves to appear before their Lord.

80. Included in this are those witnesses who will testify that they had conveyed God's message to mankind. There will also be those witnesses who will bear testimony to the deeds of people. These latter witnesses

and judgement shall be justly passed among them, and they shall not be wronged; (70) and everyone shall be paid in full for all that he did. Allah is best aware of all that they do.

(71) (After the judgement has been passed) the unbelievers shall be driven in companies to Hell so that when they arrive there, its gates shall be thrown open[81] and its keepers shall say to them: 'Did Messengers from among yourselves not come to you, rehearsing to you the Signs of your Lord and warning you against your meeting of this Day?' They will say: 'Yes indeed; but the sentence of chastisement was bound to be executed against the unbelievers.' (72) It will be said: 'Enter the gates of Hell. Herein shall you abide.' ▶

وَقُضِىَ بَيْنَهُم بِٱلْحَقِّ وَهُمْ لَا يُظْلَمُونَ ﴿٦٩﴾
وَوُفِّيَتْ كُلُّ نَفْسٍ مَّا عَمِلَتْ وَهُوَ أَعْلَمُ
بِمَا يَفْعَلُونَ ﴿٧٠﴾ وَسِيقَ ٱلَّذِينَ كَفَرُوٓا۟ إِلَىٰ
جَهَنَّمَ زُمَرًا ۖ حَتَّىٰٓ إِذَا جَآءُوهَا فُتِحَتْ
أَبْوَٰبُهَا وَقَالَ لَهُمْ خَزَنَتُهَآ أَلَمْ يَأْتِكُمْ رُسُلٌ
مِّنكُمْ يَتْلُونَ عَلَيْكُمْ ءَايَٰتِ رَبِّكُمْ
وَيُنذِرُونَكُمْ لِقَآءَ يَوْمِكُمْ هَٰذَا ۚ قَالُوا۟ بَلَىٰ
وَلَٰكِنْ حَقَّتْ كَلِمَةُ ٱلْعَذَابِ عَلَى
ٱلْكَٰفِرِينَ ﴿٧١﴾ قِيلَ ٱدْخُلُوٓا۟ أَبْوَٰبَ
جَهَنَّمَ خَٰلِدِينَ فِيهَا ۖ

---

may not necessarily be human beings. The angels, the *jinn*, the animals, the limbs of a person's own body, the physical environment and the trees and stones may also testify to men's deeds, each in its peculiar manner.

81. The gates of Hell will not be routinely open. Instead, they will be opened when the unbelievers arrive there. Once they have entered it, the gates will again be closed.

How evil is the abode of the vainglorious!

(73) And those who eschewed disobeying their Lord shall be driven in companies to Paradise so that when they arrive there its gates will have already been thrown open and its keepers shall say to them: 'Peace be upon you; you have done well. So enter. Herein you shall abide.' (74) They will say: 'All thanks and praise be to Allah Who has made His promise to us come true, and Who gave us the earth to inherit.[82] We may now dwell in Paradise wherever we please.'[83] How excellent is the reward of those who laboured![84]

فَبِئْسَ مَثْوَى ٱلْمُتَكَبِّرِينَ ﴿٧٢﴾ وَسِيقَ ٱلَّذِينَ
ٱتَّقَوْا۟ رَبَّهُمْ إِلَى ٱلْجَنَّةِ زُمَرًا ۖ حَتَّىٰٓ إِذَا
جَآءُوهَا وَفُتِحَتْ أَبْوَٰبُهَا وَقَالَ لَهُمْ خَزَنَتُهَا
سَلَـٰمٌ عَلَيْكُمْ طِبْتُمْ فَٱدْخُلُوهَا
خَـٰلِدِينَ ﴿٧٣﴾ وَقَالُوا۟ ٱلْحَمْدُ لِلَّهِ ٱلَّذِى
صَدَقَنَا وَعْدَهُۥ وَأَوْرَثَنَا ٱلْأَرْضَ نَتَبَوَّأُ مِنَ
ٱلْجَنَّةِ حَيْثُ نَشَآءُ ۖ فَنِعْمَ أَجْرُ ٱلْعَـٰمِلِينَ ﴿٧٤﴾

82. For further details see *Ṭā Hā* 20, nn. 83 and 106 and *al-Anbiyā'* 21, n. 99, *Towards Understanding the Qur'ān,* vol. V, pp. 226, 237-40 and pp. 299-302.

83. The dwellers of Paradise will own the part of it granted to them to abide and there they will enjoy full power and authority.

84. This may be the utterance of the dwellers of Paradise. Alternatively, it may be an additional observation made by God.

(75) You shall see the angels surrounding the Throne, glorifying their Lord with His praise, and judgement will have been made among them with fairness, and it will be proclaimed: 'All praise and thanks be to Allah, the Lord of the whole Universe.'[85]

وَتَرَى ٱلْمَلَـٰٓئِكَةَ حَآفِّينَ مِنْ حَوْلِ ٱلْعَرْشِ
يُسَبِّحُونَ بِحَمْدِ رَبِّهِمْ ۖ وَقُضِىَ بَيْنَهُم بِٱلْحَقِّ
وَقِيلَ ٱلْحَمْدُ لِلَّهِ رَبِّ ٱلْعَـٰلَمِينَ ﴿٧٥﴾

85. The entire universe will celebrate God's glory.

Sūrah 40

Al-Mu'min

(The Believer)

(Makkan Period)

Title

The title is derived from verse 28: 'Then a man endowed with faith *(mu'min)*, from Pharaoh's folk, who had kept his faith hidden, said...' The significance of giving the *sūrah* this title is to be found in the fact that it talks about that man of faith.

Period of Revelation

According to 'Abd Allāh ibn 'Abbās and Jābir ibn Zayd, this *sūrah* was revealed soon after the revelation of *Sūrah al-Zumar.* It is, accordingly, placed next to that *sūrah.* (Ālūsī, *Rūḥ al-Ma'ānī*, introductory remarks on *Sūrah al-Mu'min* 40.)

Background

The circumstantial setting in which the *sūrah* was revealed is indicated by its contents. At that point in time the Makkan unbelievers had initiated the following two kinds of activities against the Prophet (peace be on him): (i) On the one hand, they had raised a storm of controversy and adversarial propaganda against the Prophet (peace be on him) on all possible issues. By levelling a whole range of allegations against the Qur'ān, Islam and the Prophet (peace be on him), they tried to create myriad doubts and misgivings in people's minds. Furthermore, such negativity could not be easily removed. Perhaps inevitably then the accumulation of such misgivings created by this vicious onslaught naturally vexed the Prophet (peace be on him) and the believers. (ii) Additionally, the unbelievers had also begun to prepare the ground for the Prophet's assassination. As a part of this plan they hatched several conspiracies. On one occasion, they even took concrete steps towards assassinating him. Bukhārī has recorded the following tradition on the authority of 'Abd Allāh ibn 'Amr ibn al-'Āṣ: 'Once while the Prophet (peace be on him) was offering Prayer in the Holy Mosque [of Makkah], 'Uqbah ibn Mu'ayṭ surged forward and tied a piece of cloth around the Prophet's neck so as to strangle him. In the meantime, Abū Bakr arrived on the scene and pushed 'Uqbah away from the Prophet (peace be on him). While trying to release the Prophet (peace be on him) from 'Uqbah's grip he kept saying: "Would you kill a person simply because he says: 'My Lord in Allah?"' (Bukhārī, *Kitāb Tafsīr al-Qur'ān*, Bāb *Sūrah al-Mu'min.*) This tradition, in a slightly different form, also features in Ibn Hishām's *Sīrah* and is also cited by Nasā'ī and Ibn Abī Ḥātim. ('Abd al-Malik ibn Hishām, *al-Sīrah al-Nabawīyah*, Muṣṭafā al-Saqqā *et al.* eds., Beirut: Dār Iḥyā' al-Turāth al-'Arabī, n.d., vol. I, p. 310; Nasā'ī, *al-Sunan al-Kubrā, Kitāb al-Tafsīr, Bāb Sūrah Ghāfir*; Ibn Abī Ḥātim, *Tafsīr*, comments on *Sūrah al-Mu'min* 40: 28.)

Subject Matter and Themes:

Both these aspects of the prevalent state of affairs are clearly indicated in the *sūrah*'s opening part. The discourse that then follows represents a moving and instructive commentary on the situation.

In response to the assassination attempts on the Prophet (peace be on him) the story of the man of faith belonging to Pharaoh's community is recounted (see verses 23-55). Through this story, three different lessons are imparted to three concerned groups of people:

(i) The Makkan unbelievers are told that what they had planned to do against the Prophet Muḥammad (peace be on him) is exactly the same as what Pharaoh had planned to do against the Prophet Moses (peace be on him). The Makkan unbelievers are also warned that if they tried to repeat what Pharaoh and his community attempted to do, the consequence of their efforts will, in the end, be no different from that of Pharaoh and his followers.

(ii) The Prophet (peace be on him) and his Companions are assured that disregarding the fact that the believers are weak and helpless in comparison to the unbelievers, and that the latter are seemingly dominant and able to oppress the believers, they are nonetheless striving to exalt the faith prescribed by God, the Mightiest of all mighties. They, therefore, have no reason to be cowed down. When confronted with the unbelievers' enmity, their response should be as follows: 'I have taken refuge with my Lord and your Lord from everyone who waxes arrogant and does not believe in the Day of Reckoning' (verse 27). As believers consistently follow God's way, God will strengthen them by His support and eventually their tormentors will eat dust just as had happened with the tormentors of the past – in this case Pharaoh and his supporters. Believers should always stand valiantly firm in the teeth of such hostility and brutal repression.

(iii) Additionally, there were those who were inwardly convinced that the truth lay with the Prophet (peace be on him) and yet they watched in detached silence the unfolding conflict between truth and falsehood. God arouses the consciences of such people, reproaching them for their inaction after they have witnessed the brazen wrongdoing perpetrated by the enemies of truth. In such circumstances what behoves a man whose conscience is alive is that he speaks out in support of the truth just as the man of faith belonging to the Pharaonic folk did. It is remarkable that such a man proclaimed the truth at a time when Pharaoh was planning to assassinate Moses (peace be on him). In this respect, then, concern for one's own interests and safety, factors that prevented people in Pharaoh's time from speaking the truth was no less important now than it was in the past. So we see how the man endowed with faith disregarded all considerations of self-interest and instead valiantly declared: 'I entrust my affairs to Allah. Surely Allah is watchful over His servants' (verse 44).

As for the Makkan unbelievers' campaign against the Prophet (peace be on him), the Qur'ān adduces a number of proofs that clearly establish him to be in the right. On the one hand, weighty proofs are put forward to establish the truth of monotheism and the Hereafter, the two articles of faith which the Makkan unbelievers vehemently opposed. It is forcefully shown how the unbelievers were engaged, for no understandable reason, in a campaign to oppose the truth and that this opposition had nothing by way of solid evidence or proof to support it. The *sūrah* also lays bare the motives behind the Quraysh chiefs' opposition to Islam, which was, in essence, their own lust for power. Accordingly, it is unequivocally stated in verse 56 that their denial stems simply from pride and arrogance. They feared that they would not be able to maintain their supremacy if the Prophet Muḥammad (peace be on him) gained general recognition among people as God's Messenger. Hence their false pretexts to reject the Prophet's mission.

The Makkan unbelievers are given a severe warning whereby if they do not relinquish their adamant opposition to God's Signs, they will meet with the same terrible end that had overtaken the iniquitous nations of the past. As for the Hereafter, a much worse end awaits them. No sooner than the present life ends, they will experience great sorrow and remorse, but to no avail.

In the name of Allah, the Most Merciful, the Most Compassionate.

بِسْمِ ٱللَّهِ ٱلرَّحْمَٰنِ ٱلرَّحِيمِ

(1) *Ḥā. Mīm.* (2) This Book is a revelation from Allah, the All-Mighty, the All-Knowing; (3) the Forgiver of sins, the Accepter of repentance, the Stern in retribution, the Bountiful. There is no god but He. To Him are all destined to return.[1]

حمٓ ١ تَنزِيلُ ٱلْكِتَٰبِ مِنَ ٱللَّهِ ٱلْعَزِيزِ
ٱلْعَلِيمِ ٢ غَافِرِ ٱلذَّنۢبِ وَقَابِلِ ٱلتَّوْبِ شَدِيدِ
ٱلْعِقَابِ ذِى ٱلطَّوْلِ ۖ لَآ إِلَٰهَ إِلَّا هُوَ ۖ إِلَيْهِ
ٱلْمَصِيرُ ٣

1. This is the prelude to the *sūrah* through which the audience are alerted to the fact that the Qur'ān is not the Word of an ordinary being; rather, it has been revealed by God Himself. Some of His attributes, specifically those of vital relevance to the *sūrah*'s content, are described here.

(1) Of these is that He is All-Mighty. Hence, whatever He wills always prevails and whatever He decides is carried out regardless of whom it affects. None can resist God's will or escape His grip. Whoever believes that he will thrive by flouting God's command or will prevail against His Messenger is a victim of sheer folly. Such expectations can never come true.

(2) Additionally, God is All-Knowing. He knows everything. He says nothing on the basis of surmise or conjecture for He has direct knowledge of everything. As far as truths that lie beyond the range of perception are concerned, only that information which God provides is absolutely true and sound. Those who disregard this are necessarily pursuing a course of ignorance. Likewise, God knows what is conducive to man's felicity and necessary for his welfare. Since His guidance is rooted in knowledge and wisdom, it excludes every possibility of error. Hence, non-acceptance of God's guidance simply means opting

for one's own destruction. Furthermore, nothing is hidden from God, not even people's unexpressed intentions and motives. Hence, no pretext or excuse proffered by man can save him from God's punishment.

(3) Another major attribute of God is that He forgives sins and accepts repentance. This attribute is mentioned to provide hope to those who have been guilty of transgression such that they do not despair of God's mercy. They are asked to mend their ways in view of the fact that if they give up their erstwhile transgression, God's mercy will engulf them.

It seems pertinent to clarify that pardoning sins and accepting repentance are not necessarily tied together. At times, God pardons man's sins without the latter's repentance. It is also possible, for example, that one's good deeds may expiate for one's lapses, even though one may not have had the chance to repent and seek pardon for them from God. Likewise, the hardships that befall a man may lead to forgiveness of his sins. This privilege is, however, enjoyed only by those believers whose record is not tarnished by rebelliousness, those who might have sinned simply because of innate human weaknesses but who were not arrogant or adamantly insistent on sinful behaviour.

(4) Another attribute of God is that He is stern in retribution. This is mentioned here so as to drive it home that in the same manner that God is merciful to those who choose for themselves the course of servitude, He is severe in dealing with those who exceed the legitimate limits of His indulgence. Thereafter, such people become worthy of God's punishment, a punishment so horrendous that only a fool would consider it to be endurable.

(5) Still other attributes belonging to God are that He is bountiful, full of grace, abundantly munificent and exceedingly magnanimous. As a result, His numerous bounties constantly reach His creatures. In fact, all that creatures receive is thanks only to His grace.

After mentioning these five attributes of God, the following two truths are forcefully brought out. (a) That there is no god besides the One True God and this is notwithstanding the plethora of false gods invented by people. (b) Everyone is eventually bound to return to God. Those who set up gods other than the One True God will face the consequences of their actions. For there is no one besides Him who can hold man to account and recompense him.

(4) None but the unbelievers[2] dispute regarding the Signs of Allah.[3] So let not their strutting about in the land delude you.[4] ▶	مَا يُجَـٰدِلُ فِىٓ ءَايَـٰتِ ٱللَّهِ إِلَّا ٱلَّذِينَ كَفَـرُوا۟ فَلَا يَغْرُرْكَ تَقَلُّبُهُمْ فِى ٱلْبِلَـٰدِ ﴿٤﴾

2. *Kufr* carries the following two meanings here: (i) ingratitude, and (ii) rejection of the truth. Taken in the former sense, the verse means that thanklessness is manifest from the behaviour of those who tend to forget God's bounties that were unremittingly showered on them. Such people forget that they have been ceaselessly sustained by His bounties. The second meaning of *kufr,* viz. rejection of the truth is implied in the attitudinal trait of those who dispute God's Signs, who turn away from the truth and make up their minds not to accept it. It is clear from the context that this does not allude to unbelievers as such. For well-meaning unbelievers may raise questions about Islam in order to pursue their quest for the truth. The reproach in the verse is not meant to apply to such people's attitude.

3. What this refers to is indulgence in unnecessary disputation, resort to hair-splitting objections against God's message or distortion of its meaning so as to obstruct others and one's own self from comprehending it. Such people cannot escape God's punishment. This hostile contentiousness is one to which people are driven by evil motives. On the other hand, an objective seeker of the truth may question a proposition and do so in order to arrive at the truth. Such a person will carefully weigh his arguments, both for and against the proposition. The aim of his discussion will be to know the truth. In contrast, evil-minded people engage in specious argumentation only to discomfit and checkmate the other party. Such people shy away from facing the real problems; instead, they confine their forays to the periphery.

4. There is a subtle gap between the first statement and the second one that is left to be filled by the intelligence of the audience. It is fairly clear from the context that those who contend and wrangle about God's Signs can never escape His punishment. Yet, despite their wickedness, they strut about with impunity, their trade and commerce thrive, their states function with pomp and splendour, and they are immersed in self-indulgence without any let or hindrance. All this should not, however, delude anyone into thinking that such people will not be seized by God's punishment. Nor should anyone think that such a war against God's Signs

(5) Before them the people of Noah also gave the lie (to Messengers), and so did many parties after them. Each nation sallied forth against its Messenger to seize him, and they disputed with false arguments seeking therewith to repudiate the Truth. Then I seized them; and behold, how woeful was My retribution! (6) Thus has the decree of your Lord become due against the unbelievers. They are destined for the Fire.[5]

(7) The angels that bear the Throne and those that are around to extol your Lord's glory with His praise, they believe in Him, ▶

كَذَّبَتْ قَبْلَهُمْ قَوْمُ نُوحٍ وَٱلْأَحْزَابُ مِنۢ
بَعْدِهِمْ ۖ وَهَمَّتْ كُلُّ أُمَّةٍۭ بِرَسُولِهِمْ لِيَأْخُذُوهُ ۖ
وَجَٰدَلُوا۟ بِٱلْبَٰطِلِ لِيُدْحِضُوا۟ بِهِ ٱلْحَقَّ
فَأَخَذْتُهُمْ ۖ فَكَيْفَ كَانَ عِقَابِ ﴿٥﴾ وَكَذَٰلِكَ
حَقَّتْ كَلِمَتُ رَبِّكَ عَلَى ٱلَّذِينَ كَفَرُوٓا۟
أَنَّهُمْ أَصْحَٰبُ ٱلنَّارِ ﴿٦﴾ ٱلَّذِينَ يَحْمِلُونَ
ٱلْعَرْشَ وَمَنْ حَوْلَهُۥ يُسَبِّحُونَ بِحَمْدِ رَبِّهِمْ
وَيُؤْمِنُونَ بِهِۦ

is an entertaining game that can be continually played without facing its woeful consequences. There is no basis whatsoever for any such illusion. The fact of the matter is simple: people have been granted a respite. The more they misuse this respite to act wickedly, the more harm they will cause to themselves.

5. The unbelievers, as we know, have in the past suffered punishment in this world. That, however, is not the end of the matter. God has also decreed that such people will be cast into Hell in the World to Come.

The verse also admits another nuance. In the past, God decreed the doom of several unbelieving nations. In like manner, those who are presently engaged in disbelief have invited God's decree of chastiment upon themselves, and like the wicked nations of the past, God's decree will overtake them, consigning them to Hell.

and ask forgiveness for the believers,[6] saying: 'Our Lord! You encompass everything with Your Mercy and Knowledge.[7] So forgive[8] those that repent ▶

وَيَسْتَغْفِرُونَ لِلَّذِينَ ءَامَنُوا۟ رَبَّنَا وَسِعْتَ
كُلَّ شَىْءٍ رَّحْمَةً وَعِلْمًا فَٱغْفِرْ لِلَّذِينَ تَابُوا۟

---

6. This was said to comfort and console the Prophet's Companions. Around that time they were agonised by the Makkan unbelievers' sharp, abrasive tongues as well as their acts of brutal oppression. All this was coupled with a helplessness that naturally left the Companions dejected. In this context, they are urged not to feel distressed on account of the behaviour of such debased people. Rather, the believers should take comfort in the fact that they are held in such high esteem by God that not only the common agents of his Kingdom but even its pillars – the angels that bear God's Throne and those that stand around it and are near stationed to Him – ardently support them. The additional statement that these angels 'believe in Him, and ask forgiveness for the believers' (verse 7) indicates that faith is the common bond that joins the heavenly and earthly creatures in union. It is such angels' faith that induces interest in and sympathy for the humans who inhabit the earth.

The statement that the angels 'believe in Him' does not imply that it was possible for angels to disbelieve and that they had opted for belief in preference to disbelief. It rather means that angels are committed to obey the authority of the One True God so that no other being can command them and that they surrender to none other in obedience. When believing humans adopt the same attitude a concord is established between them and the angels and this was despite the fact that they belong to a different species and that a spatial gap also separates the two.

7. None of man's lapses and weaknesses is hidden from God for His Knowledge embraces everything. However, God's mercy too is as extensive as His Knowledge. Hence, He can forgive people despite fully knowing their lapses. The verse also means that God will forgive those who are known to Him to have sincerely repented and to have earnestly adopted His prescribed way.

8. Pardoning and saving people from the punishment of Hellfire are interrelated. To mention one also implies the other. Once again, this brings into sharp relief the angels' concern for the well-being of the believers.

and follow Your Path,[9] and guard them against the chastisement of Hell. (8) Our Lord, admit them to the everlasting Gardens You have promised them[10] and those of their fathers and spouses and progeny that were righteous.[11] Surely You alone are Most Mighty, Most Wise; (9) and guard them against all ills.[12] ▶

وَٱتَّبَعُوا۟ سَبِيلَكَ وَقِهِمْ عَذَابَ ٱلْجَحِيمِ ﴿٧﴾
رَبَّنَا وَأَدْخِلْهُمْ جَنَّـٰتِ عَدْنٍ ٱلَّتِى وَعَدتَّهُمْ
وَمَن صَلَحَ مِنْ ءَابَآئِهِمْ وَأَزْوَٰجِهِمْ
وَذُرِّيَّـٰتِهِمْ ۚ إِنَّكَ أَنتَ ٱلْعَزِيزُ ٱلْحَكِيمُ ﴿٨﴾
وَقِهِمُ ٱلسَّيِّـَٔاتِ ۚ

It is common knowledge that whoever is keen about a thing is likely to repeat and express it in a variety of ways. This seems to be manifest from what the angels are saying here.

9. That is, they have abandoned disobedience and rebellion and are following the way prescribed by God in a spirit of obeisance and devotion.

10. This is also illustrative of the angels' fervent entreaty to which we have alluded in n. 8 above. Obviously, to forgive and save someone from Hellfire implies his entry into Paradise. Hence the angels' prayer: 'Our Lord, admit them to the everlasting Gardens You have promised them and those of their fathers and spouses and progeny that were righteous...' (verse 8). Much of this prayer might appear superfluous. However, so overflowing is the angels' love and goodwill for the believers that they cannot help repeatedly asking God to bestow all of His bounties and blessings on them. They do so even though it is quite obvious that God will certainly do so as that is what He has already promised.

11. That is, may God join them with their parents, wives and children in Paradise, so as to grant them the utmost gratification. God mentions this as one of His favours, (see *al-Ra'd* 13: 23 and *al-Ṭūr* 52: 21.) The Qur'ān states: 'We shall unite the believers with those descendants of theirs who followed them in their faith', (*al-Ṭūr* 52: 21.)

12. *Sayyi'āt*, a synonym for evils or ills, is used to indicate the following: (i) Erroneous beliefs, degenerate morals and evil deeds;

He whom You guard against ills on that Day,[13] to him You have surely been Most Merciful. That is the great triumph.'

(10) It will be announced to the unbelievers (on the Day of Resurrection): 'Surely Allah's abhorrence of you when you were called to believe but you disbelieved[14] was greater than is your abhorrence of yourselves today.' (11) They will say: 'Our Lord, twice have You caused us to die and twice have ▶

وَمَن تَقِ ٱلسَّيِّـَٔاتِ يَوْمَئِذٍ فَقَدْ رَحِمْتَهُۥ وَذَٰلِكَ هُوَ ٱلْفَوْزُ ٱلْعَظِيمُ ۝٩ إِنَّ ٱلَّذِينَ كَفَرُوا۟ يُنَادَوْنَ لَمَقْتُ ٱللَّهِ أَكْبَرُ مِن مَّقْتِكُمْ أَنفُسَكُمْ إِذْ تُدْعَوْنَ إِلَى ٱلْإِيمَـٰنِ فَتَكْفُرُونَ ۝١٠ قَالُوا۟ رَبَّنَآ أَمَتَّنَا ٱثْنَتَيْنِ

(ii) terrible consequences of error and wickedness; and (iii) the calamities, sufferings and torment in this world or in *barzakh* or on the Day of Judgement. The angels' supplication embraces all these insofar as they want the believers to be protected against everything that is evil.

13. This refers to the terrible situation pervading the Grand Assembly, to the lack of shade and other comforts, to the severity of interrogation, to the public disgrace as a result of the sinners' secrets being exposed and all other hardships to which they will be subjected on the Day of Judgement.

14. On the Day of Judgement the unbelievers will witness their utter loss because they had indulged in polytheism or atheism, had denied the Hereafter, and opposed God's Messengers. They will be filled with remorse and frustration and will curse themselves for their foolishness. The angels will then remind them that when the Messengers and other pious people summoned them to the Straight Way to save them from this terrible end, they used to spurn their call which further aroused God's wrath.

You given us life.[15] We have now confessed our sins.[16] Is there, then, any way out?'[17] (12) (They will be told): 'The cause of your present state is that when Allah alone was invoked, you disbelieved; and when others instead of Him were invoked, you believed. Today all judgement lies with Allah, the Most High, the All-Great.'[18]

وَأَحْيَيْتَنَا ٱثْنَتَيْنِ فَٱعْتَرَفْنَا بِذُنُوبِنَا فَهَلْ إِلَىٰ
خُرُوجٍ مِّن سَبِيلٍ ﴿١١﴾ ذَٰلِكُم بِأَنَّهُۥٓ إِذَا
دُعِىَ ٱللَّهُ وَحْدَهُۥ كَفَرْتُمْ ۖ وَإِن يُشْرَكْ بِهِۦ
تُؤْمِنُوا۟ ۚ فَٱلْحُكْمُ لِلَّهِ ٱلْعَلِىِّ ٱلْكَبِيرِ ﴿١٢﴾

---

15. The same point is made in *Sūrah al-Baqarah* 2: 28 where it has been said that God grants man life and death twice. Human beings are asked: how can they dare disbelieve in God Who bestowed life on them when they were lifeless? They are also told that it is God Who causes their death and it is He Who will resurrect them. Quite obviously, the unbelievers could not deny that they were once lifeless and that then they were granted life and that they will meet their death at God's command for they witnessed all this. They did, however, deny the resurrection, as they had not observed it and were merely informed about it by God's Prophets. They will, however, observe it at first-hand on the Day of Judgement. It is then that they will acknowledge that what they had been told by God's Prophets was true and has now come to pass.

16. They will also acknowledge that they had committed a serious mistake by having denied the Afterlife. Thanks to a false outlook on life, they filled their lives with sin.

17. The unbelievers will enquire whether there is any way out; whether they can be rescued from their punishment by confessing their mistake.

18. Judgement on the Last Day will rest with God alone. In the past, the unbelievers had refused to believe in His exclusive Godhead. As for those deities whom they had associated with God, they are bereft of all power and authority. (For further details see *al-Zumar* 39: 45 and n. 64

(13) He it is Who shows you His Signs[19] and sends down provision for you from the sky.[20] Yet none takes heed except he who constantly turns to Allah.[21] (14) So call upon Allah, consecrating all ▶

هُوَ ٱلَّذِى يُرِيكُمْ ءَايَـٰتِهِۦ وَيُنَزِّلُ لَكُم
مِّنَ ٱلسَّمَآءِ رِزْقًا ۚ وَمَا يَتَذَكَّرُ إِلَّا مَن
يُنِيبُ ﴿١٣﴾ فَٱدْعُوا۟ ٱللَّهَ

above.) This implies that the unbelievers will find no way out of their grievous predicament. This because they not only denied the Hereafter but also displayed an aversion towards their Creator and felt uneasy unless they associated others with Him.

19. The reference here is to the signs indicating that it is the One True God Who has created the universe and it is He Who rules over it.

20. The word *rizq* used here signifies rainfall. This because rain is the source of every form of sustenance that man receives. Out of God's innumerable signs man's attention is specifically drawn to this particular sign of God – to the system pertaining to rainfall. If men were to grasp just this one ingredient of life, it would enable him to realise that the Qur'ānic worldview is entirely true. For this system could only be operative if the Creator of the earth and all its creatures, the Creator of water and wind, of sun and of heat and cold is one and the same God. Furthermore, this whole system can only operate ceaselessly for millions and billions of years because it is the same God, Who has always been and shall always be, that ensures its operation. This whole system was brought into existence by an All-Wise and Most Compassionate God Who, at the time of creating human beings and animals, created water exactly in proportion to their needs and saw to it that it should reach every corner of the earth through the astounding phenomena of rainfall. Now, who can be more iniquitous than he who observes all this and yet either denies the existence of God or associates others with Him in His Divinity?

21. In other words, anyone who turns away from God and puts blinkers of heedlessness and prejudice over his eyes becomes incapable of deriving any lesson from anything. His physical eyes observe that winds blow, clouds cover the sky, and that there is thunder and lightning and rainfall. But this does not enable him to appreciate why all this happens nor who is causing it to happen, nor what he owes that Being.

your devotion to Him,[22] howsoever much the unbelievers may dislike it.

(15) Exalted in Rank,[23] Lord of the Throne: [24] He causes the spirit to descend on whomsoever of His servants[25] He pleases so as to warn them of the Day of Encounter;[26] ▶

مُخْلِصِينَ لَهُ ٱلدِّينَ وَلَوْ كَرِهَ
ٱلْكَٰفِرُونَ ﴿١٤﴾ رَفِيعُ ٱلدَّرَجَٰتِ
ذُو ٱلْعَرْشِ يُلْقِى ٱلرُّوحَ مِنْ أَمْرِهِۦ عَلَىٰ مَن
يَشَآءُ مِنْ عِبَادِهِۦ لِيُنذِرَ يَوْمَ ٱلتَّلَاقِ ﴿١٥﴾

---

22. The idea of consecrating the whole of one's devotion to God is elaborated upon in *Sūrah al-Zumar* 39, n. 3 above.

23. That is, God is far too exalted in rank and way beyond all those that exist. Every creature – be it an angel, or Prophet of God, or saint or for that matter any other creature – all pale into insignificance in comparison with Him. However exalted a created being's rank might be, it cannot even come close to God's rank let alone be considered to share His attributes or authority.

24. That is, God is the Sovereign and Ruler of the entire universe. (For further details see *al-A'rāf* 7, n. 41, *Towards Understanding the Qur'ān*, vol. III, pp. 33-4; *Yūnus* 10, n. 4, vol. IV, p. 7, and *Ṭā Hā* 20, n. 3, vol. V, p. 182.)

25. The word *rūḥ* (lit. spirit) here signifies revelation and Prophethood. (For details see *al-Naḥl* 16, n. 3, *Towards Understanding the Qur'ān*, vol. IV, p. 312; and *Banī Isrā'īl* 17, n. 103, vol. V, pp. 69-71.) It is affirmed that God sends down this spirit on whomsoever He pleases. In other words, no one is justified in saying as to why a particular person was designated to the Prophetic office in the same way that no one has the right to say why someone was made handsome, or why he was endowed with a more retentive memory or greater intelligence than someone else.

26. 'The Day of Encounter', that is, the Day on which all men, *jinn* and devils will appear together before their Lord along with the witnesses to their deeds.

(16) the Day when they will emerge and nothing of them shall be hidden from Allah. (On that Day they will be asked): 'Whose is the kingdom today?'[27] (The whole world will cry out): 'It is Allah's, the One, the Overpowering.' (17) (It will then be said): 'Today shall everyone be fully recompensed for his deeds. None shall be wronged today.[28] Surely Allah is ▶

يَوْمَ هُم بَٰرِزُونَ ۖ لَا يَخْفَىٰ عَلَى ٱللَّهِ مِنْهُمْ
شَىْءٌ ۚ لِّمَنِ ٱلْمُلْكُ ٱلْيَوْمَ ۖ لِلَّهِ ٱلْوَٰحِدِ ٱلْقَهَّارِ ﴿١٦﴾
ٱلْيَوْمَ تُجْزَىٰ كُلُّ نَفْسٍۭ بِمَا كَسَبَتْ ۚ لَا ظُلْمَ
ٱلْيَوْمَ ۚ إِنَّ ٱللَّهَ

27. That is, many fools pompously claim to possess paramount power and glory and many fools accept those claims. On the Day of Judgement they will be asked: 'Whose is the kingdom today? Whose is all power and authority? Whose command prevails?' If a person considers all this seriously, it is bound to send a chilling shiver down his body, regardless of how mighty a king or how absolute a dictator he might be. This should also suffice to purge his mind of any delusions of grandeur from which he might suffer. It is on record that when the Sāmānid ruler Naṣr ibn Aḥmad (293-331/905-943) entered Nīsāpūr, a court was held at his behest. It commenced with recitation from the Qur'ān, and an elderly person recited these verses. When the reciter reached this very verse, Naṣr was so awe-struck that he descended from his throne, shaking from fear of God. He took off his crown, fell down in prostration, exclaiming that all kingdom was God's alone. (Niẓām al-Dīn al-Ḥasan ibn Muḥammad ibn Ḥusayn al-Qummī al-Nīsābūrī, *Gharā'ib al-Qur'ān wa Raghā'ib al-Furqān*, comments on *Sūrah al-Mu'min* 40: 16.)

28. No one will be wronged on the Day of Judgement. Obviously, when human beings make judgements, there can be errors in retributing someone in any of the following ways: one may, for example, be denied what one deserves. Also, one may receive less than one's due. It is also possible that one may be punished though one does not deserve punishment. Or one may escape a punishment though that should be

Swift in Reckoning.'[29] (18) (O Prophet), then warn them of the Day that has drawn near,[30] the Day when hearts full of suppressed grief will leap up to the throats and the wrong-doers shall neither have ▶

سَرِيعُ ٱلْحِسَابِ ﴿١٧﴾ وَأَنذِرْهُمْ يَوْمَ ٱلْآزِفَةِ
إِذِ ٱلْقُلُوبُ لَدَى ٱلْحَنَاجِرِ كَـٰظِمِينَ
مَا لِلظَّـٰلِمِينَ مِنْ

awarded. Or, one may be punished in excess of one's offence. Furthermore, victims may be denied justice if their oppressors go unpunished. Or someone may be punished for a crime committed by someone else. The Qur'ānic statement, however, clarifies that none of these wrongs will mar the judgements of God's court of justice on the Last Day.

29. It will take no time for God to recompense mankind. He incessantly provides sustenance to all the creatures of the universe. This engagement of His in providing sustenance to some of His creatures does not prevent Him from attending to the needs of others. Likewise, He sees all things in the universe and hears all sounds at the same time. He also manages all affairs simultaneously, nothing engages Him at the cost of the other. The same will happen on the Day of Judgement when attention to some matters requiring judgement will not prevent Him from judging other matters. Nor will there be cases that will cause any delay in His judgement of other cases. Nor will there be any difficulty in producing witnesses and other pieces of evidence. For the Judge will be aware of everything. Each party will stand before Him in their true colours. Incontrovertible pieces of evidence with minute details will be produced without any delay. As a result, every case will be disposed of in no time.

30. The Qur'ān repeatedly draws mankind's attention to the truth that the Last Day does not lie at some remote distance of time. In fact it is very close and can come about any moment; in other words, it is fast approaching. (Other verses of similar import are *al-Anbiyā'* 21: 1; *al-Qamar* 54: 1; *al-Naḥl* 16: 1; and *al-Najm* 53: 57.) People are thus warned that they should not become fearless of the Last Day, considering it to be an event in a far-off, distant future. Rather, they should mend their ways without wasting as much as a single moment.

any sincere friend[31] nor intercessor whose word will be heeded.[32] (19) He knows even the most stealthy glance of the eyes and all the secrets that hearts conceal. (20) Allah will judge with justice, whereas those whom they call upon beside Him cannot judge at all. Surely Allah – and He alone – is All-Hearing, All-Seeing.[33]

(21) Have they not journeyed in the land that ▶

حَمِيمٖ وَلَا شَفِيعٖ يُطَاعُ ۝١٨ يَعۡلَمُ خَآئِنَةَ
ٱلۡأَعۡيُنِ وَمَا تُخۡفِي ٱلصُّدُورُ ۝١٩ وَٱللَّهُ
يَقۡضِي بِٱلۡحَقِّۖ وَٱلَّذِينَ يَدۡعُونَ مِن دُونِهِۦ
لَا يَقۡضُونَ بِشَيۡءٍۗ إِنَّ ٱللَّهَ هُوَ ٱلسَّمِيعُ
ٱلۡبَصِيرُ ۝٢٠ ۞ أَوَلَمۡ يَسِيرُواْ فِي ٱلۡأَرۡضِ

31. *Ḥamīm* signifies the bosom friend of a person who is filled with compassionate zeal when he sees his friend in a bad predicament and who hastens to his rescue.

32. This observation is made in connection with refuting the unbelievers' idea of intercession. The fact is that in the Next World the wrongdoers will have no access to intercession with God, even though they think they can look forward to this. This because God will grant the power of intercession only to His upright servants and they can never be the friends of unbelievers, polytheists, and wicked or iniquitous folk, let alone that they would consider interceding on their behalf. It has, however, generally been the belief of unbelievers, polytheists and those immersed in wickedness, both in the past and the present, that they are strongly bound in devotion to some saints who will simply stop them from being cast into Hell, and further that these saints will secure their acquittal from God. It is for this reason that it is being affirmed that 'the wrong-doers shall neither have any sincere friend nor intercessor whose word will be heeded.'

33. Unlike the false gods of the unbelievers, God is not blind or deaf. Unlike them He knows well everyone's record of deeds.

they might observe the end of those who came before them? They were even greater in strength than they and left behind more splendid traces in the land. Then Allah seized them because of their sins and they had none who could protect them from Allah. (22) They came to this end because their Messengers would come to them with Clear Signs[34] and yet they would refuse to believe. So Allah seized them. He is indeed Strong, Terrible in Retribution.

(23) Verily We sent Moses[35] with Our Signs ▶

فَيَنظُرُواْ كَيْفَ كَانَ عَٰقِبَةُ ٱلَّذِينَ كَانُواْ
مِن قَبْلِهِمْۚ كَانُواْ هُمْ أَشَدَّ مِنْهُمْ قُوَّةً وَءَاثَارًا
فِى ٱلْأَرْضِ فَأَخَذَهُمُ ٱللَّهُ بِذُنُوبِهِمْ وَمَا كَانَ
لَهُم مِّنَ ٱللَّهِ مِن وَاقٍ ﴿٢١﴾ ذَٰلِكَ بِأَنَّهُمْ
كَانَت تَّأْتِيهِمْ رُسُلُهُم بِٱلْبَيِّنَٰتِ فَكَفَرُواْ
فَأَخَذَهُمُ ٱللَّهُۚ إِنَّهُۥ قَوِىٌّ شَدِيدُ ٱلْعِقَابِ ﴿٢٢﴾
وَلَقَدْ أَرْسَلْنَا مُوسَىٰ بِـَٔايَٰتِنَآ

---

34. *Bayyināt* signifies the following: (i) the clear, distinct signs which attest that the Messenger had been raised by God; (ii) the weighty arguments which prove that the teachings of those Messengers were utterly true; and (iii) the valuable guidance about various aspects of life that would convince every sensible person that a liar or selfish person could not have imparted such teachings as are so utterly true, morally so unblemished and superb.

35. For a detailed account of the Prophet Moses' story, see *al-Baqarah* 2: 49-61 and 164, *Towards Understanding the Qur'ān*, vol. I, pp. 73-7; *al-Mā'idah* 5: 20-6, vol. II, pp. 114-15 and p. 150; *al-A'rāf* 7: 103-60, *Yūnus* 10: 75-93, *Hūd* 11: 17, 90, 98 and 110; and *Ibrāhīm* 14: 5-13, vol. IV, pp. 54-64, 90, 131-2, 136, 147-50 and 254-8; *Banī Isrā'īl* 17: 101-4, *al-Kahf* 18: 60-83, *Maryam* 19: 51-3, *Ṭā Hā* 20: 9-98, vol. V, pp. 77-80, 116-22, 163 and 182-222; *al-Mu'minūn* 23: 45-9, vol. VI, pp. 100-1; *al-Shu'arā'* 26: 10-68, *al-Naml* 27: 7-14, and *al-Qaṣaṣ* 28: 3-43, vol. VII, pp. 55-74, 138-44

and a clear authority[36] (24) to Pharaoh and Hāmān[37] ▶

وَسُلْطَٰنٍ مُّبِينٍ ﴿٢٣﴾ إِلَىٰ فِرْعَوْنَ وَهَٰمَٰنَ

---

and 195-223; and *al-Aḥzāb* 33: 69 and *al-Ṣāffāt* 37: 114-22, vol. IX, pp. 108 and 309.

36. In other words, these distinct signs left no doubt that the Messengers had been deputed by God and that they had God's power at their backs. A careful reading of the Qur'ānic account of the Prophet Moses' story makes it clear as to which signs clearly establish that He had been designated by God as His Messenger.

First of all, it was simply astounding that a person, who had fled a country a few years ago because he had killed someone, reappeared all of a sudden in Pharaoh's court and boldly summoned the king and his courtiers to believe in God, thereby asking that they recognise him as the representative of God, the Lord of the universe, and that they follow his directives. Indeed, it was astonishing that on that occasion no one dared to seize Moses (peace be on him). This becomes all the more striking since the Prophet Moses (peace be on him) belonged to a community that was oppressed and was groaning under the yoke of slavery and subjugation. Had Moses been arrested on the charge of murder, presumably his community would not have even dared to protest, let alone rise in rebellion against it. It is evident, therefore, that even before they witnessed the miracles of the rod and the shining hand, the Egyptian courtiers were overawed by the Prophet Moses (peace be on him). In their very first encounter with Moses they realised that he was sponsored by someone truly mighty.

Furthermore, Moses presented one miracle after another, each clearly demonstrating that he was supported by God. This because mere magic cannot transform a rod into a serpent, nor can magic cause a famine to hit a whole country, nor can a vast country, spread over thousands of square miles, be hit by myriads of storms at a moment's notice and again subside at a moment's notice. Therefore, the Qur'ān states that Pharaoh and his courtiers, notwithstanding their verbal rejection of Moses, realised that he had been sent to them by God. (For further details, see *al-A'rāf* 7: 107-117, *Towards Understanding the Qur'ān,* vol. VII, pp. 61-70 and p. 143; *Ṭā Hā* 20: 56-78, vol. V, pp. 196-207; *al-Shu'arā'* 26: 30-51 and *al-Naml* 27: 12, vol. VII, pp. 61-70 and 143, along with the relevant notes.)

37. For a refutation of the opponents' objections regarding Hāmān, see *al-Qaṣaṣ* 28, n. 8, *Towards Understanding the Qur'ān,* vol. VII, pp. 197-8.

and Korah. They said: '(He is) a sorcerer, an utter liar.' (25) When Moses brought them the Truth from Us[38] they said: 'Kill the sons of all the believers who have joined him, but spare the women.'[39] The guile of the unbelievers always ends in vain.[40]

وَقَٰرُونَ فَقَالُوا۟ سَٰحِرٌ كَذَّابٌ ﴿٢٤﴾ فَلَمَّا
جَآءَهُم بِٱلْحَقِّ مِنْ عِندِنَا قَالُوا۟ ٱقْتُلُوٓا۟ أَبْنَآءَ
ٱلَّذِينَ ءَامَنُوا۟ مَعَهُۥ وَٱسْتَحْيُوا۟ نِسَآءَهُمْ ۚ
وَمَا كَيْدُ ٱلْكَٰفِرِينَ إِلَّا فِى ضَلَٰلٍ ﴿٢٥﴾

(26) One day Pharaoh said:[41] 'Let me go and ▶

وَقَالَ فِرْعَوْنُ ذَرُونِىٓ

38. By showing a series of miracles, the Prophet Moses (peace be on him) conclusively established that he was God's Messenger and by marshalling a range of weighty arguments he proved that he was on the right path.

39. Verse 127 of *Sūrah al-A'rāf* (*Sūrah* 6) mentions that Pharaoh's courtiers had asked him how long he would allow Moses to spread mischief in the land. In reply Pharaoh had expressed the resolve to slay all Israeli male children and spare female children so as to thwart Moses' mission. This verse makes it clear that this command was issued at Pharaoh's behest in order to terrorise Moses' followers and supporters into abandoning him.

40. The actual words are: 'The guile of the unbelievers always ends in vain'. These words can also mean that since all the vain tricks of the unbelievers were intended to promote injustice, iniquity, oppression and enmity to the truth, their adamant opposition grew even after the truth had become clear to them and after they had become convinced of it in their hearts. They went so far in their opposition that they spared no means, howsoever ignoble, to oppose the truth.

41. This marks the beginning of the Qur'ān's account of an important event in Israelite history, one that has been ignored by the Israelites themselves. Indeed, both the Bible and the Talmud make no reference to it. It is only the Qur'ān that tells us how this incident took place during

kill Moses;[42] then let him invoke his Lord. I fear that he will change your ▶	أَقْتُلْ مُوسَىٰ وَلْيَدْعُ رَبَّهُۥٓ ۖ إِنِّىٓ أَخَافُ أَن يُبَدِّلَ

the course of the conflict between Pharaoh and the Prophet Moses (peace be on him).

Anyone who studies this Qur'ānic account with an open mind is bound to recognise the story's immense significance. It is not unlikely that, impressed by the Prophet Moses' personality, his preaching and his amazing miracles, a member of Pharaoh's court should have embraced the true faith. Furthermore, it is not inconceivable that he should have been unable to restrain himself after noting Pharaoh's design to assassinate the Prophet Moses. However, blinded as the Orientalists are by their hostility to Islam, they throw dirt on the self-evident truths the Qur'ān embodies and do so despite all their tall claims to objectivity. Take, for instance, the article on 'Moses' in the *Encyclopedia of Islam,* especially its following passage, which is a typical illustration of their attitude:

> The Ḳur'ānic story of a believer at the court of Pharaoh who wants to save Mūsā is not quite clear (xl. 29). Ought we to compare Jethro in the Haggada who advocates clemency at Pharaoh's court? (*Sōṭa,* 11[a]; *Sanhedrin,* 106[a]; Ginzberg, v. 392, 21; v. 412, 101). (Bernhard Heller, 'Mūsā', in Martijin Theodoor Houtsma *et al.* eds., *E. J. Brill's First Encyclopaedia of Islam 1913-1936* (Leiden-New York: E. J. Brill, 1987), vol. VI, pp. 738-9; quote at p. 739.)

The presumption of these Orientalists is that every Qur'ānic account is decidedly unsound. Indeed, they dismiss almost every Qur'ānic narrative as incredible or dubious. In the above instance, the suggestion is that the Prophet Muḥammad (peace be on him) may somehow have come to know of something about Jethro, which he passed off in this *sūrah* as the account of a believer in Pharaoh's court. This is the level to which Western scholarship can stoop in regard to Islam, the Qur'ān and the Prophet (peace be on him)!

42. Pharaoh gives the impression that some people had prevented him from executing the Prophet Moses (peace be on him). However, there was no person who could have deterred him from going ahead. Rather, it was only his own fear that prevented him from fully taking on God's Messenger.

religion or cause disruption in the land.'[43]

(27) Moses said: 'I have taken refuge with my Lord and your Lord from everyone who waxes arrogant ▶

دِينَكُمْ أَوْ أَن يُظْهِرَ فِي ٱلْأَرْضِ ٱلْفَسَادَ ۝٢٦
وَقَالَ مُوسَىٰٓ إِنِّي عُذْتُ بِرَبِّي وَرَبِّكُم مِّن
كُلِّ مُتَكَبِّرٍ

---

43. Pharaoh expresses his fear that the Prophet Moses (peace be on him) was trying to bring about a revolution. Even if Moses were unable to so do, his activities were nonetheless imperilling public order in the country. Hence, in Pharaoh's opinion, even before Moses was able to commit any crime that carried death penalty, Moses should be executed in order to 'maintain public order.' Pharaoh did not, however, put forward any evidence of any criminal act committed by the Prophet Moses (peace be on him). Instead his apprehensions alone were sufficient to put into effect his desire to punish Moses. Since he considered Moses a dangerous person, his head should be chopped off!

At this point it is necessary to understand what Pharaoh meant when he accused Moses that he would 'change your religion' (verse 26). The word used in the verse that has been used is *dīn* which, in this context, denotes 'the system of government' that was then in vogue in Egypt. In other words, this meant that Pharaoh feared that Moses would subvert the Pharaonic dominance in Egypt. (See, Ālūsī, *Rūḥ al-Ma'ānī*, comments on *Sūrah al-Mu'min* 40: 25.) In other words, the religious, political, social and economic order then operating in Egypt represented the *dīn* of the country. Pharaoh feared that the Prophet Moses' call to monotheism would lead to the overthrowing of that order.

Like all cunning rulers, Pharaoh did not charge the Prophet Moses (peace be on him) with acting in opposition to his political authority. Rather, he projected Moses as a grave threat to public order insofar as the latter's success would subvert their *dīn,* meaning thereby the established system of the land. He thus invoked the support of his subjects, urging them to rise against the Prophet Moses (peace be on him) whom he depicted as their enemy, the enemy of their state and community. At the same time, Pharaoh cleverly projected himself as someone who was not worried for his own sake. Rather, he really worried that his people would suffer immensely if he were removed from the scene. He, therefore, urged that they should exterminate Moses, the enemy of their country and their nation.

and does not believe in the Day of Reckoning.'[44]

(28) Then a man endowed with faith, from Pharaoh's folk, who had kept his faith hidden, said: 'Do you kill a person simply because he says: "My Lord is Allah" even though he brought to you clear Signs from your Lord?[45] If he is a liar, ▶

لَّا يُؤْمِنُ بِيَوْمِ ٱلْحِسَابِ ﴿٢٧﴾ وَقَالَ رَجُلٌ
مُّؤْمِنٌ مِّنْ ءَالِ فِرْعَوْنَ يَكْتُمُ إِيمَـٰنَهُۥٓ
أَتَقْتُلُونَ رَجُلًا أَن يَقُولَ رَبِّىَ ٱللَّهُ وَقَدْ
جَآءَكُم بِٱلْبَيِّنَـٰتِ مِن رَّبِّكُمْ ۖ وَإِن يَكُ
كَـٰذِبًا

---

44. There are two equally plausible possibilities as regards what happened and there is no reason to prefer one over the other. One possibility is that the Prophet Moses (peace be on him) was present in court when Pharaoh expressed his intention to execute him and Moses then made these remarks while addressing Pharaoh and his courtiers. The other possibility is that Pharaoh might have suggested the same in a private council of his chiefs in Moses' absence and that the Prophet Moses (peace be on him) was subsequently informed by some believers of what Pharaoh had said in that meeting. Upon hearing this, Moses possibly made these remarks to his followers.

Whatever the case, it is clear that Pharaoh's threat did not cause Moses the least concern. Reposing his faith in God, the Prophet Moses (peace be on him) paid no heed to Pharaoh's threat and threw it with impunity at his face. The same should be the Prophet Muḥammad's response to the unbelieving Makkans who, much like Pharaoh and his supporters, were actively engaged in efforts to assassinate him.

45. The Prophet Moses (peace be on him) had shown Clear Signs to the Egyptians, indicating beyond every shadow of doubt that he was God's Messenger. The man of faith from among Pharaoh's community pointed to these signs, all of which are discussed in the following Qur'ānic passages: *al-A'rāf* 7: 107-8, 117-20 and 130-5, *Towards Understanding the Qur'ān,* vol. III, pp. 65-73; *Banī Isrā'īl* 17: 101-2, and *Ṭā Hā* 20: 56-73, vol. V, pp. 77-9 and 196-205; *al-Shu'arā'* 26: 30-51 and *al-Naml* 27: 10-13, vol. VII, pp. 63-70 and 142-3.

فَعَلَيۡهِ كَذِبُهُۥۖ وَإِن يَكُ صَادِقٗا يُصِبۡكُم
بَعۡضُ ٱلَّذِي يَعِدُكُمۡۖ إِنَّ ٱللَّهَ لَا يَهۡدِي مَنۡ
هُوَ مُسۡرِفٞ كَذَّابٞ ٢٨

his lying will recoil upon him;[46] but if he is truthful, you will be smitten with some of the awesome consequences of which he warns you. Allah does not guide to the Right Way any who exceeds the limits and is an utter liar.[47] ▶

46. This man of faith pointed out that even if Pharaoh and his courtiers considered the Prophet Moses (peace be on him) to be a liar, and this despite incontestable signs to the contrary, they should still nonetheless spare him. This because there was the possibility that Moses might be true. In that case their actions against Moses would incur God's wrath. So, even if they considered Moses a liar, they should nonetheless not harm him. For if Moses was indeed ascribing any falsehood to God, God would duly chastise him. Almost the same point was made by the Prophet Moses (peace be on him) himself in his exchange with Pharaoh: 'But if you do not believe what I say, leave me alone' *(al-Dukhān* 44: 21.)

It should also be noted that at the outset of his address this person – a believer from among Pharaoh's community – did not identify himself as a believer. Rather, he spoke as a member of Pharaoh's community and spoke in terms of their interests. However, when he learned that Pharaoh and his courtiers were bent upon rejecting the truth, he disclosed his faith. (See verses 38ff, below.)

47. This is open to two meanings. In all probability, the believer in question made an ambivalent statement so as to avoid disclosing his real intent. In essence, he stated that a person cannot be both truthful and liar at the same time. It was common knowledge that the Prophet Moses (peace be on him) was a pious person, known for his excellent demeanour and noble character. Hence, his claim to be God's Messenger could not be false. It would be hard to believe that a person with such excellent moral qualities would invent a falsehood. Alternatively, the verse might mean that if Moses' opponents were to exceed all reasonable limits, justifying their assassination plan by fabricating false accusations against him, God would nonetheless never let them succeed.

(29) My people, today the kingdom is yours, and you are supreme in the land. But if Allah's chastisement were to come upon you, who will come to our help?'[48]

Pharaoh said: 'I only counsel what I consider right; I only direct you to the Path of Rectitude.'[49]

(30) He who had faith said: 'My people, I fear that you will confront a day like that which overtook many parties before you, (31) like the day that overtook the people of Noah and 'Ād and Thamūd, and those who came after them. Allah does not wish to subject His servants to any injustice.[50] ▶

يَٰقَوْمِ لَكُمُ ٱلْمُلْكُ ٱلْيَوْمَ ظَٰهِرِينَ فِى
ٱلْأَرْضِ فَمَن يَنصُرُنَا مِنۢ بَأْسِ ٱللَّهِ إِن
جَآءَنَا ۚ قَالَ فِرْعَوْنُ مَآ أُرِيكُمْ إِلَّا مَآ أَرَىٰ
وَمَآ أَهْدِيكُمْ إِلَّا سَبِيلَ ٱلرَّشَادِ ﴿٢٩﴾ وَقَالَ
ٱلَّذِىٓ ءَامَنَ يَٰقَوْمِ إِنِّىٓ أَخَافُ عَلَيْكُم مِّثْلَ
يَوْمِ ٱلْأَحْزَابِ ﴿٣٠﴾ مِثْلَ دَأْبِ قَوْمِ نُوحٍ
وَعَادٍ وَثَمُودَ وَٱلَّذِينَ مِنۢ بَعْدِهِمْ ۚ وَمَا ٱللَّهُ
يُرِيدُ ظُلْمًا لِّلْعِبَادِ ﴿٣١﴾

---

48. The believer from among the Pharaonic community counselled his people not to incur God's displeasure by being thankless to Him and especially since it was He Who had bestowed His favours upon them.

49. Pharaoh's response reveals that he was unaware that this particular courtier had inwardly accepted faith. Therefore, he showed no displeasure at the advice he gave. However, Pharaoh did make it clear that while he had listened to the advice, he was not prepared to change his mind.

50. That is, God has no hostility towards His servants so that He will arbitrarily destroy them. Rather, He afflicts them with punishment only when they transgress all limits and when inflicting them with Divine scourge becomes an inexorable requirement of justice and equity.

وَيَٰقَوۡمِ إِنِّيٓ أَخَافُ عَلَيۡكُمۡ يَوۡمَ ٱلتَّنَادِ ٣٢
يَوۡمَ تُوَلُّونَ مُدۡبِرِينَ مَا لَكُم مِّنَ ٱللَّهِ مِنۡ
عَاصِمٖۗ وَمَن يُضۡلِلِ ٱللَّهُ فَمَا لَهُۥ مِنۡ هَادٖ ٣٣
وَلَقَدۡ جَآءَكُمۡ يُوسُفُ مِن قَبۡلُ بِٱلۡبَيِّنَٰتِ
فَمَا زِلۡتُمۡ فِي شَكّٖ مِّمَّا جَآءَكُم بِهِۦۖ حَتَّىٰٓ إِذَا
هَلَكَ قُلۡتُمۡ لَن يَبۡعَثَ ٱللَّهُ مِنۢ بَعۡدِهِۦ رَسُولٗاۚ
كَذَٰلِكَ يُضِلُّ ٱللَّهُ مَنۡ هُوَ مُسۡرِفٞ

(32) My people, I fear that you will encounter a day when there will be much wailing and you will cry out to one another for help, (33) the day when you will turn around to retreat, there will be none to protect you from Allah. He whom Allah lets go astray, none will be able to show him the Right Way. (34) Verily Joseph came to you with Clear Signs before, yet you continued to doubt his Message. Thereafter when he died, you said: "Allah shall send no Messenger after him."'[51] Thus Allah leads astray those who transgress the limits ▶

51. The unbelievers' error combined with their adamance were quite inordinate. Before Moses (peace be on him) the Prophet Joseph (peace be on him) had been sent to them and they recognised him to be a paragon of moral excellence. They further acknowledged that he had rightly interpreted the dream of the then sovereign and that this had saved them from the terrible devastations of the seven-year famine. They also conceded that during Joseph's time they enjoyed peace, justice, prosperity and well-being as never before in Egypt's history. While fully recognising all his merits, they still did not profess faith in Joseph (peace be on him) as long as he lived. Then, after he died, they mourned him, saying that none like him would to be born again. In other words, not believing in Joseph (peace be on him) despite their recognition of his extraordinary qualities provided them with an easy pretext to reject all later Prophets. In essence, what all this means is that they were not prepared to embrace true guidance.

and are given to much doubting;[52] (35) those who contend regarding Allah's Signs without any evidence that might have come to them.[53] That is exceedingly loathsome to Allah and to those that believe. Thus does Allah seal the heart of everyone who is proud and high-handed.[54]

(36) Pharaoh said: 'Hāmān, build for me ▶

مُّرۡتَابٌ ۝٣٤ ٱلَّذِينَ يُجَٰدِلُونَ فِيٓ ءَايَٰتِ
ٱللَّهِ بِغَيۡرِ سُلۡطَٰنٍ أَتَىٰهُمۡۖ كَبُرَ مَقۡتًا عِندَ
ٱللَّهِ وَعِندَ ٱلَّذِينَ ءَامَنُواْۚ كَذَٰلِكَ يَطۡبَعُ
ٱللَّهُ عَلَىٰ كُلِّ قَلۡبِ مُتَكَبِّرٖ جَبَّارٖ ۝٣٥ وَقَالَ
فِرۡعَوۡنُ يَٰهَٰمَٰنُ ٱبۡنِ لِي

52. It appears that God adds this as an observation to the opinion expressed by the believer belonging to Pharaoh's community.

53. God 'leads astray' only those who display the following traits: (i) Those who exceed all limits of wickedness. Such people are so enamoured of iniquity that they show no inclination to improve their moral conduct. (ii) Those who are disposed to entertain doubts about Prophets. They distrust them no matter how overwhelmingly persuasive the signs are that they produce to corroborate the truths of monotheism and the Hereafter. (iii) Those who, rather than reflect on the Word of God rationally, are prone to presenting all kinds of silly objections to the same. In essence, the arguments of such people are neither supported by rational proof nor by any authoritative evidence derived from the Scriptures. Their whole argument from beginning to end is rooted in obstinacy and adamance. Wherever there is a group of people displaying these three major faults, God hurls them into the pit of error from which none has the power to pull them out.

54. No one's heart is sealed arbitrarily. It is only the arrogant and overbearing whose hearts are sealed. Puffed up with vain pride such people find it beneath their dignity to submit themselves to the truth. This trait is combined with an attitude of overbearingness made manifest in their high-handedness towards others. As a result, they find it hard to follow the restrictions placed upon them by the Law.

a lofty tower that I may scale the highways – (37) the highways to the heavens – and have a look at the God of Moses, although I am certain that Moses is a liar.'[55] Thus Pharaoh's evil deed was made to seem fair to him, and he was barred from the Right Path. Pharaoh's guile only led him to his own perdition.

(38) The person endowed with faith said: 'My people, follow me; I shall direct you to the Path of Rectitude. (39) My people, the life of this world is ephemeral,[56] whereas the Hereafter, that is the permanent abode. (40) Whosoever does an evil deed will be requited ▶

صَرْحًا لَّعَلِّيٓ أَبْلُغُ ٱلْأَسْبَٰبَ ﴿٣٦﴾ أَسْبَٰبَ
ٱلسَّمَٰوَٰتِ فَأَطَّلِعَ إِلَىٰٓ إِلَٰهِ مُوسَىٰ وَإِنِّى
لَأَظُنُّهُۥ كَٰذِبًا ۚ وَكَذَٰلِكَ زُيِّنَ لِفِرْعَوْنَ
سُوٓءُ عَمَلِهِۦ وَصُدَّ عَنِ ٱلسَّبِيلِ ۚ وَمَا كَيْدُ
فِرْعَوْنَ إِلَّا فِى تَبَابٍ ﴿٣٧﴾ وَقَالَ ٱلَّذِىٓ
ءَامَنَ يَٰقَوْمِ ٱتَّبِعُونِ أَهْدِكُمْ سَبِيلَ
ٱلرَّشَادِ ﴿٣٨﴾ يَٰقَوْمِ إِنَّمَا هَٰذِهِ ٱلْحَيَوٰةُ ٱلدُّنْيَا
مَتَٰعٌ وَإِنَّ ٱلْءَاخِرَةَ هِىَ دَارُ ٱلْقَرَارِ ﴿٣٩﴾ مَنْ
عَمِلَ سَيِّئَةً فَلَا يُجْزَىٰٓ

55. Pharaoh made this statement while addressing his vizier, Hāmān, during the course of the believer's speech. The manner of the statement indicates that Pharaoh did not pay heed to the believer's speech, considering it unworthy of serious attention. He therefore, arrogantly turned his face away from him, sarcastically asking Hāmān to erect a tall building so that he might climb it and find out the truth as to God's whereabouts. (For further details see *al-Qaṣaṣ* 28, nn. 52-4, *Towards Understanding the Qur'ān,* vol. VII, pp. 220-2.)

56. The believer from among the Pharaonic community pointed out that they were exulting in the fleeting wealth and prosperity of this world, consigning God to oblivion. In short this was nothing but ignorance and folly.

only with the like of it; and whosoever acts righteously and has attained to faith – be he a male or a female – they shall enter Paradise and be provided sustenance beyond all reckoning. (41) My people, how is it that I call you to salvation while you call me to the Fire; (42) you call me to deny Allah and to associate with Him as His partners those regarding whom I have no knowledge (that they are Allah's partners in His Divinity),[57] whereas I call you to the Most Mighty, the Most Forgiving? (43) There is no doubt that those whom you call me to have no claim to be called upon in this world and in the Hereafter.[58] ▶

إِلَّا مِثْلَهَا ۖ وَمَنْ عَمِلَ صَـٰلِحًا مِّن ذَكَرٍ
أَوْ أُنثَىٰ وَهُوَ مُؤْمِنٌ فَأُو۟لَـٰٓئِكَ يَدْخُلُونَ
ٱلْجَنَّةَ يُرْزَقُونَ فِيهَا بِغَيْرِ حِسَابٍ ﴿٤٠﴾
۞ وَيَـٰقَوْمِ مَا لِىٓ أَدْعُوكُمْ إِلَى ٱلنَّجَوٰةِ
وَتَدْعُونَنِىٓ إِلَى ٱلنَّارِ ﴿٤١﴾ تَدْعُونَنِى لِأَكْفُرَ
بِٱللَّهِ وَأُشْرِكَ بِهِۦ مَا لَيْسَ لِى بِهِۦ عِلْمٌ وَأَنَا۠
أَدْعُوكُمْ إِلَى ٱلْعَزِيزِ ٱلْغَفَّـٰرِ ﴿٤٢﴾ لَا جَرَمَ
أَنَّمَا تَدْعُونَنِىٓ إِلَيْهِ لَيْسَ لَهُۥ دَعْوَةٌ فِى ٱلدُّنْيَا
وَلَا فِى ٱلْـَٔاخِرَةِ

57. The believer contended that there was no rational proof whatsoever that such false gods had any share with the One True God in His Divinity. How could he, then, accept them to be God's associates in Divinity? He, therefore, expressed his inability to endorse the outrageous proposition that there are beings that have a share in God's Divinity and that they too are objects of man's service along with God.

58. This is open to several meanings: (i) None has the right to invite people in this world or in the Next to take any as God's associate in His Divinity. (ii) Those who were being treated as deities had been arbitrarily given that status by others rather than by themselves. In fact, they had neither laid claim to Godhead in this world and nor will lay claim to it

Certainly to Allah shall be our return, and those who exceed the limits are destined to the Fire.[59] (44) Soon you shall remember what I say to you. I entrust my affairs to Allah. Surely Allah is watchful over His servants.'[60]

(45) Eventually Allah saved the person endowed with faith from all the evils of their guile,[61] ▶

وَأَنَّ مَرَدَّنَآ إِلَى ٱللَّهِ وَأَنَّ ٱلْمُسْرِفِينَ هُمْ
أَصْحَـٰبُ ٱلنَّارِ ﴿٤٣﴾ فَسَتَذْكُرُونَ مَآ
أَقُولُ لَكُمْ ۚ وَأُفَوِّضُ أَمْرِىٓ إِلَى ٱللَّهِ ۚ إِنَّ
ٱللَّهَ بَصِيرٌۢ بِٱلْعِبَادِ ﴿٤٤﴾ فَوَقَىٰهُ ٱللَّهُ سَيِّـَٔاتِ
مَا مَكَرُوا۟ ۖ

in the Next World. (iii) There is no use calling upon these deities in either of the two worlds for they are absolutely powerless. Invoking them is thus pointless.

59. The words 'those who exceed the limits' refer to those who go beyond the limits of truth and right. These words apply to those who take others as God's associates in His Divinity, or who lay claim to Divinity, or adopt a defiant posture towards God and believe that they have the right to act as they please. As a result of such false beliefs they commit all kinds of excesses against those with whom they come into contact – with their own selves, with other of God's creatures, and with other objects of the universe. Such persons are guilty of transgressing all limits of reason and justice.

60. It is evident from the believer's observation that he knew well that his affirmation of truth would incur Pharaoh's wrath upon him; in other words, he knew that he would be deprived of his exalted position, would have to sacrifice his titles of honour as well as material interests and possibly even his life. Yet, reposing full trust in God, he discharged his duty to proclaim the truth. Even at that crucial juncture he acted in accord with his conscience.

61. One thus learns that this believer enjoyed such an important position in the kingdom that, notwithstanding his public defiance of Pharaoh,

and a woeful chastisement encompassed the Pharaonites.[62] (46) They are exposed to the Fire every morning and evening; and when the Last Hour will come to pass, a command shall be given: 'Admit the Pharaonites to an even more severe chastisement.'[63] (47) Just imagine when they will remonstrate with one another in Hell. The weak ones will say to those who waxed proud: 'We were ▶

وَحَاقَ بِـَٔالِ فِرْعَوْنَ سُوٓءُ ٱلْعَذَابِ ﴿٤٥﴾
ٱلنَّارُ يُعْرَضُونَ عَلَيْهَا غُدُوًّا وَعَشِيًّا ۖ وَيَوْمَ
تَقُومُ ٱلسَّاعَةُ أَدْخِلُوٓا۟ ءَالَ فِرْعَوْنَ أَشَدَّ
ٱلْعَذَابِ ﴿٤٦﴾ وَإِذْ يَتَحَآجُّونَ فِى ٱلنَّارِ فَيَقُولُ
ٱلضُّعَفَـٰٓؤُا۟ لِلَّذِينَ ٱسْتَكْبَرُوٓا۟ إِنَّا كُنَّا

no punishment was instantly meted out to him. Rather, Pharaoh and his courtiers had to resort to a secret plot to kill him. God, however, did not allow their plans to come to fruition.

62. The wording of the text indicates that this incident took place during the last stage of the conflict between the Prophet Moses (peace be on him) and Pharaoh. Most probably Pharaoh had decided to assassinate the Prophet Moses (peace be on him). However, the public support extended to him by the believer mentioned above would have alerted Pharaoh to the fact that Moses' call had even reached his own chiefs. Therefore, he decided first to identify those among his courtiers who had been influenced by Moses' call and to eliminate them before taking any decisive action against the Prophet Moses (peace be on him) himself. While Pharaoh was preoccupied, God directed the Prophet Moses (peace be on him) and his companions to migrate. Ultimately, Pharaoh and his army were drowned while pursuing Moses and his followers.

63. This verse clearly proves that punishment in the state of *barzakh* (the transitional period between death and resurrection) is real (rather than figurative). Several *aḥādīth* describe this punishment as one that will be meted out to people in their graves. The verse under study unmistakably points to two kinds of punishment: the punishment of

your followers. Will you, then, lighten for us a part of our suffering of the Fire?'[64] ▶	لَكُمْ تَبَعًا فَهَلْ أَنتُم مُّغْنُونَ عَنَّا نَصِيبًا مِّنَ ٱلنَّارِ ﴿٤٧﴾

a lesser degree that was then being inflicted on Pharaoh and his followers, one which will last until the Day of Judgement. Such punishment consists in their being brought before Hellfire every morning and evening. This constantly fills such people with dread and horror in view of the fact that they will eventually be hurled into Hell. However, when the Day of Judgement comes, they will be subjected to the actual, major punishment destined for them – that is, they will be consigned to Hellfire, a horror the Egyptians had witnessed every day following their drowning. Such punishment will not only be meted out to Pharaoh and his community. Rather, all culprits will keep witnessing their ultimate punishment from the moment of their death until the Day of Judgement.

In contrast, the pious are shown a glimpse of their felicitous end which God has earmarked for them. Bukhārī, Muslim and Aḥmad ibn Ḥanbal narrate the tradition reported by 'Abd Allāh ibn 'Umar that the Prophet (peace be on him) said: 'If anyone of you dies, he is shown his final abode every morning and evening. If he is among the people of Paradise then the abode of the people of Paradise, and if he is among the people of Fire then the abode of the people of Fire. They are told that they will be transported to the place earmarked for them when God will resurrect them and summon them to His presence on the Day of Judgement.' (Bukhārī, *Kitāb al-Janā'iz, Bāb al-Mayyit Yu'raḍ 'alayhi Maq'aduhu bi al-Ghadāh wa al-'Ashīy*; Muslim, *Kitāb al-Jannah wa Ṣifat Na'īmihā wa Ahlihā, Bāb 'Arḍ Maq'ad al-Mayyit min al-Jannah aw al-Nār 'alayhi wa Ithbāt 'Adhāb al-Qabr wa al-Ta'awwudh minhu*; Aḥmad ibn Ḥanbal, *Musnad*, narrated by 'Abd Allāh ibn 'Umar.) (For further details see also *al-Nisā'* 4: 97; *al-Anfāl* 8: 50; *al-Naḥl* 16: 28-32; *al-Mu'minūn* 23: 99-100 and *Yā Sīn* 36, nn. 22-3, *Towards Understanding the Qur'ān*, vol. IX, pp. 253-4.)

64. They will not say this because they entertain the hope that their former guides, rulers or leaders will truly be able to rescue them from punishment or have it lightened for them. For the truth will already have dawned on them that such people are of no avail to them. However, in order to further humiliate them, they will taunt them by saying in effect: 'During the life of the world you led us with great pomp and pelf. Will you now deliver us from this torment which, thanks to you, has overtaken us?'

(48) Those who had waxed proud will reply: 'All of us are in it. Allah has already passed His judgement among His servants.'[65] (49) Those suffering in the Fire will say to the keepers of Hell: 'Call upon your Lord to lighten the chastisement for us just for a day.' (50) The keepers of Hell will ask: 'Did your Messengers not come to you with Clear Signs?' They will say: 'Yes (they did).' The keepers of Hell will say: 'Then you yourselves should call (upon the Lord). And the call of the unbelievers will end in vain.'[66]

قَالَ ٱلَّذِينَ ٱسْتَكْبَرُوٓا۟ إِنَّا كُلٌّ فِيهَآ إِنَّ ٱللَّهَ
قَدْ حَكَمَ بَيْنَ ٱلْعِبَادِ ﴿٤٨﴾ وَقَالَ ٱلَّذِينَ فِى
ٱلنَّارِ لِخَزَنَةِ جَهَنَّمَ ٱدْعُوا۟ رَبَّكُمْ يُخَفِّفْ
عَنَّا يَوْمًا مِّنَ ٱلْعَذَابِ ﴿٤٩﴾ قَالُوٓا۟ أَوَلَمْ تَكُ
تَأْتِيكُمْ رُسُلُكُم بِٱلْبَيِّنَٰتِ ۖ قَالُوا۟ بَلَىٰ ۚ
قَالُوا۟ فَٱدْعُوا۟ ۗ وَمَا دُعَٰٓؤُا۟ ٱلْكَٰفِرِينَ
إِلَّا فِى ضَلَٰلٍ ﴿٥٠﴾

65. The misguiding leaders will confess before their devotees that both they and their devotees are culprits and have been convicted by God as guilty. Now it is in no one's power to alter God's judgement or to diminish even to the slightest extent the punishment that He has ordained for them.

66. The keepers of Hell will ask the unbelievers: 'Did your Messengers not come to you with Clear Signs?' Now, since Messengers had already come to them with Clear Signs the unbelievers will be punished for they had rejected their message. The angels who are the keepers of Hell will, therefore, be left with no justifiable reason to pray to God on their behalf that they be rescued from His chastisement. If the unbelievers themselves wished to pray, they may go ahead and do so. It was clear, however, that all such prayers by those who had been transported to Hell on account of their disbelief were absolutely futile.

إِنَّا لَنَنصُرُ رُسُلَنَا وَٱلَّذِينَ ءَامَنُوا۟ فِى ٱلْحَيَوٰةِ
ٱلدُّنْيَا وَيَوْمَ يَقُومُ ٱلْأَشْهَـٰدُ ﴿٥١﴾ يَوْمَ لَا يَنفَعُ
ٱلظَّـٰلِمِينَ مَعْذِرَتُهُمْ ۖ وَلَهُمُ ٱللَّعْنَةُ وَلَهُمْ سُوٓءُ
ٱلدَّارِ ﴿٥٢﴾ وَلَقَدْ ءَاتَيْنَا مُوسَى ٱلْهُدَىٰ
وَأَوْرَثْنَا بَنِىٓ إِسْرَٰٓءِيلَ ٱلْكِتَـٰبَ ﴿٥٣﴾
هُدًى وَذِكْرَىٰ لِأُو۟لِى ٱلْأَلْبَـٰبِ ﴿٥٤﴾

(51) Surely We shall help Our Messengers and the believers in the life of this world[67] and on the Day when witnesses will rise to testify,[68] (52) the Day when the excuses offered by the wrong-doers shall not avail them. They shall be victims of the curse and a woeful abode. (53) We surely guided Moses[69] and made the Children of Israel the heirs of the Book (54) which was a guidance and good counsel to people endowed with understanding and wisdom.[70] ▶

67. For details, see *al-Ṣāffāt* 37, n. 33, *Towards Understanding the Qur'ān*, vol. IX, p. 293.

68. This refers to the Day of Judgement when God will hold His court of justice and witnesses will be summoned for testimony.

69. God makes it clear that after He directed Moses (peace be on him) to go forth and confront Pharaoh, he was not left to his own devices. Rather, God guided him at every step and this naturally culminated in his triumph.

Implicit in this is the subtle message for the Prophet Muḥammad (peace be on him) that God will show him the favour he had earlier shown to Moses. After having raised him in Makkah among the Quraysh, God will not leave him at the tender mercy of his oppressive enemies. God assures him that He stands by the Prophet (peace be on him) to support and guide him.

70. The Pharaonic community that had rejected the Prophet Moses (peace be on him) was deprived of God's blessings and favours. In sharp

(55) Be steadfast,[71] then, (O Prophet), Allah's promise is true.[72] Seek forgiveness for your shortcomings,[73] and celebrate the praise of your Lord, ▶	فَٱصۡبِرۡ إِنَّ وَعۡدَ ٱللَّهِ حَقٌّ وَٱسۡتَغۡفِرۡ لِذَنۢبِكَ وَسَبِّحۡ بِحَمۡدِ رَبِّكَ

contrast to this, the Children of Israel, who had affirmed their belief in Moses, were made to inherit the Scriptures. In like manner, it was made clear that those who reject the Prophet Muḥammad (peace be on him) will be deprived of God's blessings and favours. On the other hand, those who believe in the Prophet (peace be on him) will inherit the Qur'ān and will rise before the whole world as the standard-bearers of the guidance enshrined in it.

71. The Prophet Muḥammad (peace be on him) is being asked to patiently put up with the hardships that might come his way.

72. The allusion here is to God's promise made just above: 'We shall help Our Messengers and the believers in the life of this world and on the Day when witnesses will rise to testify,' (verse 51.)

73. It appears from the context that the 'shortcoming' to which reference is made here consists of a degree of impatience which had begun to develop in the Prophet (peace be on him) in this atmosphere of severe repression, especially by his observing his Companions' suffering and helplessness. The Prophet (peace be on him) had eagerly begun to look forward to some miracle taking place, one that would persuade the unbelievers into believing or to the appearance of something extraordinary, at God's behest, that would pacify the then raging storm of opposition and hostility. Obviously, there was nothing inherently wrong with this desire that one should call upon God, seeking His forgiveness. However, God had placed the Prophet (peace be on him) on a highly exalted pedestal which required of him utmost patience and fortitude. So high was the Prophet's station that the show of least impatience by him was considered out of tune with his exceptional position. It was for this reason that the Prophet (peace be on him) was asked to seek forgiveness from his Lord and to withstand all hardships with the strength of a rock.

evening and morning.[74] (56) Verily those who dispute regarding the Signs of Allah without any evidence that might have come to them, nothing but vain pride fills their hearts.[75] Yet they shall never be able to satisfy ▶

بِٱلْعَشِيِّ وَٱلْإِبْكَٰرِ ۝ إِنَّ ٱلَّذِينَ
يُجَٰدِلُونَ فِيٓ ءَايَٰتِ ٱللَّهِ بِغَيْرِ سُلْطَٰنٍ
أَتَىٰهُمْ إِن فِي صُدُورِهِمْ إِلَّا كِبْرٌ
مَّا هُم بِبَٰلِغِيهِ

74. Praising and glorifying God instils in believers the strength that enables them to endure all hardships in His cause.

Praising God in the morning and evening admits of two meanings: (i) that one should continually remember God; and (ii) that one should offer Prayers at the appointed hours. Taken in the latter sense, the reference is to the five obligatory Prayers that were prescribed for Muslims a little after this *sūrah*'s revelation. Evening covers the time period from the decline of the sun to early night. This obviously refers to *Ẓuhr*, *'Aṣr*, *Maghrib* and *'Ishā'* Prayers. The other expression, *ibkār,* signifies the time from dawn till sunrise when *Fajr* Prayer is offered. (For further details on this matter, see *al-Baqarah* 2, nn. 5, 59-61 and 262-3, *Towards Understanding the Qur'ān,* vol. I, pp. 46, 71-2 and 184-6; *Hūd* 11, n. 113 and *al-Ḥijr* 15, n. 53, vol. IV, pp. 137, 305; *Banī Isrā'īl* 17, nn. 1 and 92-97, and *Ṭā Hā* 20, n. 111, vol. V, pp. 5-8, 63-6 and 242; *al-'Ankabūt* 29, nn. 77-9 and *al-Rūm* 30, nn. 23-24 and 50, vol. VIII, pp. 41-6, 85-8 and 101-2.)

75. The unbelievers opposed the Qur'ān without any worthwhile reason and engaged in contentious argumentation against it. This was not because they could not understand its teachings. Nor was it their inability to appreciate the truth and the good which it embodies that made them engage in disputatious argumentation motivated by the desire to search the truth. Rather, their hostile argumentation was prompted by pride and hauteur such that they could not seriously entertain the proposition that the Prophet (peace be on him), rather than they, could guide and lead the people of Arabia. However, eventually the time came when even these opponents too had to recognise the leadership of the Prophet (peace be on him), the leadership of one whom they had once considered, as compared to themselves, utterly unworthy of leadership. At the point of time under discussion, however, they tried their utmost to obstruct the Prophet's path, sparing no means, howsoever mean and ignoble, to oppose him.

the pride with which they are puffed up.[76] So seek refuge with Allah.[77] Verily He is All-Hearing, All-Seeing.

(57) Surely the creation of the heavens[78] and the earth is a greater act than the creation of human beings. But most people do not know.[79] (58) Never can the blind and the seeing be equal; ▶

فَٱسْتَعِذْ بِٱللَّهِ ۖ إِنَّهُۥ هُوَ ٱلسَّمِيعُ ٱلْبَصِيرُ ﴿٥٦﴾
لَخَلْقُ ٱلسَّمَٰوَٰتِ وَٱلْأَرْضِ أَكْبَرُ مِنْ
خَلْقِ ٱلنَّاسِ وَلَٰكِنَّ أَكْثَرَ ٱلنَّاسِ
لَا يَعْلَمُونَ ﴿٥٧﴾ وَمَا يَسْتَوِى ٱلْأَعْمَىٰ
وَٱلْبَصِيرُ

76. Only those whom God exalts will enjoy honour. As for the petty ones who are in vain pursuit of greatness, their attempts will end in naught.

77. The Prophet Moses (peace be on him) had grown fearless of Pharaoh, having sought refuge with God, the Most Mighty and Irresistible. In like manner, the Prophet Muḥammad (peace be on him) should seek refuge with God against the threats and conspiracies of the Quraysh and should ceaselessly strive to exalt His Word.

78. After commenting on the conspiracies hatched by the Quraysh chiefs, (see verses 21-25 above), the Qur'ānic discourse is now addressed to the common people to whom the truth of the Prophet's teachings is being explained. They are told that it is in their own interest to believe in the Prophet (peace be on him); in other words, it would simply be calamitous for them to reject his teachings. In this connection reference is first made to the Hereafter along with its supporting proofs. It may be recalled that the unbelievers found the very notion of the Hereafter as weird, as something utterly incomprehensible.

79. This is meant to show that the Hereafter lies in the range of the possible. As for the unbelievers, they had ruled out resurrection as something impossible. The Qur'ān refutes their fallacious notions, pointing out that those who so think are devoid of understanding. Were they to be guided by reason, they would realise that it is pretty easy for God, Who has created this vast universe, to raise the dead to life.

nor those that believe and act righteously and those that do evil. Little do you understand.[80] (59) The Hour will indeed come; there is no doubt about that. Yet most people do not believe.[81]	وَٱلَّذِينَ ءَامَنُوا۟ وَعَمِلُوا۟ ٱلصَّٰلِحَٰتِ وَلَا ٱلْمُسِىٓءُ ۚ قَلِيلًا مَّا تَتَذَكَّرُونَ ﴿٥٨﴾ إِنَّ ٱلسَّاعَةَ لَءَاتِيَةٌ لَّا رَيْبَ فِيهَا وَلَٰكِنَّ أَكْثَرَ ٱلنَّاسِ لَا يُؤْمِنُونَ ﴿٥٩﴾

80. This proves the imminence of the Hereafter. Both reason and justice demand that there be an Afterlife. In fact it is not its occurrence but its non-occurrence that is inconsistent with reason and justice. After all, how can any reasonable person believe that those who live in the world in a state of moral blindness and who corrupt the world by their misdeeds should remain unpunished, (something that was bound to happen if there were no Afterlife)? In like manner, those who live in the world with open eyes, who believe and act righteously, will see no good result of their conduct if there is no Afterlife. If this is against the dictates of reason and justice, then denial of the Afterlife is also bound to be against the dictates of reason and justice. This because the denial of the Afterlife means that both the good and the wicked will be reduced to the earth after death, both coming to the same end. If both the good and the wicked meet the same end, what would be the point in the former living in accordance with a code of goodness? Would it not be smarter, in that case, for a person were to concentrate all his attention on the single-minded pursuit of pleasure, allowing none of his desires to remain unfulfilled?

81. The truth of the Hereafter can be categorically affirmed only on the basis of sure knowledge rather than of rational argument. The fact is that a definitive statement on this matter can only be made on the basis of Revelation. At most what can be said on the basis of rational argument is that *the occurrence of the Hereafter is possible and that it should take place.* It is only for God and no one else to go beyond that and categorically affirm *that the Hereafter will certainly take place for He alone knows for sure about that.* At this point it becomes quite evident that if the foundation of religious faith is to be rooted in true, dependable knowledge, it will have to be anchored in Revelation.

(60) Your Lord said: [82] 'Pray to Me, and I will accept your prayers.[83] ▶	وَقَالَ رَبُّكُمُ ٱدْعُونِىٓ أَسْتَجِبْ لَكُمْ

82. From here on the discourse on the Hereafter is replaced by one on monotheism which was another point of contention and dispute between the unbelievers and the Prophet (peace be on him).

83. God makes it clear that He alone has the power to accept prayers or not. Hence it stands to reason that people should address their prayers only to Him. In order to understand the underlying spirit of this verse one should fully grasp the following points:

(1) Man naturally addresses his prayers to the One Whom he considers to be All-Hearing, All-Seeing and possessed of supernatural powers. What motivates a man to pray is His feeling that the ordinary means that form part of natural causation are not sufficiently effective to deliver him from his affliction or to fulfil his needs. It is only in such a state of mind that man considers it inevitable to call upon a being possessed of supernatural powers. It is for this reason that he turns to the Supreme Being. He invokes Him even though He does not see Him and makes supplications to Him whenever and wherever he likes. He invokes Him in utter solitude and prays to Him both loudly and in a low voice and even calls upon Him in his heart. All this is done in the belief that the Supreme Being is All-Seeing, that He knows even that which lies in the recesses of a person's heart. This is further done in the belief that the Almighty Being can come to his aid and deliver him from distress. This being the nature of prayer to God, it is not difficult for man to realise that the person who invokes someone besides God for help is guilty of gross polytheism for he ascribes to whom he invokes those attributes that belong to God alone.

(2) If a person believes that someone has power and authority this does not necessarily mean that that belief is correct. Possession of authority relates to fact rather than to anyone's assumptions about it. If someone is possessed of power and authority he will remain so regardless of whether people affirm this or not. Now, it is a fact that God alone is All-Mighty, that He rules over the universe, that He is All-Hearing and All-Seeing and that He is

Surely those who wax too proud to worship Me shall enter Hell, utterly abased.'[84]

(61) Allah it is Who made the night so that you may ▶

إِنَّ ٱلَّذِينَ يَسْتَكْبِرُونَ عَنْ عِبَادَتِي سَيَدْخُلُونَ جَهَنَّمَ دَاخِرِينَ ﴿٦٠﴾ ٱللَّهُ ٱلَّذِي جَعَلَ لَكُمُ ٱلَّيْلَ

the One Who has absolute power over everything. There is none else who has the power to hear people's prayers and to decide how to respond to them. If in contravention of this basic fact, some people believe that there are any Prophets, or saints, or angels, or *jinn,* or planets or idols who have a share in God's power and authority, this will not at all change the objective reality. The Lord will remain what He is and the servant will remain what he actually is.

(3) The likeness of addressing prayers to anyone other than God is that of carrying a petition to a governmental bureau. However, instead of handing it over to the actual sovereign, one hands it over to other petitioners like himself, fervently entreating them to accept it. It is an act of sheer folly and ignorance that one should turn to incapable beings like oneself for help. However, if someone petitions others in the very presence of the Sovereign, this also becomes an act of outrageous provocation. This act reaches the climax of folly and ignorance when those to whom the petitions are presented repeatedly point out that they are as helpless as the petitioner himself and that he would do well to address his petition to the Sovereign Who is right there. This folly assumes ridiculous proportions when the petitioner, despite being told that all except the Sovereign are helpless, keeps repeating to others that they alone have the power to deliver him from his awful situation.

It is against this backdrop that one should understand the implications of God's directive: 'Pray to Me, and I will accept your prayers', making it clear that accepting the prayers of God's creatures rests with Him alone.

84. The following two points in this verse merit particular attention: (i) Prayer and worship have been used as synonyms. This reinforces the notion that prayer or supplication is the quintessence of worship. (ii) The following observation is significant: 'Surely those who wax too proud

to worship Me...' (see verse 60.) This implies that to pray is the essence of servitude to God. It is the very zenith of man's servitude to God to supplicate to Him. Those who wilfully refrain from praying in fact do so because they have been puffed up by pride and arrogance. The Prophet's own observations also amplify this point. Nu'mān ibn Bashīr narrates that the Prophet (peace be on him) said: 'Supplication is the essence of worship. ' Then he recited the verse 60 of *Sūrah al-Mu'min*. (Aḥmad ibn Ḥanbal, *Musnad*, narrated by Nu'mān ibn Bashīr; Tirmidhī, *Kitāb Tafsīr al-Qur'ān 'an Rasūl Allāh Ṣallā Allāh 'alayhi wa Sallam, Bāb wa min Sūrat al-Mu'min*; Abū Dā'ūd, *Kitāb al-Ṣalāh, Bāb al-Du'ā'*; Nasā'ī, *Kitāb al-Tafsīr, Bāb Sūrah Ghāfir*; Ibn Mājah, *Kitāb al-Du'ā', Bāb Faḍl al-Du'ā'*; Ibn Abī Ḥātim, *Tafsīr*, comments on *Sūrah al-Mu'min* 40: 60; and Ṭabarī, *Tafsīr*, comments on *Sūrah al-Mu'min* 40: 60.) According to Anas, the Prophet (peace be on him) spoke of supplication as the quintessence of worship, (Tirmidhī, *Kitāb al-Da'wāt 'an Rasūl Allāh Ṣallā Allāh 'alayhi wa Sallam, Bāb minhu*.) Abū Hurayrah narrated the following on the Prophet's authority: 'God becomes wrathful with him who does not invoke Him for help and support,' (Tirmidhī, *Kitāb al-Da'wāt 'an Rasūl Allāh Ṣallā Allāh 'alayhi wa Sallam, Bāb minhu*.)

These observations also resolve a perplexing dilemma. Some people think that since God exercises total control over man's destiny, both good and bad, and since God has already decreed something for man out of His wisdom and dispensation, nothing but that is bound to happen. In view of this, they argue, it is pointless to make supplication [for what will happen has already been decreed.]

The present verse, however, removes such misperceptions: (i) God pointedly says in this verse: 'Pray to Me, and I will accept your prayers.' Thus what is called 'fate' does not prevent God from doing anything that He pleases or from accepting any supplication. *Man obviously cannot alter the Divine Decree. However, God can change His decision in response to someone's supplication.* (ii) Whether someone's supplication is granted or not, it is nonetheless not devoid of blessing because by the act of supplication one acknowledges God's supremacy and one's own servitude and helplessness. This admission of servitude is the very essence of worship. One is rewarded for this irrespective of whether one's supplication is granted or not. The Prophet's following sayings on this issue further clarify both these points. Salmān al-Fārisī states that the Prophet (peace be on him) said: 'Nothing but prayer can alter fate', (Tirmidhī, *Kitāb al-Qadr 'an Rasūl Allāh Ṣallā Allāh 'alayhi wa Sallam, Bāb mā Jā'a lā Yarudd al-Qadr illā al-Du'ā'*.) In other words, God can change His decision after listening to a man's entreaty whereas no one else can change his fate. According to Jābir ibn 'Abd Allāh, the Prophet (peace be on him) observed: 'As one invokes God to grant one something,

He either grants it to the person or averts some disaster that would otherwise have afflicted him, providing that it does not entail any sin or the severing of kinship ties', (Tirmidhī, *Kitāb al-Da'wāt 'an Rasūl Allāh Ṣallā Allāh 'alayhi wa Sallam, Bāb mā Jā'a anna Da'wat al-Muslim Mustajābah.*) Another tradition is narrated by Abū Sa'īd al-Khudrī in the following words: 'When a believer makes a supplication to God, provided that it does not entail any sin or the serverance of ties of kinship, He accepts it in one of three ways: (i) The person's supplication is granted in this world, (ii) He is compensated for it in the Hereafter, (iii) Some disaster about to befall him is averted to some extent.' (Aḥmad ibn Ḥanbal, *Musnad*, narrated by Abū Sa'īd.) Abū Hurayrah narrates that the Prophet (peace be on him) said: 'If any of you prays to God, let him not say: "Grant me deliverance or mercy or sustenance, if You please." Rather, he should pray categorically for what he wants,' (Bukhārī, *Kitāb al-Tawḥīd, Bāb fī al-Mashī'ah wa al-Irādah.*) Another *ḥadīth* of similar import, also related by Abū Hurayrah, is as follows: 'Pray to God with the conviction that He will answer your prayer,' (Tirmidhī, *Kitāb al-Da'wāt 'an Rasūl Allāh Ṣallā Allāh 'alayhi wa Sallam, Bāb mā Jā'a fī Jāmi' al-Da'wāt 'an Rasūl Allāh Ṣallā Allāh 'alayhi wa Sallam.*) Abū Hurayrah also narrates yet another *ḥadīth:* 'A servant's prayer is answered if it does not involve sin or severing of ties of kinship providing he does not hasten.' On being requested to clarify the meaning of haste in this context, he replied: '[It means] his saying: "I prayed and prayed and did not see that my prayer was answered," so he grew weary and gave up praying.' (Muslim, *Kitāb al-Dhikr wa al-Du'ā' wa al-Tawbah wa al-Istighfār, Bāb Bayān annahu Yustajāb li al-Dā'ī mā lam Ya'jal fa Yaqūl: 'Da'awtu falam Yustajab lī'.*)

The following *aḥādīth* shed light on the excellence of supplications: Abū Hurayrah narrates that the Prophet (peace be on him) said: 'Nothing is more valuable in God's sight than man's supplication to Him', (Tirmidhī, *Kitāb al-Da'wāt 'an Rasūl Allāh Ṣallā Allāh 'alayhi wa Sallam, Bāb mā Jā'a fī Faḍl al-Du'ā'*; Ibn Majah, *Kitāb al-Du'ā', Bāb Faḍl al-Du'ā'.*) 'Abd Allāh ibn Mas'ūd says: 'Seek God's munificence. God loves those who invoke Him to bestow His grace upon them', (Tirmidhī, *Kitāb al-Da'wāt 'an Rasūl Allāh Ṣallā Allāh 'alayhi wa Sallam, Bāb mā Jā'a fī Intiẓār al-Faraj wa Ghayr Dhālik.*) 'Abd Allāh ibn 'Umar and Mu'ādh ibn Jabal relate that the Prophet (peace be on him) said: 'Your supplication is beneficial for you. It protects you against the calamities that have struck you before as well as against those that are to afflict you. O servants of God, it is imperative that you turn to God, invoking His help,' (Tirmidhī, *Kitāb al-Da'wāt 'an Rasūl Allāh Ṣallā Allāh 'alayhi wa Sallam, Bāb fī Du'ā' al-Nabī Ṣallā Allāh 'alayhi wa Sallam*; Aḥmad ibn Ḥanbal, *Musnad*, narrated by Mu'ādh ibn Jabal.) Similarly, Anas ibn Mālik narrates: 'Let each of you ask God for what he needs, so much so that he should even ask him for his shoelace,' (Tirmidhī, *Kitāb*

seek repose in it, and made the day radiant. Surely Allah is Most Bounteous to people; but most people do not give thanks.[85] (62) Allah (Who bestowed all these favours upon you) is your Lord, the Creator of everything. There is no god but He.[86] ▶

لِتَسْكُنُوا۟ فِيهِ وَٱلنَّهَارَ مُبْصِرًا ۚ إِنَّ ٱللَّهَ لَذُو
فَضْلٍ عَلَى ٱلنَّاسِ وَلَـٰكِنَّ أَكْثَرَ ٱلنَّاسِ
لَا يَشْكُرُونَ ﴿٦١﴾ ذَٰلِكُمُ ٱللَّهُ رَبُّكُمْ خَـٰلِقُ
كُلِّ شَىْءٍ لَّآ إِلَـٰهَ إِلَّا هُوَ ۖ

---

al-Da'wāt 'an Rasūl Allāh Ṣallā Allāh 'alayhi wa Sallam, Bāb liyas'al al-Ḥājah mahmā Ṣaghurat.)

The fact is that one should invoke God's help even in such ordinary matters that lie within one's power and which can easily be accomplished. For one cannot gain any success without God's help and support. To pray to God for one's needs before taking the practical steps that one should take amounts to a fulsome acknowledgement by man of his utter helplessness on the one hand and of God's supremacy on the other.

85. This verse comprises two important truths: (i) The phenomenon of day and night is put forward as a proof in support of monotheism. The constant alternation of day and night underscores that the One True God reigns supreme over the whole universe and that He exercises full control over both the earth and the sun. That their alternation is immensely beneficial for God's creatures only serves to underline that God is the Creator of everything and that He has devised the whole system with such perfect wisdom that it is beneficial for all His creatures. (ii) Polytheists and atheists have been sensitised to the immense benefits of the alternation of day and night. In view of these benefits it becomes all the more evident how starkly ungrateful both unbelieving groups are to their Beneficent Creator. Even though they constantly benefit from God's bounties they nonetheless remain disloyal and thankless to Him. (For further details, see *Yūnus* 10, n. 65, *Towards Understanding the Qur'ān*, vol. IV, pp. 48-50; *al-Furqān* 25, n. 77, *al-Naml* 27, n. 105, and *al-Qaṣaṣ* 28: 71-3, vol. VII, pp. 36 and 187-8; *al-Rūm* 30, n. 33 and *Luqmān* 31: 29 and n. 50, vol. VIII, pp. 93-5 and 144; and *Yā Sīn* 36: 37 and n. 32, vol. IX, p. 257.)

86. The alternation of day and night demonstrates that God is the Creator of man and of everything else. The numerous benefits accruing

Whence are you, then, being led astray?[87] (63) Thus it is only those who had denied Allah's Signs that were led astray.[88]

(64) Allah it is Who made the earth a dwelling place for you[89] and made the sky a canopy,[90] Who shaped you – and shaped you exceedingly well – ▸

فَأَنَّىٰ تُؤْفَكُونَ ﴿٦٢﴾ كَذَٰلِكَ يُؤْفَكُ ٱلَّذِينَ
كَانُوا۟ بِـَٔايَـٰتِ ٱللَّهِ يَجْحَدُونَ ﴿٦٣﴾ ٱللَّهُ
ٱلَّذِى جَعَلَ لَكُمُ ٱلْأَرْضَ قَرَارًا
وَٱلسَّمَآءَ بِنَآءً وَصَوَّرَكُمْ فَأَحْسَنَ صُوَرَكُمْ

---

to mankind from the alternation of day and night highlight the fact that God is the Most Merciful Lord. It leaves no room to doubt that He is the Lord of the whole universe. What naturally follows from this is that God should also be their deity. For it is altogether discordant with both reason and justice that while God should be man's creator and sustainer, he should consecrate his worship and service to any other than Him.

87. The unbelievers are asked as to who misguides them into worshipping those who neither created them nor provide them with sustenance.

88. Human beings have been misled simply because they paid no heed to the Messengers' teachings. As a result, they fell prey to misguided and selfish people who deceived them in order to promote their own selfish ends.

89. For further details, see *al-Naml* 27, n. 74-5, *Towards Understanding the Qur'ān*, vol. VII, pp. 172-3.

90. Human beings have not been left unprotected against the natural calamities from outer space that would annihilate them. Instead, God has erected a firm celestial barrier which appears to the naked eyes as though it were a canopy. No destructive object, not even devastating cosmic rays, can reach human beings without first passing through this celestial obstacle. It is thanks to this protection that man has enjoyed a secure and comfortable living on earth.

and gave you good things as sustenance.[91] That is Allah, your Lord; blessed be Allah, the Lord of the Universe. (65) He is the Ever-Living: [92] there is no god but He. ▸	وَرَزَقَكُم مِّنَ ٱلطَّيِّبَٰتِ ۚ ذَٰلِكُمُ ٱللَّهُ رَبُّكُمْ ۖ فَتَبَارَكَ ٱللَّهُ رَبُّ ٱلْعَٰلَمِينَ ﴿٦٤﴾ هُوَ ٱلْحَىُّ لَآ إِلَٰهَ إِلَّا هُوَ

91. That is, before creating man God arranged for him an exceedingly safe and secure dwelling place. Thereafter, when God created man He made sure that he was possessed of a very wholesome body, of extremely well-proportioned limbs and of sterling physical and mental faculties. Man's straight posture, his hands and feet, his eyes and ears, his articulate tongue, and his brain – that outstanding treasure-house of excellent potentialities – none of these was created by man himself, nor did his parents make them, nor did any Prophet or saint or deity have the power to bring them into existence. It is only the All-Powerful, All-Compassionate and All-Merciful God Who, on deciding to create man, bestowed on him an exquisite body to enable him to function effectively on earth.

No sooner than man opened his eyes did he find a vast table of wholesome dishes spread around him for his sustenance. Notably, the sustenance that had already been arranged for him is nutritious, delicious and palatable rather than injurious, bitter and foul-tasting. It does not consist of good-for-nothing ruffage but is rich in vitamins and beneficial nutrients and is most vitally suited for his physical growth and development. Take for instance water, iron, vegetables, fruits, milk, honey, meat, salt and spices. All these provide exceedingly appropriate nourishment. Besides, they not only provide man with ample vitality to live but are also exceedingly conducive for life's enjoyment. Who, after all, has made these valuable objects available in such abundance? Who has made sure that these limitless resources of food constantly well out of earth in uninterrupted continuity, their supply never coming to an end? Had people been brought into existence without creating this excellent arrangement, what would human life have been like? Is this not clear proof that man's Creator did not simply create, but that He is also an immensely Wise Creator and a Most Compassionate Sustainer?

92. God alone enjoys eternal life. He exists by Himself and no one else shares eternity with Him. None other than God owes his life to himself for all received it from God. Therefore, all beings are mortal and live only for a relatively short time.

So call upon Him, consecrating to Him all your devotion.[93] All praise and thanks be to Allah, the Lord of the whole Universe.[94]

(66) Say, (O Prophet): 'I have been forbidden to worship those beside Allah whom you call upon.[95] (How can I worship any beside Allah) when clear Signs have come to me from my Lord and I have been commanded to surrender to Allah, the Lord of the Universe?'

(67) He it is Who created you from dust, then from a sperm-drop, then from a clot; then He brings you out as an infant, then causes you to grow into full maturity, and then causes you to grow further so that you may reach old age, while some of you He recalls earlier.[96] ▶

فَٱدۡعُوهُ مُخۡلِصِينَ لَهُ ٱلدِّينَۗ ٱلۡحَمۡدُ لِلَّهِ رَبِّ
ٱلۡعَٰلَمِينَ ﴿٦٥﴾ ۞ قُلۡ إِنِّي نُهِيتُ أَنۡ أَعۡبُدَ
ٱلَّذِينَ تَدۡعُونَ مِن دُونِ ٱللَّهِ لَمَّا جَآءَنِيَ
ٱلۡبَيِّنَٰتُ مِن رَّبِّي وَأُمِرۡتُ أَنۡ أُسۡلِمَ لِرَبِّ
ٱلۡعَٰلَمِينَ ﴿٦٦﴾ هُوَ ٱلَّذِي خَلَقَكُم مِّن تُرَابٖ
ثُمَّ مِن نُّطۡفَةٖ ثُمَّ مِنۡ عَلَقَةٖ ثُمَّ يُخۡرِجُكُمۡ
طِفۡلٗا ثُمَّ لِتَبۡلُغُوٓاْ أَشُدَّكُمۡ ثُمَّ لِتَكُونُواْ
شُيُوخٗاۚ وَمِنكُم مَّن يُتَوَفَّىٰ مِن قَبۡلُۖ

93. For further details, see *al-Zumar* 39, nn. 3-4 above.

94. None other than God deserves absolute praise and glorification.

95. Once again, prayer and worship are used as synonyms.

96. Some die even before birth, while others die before reaching youth or old age.

All this is in order that you may reach an appointed term[97] and that you may understand (the Truth).[98] (68) He it is Who gives life and causes death. Whenever He decrees a thing, He only commands to it 'Be', and it is.

وَلِتَبْلُغُوٓاْ أَجَلًا مُّسَمًّى وَلَعَلَّكُمْ تَعْقِلُونَ
﴿٦٧﴾ هُوَ ٱلَّذِى يُحْىِۦ وَيُمِيتُ ۖ فَإِذَا قَضَىٰٓ
أَمْرًا فَإِنَّمَا يَقُولُ لَهُۥ كُن فَيَكُونُ ﴿٦٨﴾

---

97. The expression 'appointed term' used here might refer to the time of one's death or to resurrection when everyone will be raised to stand before God. In the former sense, it means that God carries man through several stages until the hour appointed for each person's return to Him arrives. Before that hour a person cannot die, even if he were to make a concerted effort to end his life. On the contrary, should the whole world try to restore life to a dead person, they will not succeed. Were we, however, to adopt the latter meaning, it would mean that God has not created human beings to simply die and be reduced to dust and extinction. On the contrary, God has made sure that human beings should pass through various stages until they are made to stand before Him at the Hour He Himself has determined.

98. That is, God does not cause humans to go through these various stages in order that they live and then become extinct like animals; rather, they are made to go through these stages in order that they use the reason that He has granted them to try to comprehend the system through which they pass.

The emergence of the astonishing phenomenon of life in lifeless matter, the growth of a microscopic sperm into the wondrous being that a human is, the development of the sperm in the mother's womb right from the time of inception in such manner that its gender, its form and appearance, its faculties, mental abilities and other potentialities are so clearly determined that no external factor can affect them. Then the one who is fated to suffer miscarriage is inevitably eliminated by miscarriage and the one who is destined to die an early death dies early. Likewise, those who are destined to reach the age of youth or old age inexorably reach that age despite the graveness of circumstances that should ordinarily have caused them to die. On the other hand, anyone who is destined to die at a certain age inevitably dies at that very age notwithstanding the best medical care available to him under the most effective supervision. All this clearly

(69) Did you not see those who dispute concerning Allah's Signs? Whence are they, then, being turned astray?[99] (70) Those who gave the lie to this Book and all the Books which We had sent with Our Messengers[100] shall soon come to know the Truth (71) when fetters and chains shall be on their necks, and they shall be dragged into (72) boiling water, and cast into the Fire.[101] ▶

أَلَمْ تَرَ إِلَى ٱلَّذِينَ يُجَٰدِلُونَ فِىٓ ءَايَٰتِ
ٱللَّهِ أَنَّىٰ يُصْرَفُونَ ﴿٦٩﴾ ٱلَّذِينَ كَذَّبُوا۟
بِٱلْكِتَٰبِ وَبِمَآ أَرْسَلْنَا بِهِۦ رُسُلَنَا ۖ فَسَوْفَ
يَعْلَمُونَ ﴿٧٠﴾ إِذِ ٱلْأَغْلَٰلُ فِىٓ أَعْنَٰقِهِمْ
وَٱلسَّلَٰسِلُ يُسْحَبُونَ ﴿٧١﴾ فِى ٱلْحَمِيمِ ثُمَّ
فِى ٱلنَّارِ يُسْجَرُونَ ﴿٧٢﴾

---

shows that man's life and death are in the Hand of the Omnipotent Being. Since this is the case, no Prophet, saint, angel, star or planet deserves to be worshipped. No creature occupies such an exalted position that justifies that we address prayers to it or consider it to have the power to make or mar our destiny. Nor does anyone possess the power and authority to warrant blind obedience to his law or that others should unquestioningly carry out his do's and dont's. (For further elaboration, see *al-Ḥajj* 22, n. 9, *Towards Understanding the Qur'ān,* vol. VI, pp. 9-11.)

99. This lays bare the root cause of the unbelievers' erroneous perception and conduct, one that has caused them to fall in the ditch of waywardness? It goes without saying that the address here is not directed specifically to the Prophet (peace be on him); it is, rather, directed to every serious student of the Qur'ān.

100. This is the root cause of the unbelievers' error. They refuse to believe in the Qur'ān and the teachings of the Messengers and contest God's Signs instead of seriously reflecting upon them. As a result, they are led astray and it is no longer possible for them to pursue the Straight Way.

101. Driven by extreme thirst, those who had contested God's Signs will ask for water but the custodians of Hell will drag them by their

(73) It will then be said to them: 'Where are those whom you (74) associated with Allah in His Divinity?'[102] They will say: 'We have lost them; rather, we never used to call upon anyone before.'[103] Thus will Allah cause them to stumble in error. (75) (They will be told): 'This is because while you were on earth you took delight in untruth and exulted in it.[104] (76) Enter Hell now to abide in it. How woeful is the abode of those who wax proud!' ▶

ثُمَّ قِيلَ لَهُمْ أَيْنَ مَا كُنتُمْ تُشْرِكُونَ ﴿٧٣﴾ مِن
دُونِ ٱللَّهِ ۖ قَالُوا۟ ضَلُّوا۟ عَنَّا بَل لَّمْ نَكُن نَّدْعُوا۟
مِن قَبْلُ شَيْـًٔا ۚ كَذَٰلِكَ يُضِلُّ ٱللَّهُ
ٱلْكَـٰفِرِينَ ﴿٧٤﴾ ذَٰلِكُم بِمَا كُنتُمْ تَفْرَحُونَ
فِى ٱلْأَرْضِ بِغَيْرِ ٱلْحَقِّ وَبِمَا كُنتُمْ
تَمْرَحُونَ ﴿٧٥﴾ ٱدْخُلُوٓا۟ أَبْوَٰبَ جَهَنَّمَ
خَـٰلِدِينَ فِيهَا ۖ فَبِئْسَ مَثْوَى ٱلْمُتَكَبِّرِينَ ﴿٧٦﴾

---

fetters and take them to springs of hot, boiling water. After partaking of this, they will be dragged back and hurled into Hellfire.

102. That is, if they were really gods or God's associates in His Divinity whom they worshipped under the impression that they would rescue them from their distress, why is it that those gods or God's associates are doing nothing to deliver them from their woeful predicament?

103. This does not mean that they will deny that in their worldly life they had associated others with God in His Divinity. What it rather means is that they have come to know fully well that their false gods are totally helpless, even though they had invoked them in the phase of their worldly existence. For such false gods have simply turned out to be as good-for-nothing as corpses.

104. They were not simply content with pursuing falsehood, but were so intoxicated with devotion to untruth that they impudently spurned the truth and exulted in their devotion to falsehood.

(77) So be patient,[105] (O Prophet). Surely Allah's promise is true. Whether We show them a part of the woeful consequences against which We warn them (while you are still in their midst) or We recall you (from this world) before that, eventually it is to Us that they shall be brought back.[106]

(78) Indeed We sent many Messengers before you: [107] of them there are some whose account We have narrated to you and there are others whose account We have not narrated to you. ▶

فَٱصْبِرْ إِنَّ وَعْدَ ٱللَّهِ حَقٌّ ۚ فَإِمَّا نُرِيَنَّكَ بَعْضَ
ٱلَّذِى نَعِدُهُمْ أَوْ نَتَوَفَّيَنَّكَ فَإِلَيْنَا يُرْجَعُونَ ﴿٧٧﴾
وَلَقَدْ أَرْسَلْنَا رُسُلًا مِّن قَبْلِكَ مِنْهُم مَّن
قَصَصْنَا عَلَيْكَ وَمِنْهُم مَّن لَّمْ نَقْصُصْ عَلَيْكَ ۗ

105. The Prophet (peace be on him) is directed to persevere in the face of the petty contentiousness of his opponents who are out to humiliate and degrade him by recourse to ignoble means.

106. It is clarified that God will not necessarily punish each of the Prophet's enemies in this world or during the Prophet's life-time. What is, nonetheless, quite certain is that they cannot escape being seized by Him. For, after all, everyone is destined to return to God. No way will be left for these culprits to escape full punishment for their misdeeds.

107. The Qur'ān here broaches another subject. The Makkan unbelievers used to say to the Prophet (peace be on him) that they would not accept him as God's Messenger until he presented them with a miracle of their choosing. In the verses that follow, the Qur'ān responds to this contention without directly referring to it. As to the miracles demanded by the Makkan unbelievers, these are discussed elsewhere in the Qur'ān. (See *Hūd* 11: 12; *al-Ḥijr* 15: 7; *Banī Isrā'īl* 17: 90-5 and *al-Furqān* 25: 21.)

It did not lie in any Messenger's power to bring any Sign except with Allah's leave.[108] So when Allah's decree came, the matter was decided with justice, and those steeped in error courted utter loss,[109] then and there. (79) Allah it is Who has made cattle for you so that you ride some of them and from some of them you derive food. (80) In them there are also other benefits for you, and through them you fulfil your heartfelt need (to reach places), and you are borne along upon them ▶

وَمَا كَانَ لِرَسُولٍ أَن يَأْتِيَ بِـَٔايَةٍ إِلَّا بِإِذْنِ
ٱللَّهِ ۚ فَإِذَا جَآءَ أَمْرُ ٱللَّهِ قُضِىَ بِٱلْحَقِّ وَخَسِرَ
هُنَالِكَ ٱلْمُبْطِلُونَ ﴿٧٨﴾ ٱللَّهُ ٱلَّذِى جَعَلَ
لَكُمُ ٱلْأَنْعَٰمَ لِتَرْكَبُوا۟ مِنْهَا وَمِنْهَا
تَأْكُلُونَ ﴿٧٩﴾ وَلَكُمْ فِيهَا مَنَٰفِعُ وَلِتَبْلُغُوا۟
عَلَيْهَا حَاجَةً فِى صُدُورِكُمْ وَعَلَيْهَا

---

108. No Prophets have ever produced miracles of their own accord; they are simply not authorised to do so. It is by God's leave alone that Prophets present miracles. A miracle is presented when God decides that it may be produced before an unbelieving community. This, then, is the first rejoinder to the unbelievers' demand for a miracle.

109. No miracle was ever presented by way of mere sport and play. Rather, a miracle is something of a grave and decisive character. If a community persists in unbelief even after witnessing a miracle, it is obliterated. The Makkan unbelievers' demand for miracle lacked seriousness. They failed to realise that by making this demand they were inviting destruction upon themselves. This is another rejoinder to the unbelievers' demand for miracles. (The same point is also made in the following *sūrahs* of the Qur'ān: *al-Ḥijr* 15, nn. 5, 30 and 33, *Towards Understanding the Our'ān,* vol. IV, pp. 282-3 and 295; *al-Anbiyā'* 21, n. 8, vol. V, pp. 254-5; *al-Furqān* 25, n. 36 and al-*Shu'arā'* 26, n. 29, vol. VII, pp. 19 and 64-5.

as upon the ships. (81) Allah shows His Signs to you; then which of Allah's Signs will you deny?[110]

وَعَلَى ٱلْفُلْكِ تُحْمَلُونَ ﴿٨٠﴾ وَيُرِيكُمْ ءَايَٰتِهِۦ
فَأَىَّ ءَايَٰتِ ٱللَّهِ تُنكِرُونَ ﴿٨١﴾

---

110. The unbelievers are told that if they are serious in their demand for a miracle, and they need it in order to believe in the Prophet's message, then there are countless Signs of God that suffice for that purpose. Indeed, they observe those signs day in and day out. In the presence of these signs there is hardly any need for any further miracles. This represents the next rejoinder to their demand. (For further details, see *al-An'ām* 6, nn. 26-7 and 29, *Towards Understanding the Qur'ān*, vol. II, pp. 229-33; *Yūnus* 10, n. 105, *al-Ra'd* 13, nn.15-18 and 20, vol. IV, pp. 69, 226-9; *al-Shu'arā'* 26, nn. 1, 3 and 5, vol. VII, pp. 52-3 and p. 55.)

God has created animals, especially those that serve mankind such as the cows, oxen, sheep, goats, camels and horses, and has endowed them with such characteristics that they can easily be domesticated, enabling mankind to derive numerous benefits from them. They are used for transportation, dairy products, meat, fat, wool, hair, skin, entrails, bones, blood and excreta. All animal products are of immense use to mankind. This proves beyond all doubt that even before man's creation God took into full account his needs and so fashioned these animals that they would prove useful to him.

Another point worth considering is that three-fourths of the earth is filled with water, while only one-fourth is dry land. Again, water divides several regions of dry land. The settlement of human populations on dry lands and their transport and trade links could not have evolved without water, the seas and winds being governed by the laws that facilitate navigation. Again it is God Who provided the necessary means for ship building. This once again establishes that the Almighty God, Who is Most Merciful and All-Wise, has made everything – mankind, the earth, the seas and wind – according to a grand design of His. Even if one studies the specifics of navigation one clearly sees how planetary movements are of immense help to mankind. All this because God the Creator of both the earth and the heavens, is the One, Most Compassionate Lord. Since He has placed numerous resources at man's disposal, it is unimaginable that He will not call man to account for all these bounties.

(82) Did they not journey in the land[111] that they may behold the end of those who had gone before them? They were more numerous and greater in strength and left behind more splendid traces in the land. Yet their attainments did not avail them. (83) When their Messengers came to them with Clear Signs, they arrogantly exulted in whatever knowledge they had.[112] They were then encompassed by what they had mocked. (84) When they saw Our chastisement, they said: 'We have come to believe in Allah, the Only One, and we reject all what we had associated (with Allah in His Divinity).' (85) But their believing after they had seen Our chastisement did not avail them. ▶

أَفَلَمْ يَسِيرُوا۟ فِى ٱلْأَرْضِ فَيَنظُرُوا۟ كَيْفَ كَانَ
عَـٰقِبَةُ ٱلَّذِينَ مِن قَبْلِهِمْ ۚ كَانُوٓا۟ أَكْثَرَ مِنْهُمْ
وَأَشَدَّ قُوَّةً وَءَاثَارًا فِى ٱلْأَرْضِ فَمَآ أَغْنَىٰ
عَنْهُم مَّا كَانُوا۟ يَكْسِبُونَ ﴿٨٢﴾ فَلَمَّا جَآءَتْهُمْ
رُسُلُهُم بِٱلْبَيِّنَـٰتِ فَرِحُوا۟ بِمَا عِندَهُم مِّنَ
ٱلْعِلْمِ وَحَاقَ بِهِم مَّا كَانُوا۟ بِهِۦ يَسْتَهْزِءُونَ ﴿٨٣﴾
فَلَمَّا رَأَوْا۟ بَأْسَنَا قَالُوٓا۟ ءَامَنَّا بِٱللَّهِ وَحْدَهُۥ
وَكَفَرْنَا بِمَا كُنَّا بِهِۦ مُشْرِكِينَ ﴿٨٤﴾ فَلَمْ يَكُ
يَنفَعُهُمْ إِيمَـٰنُهُمْ لَمَّا رَأَوْا۟ بَأْسَنَا ۖ

111. This marks the conclusion of this passage, which may be better appreciated if it is studied in conjunction with verses 4, 5 and 21 of this *sūrah.*

112. The unbelievers were engrossed in the study of the disciplines of their choice, such as philosophy, science, law, mythology and theology, considering them to represent the truth. At the same time, they looked down upon the knowledge bestowed upon the Prophets as unworthy of serious attention.

That has been Allah's Way concerning His servants.[113] And the unbelievers courted utter loss, then and there.	سُنَّتَ ٱللَّهِ ٱلَّتِى قَدْ خَلَتْ فِى عِبَادِهِۦ ۖ وَخَسِرَ هُنَالِكَ ٱلْكَـٰفِرُونَ ﴿٨٥﴾

113. Belief and repentance can benefit man only before he is seized by God's punishment or death. Once a man is confronted with God's punishment or death, his act of belief or repentance becomes unacceptable to God.

Sūrah 41

Ḥā Mīm Al-Sajdah

(Makkan Period)

Title

A compound word *Ḥā Mīm al-Sajdah* constitutes this *sūrah*'s title. *Ḥā Mīm* signifies that it is the *sūrah* that commences with this expression and *al-Sajdah* indicates that it contains a verse that requires prostration.

Period of Revelation

Authentic traditions indicate that this *sūrah* was revealed after Ḥamzah's but before 'Umar's acceptance of Islam. On the authority of Muḥammad ibn Ka'b al-Quraẓī, a leading Successor, Muḥammad ibn Iṣhāq, the Prophet's earliest biographer, records the following: Once some Quraysh chiefs were assembled in the Mosque. The Prophet (peace be on him) was there all alone, seated in a corner of the Sacred Mosque. By that time Ḥamzah had embraced Islam and the Quraysh were getting panicky over the conversion of an increasing number of people to Islam. On that occasion 'Utbah ibn Rabī'ah, Abū Sufyān's father-in-law, spoke to the chiefs of the Quraysh. He suggested that if they agreed, he would approach Muḥammad (peace be on him) and would put forward a few ideas to him in the hope that if any of these were acceptable to the Quraysh, that would put an end to the discord between them and the Prophet (peace be on him). All those present agreed. As a result, 'Utbah went to the Prophet (peace be on him) and sat beside him. When the Prophet (peace be on him) turned towards him, 'Utbah said: 'Nephew, you know what esteem you enjoy among your people because of your family and lineage. But you have brought about huge hardship for your people. You have destroyed their unity and you are declaring them to be imbeciles. You have decried their deities and have begun to say things which mean that our ancestors were infidels. Now pay heed to what I say: I am putting forward a few suggestions to you. Consider them, maybe some of them will appeal to you.' The Prophet (peace be on him) asked 'Utbah to say what he wanted to, assuring him that he would pay heed. 'Utbah said: 'If you have started your mission for pecuniary gains we will grant you so abundantly that you will become the wealthiest person among us. If you seek personal glory and status, we will appoint you our chief. If you are after kingship, we will make you our king. If you are afflicted by some *jinn*, we will bear all the expenses incurred on your treatment.'

While 'Utbah made these offers, the Prophet (peace be on him) remained silent. Thereafter, he asked: 'O Abū al-Walīd, are you finished?' After he replied in the affirmative, the Prophet (peace be on him) said: 'Now listen to me.' He then pronounced the *Basmalah* and then began to recite this particular *sūrah*. 'Utbah listened to him in rapt attention. When the Prophet (peace be on him) recited the verse 38 of this *sūrah*, he prostrated. He then raised his head and said: 'O Abū al-Walīd, you now know my response. You may do as you please.' 'Utbah returned to the Quraysh chiefs. When they saw him they said among themselves that 'Utbah's countenance had changed. Thereafter 'Utbah reported to them all that had transpired: 'By Lord! Never before did I listen to such a discourse. By Lord! It is neither poetry, nor magic, nor soothsaying. O chiefs of the Quraysh! Listen to me and leave this person alone. I think his message will bear fruit. Suppose other Arabs prevail against him, you will bear no blame for raising your hands against your brother. On the contrary, if he prevails, you will receive your share in his success and you will bask in his glory.' No sooner had the Quraysh chiefs heard this than they said: 'O father of Walīd, eventually his spell has also charmed you!' 'Utbah replied that he had placed his opinion before them and now it was for them to do whatever they pleased. (Ibn Isḥāq, *The Life of Muḥammad*, tr. and notes by A. Guillaume, Karachi: Oxford University Press, 1955, 6th impression, 1980, pp. 132-33.)

Ḥadīth scholars have recorded variants of the same narration on the authority of Jābir ibn 'Abd Allāh. Some state that as the Prophet (peace be on him) recited verse 13: 'I warn you against a sudden scourge like that which struck the 'Ād and Thamūd', 'Utabah rushed to seal the Prophet's mouth, urging him to have mercy on his own tribe. Later, he justified his actions, saying: 'Muḥammad's word always comes true. So I stopped him from saying anything further lest a scourge might overtake us.' (Ibn Kathīr, *Tafsīr*, Comments on *Sūrah Ḥā Mīm al-Sajdah* 41: 5 and idem, *al-Bidāyah wa al-Nihāyah*, 'Alī Shayrī, ed., Cairo: Dār Iḥyā' al-Turāth al-'Arabī, 1408/1988, vol. III, p. 80.)

Subject Matter and Themes:

The Qur'ān paid no attention to the suggestions made by 'Utbah to the Prophet (peace be on him), for they implicitly attacked the Prophet's integrity and cast aspersions on his intelligence, wisdom and rationality. The underlying assumption behind 'Utbah's suggestions were an unmistakable denial of Muḥammad's Prophethood and of the Divine provenance of the Qur'ān. The Quraysh simply thought that the Prophet (peace be on him) was in pursuit of power or money. Alternatively, they thought that maybe he suffered from some kind of mental instability. In the first case, they wanted to strike a bargain with him, and in the second, they wanted to insult him by calling him insane and offering to bear the expenses of the treatment of his insanity. Obviously, when such outrageous statements were made, they deserved no response.

These blatantly foolish contentions were thus ignored and attention was paid instead to expounding the message of the Prophet (peace be on him). While totally disregarding the materially seductive offers made to the Prophet (peace be on him), attention was directed on the unbelievers' obstinate and ill-mannered opposition to the Prophet (peace be on him). His opponents had clearly told the Prophet (peace be on him) that they would never listen to his message. They had also arrogantly declared that their hearts and ears were sealed against it and that there stood an unbridgeable chasm between them and the Prophet (peace be on him), a chasm that would keep them apart for ever. They had openly challenged the Prophet (peace be on him) to continue his mission but it would be in the face of their very fierce opposition. As part of the same strategy, the unbelievers used to disturb the gatherings in which the Prophet (peace be on him) or any of his Companions recited the Qur'ān. They created such a din that no one could hear the Qur'ān's recital. Furthermore, they always made a point of twisting and subverting the Qur'ān's message. They would deliberately misinterpret the Qur'ān, speak of things out of context, or even present a corrupted version of it to others. Their only purpose was to discredit both the Qur'ān and its bearer, the Prophet Muḥammad (peace be on him).

As for their objections with regard to the Qur'ān, these were both numerous and ill-founded. This *sūrah* cites one such silly objection whereby they took exception to the Qur'ān's revelation in Arabic. According to them, had it been revealed in a language other than Arabic, that would have been a miracle, for then an Arab would have suddenly and fluently presented a discourse in some foreign tongue. Had that been the case, it could have been regarded as not to be his own composition but a piece revealed to him from on High, from God.

The following main points were brought out in response to the unbelievers' bigoted opposition:

(1) The Qur'ān is God's Own Word and it is in the Arabic language. It clearly expounds truths, truths that the ignorant find to be of no value whereas those endowed with understanding consider them to embody the light and guidance of which they can constantly avail themselves. Out of His Mercy God has revealed the Qur'ān to guide mankind. Wretched and unfortunate are those who resent

its revelation. Yet, it is an especially welcome event for those blessed souls who wish to be guided by it. As for those who reject it, they should be fearful of the consequences of their disbelief.

(2) If the unbelievers have sealed their hearts and have turned deaf to the Qur'ān's message, then let it be known that it is not the Prophet's job to force to hear those who do not wish to hear or to force to understand those who disdain to do so. The Prophet (peace be on him) can make them hear the Qur'ānic message only if they are willing to hear it and to make them understand only if they are willing to do so. After all he is only a mortal human being like his addressees.

(3) The unbelievers can close their eyes and ears and seal their hearts. However, the truth remains that there is One True God and human beings are servants and creatures of no other god. The unbelievers' adamance in this regard cannot alter the truth. If they accept the truth that there is no other deity than the One True God, then this will be conducive to their own good. On the other hand, should they refuse to accept it, they will incur their own ruin.

(4) The unbelievers should realise the enormity of their guilt in associating others with God in His Divinity and in denying Him as the Only True God. For God indeed is the Creator, Sovereign and Sustainer of this vast universe, and all creatures derive benefit from His bounties and receive their sustenance from Him. How pitiful it is that people take God's humble creatures as associates in His Divinity!

(5) If people refuse to believe, they should prepare themselves for God's scourge that may suddenly overtake them unawares just as happened in the case of the 'Ād and Thamūd. That, however, will not be the end of the matter for it will be followed by their strict reckoning on the Day of Judgement and possibly torment in Hell.

(6) Unfortunate is he who falls prey to the devils among men and *jinn* who make his follies appear in an alluring light, who do not let him reflect as to what is right, nor let him pay proper heed to the matter when others direct him to

it. Such ignorant folk encourage each other to vie in committing wrongs with impunity. However, on the Day of Judgement, each of them will simply want to trample those who misled him under his feet.

(7) The Qur'ān embodies the truth in clear, unalterable terms. The unbelievers cannot checkmate it by recourse to dishonourable means. Whether falsehood assaults it publicly from the front or assails it stealthily, using indirect strategy, it can never cause the Qur'ān to be defeated.

(8) The unbelievers contend that the Qur'ān should have been sent down in a non-Arabic tongue. Had that indeed been done, the unbelievers would have made that very fact the butt of their ridicule, criticising that the Book meant for the guidance of Arabs was revealed in a language they cannot even understand. What this kind of pickish objection shows, however, is that the unbelievers are simply not interested in God's guidance and there is no end to their pretexts to justify their disbelief.

(9) Have the unbelievers given any thought to how terrible their end will be if it indeed turns out, as it will, that the Qur'ān is God's Own Revelation? How horrendous, then, will the consequences of their rejecting and fiercely opposing it be?

(10) They have presently gone quite far in opposing the Qur'ān. They will, however, soon observe that the Qur'ān's message has spread all around and has come to pervade not only the world around them but also they themselves have been overcome by it. It will then dawn upon them that what they were being told has indeed come true.

Apart from thus responding to the unbelievers, the *sūrah* deals with some of the issues with which the Prophet (peace be on him) and his Companions were confronted in this fiercely charged and hostile atmosphere. So adverse was the situation that, let alone being able to propagate their faith, it was extremely difficult for the believers even to live according to its requirements. Those who were discovered to have converted to Islam found themselves utterly helpless before the fierce enmity of their powerful and resourceful opponents. The believers are, therefore, consoled and told that in point of fact they are neither alone nor helpless. Rather, whoever makes up his mind to take God as His Lord and remains firm in that regard, God's angels come to his aid throughout the life of this world as well as in the Hereafter. They are further comforted by the information that the best person in God's sight is he who does good, who calls people to God's way and who fearlessly declares himself to be one of those who submit to God's command. Likewise, the Prophet (peace be on him) is apprised that he was armed with a powerful weapon: that of excellent conduct. So overwhelming is this weapon that in time it will make inroads into the ranks of Islam's inveterate enemies and their hostility will crack into pieces and then simply dissolve and disappear. The believers are, therefore, required to be patient. Whenever Satan prompts them to act in a state of provocation they should seek refuge with God.

In the name of Allah, the Most Merciful, the Most Compassionate.

بِسۡمِ ٱللَّهِ ٱلرَّحۡمَٰنِ ٱلرَّحِيمِ

(1) *Ḥā. Mīm.* (2) This is a revelation from the Most Merciful, the Most Compassionate, (3) a Book whose verses have been well-expounded; an Arabic Qur'ān for those who have knowledge, (4) one bearing good news and warning.[1] ▶

حمٓ ﴿١﴾ تَنزِيلٞ مِّنَ ٱلرَّحۡمَٰنِ ٱلرَّحِيمِ ﴿٢﴾
كِتَٰبٞ فُصِّلَتۡ ءَايَٰتُهُۥ قُرۡءَانًا عَرَبِيّٗا
لِّقَوۡمٖ يَعۡلَمُونَ ﴿٣﴾ بَشِيرٗا وَنَذِيرٗا

---

1. This is a brief introduction to the *sūrah*. Were one to carefully reflect over the discourse that follows, it will become clear how closely interlinked the introductory statement and the later discourse are.

The first point emphasised is that the Qur'ān is revelation from God. Notwithstanding the unbelievers' parrot-like cry that it is the product of the Prophet's own mind, the plain fact is that it was sent down by none other than God. Implicit in this is the warning that if the unbelievers resent the fact that it was revealed, their resentment is in fact not directed against the Prophet (peace be on him); but, it is directed against God Himself. If the unbelievers reject the Qur'ān, they are not rejecting the word of Muḥammad (peace be on him), but God's Own Word. The One they are contemptuously turning away from is thus God and not another human being.

Another truth enunciated here is that the One Who caused the Qur'ān's revelation is Most Compassionate and Merciful towards His creatures. This pointed reference to God's Compassion and Mercy conveys the idea that the Qur'ān was revealed as a necessary corollary of His Mercy and Compassion. By means of this observation the unbelievers are told that if they pay no heed to the Qur'ān or reject it or raise their eyebrows at it, they will court their own ruin. The Qur'ān is an immense bounty that God has bestowed out of His abundant grace upon mankind for their welfare and guidance. Had God been indifferent to human beings' well-being, He could have left them to grope about in darkness, with indifference to the calamitous end that might meet them because of the non-availability of adequate guidance. However, the fact is that God is much concerned with mankind's welfare. As a result, He not only provided for man's sustenance but took upon Himself the task of providing the knowledge that would set his life on the right course. It is with this end in view that He revealed this Book to one of His servants. Now, who would be more thankless and more inimical to himself than he who fails to benefit from this treasure of grace, and rises instead, in rebellion against it?

The third point stressed here is that the verses of the Qur'ān are 'well-expounded.' In other words, there is no ambiguity or complication in the Qur'ānic teachings. Hence, no one can excuse himself from not accepting the Qur'ān on the grounds that its contents are incomprehensible. On the contrary, the Qur'ān clearly enunciates what is true and what is false; explains which are the right articles of belief and which are the wrong ones; what are good and what are bad morals; which kind of behaviour leads to success and well-being and which kind of behaviour to suffering, loss and failure. If someone tries to prevent others from accepting such clear and unambiguous guidance or adopts apathy towards it, he has no justifiable excuse for so doing. His attitude simply demonstrates that he wants to persist in error.

The fourth point emphasised is that the Qur'ān is an 'Arabic Qur'ān.' What this implies is that had the Qur'ān been delivered in some foreign tongue, the Arabs could have claimed that they were unable to comprehend it, not knowing the language of the Book. The Qur'ān, however, was given to them in their own language. Hence, they could not advance the pretext that they cannot understand what it says. (Verse 44 of this *sūrah* also drives home the same point although it has been expressed in a somewhat different form. See also *Yūsuf* 12: n. 5, *Towards Understanding the Qur'ān,* vol. IV, pp. 152-3 and the author's work in Urdu, *Rasā'il-o Masā'il,* Lahore: Islamic Publications Limited, n.d., vol. I, pp. 20-5.)

The fifth point emphasised is that the Qur'ān is meant for only those who are endowed with knowledge. In other words, only those who have common sense and reason can draw upon it. So for the ignorant, the Qur'ān is as useless as a precious stone is for those who do not know the difference between a diamond and a piece of rock.

The sixth point emphasised is that the Qur'ān announces good tidings as well as deliver warnings. To put it differently, the Qur'ān is not the figment of a rich creative imagination, or a philosophical idea, or a literary masterpiece whose acceptance or rejection has no practical bearing on human life. On the contrary, the Qur'ān vehemently claims

Yet most of them turned away and are not wont to give heed. (5) They say: 'Our hearts are securely wrapped up against what you call us to,[2] and in our ears is a heaviness, and between you and us there is a veil.[3] So act; we too are acting.'[4]

(6) Tell them, (O Prophet): 'I am only a human being like you.[5] It is revealed ▶

فَأَعْرَضَ أَكْثَرُهُمْ فَهُمْ لَا يَسْمَعُونَ ﴿٤﴾
وَقَالُوا قُلُوبُنَا فِي أَكِنَّةٍ مِّمَّا تَدْعُونَا إِلَيْهِ
وَفِي آذَانِنَا وَقْرٌ وَمِن بَيْنِنَا وَبَيْنِكَ حِجَابٌ
فَاعْمَلْ إِنَّنَا عَامِلُونَ ﴿٥﴾ قُلْ إِنَّمَا أَنَا بَشَرٌ
مِّثْلُكُمْ يُوحَىٰ

---

that its acceptance will yield magnificent results and its rejection will lead to horrendous consequences. Only an imbecile can summarily set aside such a Book.

2. That is, none of the avenues that can carry the Qur'ān to their hearts has been left unused.

3. The unbelievers claimed that the Prophet's message created a wedge between them and him. As a result, it was impossible for the two opposing camps to come to any point of agreement.

4. This carries the following two meanings: (i) That the two groups had nothing to do with each other. (ii) That if the Prophet (peace be on him) cannot desist from working for his cause, he may do so. In this case, however, the unbelievers too will not desist from opposing him and will not cease their efforts to reduce his mission to naught.

5. The Prophet (peace be on him) made it clear that it did not lie in his power to remove the coverings that had sealed their hearts, or to restore hearing to their deaf ears, or to tear down the barriers they had erected between themselves and him. After all, he was merely a human being. He can drive home his point only to those who are prepared to pay attention; communicate his message only to those who are prepared to listen; and can meet and explain things only to those who care to meet him.

to me that your God is One God;[6] so direct yourselves straight to Him,[7] and seek His forgiveness.[8] Woe to those who associate others with Allah in His Divinity, (7) who do not pay *Zakāh*,[9] ▶

إِلَىَّ أَنَّمَآ إِلَـٰهُكُمْ إِلَـٰهٌ وَٰحِدٌ فَٱسْتَقِيمُوٓا۟ إِلَيْهِ وَٱسْتَغْفِرُوهُ ۗ وَوَيْلٌ لِّلْمُشْرِكِينَ ۝٦ ٱلَّذِينَ لَا يُؤْتُونَ ٱلزَّكَوٰةَ

6. Even if they seal their hearts and make their ears deaf to the truth, this will not change the fact that there is only One True God and that human beings are His born servants. This is not a philosophical doctrine invented by the Prophet (peace be on him) after due thought and reflection. Had that been the case, there was clearly the possibility of its being either right or wrong. However, what the Prophet (peace be on him) was communicating to people was the truth that had been disclosed to him through revelation and hence was immune from error.

7. The unbelievers are asked not to take aught as God or to serve and worship aught but God, nor to invoke others than God to come to their aid. Likewise, they are required not to bind themselves to the unreserved obedience of anyone other than God, nor to consider any custom or usage, any law or regulation which is devoid of God's sanction as necessarily binding upon them.

8. That is, they should seek God's forgiveness for the disloyalty they had shown Him, for the polytheism, disbelief and disobedience of which they had been guilty.

9. The Qur'ānic commentators differ in their opinions as regards what *zakāh* means here. Ibn 'Abbās and his distinguished students, 'Ikrimah and Mujāhid, believe that the word *zakāh* here denotes the purity of self one attains by dint of subscribing to monotheism and obeying God. (Ṭabarī, *Tafsīr*, comments on *Sūrah Ḥā Mīm al-Sajdah* 41: 7.) Taken in this sense, the meaning would be as follows: 'Woe to the associators with Allah in His Divinity who fail to attain self-purification.' However, Qatādah, Suddī, al-Hasan al-Baṣrī, Ḍaḥḥāk, Muqātil and Ibn al-Sā'ib interpret *zakāh* in the usual sense of paying obligatory alms from one's wealth. (Ṭabarī, *Tafsīr*, comments on *Sūrah Ḥā Mīm al-Sajdah* 41: 7.) In their opinion, the verse conveys the message that those who associate others with God in His Divinity and do not pay *zakāh*, thereby depriving their fellow human beings of their due, are doomed to destruction.

and who deny the Hereafter. (8) As to those who have faith and do good works, surely theirs shall be a never-ending reward.'[10]

(9) Tell them, (O Prophet): 'Do you indeed disbelieve in Him and assign compeers to Him Who created the earth in two days? He is the Lord of all beings of the Universe.' (10) (After creating the earth) He set up firm mountains on it, blessed it,[11] and provided it with sustenance in proportion to the needs of all who seek (sustenance).[12] ▶

وَهُم بِٱلْـَٔاخِرَةِ هُمْ كَـٰفِرُونَ ﴿٧﴾ إِنَّ ٱلَّذِينَ
ءَامَنُوا۟ وَعَمِلُوا۟ ٱلصَّـٰلِحَـٰتِ لَهُمْ أَجْرٌ غَيْرُ
مَمْنُونٍ ﴿٨﴾ ۞ قُلْ أَئِنَّكُمْ لَتَكْفُرُونَ بِٱلَّذِى
خَلَقَ ٱلْأَرْضَ فِى يَوْمَيْنِ وَتَجْعَلُونَ لَهُۥٓ
أَندَادًا ۚ ذَٰلِكَ رَبُّ ٱلْعَـٰلَمِينَ ﴿٩﴾ وَجَعَلَ
فِيهَا رَوَٰسِىَ مِن فَوْقِهَا وَبَـٰرَكَ فِيهَا وَقَدَّرَ
فِيهَآ أَقْوَٰتَهَا

---

10. Those who have faith and do good are promised 'a never-ending reward.' This expression admits of two meanings: (i) That the reward will never decrease. (ii) That none will discomfort the recipients of the reward by offensively impressing that its grant was an act of favour. This is so unlike the grudging grant of a gift made by a miser, who never ceases to rub the fact that a favour has been granted to the gift's recipient.

11. '(After creating the earth), He set up firm mountains in it, blessed it, and provided it with sustenance in proportion to the need of all.' Blessing the earth refers to the vast reservoir of provision that has supported the needs of billions of creatures, ranging from microscopic insects to human beings. One of the greatest blessings is air because of which plant, animal and human life on earth became possible.

12. Qur'ānic scholars differ in their interpretations of the words: قَدَّرَ فِيهَا أَقْوَاتَهَا فِي أَرْبَعَةِ أَيَّامٍ سَوَاءً لِلسَّائِلِينَ '...provided it with sustenance in proportion to the needs of all who seek (sustenance).' Some take it to mean that the sustenance needed by the earth's inhabitants was placed there in the right

proportion in exactly four days. (Ṭabarī, *Tafsīr*, comments on *Sūrah Ḥā Mīm al-Sajdah* 41: 10.) However, Ibn 'Abbās, Qatādah and al-Suddī offer the following explanation of the verse: 'In four days sustenance was placed on earth. This answers the question of those who asked it.' (Ṭabarī, *Tafsīr*, comments on *Sūrah Ḥā Mīm al-Sajdah* 41: 10.) In other words, if someone asks about the time duration in which this arrangement was made, the answer is that the task was completed in four days.

Ibn Zayd, however, believes that the verse means that sustenance was placed in the earth for its inhabitants in four days, in perfect measure, and in accord with the requirements of all of the inhabitants. (Ṭabarī, *Tafsīr*, comments on *Sūrah Ḥā Mīm al-Sajdah* 41: 10.)

As to the textual construction of the verse under study, it admits all the above three meanings. In our opinion, however, the first two interpretations do not take the readers anywhere. In the context of the verse it is unimportant whether the completion of the task took exactly four days or a few hours less or a few hours more. What would be left wanting in the consummate perfection of God's power, or of His sustenance or His wisdom which requires that the task be completed in exactly four days, neither more nor less. Thus, this interpretation too is not very persuasive. Likewise, the interpretation that the verse means that all what people seek was revealed in order to answer someone's query about the precise duration in which this task was accomplished, and that by mentioning four days as the duration that duly answered the question. Therefore, we prefer Ibn Zayd's interpretation. To the best of our understanding, the thrust of the verse is that God has placed in the earth every kind of sustenance needed by all those creatures who will ever live on it from the beginning of time until its end. Needless to add that countless varieties of plant life on both land and in the water require myriad types of sustenance. God has created immeasurable species of creatures with their habitats on land and in water. Each species has its own unique food habits which are different from those of others. Above all, there is the human being who stands out distinct from all other creatures. Humans need food not only for nourishing their bodies but also to cater for their varying tastes with which they are endowed. Only God knew how much sustenance would be required by all of His creatures from the beginning until the end of time. His scheme of creation, thus, envisaged the food requirements of all His creatures over an extremely long period of time.

Those who are swayed in our own times by Marxist ideas and have had the audacity to superimpose an Islamised version of these ideas which they call '*Qur'ānī Niẓām-i Rubūbīyat*', insist that God has provided sustenance for everyone in equal measure. (Ghulām Aḥmad Parvaiz,

All this was done in four days.[13] (11) Then He turned to the heaven while it was ▶	فِىٓ أَرْبَعَةِ أَيَّامٍ سَوَآءً لِّلسَّآئِلِينَ ﴿١٠﴾ ثُمَّ ٱسْتَوَىٰٓ إِلَى ٱلسَّمَآءِ وَهِىَ

Niẓām-i Rubūbīyat, Karachi: Idārah-'i Ṭulū'-i Islām, 1954, p. 131.) Therefore, they argue, that the state must ensure equal distribution of food and this cannot be achieved in a system that admits private ownership.

In making such outrageous assertions they disregard the important truth that the verse is not specific to man. Rather, it refers to all creatures who stand in need of food to be able to live. As it is, God has not laid down equality among all creatures' need for sustenance. To say contrary to this is not supported by natural or by the actual workings of the universe. In both the plant and animal kingdoms, God has not implanted any mechanism by means of which equal food rations might be made available to plants and animals, or even to all members of the same species. This evidently cannot be regarded as an injustice on God's part. Let us also clarify that the Qur'ānic account also includes cattle and poultry, i.e. the creatures under man's care for his sustenance. If a state were ever established with the purpose of providing equal sustenance to all, would it ensure equality between human beings and the animals under his care?

13. Some Qur'ānic scholars find the number of days mentioned here somewhat problematic. If it took two days to create the earth and four days to place mountains on it and provide the means of sustenance for earth's inhabitants and another two days for the creation of the heavens, then the total number of days would be eight. (Rāzī, *al-Tafsīr al-Kabīr*, comments on *Sūrah Ḥā Mīm al-Sajdah* 41: 10.) This poses a difficulty insofar as the Qur'ān specifically mentions on several occasions that the earth and the heavens were created in six days. (See *al-A'rāf* 7: 54, *Yūnus* 10: 3, *Hūd* 11: 7 and *al-Furqān* 25: 59.) Therefore, Qur'ānic commentators are unanimously of the opinion that the four days mentioned here also include the two days devoted to the earth's creation. (Rāzī, *al-Tafsīr al-Kabīr*, comments on *Sūrah Ḥā Mīm al-Sajdah* 41: 10.) In other words, it took two days for the creation of the other things that are mentioned. The earth was, thus, brought into working order in four days. However, this is contrary to the Qur'ān's wording. Moreover, the problem which these scholars tried to resolve was an imaginary one. The fact is that the earth was created in two days and it was in this time span that the whole universe was created. Consider the other verses which mention the creation of the heavens and the earth together. It is also stated that God created the seven firmaments in two days. (*Sūrah Ḥā Mīm al-Sajdah* 41: 12.) This signifies the creation of the

all smoke.[14] He said to the heaven and the earth: 'Come (into being), willingly or unwillingly.' They said: ▶	دُخَانٌ فَقَالَ لَهَا وَلِلْأَرْضِ ٱئْتِيَا طَوْعًا أَوْ كَرْهًا قَالَتَآ

entire universe of which the earth is a part. Once the earth was created along with other planets, God placed in it all the means of sustenance in four days, to which reference is made in this verse. God has not said anything about His dispensation as being applicable to other stars and planets. It is evident that mention of anything in that regard would be hard to grasp even today, which only highlights how very difficult it would have been to understand them fourteen hundred years ago.

14. Here three points merit explanation: (i) The word 'heaven' in this instance signifies the universe, as will be clear by the verses that follow. In other words, 'then He turned to the heaven' means that God turned His attention to the creation of the universe. (ii) The word 'smoke' stands for the initial form of matter in which it appeared before the universe took any distinct shape. At that stage matter lay diffused in space, shapeless and dustlike. Scientists today brand this as nebula. They are of the opinion that prior to creation, the matter out of which this universe was made, lay diffused in a smoke-like nebulous form. (iii) To say that God *then* turned to the heaven does not indicate any time sequence. It should not, therefore, be taken to mean that God first created the earth, then placed mountains on it, and then devised an elaborate system to provide sustenance to all His creatures, and then finally turned to the act of creating the universe. This misconception is removed by the very next verse which states: 'He said to the heaven and the earth: "Come (into being), willingly or unwillingly." They said: "Here we come (into being) in willing obeisance."' (verse 11). It is clear from the context that this happened at a time when the heavens and the earth did not exist. Rather, it dates back to an era when creation was only in the offing. The Qur'ānic expression *thumma* (then), as employed in the verse, is, therefore, not a marker of time sequence. (See, for instance, *al-Zumar* 39, n. 12 above.)

Classical Qur'ānic scholars have debated for long as to which was created first – the heavens or the earth. On the basis of this verse and *Sūrah al-Baqarah* 2: 29 some argue that the first to be created was the earth. Others cite *al-Nāzi'āt* 79: 27-33 in order to stress that the heavens were created first. For them, this passage also clarifies that the creation of the earth followed the creation of the heavens. (Rāzī, *al-Tafsīr al-Kabīr*,

'Here we come (into being) in willing obeisance.'[15] ▶	أَتَيۡنَا طَآئِعِينَ ﴿١١﴾

comments on *Sūrah Ḥā Mīm al-Sajdah* 41: 11.) Let us remind ourselves here that at no point does the Qur'ān discuss the phenomenon of creation with reference to physics or astronomy. Rather, it mentions the creation of the universe as one of the many signs for reflection while inviting people to believe in monotheism and the Afterlife. Accordingly, the Qur'ān altogether disregards the question: what was created first, the earth or the heavens? What is rather important is that both the heavens and the earth point to God's Oneness and that this whole universe was not created in vain as though it were a child's plaything. At times, the Qur'ān speaks first of the earth and at others of the heavens. Wherever the Qur'ān seeks to remind man of God's blessings, it speaks first of the earth insofar as it is closer to him in terms of space. In those instances in which the purpose of the Qur'ān is to press home the glory and creative wonders of God, it talks of the heavens. For it is this spectacle which fills man's heart with awe.

15. The manner in which God has laid bare the process of His creation here makes it stand out from human workmanship. When man wants to do something, he first draws a blueprint of the task in his mind, collects the requisite materials to execute the task, and then proceeds to make that thing according to his design. However, he has to struggle constantly in adapting those materials to his scheme. At times, he fails in his plan while at others he succeeds. Take the analogy of a shirt sewn by a tailor. First, he conceives a mental image of the shirt's design. Then he procures the necessary materials and tries his best to prepare the shirt according to that design. While trying to do so, he is likely to face some difficulties. Sometimes he is not at all successful in preparing the shirt the way he intended to, whereas in other instances he accomplishes the task satisfactorily.

Let us now see how God created the universe. There was matter which existed in the form of smoke. God decided to give shape to the universe out of it. Unlike humans, He did not have to erect the earth, the sun, the moon and other stars and planets. He simply decreed that they take the form in accordance with what He desired. The smoke assumed the form of galaxies, stars and planets which He intended to create. Within no time, His command was executed. Within two days the entire universe, including the earth, was ready. God's act of creation is also described in

(12) Then He made them seven heavens in two days and revealed to each heaven its law. And We adorned the lower heaven with lamps, and firmly secured it.[16] All this is the firm plan of the All-Mighty, the All-Knowing.

(13) But if they turn away,[17] tell them: 'I warn you against a sudden scourge like that which struck 'Ād and Thamūd.' (14) When the Messengers (of Allah) came to them from the front and from the rear,[18] ▶

فَقَضَىٰهُنَّ سَبْعَ سَمَٰوَاتٍ فِى يَوْمَيْنِ وَأَوْحَىٰ
فِى كُلِّ سَمَآءٍ أَمْرَهَا ۚ وَزَيَّنَّا ٱلسَّمَآءَ ٱلدُّنْيَا
بِمَصَٰبِيحَ وَحِفْظًا ۚ ذَٰلِكَ تَقْدِيرُ ٱلْعَزِيزِ
ٱلْعَلِيمِ ﴿١٢﴾ فَإِنْ أَعْرَضُوا۟ فَقُلْ أَنذَرْتُكُمْ
صَٰعِقَةً مِّثْلَ صَٰعِقَةِ عَادٍ وَثَمُودَ ﴿١٣﴾ إِذْ
جَآءَتْهُمُ ٱلرُّسُلُ مِنۢ بَيْنِ أَيْدِيهِمْ وَمِنْ خَلْفِهِمْ

---

the following passages of the Qur'ān: *al-Baqarah* 2: 117 and *Āl 'Imrān* 3: 47 and 59, *Towards Understanding the Qur'ān,* vol. I, pp. 104 and 252-60; *al-Naḥl* 16: 40, vol. IV, pp. 329-30; *Maryam* 19: 35, n. 22, p. 157, *Yā Sīn* 36: 82, and *al-Mu'min* 40: 68.

16. For a better understanding of this verse, see *al-Baqarah* 2: 29, n. 34, *Towards Understanding the Qur'ān,* vol. I, p. 58; *al-Ra'd* 13: 2 and *al-Ḥijr* 15, nn. 16-19, nn. 8-12, vol. IV, pp. 219-20 and 284-6; *al-Anbiyā'* 21: 30-3, nn. 34-5; *al-Ḥajj* 22: 65, vol. V, p. 265; *al-Mu'minūn* 23, n. 15, vol. VI, p. 89: *Yā Sīn* 36, n. 37 and *al-Ṣāffāt* 37, nn. 5-6, vol. IX, pp. 261-2 and 282.

17. The unbelievers are guilty of refusing to believe that God alone, Who created the earth and the entire universe, has the right to be worshipped. They persist in their false beliefs, taking others as His partners and crediting them with God's attributes and authority.

18. This admits of more than one meaning: (i) That many Messengers appeared successively among those people. (ii) That the Messengers tried to convince them in every possible manner, sparing no effort to direct

saying: 'Do not serve any but Allah'; they said: 'Had our Lord so willed, He would have sent down angels. So we deny the Message you have brought.'[19]

(15) As for 'Ād, they waxed proud in the land without justification and said: 'Who is greater than we in strength?' Did they not see that Allah, Who created them, is greater in strength than they? They continued to deny Our Signs, (16) whereupon We sent upon them a fierce wind on inauspicious days[20] that ▶

أَلَّا تَعْبُدُوٓا۟ إِلَّا ٱللَّهَ ۖ قَالُوا۟ لَوْ شَآءَ رَبُّنَا لَأَنزَلَ
مَلَـٰٓئِكَةً فَإِنَّا بِمَآ أُرْسِلْتُم بِهِۦ كَـٰفِرُونَ ﴿١٤﴾
فَأَمَّا عَادٌ فَٱسْتَكْبَرُوا۟ فِى ٱلْأَرْضِ بِغَيْرِ ٱلْحَقِّ
وَقَالُوا۟ مَنْ أَشَدُّ مِنَّا قُوَّةً ۖ أَوَلَمْ يَرَوْا۟ أَنَّ ٱللَّهَ
ٱلَّذِى خَلَقَهُمْ هُوَ أَشَدُّ مِنْهُمْ قُوَّةً ۖ وَكَانُوا۟
بِـَٔايَـٰتِنَا يَجْحَدُونَ ﴿١٥﴾ فَأَرْسَلْنَا عَلَيْهِمْ رِيحًا
صَرْصَرًا فِىٓ أَيَّامٍ نَّحِسَاتٍ

---

them to the Right Way. (iii) That the Messengers were raised in their own respective countries, be it Arabia or other neighbouring countries.

19. They argued that had God disapproved of their faith and sent a Messenger to keep them away from such false faith, He would have sent down an angel for that purpose. Since the Prophet (peace be on him) is only a human being like themselves and not an an angel, their refusal to believe that he had been sent by God so that people might abandon their ancestral faith and adopt some new faith in its place was justified. They sarcastically asserted 'so we deny the Message you have brought' (verse 14.) The same attitude had earlier been displayed by Pharaoh when he disdainfully introduced the Prophet Moses (peace be on him) to his courtiers: 'This Messenger of yours who has been sent to you is simply mad' (*al-Shu'arā'* 26: 27). (For further details, see *Yā Sīn* 36, n. 11; *Towards Understanding the Qur'ān,* vol. IX, pp. 247-9.)

20. The expression 'inauspicious days' in the verse does not mean that the days on which fierce winds blew were inauspicious as such.

We might make them taste a degrading chastisement in the life of this world.[21] And surely the chastisement of the Hereafter is even more degrading. There will be none to help them there.

لِّنُذِيقَهُمۡ عَذَابَ ٱلۡخِزۡيِ فِي ٱلۡحَيَوٰةِ
ٱلدُّنۡيَاۖ وَلَعَذَابُ ٱلۡأٓخِرَةِ أَخۡزَىٰۖ وَهُمۡ
لَا يُنصَرُونَ ١٦

Rather, it is because God's scourge overtook the 'Ād during those days that they are referred to as inauspicious. The verse does not suggest that some days are inauspicious and others are not. Had the days themselves been inauspicious the scourge would have struck all nations, far and near. But since it is the 'Ād who were destroyed by the storm, those days were inauspicious for that nation. This fact, however, cannot be made a basis for declaring some days to be inherently inauspicious and others as auspicious.

Here the words *rīḥ ṣarṣar* ('fierce winds') have been used for tempestuous winds. Lexicographers disagree as to what this expression precisely means. Some consider it to be a fiercely hot wind while others consider it to mean a fiercely cold wind. There are still others who consider it to mean a fiercely noisy wind. All agree, however, that it denotes a fierce windstorm. (Ibn 'Aṭīyah, *al-Muḥarrar al-Wajīz,* comments *Sūrah Ḥā Mīm al-Sajdah* 41: 16.)

The details of the windstorm that struck the 'Ād are mentioned at other places in the Qur'ān. It has, for instance, been said that this fierce windstorm continually raged over them for seven nights and eight days (*al-Ḥāqqah* 69: 7.) It was a devastating storm, one that killed everyone, destroying them just as if they were the 'uprooted trunks of hollowed palm trees' (*al-Ḥāqqah* 69: 7.) 'Such was this wind that it left nothing that it came upon without reducing it to rubble', (*al-Dhāriyāt* 51: 41-2.) When people saw that this fierce wind was approaching them in the form of a cloud, they were jubilant and mirthful: 'When they saw the scourge approaching their valleys, they said: This is a cloud which will bring much rain to us'. 'By no means; it is what you had sought to hasten – a windstorm bearing a grievous chastisement', (*al-Aḥqāf* 46: 24-5.)

21. This degrading chastisement was in response to their arrogance because of which they boastfully proclaimed: 'Who is greater than we in strength?' (verse 15.) God, however, disgraced them; a great many of them were killed and their civilisation was effaced. As for those who

(17) As for Thamūd, We bestowed guidance upon them, but they preferred to remain blind rather than be guided. At last a humiliating scourge overtook them on account of their misdeeds. (18) Yet We delivered those who believed and were God-fearing.[22]

(19) Imagine the Day when Allah's enemies will be mustered to the Fire,[23] and the people of the former times will be detained until the arrival of people of the later times,[24] ▶

وَأَمَّا ثَمُودُ فَهَدَيْنَٰهُمْ فَٱسْتَحَبُّوا۟ ٱلْعَمَىٰ عَلَى
ٱلْهُدَىٰ فَأَخَذَتْهُمْ صَٰعِقَةُ ٱلْعَذَابِ ٱلْهُونِ
بِمَا كَانُوا۟ يَكْسِبُونَ ﴿١٧﴾ وَنَجَّيْنَا ٱلَّذِينَ ءَامَنُوا۟
وَكَانُوا۟ يَتَّقُونَ ﴿١٨﴾ وَيَوْمَ يُحْشَرُ أَعْدَآءُ ٱللَّهِ
إِلَى ٱلنَّارِ فَهُمْ يُوزَعُونَ ﴿١٩﴾

survived, they became subject to the domination of other communities and were oppressed by them. These were the same communities that they had earlier oppressed. (For details of the story of the People of 'Ād, see *al-A'rāf* 7, nn. 51-6, *Towards Understanding the Qur'ān*, vol. III, pp. 42-5; *Hūd* 11, n. 54-65, vol. IV, pp. 108-11; *al-Mu'minūn* 23, nn. 34-36a, vol. VI, pp. 96-9; *al-Shu'arā'* 26, nn. 88-94; vol. VII, pp. 91-4, and *al-'Ankabūt* 29, n. 65, vol. VIII, p. 36.)

22. For details about the Thamūd's story, see *al-A'rāf* 7: 73-79, *Towards Understanding the Qur'ān,* vol. III, pp. 45-9; *Hūd* 11: nn. 66-74, and *al-Ḥijr,* 15: nn. 42-6, vol. IV, pp. 112-16 and pp. 300-1; *al-Shu'arā'* 26: nn. 95-6.

23. The reference here is to the fact that people will be mustered to appear before God. The expression used, however, is that 'Allah's enemies will be mustered to the Fire.' This is because of the fact that their ultimate end will be their hurling into Hell.

24. On the Day of Judgement what will happen is not that various generations of people will be recompensed one after the other. Rather,

(20) and when all have arrived, their ears, their eyes, and their skins shall bear witness against them, stating all that they had done in the life of the world.[25] (21) They will ask their skins: 'Why did you bear witness against us?' The skins will reply: ▶

حَتَّىٰٓ إِذَا مَا جَآءُوهَا شَهِدَ عَلَيۡهِمۡ سَمۡعُهُمۡ
وَأَبۡصَٰرُهُمۡ وَجُلُودُهُم بِمَا كَانُواْ يَعۡمَلُونَ ﴿٢٠﴾
وَقَالُواْ لِجُلُودِهِمۡ لِمَ شَهِدتُّمۡ عَلَيۡنَاۖ قَالُوٓاْ

all generations will be brought together and judged at one time. This because one's deeds do not come to an end with one's death; rather, the impact of these deeds continues till long after one's death and, therefore, one will be held accountable for the totality of the effect one's acts had upon all the generations combined. What holds true for an individual, also holds true for a whole generation insofar as each generation has its effect on subsequent generations. All pieces of evidence, including the effects of one generation on subsequent generations, will be marshalled at the time of the Final Judgement. On the Day of Judgement, therefore, generation after generation will be gathered together and detained and their reckoning will take place. For further details, see *al-A'rāf* 7, n. 30, *Towards Understanding the Qur'ān*, vol. III, pp. 23-6.

25. *Aḥādīth* indicate that when a diehard criminal denies his misdeeds and contests the evidence brought against him, then by God's command the different organs of his body will testify against him. Each of these organs will relate to what use they were put by that person. This has also been narrated by Anas, Abū Mūsā al-Ash'arī, Abū Sa'īd al-Khudrī and 'Abd Allāh ibn 'Abbās from the Prophet (peace be on him). Furthermore, these reports are cited by Muslim, Nasā'ī, Ibn Jarīr al-Ṭabarī, Ibn Abī Ḥātim, and al-Bazzār. (Muslim, *Kitāb Ṣifāt al-Munāfiqīn wa Aḥkāmihim;* Nasā'ī, *al-Sunan al-Kubrā, Kitāb al-Tafsīr, Bāb Qawlihi Ta'ālā: 'Wa mā Kuntum Tastatirūna an Yashhad 'alaykum Sam'ukum'*; Ṭabarī, *Tafsīr*, comments on *Sūrah Ḥā Mīm al-Sajdah* 41: 21; Ibn Abī Ḥātim, *Tafsīr*, comments on *Sūrah Ḥā Mīm al-Sajdah* 41: 22; Aḥmad b. 'Alī al-Bazzār, *Musnad*, narrated by Anas b. Mālik. For further details, see *Yā Sīn* 36, n. 55, *Towards Understanding the Qur'ān*, vol. VIII, pp. 270-6.)

This is among those verses that make it quite clear that the Hereafter will not merely be in the realm of the spirit; instead, human beings will

'Allah gave us speech, as He gave speech to all others.[26] He it is Who created you for the first time and it is to Him that you will be sent back. (22) When you used to conceal yourselves (while committing misdeeds) you never thought that your ears or your eyes or your skins would ever bear witness against you; you rather fancied that Allah does not know a great deal of what you do. (23) This thought of yours about your Lord has led to your perdition and you have become ▶

أَنطَقَنَا ٱللَّهُ ٱلَّذِىٓ أَنطَقَ كُلَّ شَىْءٍ وَهُوَ
خَلَقَكُمْ أَوَّلَ مَرَّةٍ وَإِلَيْهِ تُرْجَعُونَ ﴿٢١﴾
وَمَا كُنتُمْ تَسْتَتِرُونَ أَن يَشْهَدَ عَلَيْكُمْ
سَمْعُكُمْ وَلَآ أَبْصَـٰرُكُمْ وَلَا جُلُودُكُمْ
وَلَـٰكِن ظَنَنتُمْ أَنَّ ٱللَّهَ لَا يَعْلَمُ كَثِيرًا
مِّمَّا تَعْمَلُونَ ﴿٢٢﴾ وَذَٰلِكُمْ ظَنُّكُمُ ٱلَّذِى
ظَنَنتُم بِرَبِّكُمْ أَرْدَىٰكُمْ

be resurrected both in body and soul. In this respect, their state will be similar to their state in the present world. People will be restored to the bodies they had earlier occupied in this world, with the same particles and atoms of which they were comprised before. In other words, people will be raised in their worldly bodies. The reference to the testimony made by the parts of a person's body underscores that the same body will be granted to each individual or else the testimony of those organs would be meaningless. The following Qur'ānic verses also make this point: *Banī Isrā'īl* 17: 49-51 and 98; *al-Mu'minūn* 23: 35-38 and 82-83; *al-Nūr* 24: 24; *al-Sajdah* 32: 10; *Yā Sīn* 36: 65 and 78-79; *al-Ṣāffāt* 37: 16-18; *al-Wāqi'ah* 56: 47-50, and *al-Nāzi'āt* 79: 10-14.

26. Not only will the parts of one's own body bear testimony on the Day of Judgement, but the very objects that witnessed one's misdeeds will speak out. This same point is made eloquently in the following verses: 'And the earth will throw up all her burdens, and man will cry out: "What is the matter with her?" On that Day it will relate all her news, for your Lord will have commanded her (to do so)', (*al-Zilzāl* 99: 2-5.)

among the losers.'[27] (24) In this state, whether they bear with patience (or not), Fire alone shall be their abode. And if they seek to make amends, they will not be allowed to do so.[28] (25) We had assigned to them companions who embellished for them all that was before them and behind them.[29] Thus the same decree (of chastisement) which had overtaken the previous generations of *jinn* and human beings (also) ▶

فَأَصْبَحْتُم مِّنَ ٱلْخَـٰسِرِينَ ﴿٢٣﴾ فَإِن
يَصْبِرُوا۟ فَٱلنَّارُ مَثْوًى لَّهُمْ ۖ وَإِن يَسْتَعْتِبُوا۟
فَمَا هُم مِّنَ ٱلْمُعْتَبِينَ ﴿٢٤﴾ ۞ وَقَيَّضْنَا لَهُمْ
قُرَنَآءَ فَزَيَّنُوا۟ لَهُم مَّا بَيْنَ أَيْدِيهِمْ وَمَا خَلْفَهُمْ
وَحَقَّ عَلَيْهِمُ ٱلْقَوْلُ فِىٓ أُمَمٍ قَدْ خَلَتْ مِن
قَبْلِهِم مِّنَ ٱلْجِنِّ وَٱلْإِنسِ ۖ

---

27. Al-Ḥasan al-Baṣrī offers an insightful interpretation of this verse, stating that each person's attitude will be determined by his concept of the Lord. A true believer behaves rightly because he entertains a sound concept of his Lord. By the same token, the hypocrites, the wicked and the wrong-doers act erroneously because they have a false concept of their Lord. (Ṭabarī, *Tafsīr*, comments *Sūrah Ḥā Mīm al-Sajdah* 41: 23.) The Prophet (peace be on him) draws attention to the same in his observation: 'Your Lord says that He is in keeping with the idea that His servant entertains about Him'. (Bukhārī, *Kitāb al-Tawḥīd, Bāb Qawl Allāh Ta'ālā: 'Wa Yuḥadhdhirukum Allāh Nafsah'*; and Muslim, *Kitāb al-Dhikr wa al-Du'ā' wa al-Tawbah wa al-Istighfār, Bāb Faḍl al- Dhikr wa al-Du'ā' wa al-Taqarrub ilā Allāh Ta'ālā.*)

28. This can mean that the unbelievers will not be able to return to the world. Alternatively, it might mean that they will not be able to escape from Hell, nor will their repentance be accepted.

29. It is part of Divine dispensation that those inclined towards evil are never granted the company of pious and righteous people. On the contrary, they are provided the company of the wicked and iniquitous.

became due against them. Surely they became the losers.

(26) The deniers of the Truth say: 'Do not give ear to the Qur'ān and cause interruption when it is recited; thus perhaps you will gain the upper hand.'[30] ▶

إِنَّهُمْ كَانُوا۟ خَـٰسِرِينَ ۝٢٥ وَقَالَ ٱلَّذِينَ كَفَرُوا۟ لَا تَسْمَعُوا۟ لِهَـٰذَا ٱلْقُرْءَانِ وَٱلْغَوْا۟ فِيهِ لَعَلَّكُمْ تَغْلِبُونَ ۝٢٦

The more one descends into a morass of evil and error, the worse possible persons becomes one's boon companions, advisers and collaborators. It is wrong to say, therefore, that such a person is himself good but is surrounded by evil people. Such is the law of nature that one is attracted towards people of like nature. If some evil person happens to join the company of a good person, this cannot continue for long. The same holds true for an interaction between a good person and a wicked person; their companionship cannot endure. The mutual attraction of wicked people is like that of flies and filth: filth attracts flies for they have an inherent bent towards filth.

The Qur'ānic observation that the devils' companions 'embellished for them all that was before them and behind them' means that those evil companions will continue to flatter them by saying how great was their past and how equally resplendent will their future be. They draw their image in golden colours and provide them with such tainted glasses that everything appears as golden. They make them believe that their critics were utterly stupid for they were doing nothing bizarre. Instead, they were doing exactly what was done by those who sought worldly progress in the past. They also assured them that, in the first instance, there is no Afterlife in which they will have to face the reckoning of their deeds. However, if there turns out to be one, as some crackpots claim, then the same God Who is lavishing favours upon them in the present world will again lavish favours upon them in the Next Life. As for Hell, it is meant to be the abode of those who have been denied God's bounties in the life of this world!

30. This was one of the methods to which the Makkan unbelievers resorted in order to frustrate the Prophet's mission. They were cognizant

فَلَنُذِيقَنَّ ٱلَّذِينَ كَفَرُوا۟ عَذَابًا شَدِيدًا
وَلَنَجْزِيَنَّهُمْ أَسْوَأَ ٱلَّذِى كَانُوا۟ يَعْمَلُونَ ﴿٢٧﴾
ذَٰلِكَ جَزَآءُ أَعْدَآءِ ٱللَّهِ ٱلنَّارُ ۖ لَهُمْ فِيهَا دَارُ
ٱلْخُلْدِ ۖ جَزَآءًۢ بِمَا كَانُوا۟ بِـَٔايَٰتِنَا يَجْحَدُونَ ﴿٢٨﴾
وَقَالَ ٱلَّذِينَ كَفَرُوا۟ رَبَّنَآ أَرِنَا ٱلَّذَيْنِ أَضَلَّانَا
مِنَ ٱلْجِنِّ وَٱلْإِنسِ نَجْعَلْهُمَا تَحْتَ أَقْدَامِنَا
لِيَكُونَا مِنَ ٱلْأَسْفَلِينَ ﴿٢٩﴾

(27) We shall certainly make these unbelievers taste a terrible chastisement and shall fully requite them according to the worst deeds that they committed. (28) That is the recompense of the enemies of Allah – the Fire, their abiding home. That will be the recompense for their denying Our Signs. (29) There the unbelievers will say: 'Our Lord, show us those that led us astray, both *jinn* and humans, and we will trample them under our feet so that they are utterly degraded.'[31]

---

of the immense appeal that the Qur'ān and its bearer had on people who came into contact with them. Taken together, both exercised enormous influence on everyone. A great many realised that this unique message, delivered by such a distinguished person, was bound in the course of time to win over people's hearts and minds. Therefore, they planned that nobody will be allowed to listen to the Qur'ān. To ensure this, they made horrendous noises as the Prophet (peace be on him) recited the Qur'ān to someone. Such opponents also shouted, jeered, clapped, raised a volley of objections and took noise to such a pitch that the Prophet's recitation was lost in the din. They believed that they would thus be successful in defeating the Prophet's call.

31. Misguided people are no doubt under the spell of their chiefs, their religious clergy and devilish folk, all of whom are out to mislead others. However, when the truth dawns upon them on the Day of Judgement, they will curse these leaders for misguiding them. Indeed, they would simply want to trample on them.

(30) Those who say[32] 'Allah is our Lord' and then remain steadfast,[33] upon them descend angels (and say): [34] 'Do not fear ▶	إِنَّ ٱلَّذِينَ قَالُوا۟ رَبُّنَا ٱللَّهُ ثُمَّ ٱسْتَقَـٰمُوا۟ تَتَنَزَّلُ عَلَيْهِمُ ٱلْمَلَـٰٓئِكَةُ أَلَّا تَخَافُوا۟

32. After having warned the unbelievers against the consequences of their adamance and rejection of the truth, the address is now directed to the Prophet (peace be on him) and his Companions.

33. True believers, once they have embraced faith in God, remain fully devoted and committed to Him. They do not commit the mistake of taking any others as lords besides God. After they have embraced true faith, they remain constant throughout their lives. After they have decided to take God for their Lord, they never entertain any erroneous doctrine. Nor do they taint their religious faith with falsehood. Instead, they fulfil its requirements and implications. The Prophet (peace be on him) and his Companions define the steadfastness in faith mentioned in this verse as follows: Anas ibn Mālik narrated that the Prophet (peace be on him) said: 'Many took God as their Lord. However, most of them turned later into unbelievers. A steadfast believer is he who adheres to monotheism until his last breath.' (Ṭabarī, *Tafsīr*, comments on *Sūrah Ḥā Mīm al-Sajdah* 41: 30; Nasā'ī, *al-Sunan al-Kubrā, Kitāb al-Tafsīr, Bāb Qawlihi Ta'ālā: 'Inna al-ladhīna Qālū Rabbunā Allāh thumma Istaqāmū'*.) According to Abū Bakr, faith consists in not taking anyone as partner with God and in not turning to anyone, considering him to be the Lord, (Ṭabarī, *Tafsīr*, comments on *Sūrah Ḥā Mīm al-Sajdah* 41: 30.) Once while reciting this verse from the pulpit, 'Umar observed: 'By Allah! The steadfast are those who firmly adhere to obeying God. They do not run from one direction to the other in the manner of foxes.' (Ṭabarī, *Tafsīr*, comments on *Sūrah Ḥā Mīm al-Sajdah* 41: 30.) 'Uthmān defined the faithful as those who work exclusively for God. (Zamakhsharī, *al-Kashshāf*, comments on *Sūrah Ḥā Mīm al-Sajdah* 41: 30.) According to 'Alī, the verse speaks of those who sincerely discharge the obligations prescribed by God. (Zamakhsharī, *al-Kashshāf*, comments on *Sūrah Ḥā Mīm al-Sajdah* 41: 30.)

34. The descent of angels does not take any palpable form. In other words, the believers do not necessarily see or hear the angels. God may, however, direct the angels to appear publicly whenever He so pleases. Generally speaking, an angel visits true believers in an imperceptible form

nor grieve,[35] and receive good tidings of Paradise which you were promised. (31) We are your companions in this world and in the Hereafter. There you shall have all that you desire and all what you will ask for. (32) This is by way of hospitality from Him Who is Most Forgiving, Most Merciful.'

وَلَا تَحْزَنُوا۟ وَأَبْشِرُوا۟ بِٱلْجَنَّةِ ٱلَّتِى كُنتُمْ
تُوعَدُونَ ﴿٣٠﴾ نَحْنُ أَوْلِيَآؤُكُمْ فِى ٱلْحَيَوٰةِ
ٱلدُّنْيَا وَفِى ٱلْـَٔاخِرَةِ ۖ وَلَكُمْ فِيهَا مَا تَشْتَهِىٓ
أَنفُسُكُمْ وَلَكُمْ فِيهَا مَا تَدَّعُونَ ﴿٣١﴾ نُزُلًا
مِّنْ غَفُورٍ رَّحِيمٍ ﴿٣٢﴾

when the latter are persecuted by the enemies of the truth. They bless believers with peace and tranquillity. Some Qur'ānic scholars believe that angels visit human beings only in his graves, on their deathbed, or in the Hereafter. In the context of the verse under study, however, the sending down of angels is mentioned in order to comfort and console believers, to boost their morale and to reinforce their faith in God's help and support. What the angels communicate to them in this regard goes down to the depths of their hearts rather than simply strike a chord in their ears. At the time of their death, true believers are warmly welcomed by the angels. The angels also greet them in their graves. They will also accompany them in the Grand Assembly until the time they enter Paradise. The angels' company of the true believers, however, is not confined to the Hereafter. They also accompany them constantly in this life.

It also becomes clear from the context of the verse that just as devils and evil ones collude with wicked people, in the same way the angels stand by the side of those true in faith. On the one hand, the collaborators of the wicked further embellish their evil deeds, encouraging them to continue with their oppression and dishonesty, assuring them that this is the road to their success. Conversely, angels approach the devotees of truth and deliver the message as mentioned in verses 30-32.

35. This expression is of pervasive import, rich with a new message of comfort for believers and covering all stages of life ranging from the present world to the Next. The angels' assuring statement to the believers that they are 'their companions in this world and the Hereafter' carries the

(33) And who is fairer in speech than he who calls to Allah and acts righteously and says: 'I am a Muslim'?[36]	وَمَنْ أَحْسَنُ قَوْلًا مِّمَّن دَعَآ إِلَى ٱللَّهِ وَعَمِلَ صَـٰلِحًا وَقَالَ إِنَّنِى مِنَ ٱلْمُسْلِمِينَ ﴿٣٣﴾

message that they should not feel cowed down by the forces of falsehood, howsoever preponderant and oppressive those might be. Nor should they grieve over the hardships and losses they might suffer in the cause of truth, for they will soon be compensated with something far superior to all worldly goods. When these same words are said by the angels to believers on their deathbeds, they are meant to assure them that they should have no fear for they are proceeding to a terminus where Paradise awaits them. As for their dear ones whom they are leaving behind in this world, they should not feel grieved, for the angels are their guardians and companions. When the angels will utter these words in *barzakh* and the Grand Assembly, it will signify that there is no reason for the believers to sorrow over the difficulties they faced in the course of their worldly life nor to have any fear with regard to Afterlife for from now on only bliss will greet them. This because the angels themselves were giving the believers tidings of Paradise.

36. After providing consolation to the believers and reinforcing their morale, they are now being urged to turn their attention to their mission. In the preceding verse, they were told that steadfastness in devotion to God and firm adherence to it is the basic goodness which endears them to the angels and makes them worthy of Paradise. They are further being told what will place them on an even higher pedestal, causing their further exaltation: This whereby they should act righteously, call others to serve God, and fearlessly proclaim themselves to be Muslims. So intense was the unbelievers' hostility to Islam at this time that anyone's declaration that he had embraced Islam amounted to him having set his foot in a wild forest teeming with ravenous beasts all ready to pounce upon him and tear him to pieces. If a believer were to go a step further and begin summoning others to Islam, then this was tantamount to inviting those beasts to devour him. Despite such severe opposition to Islam, when identification with it amounts to inviting hardship upon oneself, one should nevertheless ensure that one's conduct is impeccable so that Islam's enemies have no pretext to point blaming fingers.

وَلَا تَسْتَوِى ٱلْحَسَنَةُ وَلَا ٱلسَّيِّئَةُ ٱدْفَعْ بِٱلَّتِى هِىَ أَحْسَنُ فَإِذَا ٱلَّذِى بَيْنَكَ وَبَيْنَهُۥ عَدَٰوَةٌ كَأَنَّهُۥ وَلِىٌّ حَمِيمٌ ﴿٣٤﴾

(34) (O Prophet), good and evil are not equal. Repel (evil) with that which is good, and you will see that he, between whom and you there was enmity, shall become as if he were a bosom friend (of yours)[37]. ▶

37. This Qur'ānic directive may be better appreciated against the backdrop in which it was given. At that time, whoever embraced Islam found himself in a bitterly hostile atmosphere. Likewise, whoever invited people to Islam aroused the wrath of the Makkan unbelievers. In such circumstances, believers are told that while it is a virtue to take God as one's Lord and to remain steadfast in following His way, nonetheless the height of virtue consists in declaring one's faith and summoning others to that faith, in total disregard of the consequences that might ensue. Furthermore, while pursuing this mission one's conduct should be so transparently clean and unblemished that detractors fail to find any fault with Islam and its votaries.

In order to fully appreciate the significance of this directive, one should call to mind the circumstances in which it was given. The directive was given when Islam's message was being generally spurned and facing obstinate and aggressive opposition. In pursuing their blind hostility, the unbelievers had exceeded all limits of morality, humanity and decency. In their zealotry, these opponents did not shrink from recourse to all kinds of lies against the Prophet (peace be on him) and his followers. Indeed, all possible means were employed in a bid to discredit the Prophet (peace be on him) and turn people against him. A whole range of allegations was fabricated to bring this about. Virtually a whole army of persons was mobilised in order to create doubts in people's minds. Not only this, but the Muslims were also being subjected to myriads of hardships and torments so that quite a few of them had to migrate for their safety. In order to render the Prophet's preaching ineffective, no sooner would he rise to preach than his opponents would create a din such as to drown out whatever he was saying. The conditions obtaining at that time were so demoralising that all avenues of preaching Islam seemed to be effectively blocked.

It was at this stage that the Prophet (peace be on him) was taught how to smash the force of his enemies.

In such adverse circumstances, it is significant that the Qur'ān directed the Prophet (peace be on him) to follow the golden rule: 'Repel (evil) with that which is good, and you will see that he, between whom and you there was enmity, shall become as if he were a bosom friend (of yours).' The first point emphasised is that good and evil are not alike. When a fierce storm of opposition is raised by the enemies of truth, believers may find themselves helpless and resourceless. Notwithstanding this, evil is intrinsically weak and fragile. It is bound to perish. The standard-bearers of evil are themselves bound to realise that they are wrongdoers, oppressors, and that they are being stubborn on account of their own self-interests. Humans, as long as they are so, can simply not help despising evil. As a result, let alone gaining the esteem of others, evil-doers lose esteem in their own sight. There also surges within them a sense of guilt which weakens them from within. Virtue, on the contrary, which apparently looks weak, has an intrinsic strength and ultimately triumphs if it remains active. Even an evil-doer recognises the value of virtue. In an open encounter between good and evil, only very few will support the latter. It is also emphasised that evil should be repulsed not simply by good but by good of the highest kind. The point is that if someone ill-treats you and you forgive him then this is surely an act of goodness. But a good act of the highest order is that you treat well even those who treat you badly. The expected result of this behaviour is intensified: the worst enemy is likely to become your bosom friend. This because human nature is such.

Suppose, then, that if one keeps quiet in response to someone's abuse, undoubtedly it is a good act. Such inaction might, however, not prompt him to stem his abusive tongue. Now, consider what would happen if the person so attacked were to go further and act benevolently towards his enemy, earnestly seeking his wellbeing in response to his abuse. Such an attitude would inevitably cause embarrassment and silence the detractor once and for all.

It is also likely, however, that in some cases if one does not retaliate, one's enemy might be further emboldened and cause one further harm. In the long run, however, evil cannot compete with goodness. This observation that goodness will always overcome one's enemies should, nonetheless, not be taken as an inexonerable law of nature. There are wicked people who will continue to cause mischief, no matter what favours one might do them. Such are the exception, however, rather than the rule.

(35) But none attains to this except those who are steadfast;[38] none attains to this except those endowed with mighty good fortune.[39] (36) And if you are prompted by a provocation from Satan, seek refuge with Allah.[40] ▶

وَمَا يُلَقَّىٰهَآ إِلَّا ٱلَّذِينَ صَبَرُواْ وَمَا يُلَقَّىٰهَآ
إِلَّا ذُو حَظٍّ عَظِيمٍ ﴿٣٥﴾ وَإِمَّا يَنزَغَنَّكَ مِنَ
ٱلشَّيْطَٰنِ نَزْغٌ فَٱسْتَعِذْ بِٱللَّهِ ۖ

---

38. Although the directive is very effective, it is nonetheless not easy to put it into practice. It calls for exemplary patience, large-heartedness, firm resolve and self-control. Occasionally one may behave in this manner. However, if one is dealing with a wickedness intoxicated with power and which lacks all scruples, it is hard to constantly act with such a high degree of self-restraint. It is only the person who is wedded fully to the cause of truth who will be able to maintain his poise, exercise self-control to the full and not be provoked at others' mischief. In other words, he will be the person of such sterling resolve and nerve that no viciousness from his opponents, howsoever despicable, will succeed in prevailing upon him to lower his lofty moral standards.

39. This is the law of nature. Only people of superb stature possess these qualities, and none can prevent them from reaching the heights of success. It is simply impossible for those of low moral stature to defeat such people by recourse to debased manoeuvres, ignoble tactics and vile acts.

40. Satan is greatly upset when he observes that in the conflict between truth and falsehood the virtuous respond to evil with good and decency. Satan longs to see the votaries of truth, especially its leading figures, commit a moral lapse, one that he can then publicise to their discredit. This lapse would be used to argue that the difference between the forces of evil and good was not all that clear for ignoble acts were not confined to one party alone; rather, they characterise both parties, whereby those who are considered good have also been guilty of unworthy actions. Superficially, this line of argument appeals to many, for common people do not have the ability to differentiate between the initial excesses that were committed and those actions that came in response to them. Hence, as long as they see the party representing

truth and goodness acting with conspicuous decency in response to the vileness of those who are evil, they remain impressed. However, if in a moment of weakness the party of good and truth also commit an untoward act, or an act that does not behove good people, then the common folk will tar both parties with the same brush though the act might have been committed in reaction to a major excess committed by those who are evil. Hence, it was pointed out that people should be constantly on guard against Satan's deception. For Satan is likely to approach them in the garb of a sincere well-wisher, provoking the good not to put up with any of the enemy's high-handedness, and emphasising that the excess to which they were subjected was simply unbearable and should be duly paid back, punch for punch. Hence why, on those occasions when one feels unduly provoked, one should be on the alert against Satan's promptings.

Such feelings of provocation are an indication that Satan is prompting the person concerned so that in a fit of rage he should take a mistaken step. However, even in full consciousness, it is still not right to be complacent for one nevertheless runs the risk of succumbing to another mistake. This because one is likely to entertain the illusion that one has such an exceeding degree of self-control that even Satan has failed to push him to committing mistakes. Such illusion is another grave act of self-deception, one caused by Satan, one that is highly dangerous. On such occasions one should seek refuge with God, for it is thanks to His succour and protection alone that man can avoid falling prey to serious mistakes.

This is best explained by the following incident narrated by Imām Aḥmad ibn Ḥanbal in his *Musnad,* on the authority of Abū Hurayrah: Once someone started hurling abuses at Abū Bakr in the Prophet's presence. Abū Bakr listened quietly while the Prophet (peace be on him) watched him with a smile on his face. At long last, Abū Bakr could no longer hold himself and made a harsh remark about the other person. When he uttered that, the Prophet's complexion changed, indicating that he felt disconcerted and then he immediately left. Abū Bakr followed the Prophet (peace be on him) and asked him on the way why he had kept smiling while he was being insulted and why he had left in anger when he [to wit, Abū Bakr] retaliated. To this the Prophet (peace be on him) replied: 'As long as you remained quiet, an angel remained with you and kept answering him on your behalf. However, when you retorted Satan replaced the angel and I could not sit in a place where Satan was present.'

He, and He alone, is All-Hearing, All-Knowing.[41]

(37) And of His Signs[42] are the night and the day, and the sun and the moon.[43] Do not prostrate yourselves before the sun, nor before the moon, ▶

إِنَّهُۥ هُوَ ٱلسَّمِيعُ ٱلْعَلِيمُ ﴿٣٦﴾ وَمِنْ ءَايَٰتِهِ ٱلَّيْلُ وَٱلنَّهَارُ وَٱلشَّمْسُ وَٱلْقَمَرُ ۚ لَا تَسْجُدُوا۟ لِلشَّمْسِ وَلَا لِلْقَمَرِ

41. After having sought refuge with God in the face of severe opposition, what fills a believer's heart with patience, steadfastness and tranquillity, peace and calm is the conviction that God is well aware of everything, including what both the believers and the unbelievers do;. He sees the acts of both the parties and also hears whatever they say. With this belief, a true believer entrusts all matters relating to themselves and the enemies of truth to God and so doing feels fully satisfied.

This is the fifth instance in which the Qur'ān imparts this wisdom to the Prophet (peace be on him) and through him to the believers, a wisdom that pertains to summoning people to Islam and bringing about reforms in the lives of fellow human beings. For the other instances in point, see *al-A'rāf* 7, nn. 149-53, *Towards Understanding the Qur'ān*, vol. III, pp. 111-16; *al-Naḥl* 16, nn. 122-3, vol. IV, pp. 375-7.

42. From here on the address turns to the generality of people. A few sentences are devoted to explaining the basic truth to them.

43. Objects of nature should not be worshipped in the mistaken belief that they are God's manifestations. Instead, they are only His signs. When one reflects on those signs, one grasps the essential truth of monotheism permeating the universe and its working. Day and night are mentioned before referring to the sun and the moon in order to bring home the point that the setting of the sun and the rising of the moon at night, and the appearance of the sun and the disappearance of the moon at day time, show that neither of them is Divine or a manifestation of the Divine. On the contrary, the sun and the moon are helpless entities bound to God's laws and as such simply revolve in their respective orbits.

but prostrate yourselves before Allah Who created them, if it is Him that you serve.[44] (38) But if they wax proud[45] (and persist in their attitude, it does not matter, for) the angels near-stationed to your Lord glorify Him night and day, and never grow weary.[46]

(39) And of His Signs is that you see the earth withered, then We send down water upon it, and lo! it quivers and swells. ▶

وَٱسْجُدُوا۟ لِلَّهِ ٱلَّذِى خَلَقَهُنَّ إِن كُنتُمْ إِيَّاهُ
تَعْبُدُونَ ﴿٣٧﴾ فَإِنِ ٱسْتَكْبَرُوا۟ فَٱلَّذِينَ عِندَ
رَبِّكَ يُسَبِّحُونَ لَهُۥ بِٱلَّيْلِ وَٱلنَّهَارِ وَهُمْ
لَا يَسْـَٔمُونَ ۩ ﴿٣٨﴾ وَمِنْ ءَايَٰتِهِۦٓ أَنَّكَ
تَرَى ٱلْأَرْضَ خَٰشِعَةً فَإِذَآ أَنزَلْنَا عَلَيْهَا
ٱلْمَآءَ ٱهْتَزَّتْ وَرَبَتْ ۚ

44. This constitutes a rejoinder to the philosophy that has been dexterously developed by the more intelligent of the polytheists. They insist that they do not prostrate themselves before objects of nature, but rather prostrate before God. In response they are asked why, if they truly worship God, they do not directly prostrate themselves before God rather than do so before any intermediaries?

45. 'But if they wax proud' means that the unbelievers thought it to be inconsistent with their pride to pay due heed to the Prophet (peace be on him) they preferred instead to intransigently cling to their ignorance.

46. The entire system of the universe is in operation through the angels, who are diligently engaged in celebrating God's unity, and in obeying and serving Him. The angels associated with the affairs of the universe constantly testify that their Lord is far too glorious to have any partners in His Divinity. Yet if there are some fools who do not take heed, even after things have been explained to them and who insist on adhering to polytheism, then these may be left alone to wallow in the foolishness which they have chosen for themselves.

There is consensus among scholars that while reciting this part of the Qur'ān prostration should be performed. There is disagreement,

Surely He Who gives life to the dead earth will also give life to the dead.[47] Surely He has power over everything.

إِنَّ ٱلَّذِىٓ أَحْيَاهَا لَمُحْىِ ٱلْمَوْتَىٰٓ ۚ إِنَّهُۥ عَلَىٰ كُلِّ شَىْءٍ قَدِيرٌ ﴿٣٩﴾ إِنَّ ٱلَّذِينَ يُلْحِدُونَ فِىٓ ءَايَٰتِنَا

(40) Those who pervert[48] Our Signs[49] are not ▶

---

however, about which of the two verses requires prostration. It is reported that 'Alī and 'Abd Allāh ibn Mas'ūd used to prostrate themselves on reciting verse 37. This view is shared by Imām Mālik, and according to one report, by Imām Shāfi'ī as well. As opposed to this, 'Abd Allāh ibn 'Abbās, 'Abd Allāh ibn 'Umar, Sa'īd ibn al-Musayyab, Masrūq, Qatādah, al-Ḥasan al-Baṣrī, Abū 'Abd al-Raḥmān al-Sulamī, Ibn Sīrīn, Ibrāhīm al-Nakha'ī and several others refer to verse 38 in this regard. This view is also held by Imām Abū Ḥanīfah, The Shāfi'īs too subscribe to the same view. (Qurṭubī, *al-Jāmi' li Aḥkām al-Qur'ān*, comments on *Sūrah Ḥā Mīm al-Sajdah* 41: 38; Nasafī, *Madārik al-Tanzīl wa Ḥaqā'iq al-Ta'wīl*, comments on *Sūrah Ḥā Mīm al-Sajdah* 41: 38.)

47. For further details see *al-Naḥl* 16: n. 53, *Towards Understanding the Qur'ān,* vol. IV, p. 340; *al-Ḥajj* 22, nn. 8-9, vol. VI, p. 9; *al-Rūm* 30, n. 25, vol. VIII, p. 88, and *Fāṭir* 35, n. 19, vol. IX, p. 215.

48. It is stated in just a few sentences that the doctrines of monotheism and the Afterlife, which the Prophet (peace be on him) summoned people to accept, were true and reasonable and that the phenomena of the universe also testifies to their truth. After this, the discourse turns to Islam's opponents, those who were inveterately bent upon opposing these doctrines.

49. The actual words are يُلْحِدُونَ فِي آيَاتِنَا ('pervert Our Signs'). The word *ilḥād* means to deviate, to turn away from the straight to the crooked way, to adopt a crooked course. To prevent God's Signs means to try to dig out something crooked in a way that is straight. In other words, while going through the verses, instead of turning to the clear, explicit meaning of those verses one commits the mistake of forcing them to yield all kinds of erroneous meanings, thereby misleading one's own self as well as others. The unbelievers of Makkah had adopted various

hidden from Us.[50] Is he who will be cast into the Fire better, or he who comes secure on the Day of Resurrection? Do as you wish; He sees all what you do. (41) These are the ones who rejected the Good Counsel when it came to them, although it is certainly a Mighty Book.[51]

(42) Falsehood may not enter it from the front or from the rear.[52] ▶

لَا يَخْفَوْنَ عَلَيْنَآ ۗ أَفَمَن يُلْقَىٰ فِى ٱلنَّارِ خَيْرٌ أَم
مَّن يَأْتِىٓ ءَامِنًا يَوْمَ ٱلْقِيَـٰمَةِ ۚ ٱعْمَلُوا۟
مَا شِئْتُمْ ۖ إِنَّهُۥ بِمَا تَعْمَلُونَ بَصِيرٌ ﴿٤٠﴾ إِنَّ
ٱلَّذِينَ كَفَرُوا۟ بِٱلذِّكْرِ لَمَّا جَآءَهُمْ ۖ وَإِنَّهُۥ
لَكِتَـٰبٌ عَزِيزٌ ﴿٤١﴾ لَّا يَأْتِيهِ ٱلْبَـٰطِلُ مِنۢ
بَيْنِ يَدَيْهِ وَلَا مِنْ خَلْفِهِۦ ۖ

---

means to deviate from the Qur'ān. One of these was that they would detach Qur'ānic verses from their context, or interpolate them, or wrongly interpret a word or passage. By so doing it became possible for them to subject the Qur'ān to a variety of objections and thereby deviate from it.

50. This implies a severe warning. Suppose a sovereign were to proclaim that those who are engaged in misdeeds 'are not hidden from Us.' Obviously, this proclamation means that such people will not escape punishment.

51. The Qur'ān stands out as the eternal truth. Its message cannot be defeated by the unbelievers' recourse to the tricks they employed against it. The votaries of falsehood employed whatever means they could against the Qur'ān. In so doing, they clearly did not appreciate that the Qur'ān represents the power of honesty, of true knowledge, of a powerful language and its eloquence, let alone the power of God, its Author as well as the force of the personality of the great Messenger (peace be on him) who brought it. The Qur'ān, in short, cannot be checkmated by falsehood or malicious propaganda.

52. 'Falsehood may not enter it from the front or from the rear.' In other words, if someone tries to refute the Qur'ān directly from the front

It is a revelation that has been sent down from the Most Wise, the Immensely Praiseworthy.

(43) (O Prophet), nothing is said to you but what was already said to the Messengers before you. Surely your Lord is the Lord of forgiveness[53] and the Lord of grievous chastisement.

(44) Had We revealed this as a non-Arabic Qur'ān they would have said: 'Why were its verses not clearly expounded? How strange, ▶

تَنزِيلٌ مِّنْ حَكِيمٍ حَمِيدٍ ﴿٤٢﴾ مَّا يُقَالُ لَكَ
إِلَّا مَا قَدْ قِيلَ لِلرُّسُلِ مِن قَبْلِكَ ۚ إِنَّ رَبَّكَ
لَذُو مَغْفِرَةٍ وَذُو عِقَابٍ أَلِيمٍ ﴿٤٣﴾ وَلَوْ
جَعَلْنَٰهُ قُرْءَانًا أَعْجَمِيًّا لَّقَالُوا۟ لَوْلَا
فُصِّلَتْ ءَايَٰتُهُۥٓ ۖ

and seeks to prove any item or teaching of it to be false and flawed, he is bound to fail. On the other hand, the statement that falsehood will not be able to enter the Qur'ān from the rear means that never can any truth or knowledge come to light which is opposed to the truths expounded by the Qur'ān. There will never be any knowledge which will negate the knowledge expounded by the Qur'ān. Nothing can ever be established through sound experiment and observation that will be able to establish the falsity of the guidance provided to mankind in the domain of beliefs, morality, law, culture and civilisation, economy, society and polity that the Qur'ān has declared to be true or vice versa. Moreover, this also means that whether falsehood attacks the Qur'ān directly or deviously, it can never thwart its message. Despite all the open and hidden tactics employed by the Qur'ān's opponents, its message will spread far and wide and none will be able to repulse it.

53. God is surely Most Forbearing and Most Forgiving. This is evident from the fact that His Messengers were rejected as liars, were reviled, persecuted and tormented and yet God continued to grant respite for a long time to those who were responsible for these actions.

a non-Arabic scripture and an Arab audience!'[54] Tell them: 'It is a guidance and a healing to the believers. But to those who do not believe, it serves as a plug in their ears and a covering over their eyes. It is as if they are being called from a place far away.'[55] (45) And in the past We gave Moses ▶

ءَا۬عْجَمِيٌّ وَعَرَبِيٌّ ۗ قُلْ هُوَ لِلَّذِينَ ءَامَنُوا۟ هُدًى
وَشِفَآءٌ ۖ وَٱلَّذِينَ لَا يُؤْمِنُونَ فِىٓ ءَاذَانِهِمْ وَقْرٌ
وَهُوَ عَلَيْهِمْ عَمًى ۚ أُو۟لَـٰٓئِكَ يُنَادَوْنَ مِن
مَّكَانٍ بَعِيدٍ ﴿٤٤﴾ وَلَقَدْ ءَاتَيْنَا مُوسَى

54. This is another example of the Makkan unbelievers' diehard opposition to the Prophet (peace be on him). They used to contend that since the Prophet was an Arab and Arabic was his mother tongue, how could one believe the Qur'ān to be the Word of God rather than the product of Muḥammad's own mind? They argued that they might have considered the Qur'ān to be of Divine provenance had the Prophet (peace be on him) suddenly burst forth into eloquence in some foreign tongue such as Persian, Greek or Latin that he did not know. In response, God makes it clear that the Qur'ān has been sent down in their own tongue precisely in order that they may easily understand it. It is nothing short of folly on their part to raise questions as to why it was revealed in Arabic. Had it been revealed in some other tongue, they would have found this odd and would have said: 'Isn't it weird? An Arab Messenger has been raised among Arabs, but the Book he has brought is in a foreign tongue, one that neither he understands nor his people.'

55. When one is called out to from a distance, one only hears a faint sound and is unable to comprehend the precise words spoken. This similitude brings out in full the psychological state that marked the obdurate opponents. It is common knowledge that if a person is unbiased and someone talks to him he tries to listen in order to grasp what is said, and is willing to accept whatever he finds reasonable. In contrast, anyone who is filled with prejudice, spite and hostility will understand nothing. It appears that only the sound reaches his ears while he is able to pay no heed to the message itself. The impression of the speaker will also be the same: what had reached the audience were just stray sounds rather than his actual words.

the Book and yet it became an object of dispute.[56] If your Lord's decree had not gone forth before, a decisive judgement would have been made among them, once and for all.[57] Surely they are in a disquieting doubt about it.[58]

ٱلْكِتَـٰبَ فَٱخْتُلِفَ فِيهِ ۗ وَلَوْلَا كَلِمَةٌ
سَبَقَتْ مِن رَّبِّكَ لَقُضِىَ بَيْنَهُمْ ۚ وَإِنَّهُمْ لَفِى
شَكٍّ مِّنْهُ مُرِيبٍ ﴿٤٥﴾

---

56. In other words, while some believed in the Scripture revealed to the Prophet Moses (peace be on him), others turned to it in hostility.

57. This statement carries the following two meanings: (i) That should God not have ordained that mankind be granted due respite to reflect over and respond to His message, the opponents of the truth would have instantly been obliterated. (ii) That had God not ordained that all the differences among mankind would be settled ultimately on the Day of Judgement, the truth would have been incontrovertibly unravelled in the world, and it would have been made absolutely clear who is in the right and who is in error.

58. This short statement identifies the malaise that afflicted the Makkan unbelievers. They doubted the veracity of the Qur'ān and the Prophet (peace be on him). Indeed, they vociferously rejected both the Qur'ān and the Prophet (peace be on him). However, their rejection was not rooted in conviction; rather, in the heart of their hearts they suffered from uncertainty and anxiety. Swayed by selfish motives and idiosyncratic prejudice, they felt compelled to reject and stoutly oppose the Qur'ān and the Prophet (peace be on him). On the other hand, they realised in the depths of their hearts that the Qur'ān was a consummate piece of discourse, the like of which had never been heard from any litterateur or poet. Nor could any person utter anything like the Qur'ān. Nor could devils and demons approach people, urging them to embrace godliness, righteousness and moral purity. Likewise, when they gave the lie to Muḥammad (peace be on him), claiming that he was saying and doing everything for self-exaltation, their consciences upbraided them. For they were inwardly aware of their own guilt and wondered how they could attribute such vile motives to someone who had never tried to acquire

مَّنْ عَمِلَ صَٰلِحًا فَلِنَفْسِهِۦ ۖ وَمَنْ أَسَآءَ
فَعَلَيْهَا ۗ وَمَا رَبُّكَ بِظَلَّٰمٍ لِّلْعَبِيدِ ﴿٤٦﴾ ۞ إِلَيْهِ
يُرَدُّ عِلْمُ ٱلسَّاعَةِ ۚ وَمَا تَخْرُجُ مِن ثَمَرَٰتٍ
مِّنْ أَكْمَامِهَا وَمَا تَحْمِلُ مِنْ أُنثَىٰ
وَلَا تَضَعُ إِلَّا بِعِلْمِهِۦ ۚ

(46) Whoever does good, does so to his own benefit; and whoever does evil, will suffer its evil consequence. Your Lord does no wrong to His servants.[59]

(47) The knowledge of the Hour[60] rests solely with Him.[61] Not a fruit comes forth from its sheath, nor does any female conceive nor give birth to a child but it is in His knowledge.[62] ▶

---

wealth, power or fame, someone who in fact was free of every taint of self-indulgence. On the contrary, he had always worked for the cause of goodness and virtue and did nothing unbecoming to serve any of his personal interests.

59. That is, their Lord can never commit the injustice of causing a person's good deeds to go to waste; nor can He let the evil-doers escape retribution for their misdeeds.

60. The reference here is to the appointed Hour when the wicked will be punished for their misdeeds and the wrongs to which good people were subjected will be redressed.

61. God alone knows when the appointed Hour will be. This represents the Qur'ānic rejoinder to the Makkan unbelievers' query as to when God's punishment, with which the Prophet (peace be on him) threatened them, will come to pass. God responds to their query without clearly stating that query in so many words.

62. This directive is meant to urge the audience to take note of two things: (i) That not only knowledge of matters relating to the Last Day but of all matters relating to the realm beyond the ken of perception is the exclusive preserve of God alone. (ii) That God is aware of even the minutest details of everything. It is inconceivable that any of man's deeds

On that Day He will call out to them: 'Where are those associates of Mine?' They will answer: 'We have declared to You that none of us can bear witness to that.'[63] (48) Then all those deities whom they once used to call upon ▶

وَيَوْمَ يُنَادِيهِمْ أَيْنَ شُرَكَآءِى قَالُوٓا۟ ءَاذَنَّٰكَ
مَا مِنَّا مِن شَهِيدٍ ﴿٤٧﴾ وَضَلَّ عَنْهُم مَّا كَانُوا۟
يَدْعُونَ مِن قَبْلُ

---

will escape His knowledge. Therefore, no person should act whimsically in God's dominion. It is in this sense that this observation is thematically linked with the verses that follow.

Pondering on what immediately follows makes it quite clear that the point being driven home is that people should not waste their time and energy on trying to ascertain the exact time when the Day of Judgement will come. What should rather concern them is what punishment will be meted out to people for their iniquity when the Day arrives. In this respect, what the Prophet (peace be on him) once said is very significant. This occurs in a tradition which has been narrated through myriad channels in the *Sīrah*, *Sunan* and *Musnad* works so that it has reached the point of *tāwātur* (massive transmission), thereby signifying absolute authenticity. According to the tradition, the Prophet (peace be on him) was travelling when someone called out to him from a distance, saying: "O Muḥammad! When will the Last Day be?' He replied: 'It is imminent. What preparations have you made for it?' (Bukhārī, *Kitāb al-Manāqib, Bāb Manāqib 'Umar b. al-Kaṭṭāb*; and Muslim, *Kitāb al-Birr wa al-Ṣilah wa al-Ādāb, Bāb al-Mar' ma'a man Aḥabb*; Nasā'ī, *al-Sunan al-Kubrā, Kitāb al-'Ilm, Bāb idhā Su'ila al-'Ālim 'anmā Yakrahuhu*; Aḥmad ibn Ḥanbal, *Musnad*, narrated by Anas b. Mālik.)

63. The unbelievers will realise on the Day of Judgement that they were in gross error. On that Day, no one will entertain any notion that God has any partner whatsoever. It is clear from the verse's wording that at each stage on the Day of Judgement, the unbelievers will be asked whether they were in the right or in error. Inevitably, at every stage they will admit that they were misguided and that the Prophet's message alone was true, and that they constantly disregarded it, persisting in error and ignorance.

shall vanish[64] and they will come to know for sure that there is no escape for them.

(49) Man wearies not of praying for good,[65] but when evil visits him, he despairs and gives up all hope. (50) And if We bestow Our Mercy upon him after hardship, he will surely say: 'This is what I truly deserve,[66] and I do not believe that the Hour (of Resurrection) will ever come to pass; and if I am ▶

وَظَنُّوا۟ مَا لَهُم مِّن مَّحِيصٍ ﴿٤٨﴾ لَّا يَسْـَٔمُ
ٱلْإِنسَـٰنُ مِن دُعَآءِ ٱلْخَيْرِ وَإِن مَّسَّهُ ٱلشَّرُّ
فَيَـُٔوسٌ قَنُوطٌ ﴿٤٩﴾ وَلَئِنْ أَذَقْنَـٰهُ رَحْمَةً
مِّنَّا مِنۢ بَعْدِ ضَرَّآءَ مَسَّتْهُ لَيَقُولَنَّ هَـٰذَا لِى
وَمَآ أَظُنُّ ٱلسَّاعَةَ قَآئِمَةً وَلَئِن

64. In a state of sheer desperation the unbelievers will look around, hoping to receive help from those whom they had worshipped during their lives. They will look here and there for someone to rescue them, or at least to lighten their punishment. However, they will find neither helper nor supporter anywhere.

65. 'Good' here means prosperity, abundance of sustenance, good health and the well-being of the family. As for the word *al-insān* (man) used here it does not refer to the entirety of mankind. For if that were the case, it would also include Prophets and pious people who do not suffer from the weakness mentioned in this verse. Rather, the verse mentions those who fervently invoke God when they are engulfed in a crisis but who, no sooner than they receive any portion of good fortune, throw all their scruples aboard and pounce on self-indulgence. Since the majority of human beings are vulnerable to this weakness, it is projected as a common failure pertaining to mankind.

66. Such a person tends to boast that he has earned all his good fortune as a result of his own talent and competence. He, thus, considers himself quite worthy of the well-being that he enjoys.

returned to my Lord, there too I shall enjoy the best.' Surely We shall fully apprise the unbelievers of what they have done, and We shall certainly make them taste a severe chastisement.

(51) When We bestow Our favour upon man, he turns away and waxes proud;[67] but when a misfortune touches him, he is full of supplication.[68]

(52) Tell them, (O Prophet): 'Did you ever consider: if this Qur'ān is indeed from Allah and you still deny it, who can be in greater error than he who goes far in fiercely opposing it?'[69]

رُّجِعْتُ إِلَىٰ رَبِّيٓ إِنَّ لِي عِندَهُۥ لَلْحُسْنَىٰ ۚ
فَلَنُنَبِّئَنَّ ٱلَّذِينَ كَفَرُوا۟ بِمَا عَمِلُوا۟ وَلَنُذِيقَنَّهُم
مِّنْ عَذَابٍ غَلِيظٍ ﴿٥٠﴾ وَإِذَآ أَنْعَمْنَا عَلَى
ٱلْإِنسَٰنِ أَعْرَضَ وَنَـَٔا بِجَانِبِهِۦ وَإِذَا مَسَّهُ
ٱلشَّرُّ فَذُو دُعَآءٍ عَرِيضٍ ﴿٥١﴾ قُلْ أَرَءَيْتُمْ إِن
كَانَ مِنْ عِندِ ٱللَّهِ ثُمَّ كَفَرْتُم بِهِۦ
مَنْ أَضَلُّ مِمَّنْ هُوَ فِى شِقَاقٍۭ بَعِيدٍ ﴿٥٢﴾

67. The unbelievers turn away from God, neither obeying nor worshipping Him. Essentially, they consider it beneath their dignity to surrender themselves to God.

68. We have come across several Qur'ānic verses which make this point. In order to gain a better understanding of the issue under consideration, it is pertinent to refer to the following: *Yūnus* 10: 12 and *Hūd* 11: 9-11, *Towards Understanding the Qur'ān,* vol. IV, pp. 16, 84-5; *Banī Isrā'īl* 17: 83, vol. V, p. 69, *al-Rūm* 30: 33-6, vol. VIII, pp. 103-4, and see *al-Zumar* 39: 8-9 and 49 above.

69. This does not mean that one should believe, on grounds of contingency, that if this Qur'ān indeed turns out to be God's Revelation then they will be spared chastisement. What it really means is that they were thoughtlessly rejecting the truth, sealing their ears against it and

(53) Soon shall We show them Our Signs on the horizons and in their own beings until it becomes clear to them that it is the Truth.[70] Is it not enough ▶	سَنُرِيهِمْ ءَايَٰتِنَا فِى ٱلْءَافَاقِ وَفِىٓ أَنفُسِهِمْ حَتَّىٰ يَتَبَيَّنَ لَهُمْ أَنَّهُ ٱلْحَقُّ ۗ أَوَلَمْ يَكْفِ

were, in a fit of adamance, bent on opposing it. All this was nothing short of foolishness. After all, they had no means of knowing that the Qur'ān was not from God; there was no definite basis for them to contend that it had not been revealed by God. Quite obviously, their refusal to believe in the Qur'ān was based on conjecture rather than on definite knowledge, and every conjecture can be true or false.

Let us now proceed to consider both possibilities: that the conjecture might be true or false. Let us assume for a moment that their conjecture turns out to be true. In this case, at most, all those who believe and those who don't will come to the same end. This because all will be reduced to dust and that will be the end of things. However, if on the contrary, it turns out that the Qur'ān was from God and whatever it says about Afterlife does come about, how horrendous will the end of those who gave the lie to Afterlife be? It is their own interest which requires them to abjure obstinacy and adamance and give serious and open-minded thought to the truth of the Qur'ānic claim. If, after serious reflection, they decide not to believe, they may do so. There is, however, no justification for them going to the extreme opposition which they did. There was no reason why they should go so far as to lie, defraud, beguile, oppress and torment people so as to arrest Islam's spread.

70. This verse admits two meanings and both have been given by highly regarded Qur'ānic commentators: (i) That the unbelievers will themselves soon see that the Qur'ān's message has come to prevail in and around Arabia and they themselves will pledge loyalty and commitment to it. It is then that it will dawn upon them that what is being propounded, something whose acceptance they had resisted, is indeed fully true. (Ṭabarī, *Tafsīr*, comments on *Sūrah Ḥā Mīm al-Sajdah* 41: 53.) Some people have objected to this on the grounds that the mere fact of an ideology's prevalence does not necessarily prove its truth. For, as we know, false ideologies too have achieved dominance and their followers succeeded in conquering territory after territory.

This objection, however, is superficial, one that is made without fully understanding the whole matter. The astounding Islamic expansion in the time of the Prophet (peace be on him) and the Rightly-Guided Caliphs was not simply a token of Islam's truth by dint of the believers' success to conquer vast stretches of land. These conquests were rather tokens of truth in the sense that they were unlike other conquests in history which made a person, or a nation, the master of the lives and properties of others, thereby filling God's earth with tyranny and oppression. As distinguished from other examples of conquest, the Islamic conquests brought in their trail a tremendous religious, moral, intellectual, cultural, political, civilisational and economic revolution. As the effects of this revolution radiated, the best potentials of human beings came into fruition and their evil potentials were quelled. The world has been in the habit of expecting moral excellence and loftiness of conduct only from devoted ascetics and godly hermits, who renounce the world to constantly remember God. Hardly was it thought that excellence of the most sublime kind can be found in the lives of those who run the affairs of the world. The revolution we are talking about has enabled us to find moral excellence in the courts of those who administered justice, in the conduct of army commanders engaged in warfare and conquest, in the revenue administration of tax-collectors, and in the trade and commerce of businessmen. This revolution brought into existence a society in which ordinary human beings reached the heights of moral excellence that were way beyond those attained by the moral elites of other societies. This revolution liberated human beings from superstitions and myths and led them along the high road of knowledge, research and rational thinking and behaviour. It treated those ills of life which other societies had not even thought of treating or which they had failed to treat. In this regard we may mention the class divisions within each society and the differences between the high and the low, let alone the vogue of untouchability, legal and social inequality, suppression of women, denial of basic human rights, extensive spread of crimes, addiction to drugs and alcohol, exaltation of rulers to the extent of rendering them beyond accountability, helplessness of the masses, wanton violation of covenants and treaties in international relations, savagery in warfare and myriad other evils.

Arabia, which was once notorious for its lawlessness, wickedness and moral degeneration, changed altogether thanks to Islam. Schism and wanton feuding were replaced by order; internecine bloodshed and lawlessness were replaced by peace and security; instead of wickedness and corruption there was piety and moral propriety; instead of oppression and tyranny there was justice; instead of impurity and defilement there was grace and refinement; instead of ignorance there was knowledge, and instead of vengeful fighting lasting for several generations there was brotherhood and love. Those people who could not even dream of anything higher than becoming the chieftains of their own tribes became leaders of the world. Those to whom the Prophet (peace be on him) had recited this verse for the first time observed these signs with their own eyes. From that time on God has constantly been showing such signs.

Even in the present phase of decline Muslims have continued to display a grandeur in their conduct which is way above the moral standards acceptable to the embodiments of refinement and cultivation. The brutal treatment to which 'civilised' nations have subjected the colonised peoples of Asia, Africa, America and even Europe has no parallel in any period of Muslim history. It is thanks to the Qur'ān that we find such tender humanity among Muslims that after becoming dominant they never adopted the brutality that characterises every period of non-Muslims' history. It is for anyone to see how Muslims treated Christians in Spain when they were in power there and conversely how the Christians treated the Muslims during the period of their control of that land: how the Muslims' magnanimous treatment of Christians utterly contrasts with the brutality of the Christians towards Muslims after they became the rulers of Spain. Let us consider another case, that of India. Muslim rule over the Subcontinent lasted for eight centuries. It is worth noting how the Muslims treated the Hindus of India during their hegemony and how they are now being treated by Hindus who presently dominate India. The same needs be said about the Muslims' treatment of Jews and vice versa.

The second meaning of the verse is that God will show to people His signs in the phenomena of the universe, of the earth and the sky as well as in their own beings, signs that will make it evident that the teachings of the Qur'ān embody the truth. (Ṭabarī, *Tafsīr*, comments on *Sūrah Ḥā Mīm al-Sajdah* 41: 53.) Some people raise strong objection to this, saying that these signs were already there, so why have they been associated with the future? This objection is as shallow as the one with regard to the first meaning of the verse. Certainly the heavens and the earth have been there for people to see and so has been man's own being. However, the signs so embedded in them are virtually countless, so that man has neither been able to encompass them in the past nor he will be able to encompass all of them in the future. However, in every age ever new signs of God have attracted man's attention and this will continue till the Day of Resurrection.

that your Lord is a witness over everything?[71] (54) Lo, they are in doubt concerning their meeting with their Lord.[72] Surely He fully encompasses everything.[73]

بِرَبِّكَ أَنَّهُۥ عَلَىٰ كُلِّ شَيْءٍ شَهِيدٌ ﴿٥٣﴾
أَلَآ إِنَّهُمْ فِي مِرْيَةٍ مِّن لِّقَآءِ رَبِّهِمْ ۗ أَلَآ إِنَّهُۥ
بِكُلِّ شَيْءٍ مُّحِيطٌ ﴿٥٤﴾

---

71. God is well aware of every effort aimed to give the lie to and frustrate His Message. Does the fact that God is well aware of their deeds not suffice to strike awe among them, filling their hearts with fear?

72. What explains their behaviour on the Last Day is that they do not believe that they have to stand before their Lord and render an account of their deeds.

73. That is, they cannot escape God's grip. Let it also be noted that none of their deeds have remained unrecorded.

Sūrah 42

Al-Shūrā

(Consultation)

(Makkan Period)

Title

The title is taken from the phrase وَأَمْرُهُمْ شُورَىٰ بَيْنَهُمْ (verse 38 of the *sūrah*) in which the word *shūrā* occurs.

Period of Revelation

Although it is not clearly stated in any authentic tradition when this *sūrah* was revealed, reflection over its content indicates that it was revealed after *Ḥā Mīm al-Sajdah* (*Sūrah* 41). This becomes further evident if the two *sūrah*s are read in sequence. Indeed, such a reading would make the present *sūrah* appear to be a supplement to the former one.

It is noteworthy that the present *sūrah* vehemently denounces the blind opposition to Islam that had been propelled by the Quraysh chiefs. This was done with a view to prick the consciences of those living in and around Makkah: if they had any vestige of moral sensitivity, decency and reasonableness left in them, for that would make them appreciate that the way in which they were treating the Prophet (peace be on him) was utterly unjustified.

Their atrocious treatment of the Prophet (peace be on him) was in sharp contrast to his own discourse which was marked by a dignified seriousness. Furthermore, his standpoint was consummately reasonable, and his attitude singularly gracious and decent. The note of disapproval contained in the earlier *sūrah, Sūrah* 41, was followed by the revelation of the present one, a *sūrah* which rendered a yeoman's service to elucidating the message of Truth and articulating the Prophet's Mission so persuasively that people in general could hardly resist being favourably impressed by it. It was only those who were altogether devoid of any love for Truth or who had been blinded by their fascination with the ways of Ignorance who could resist being attracted to the Prophet's Mission.

Subject Matter and Theme

The *sūrah* commences with a comment about the Prophet's discourse. It expresses surprise at the hostility shown to it by the Quraysh, for neither was the Prophet's discourse something altogether novel and unprecedented nor was it bizarre that Prophets were raised and provided with revelation so as to guide human beings. In the past God had raised a series of Prophets (peace be on them) and had endowed them with the same kind of revelation and guidance. It is not at all weird that the Lord of the heavens and the earth should be recognised as the Deity and the Sovereign. What indeed is weird is that despite being God's born servants, and while living in His dominion and deriving sustenance from Him, people should acknowledge the Godhead of any other than the One True God. The unbelievers were amazed at those who call people to monotheism. The fact, however, was that their acceptance of others as God's associates in His Divinity is a monstrosity, one grave enough to cause the sky to be rent asunder. Angels are aghast at their brazenness and ever apprehensive that some scourge might overtake them.

From here on, it is stressed that the designation of any person as a Prophet and his introducing himself to people in that capacity does not at all mean that people's destinies have been entrusted to him and that he may make or mar them at his pleasure. The fact is that men's destinies lie entirely with God. A Prophet's task is no more than to arouse people from their heedlessness and negligence and direct to the Straight Way those who have strayed from it. The task of holding to task those who do not pay heed to a Prophet's call, and to punish or not punish them, are matters that lie totally in God's Hand; such matters have not been entrusted even to Prophets. Hence people should disabuse their minds of all false perceptions that Prophets appear on the public scene with the kind of tall claims often made by religious clergy or charlatans who parade their holiness and go about swaggering that they will reduce to dust all those who do not follow them or are insolent to them. It is made very clear that Prophets are not sent to destroy their peoples. On the contrary, they are their people's well-wishers, warning them that they are pursuing a road that leads to their doom.

It is also explained why God did not make all human beings to compulsively follow the Right Way, and why He kept the other option open to them. As a result of that, men are traversing numerous erroneous paths. This arrangement, however, also enables them to have access to God's special Grace, which is denied to other creatures who cannot choose any other options. This unique opportunity is available only to man who has been granted free will. Once man resolves to turn to the Straight Way, God supports and guides him, enables him to do good deeds and this makes him deserving of God's special favour. This is a privilege enjoyed only by humans who consciously take God as their Patron and Guardian. On the contrary, anyone who misuses his freedom of choice and takes as his Patron and Guardian those who are not and can never be his Patron and Guardian, is deprived of this favour. In this regard it is made clear that in the true sense of the term God alone is the Patron and Guardian of man and no other creature has any rightful claim to this position, nor the power to function as such. Man's success lies in his not committing any mistake while exercising his freedom to choose his Patron and Guardian: he should opt for God alone.

This is followed by enunciating the religion promulgated by Muḥammad (peace be on him). The very first foundation of this religion is that since God is the Creator of both the universe and mankind, as well as mankind's Lord and Patron and Sovereign, He alone has the right to provide man with the right system of belief and conduct. He also has the right to resolve all matters on which men differ and to definitively lay down what is right and what is wrong. No other creature has the right to be the lawgiver for mankind. In other words, God alone enjoys legal-prescriptive sovereignty even as He enjoys sovereignty over the domain of nature. No human being nor any other creature is possessed of this sovereignty. Any person who does not subscribe to God's legal sovereignty, and merely accepts Him as sovereign over the natural domain, falls short of what is needed.

It is on this basis that God has prescribed from the very beginning a religion for mankind. The religion so prescribed has been one and the same religion that was entrusted to Prophets in their respective times. No Prophet was the founder of any specific religion of his own. It is the one and same religion that was prescribed by God for all mankind and all Prophets adhered to it, calling people to the same.

This religion was not bestowed on people merely for passive acceptance. It was rather given to them in order that it might be made operative on earth and prevail in human affairs. It was meant that God's religion, rather than the systems devised by others than God, should hold sway. Prophets had been raised not simply to propound this religion but also to establish it.

This was the true original religion of mankind. Yet it constantly happened that selfish people, after the demise of Prophets, were swayed by their own opinions and the desire to achieve prominence, succumbed to schisms and gave rise to ever new religions. All the religions presently found in the world are in fact distortions of the one original religion prescribed by God.

Then came the era when the Prophet Muḥammad (peace be on him) was raised to expound this original faith to the followers of these multifarious ways, counterfeit cults and man-made religions. Furthermore, apart from expounding this religion, it was also his task to translate it into practice. People should have been grateful to God for this great favour. Instead, they were annoyed, hostile and belligerent. This is nothing but rank folly. However, their stupidity will not deter the Prophet (peace be on him) from pursuing his mission. He is mandated to stick to his way with constancy and perseverance and to accomplish the task entrusted to him. The unbelievers should entertain no hope that he will give up his task and will allow the same corruptions, superstitions and *Jāhilī* usages to penetrate and corrupt the body politic of God's religion, as they had done in the past. How brazenly audacious of them to cast aside the religious faith prescribed by God and accord preference to a faith and way of life sanctioned by others than God! They consider this an ordinary matter which scantly deserves any blame. In God's sight, however, it is the worst kind of polytheism and a very grave offence. It is so grave that all those who were guilty of operationalising the religions of their contriving, and all those guilty of following them, will have to face a terrible punishment.

Thus, after having expounded a clear, unequivocal concept of religion it was pointed out that the best possible means to direct the unbelievers to the Right Way had already been adopted. On the one hand, God had revealed His Book in their own language, enunciating the Truth in the most appealing form. Additionally, there were the illustrious lives of the Prophet (peace be on him) and his Companions. These provided role models *par excellence* of humanity as their lives were moulded primarily under the influence of the Qur'ān. If all these failed to direct them to the Right Way, nothing could. Their inability to mend themselves clearly showed that they should be left mired in error, as they had been for centuries. They should face the woeful end ordained for those immersed in error and misguidance.

Alongside enunciating these truths, sufficient proofs are brought forth in support of monotheism and the Afterlife. Moreover, the dire consequences of excessive worldliness have also been brought out in order to impress upon people the need to hold in dread the punishment of the Hereafter. They are also reproached for having lapsed into moral weakness as a result of aversion to Divine Guidance.

While concluding the discourse, two important points are made: (i) During the entire 40 years of his life prior to being designated a Prophet, Muḥammad (peace be on him) was totally unaware of the concepts of the Heavenly Book and unacquainted with matters pertaining to religious faith. The fact that all of a sudden he began to expound the Book and expatiate on matters of religious faith is clear evidence of his being a genuine Prophet. (ii) The Prophet (peace be on him) does not claim to be in direct, face-to-face interaction with God. Like all other Prophets, God communicated with him in the following three ways: (a) by revelation, (b) by address from behind a veil, and (c) by communication of messages to him through an angel (see verse 51). This clarification sought to forestal the opponents' accusation that the Prophet (peace be on him) claimed to have a direct, face-to-face communication with God. It also informed believers as regards the modes through which God communicates with those who are elevated to the august office of Prophethood.

In the name of Allah, the Most Merciful, the Most Compassionate.

(1) *Ḥā. Mīm.* (2) *'Ayn. Sīn. Qāf.* (3) Thus does Allah, the Most Mighty, the Most Wise reveal to you even as (He revealed) to those (Messengers) who preceded you.[1] ▶

بِسْمِ ٱللَّهِ ٱلرَّحْمَٰنِ ٱلرَّحِيمِ

حمٓ ﴿١﴾ عٓسٓقٓ ﴿٢﴾ كَذَٰلِكَ يُوحِىٓ إِلَيْكَ
وَإِلَى ٱلَّذِينَ مِن قَبْلِكَ ٱللَّهُ ٱلْعَزِيزُ
ٱلْحَكِيمُ ﴿٣﴾

---

1. The style of the opening verses clearly implies that a hostile whispering campaign was fully in action throughout Makkah against the Prophet's message and the Qur'ān. In every bazaar, on every street, in every house and shop, and wherever a few people got together they engaged in a hostile, gossipy chatter against the Prophet (peace be on him). His opponents accused him of having brought forth a discourse full of absolutely bizarre ideas that had never been heard of before. They expressed their outrage at his having openly proclaimed their centuries-old, ancestral faith, which was followed by the whole community, to be utterly false, offering a faith all his own to replace it. Had he suggested some partial modifications to their ancestral faith and way of life, they could have condescended to give some consideration. However, the Prophet (peace be on him) claimed that he was expounding to them the Word of God verbatim. What could possibly prompt them to accept that? Is it the Word of God because God seeks out Muḥammad or Muḥammad goes to Him? Or, does any conversation take place between the two?

What is being said here on these matters is ostensibly addressed to the unbelievers, but is actually meant for the Prophet's attention. It is being affirmed that the revelation received by the Prophet Muḥammad (peace be on him) had earlier been communicated to the Prophets of yore. Both the content of the teaching and the mode of communicating it were the same.

As for *waḥy*, it denotes a quick, secret suggestion, one that is known only to him who makes it and to him who receives it. As a term it stands for the Guidance communicated with the speed of lightning by God to the hearts of any of His chosen servants. What the verse states is that there is no question of anyone visiting God or of God visiting anyone and, thus, of face-to-face communication. God is Most Mighty and Most Wise.

(4) His is all that is in the heavens and all that is in the earth;[2] He is the Most High, the All-Great. (5) The heavens may well nigh rend asunder from above[3] while the angels proclaim ▶

لَهُۥ مَا فِى ٱلسَّمَـٰوَٰتِ وَمَا فِى ٱلْأَرْضِ ۖ
وَهُوَ ٱلْعَلِىُّ ٱلْعَظِيمُ ﴿٤﴾ تَكَادُ ٱلسَّمَـٰوَٰتُ
يَتَفَطَّرْنَ مِن فَوْقِهِنَّ ۚ وَٱلْمَلَـٰٓئِكَةُ

Whenever He decides to communicate His Guidance to any of His servants, He encounters no difficulty in doing so. Thanks to His Wisdom, He resorts to *waḥy* (revelation). The same idea is repeated in the concluding verses of this *sūrah* and even in clearer terms (see verses 51-52 below).

The unbelievers thought that the Prophet's message consisted of things that were outlandish and bizarre. In response, they are told that that impression is false, for the Prophets who had been raised before the Prophet Muḥammad (peace be on him) had also received similar teachings.

2. These introductory remarks are not simply aimed at glorifying God. Rather, all that has been said here profoundly relates to the background against which these verses were revealed. The primary reason motivating those engaged in a virulent campaign of opposition against the Prophet (peace be on him) and the Qur'ān was that the Prophet was calling people to monotheism. Astounded by this, they vociferously shrieked at the idea that if God alone were the Deity, the Lord, the Provider and the Law-giver, then what was the *locus standi* of their venerated ancestors who worshipped other deities? In this regard they were firmly told that the whole universe belongs to God. Since God is the Lord of the universe, how can there be any other's lordship? This is specially so because those that are accepted as deities or would like to be treated as lords and masters themselves belong to God. It is also stated that God is 'the Most High, the All Great' (verse 4), which implies that none can be His compeer, that none can share with Him His essence, attributes, and rights.

3. It is the height of blasphemy that a created being's lineage be established with God by declaring someone to be His son or daughter. Likewise, it is outrageous to invoke or and address supplications to anyone other than God for the fulfilment of one's needs. No less heinous is the fact that someone – say a saint – be considered to have the power

the praise of their Lord and ask forgiveness for those on earth.[4] Lo, it is Allah, and He alone, Who is Most Forgiving, Most Merciful.[5] (6) Those who have taken others than Him as their protectors beside Him,[6] ▶

يُسَبِّحُونَ بِحَمْدِ رَبِّهِمْ وَيَسْتَغْفِرُونَ لِمَن فِى
ٱلْأَرْضِ ۗ أَلَآ إِنَّ ٱللَّهَ هُوَ ٱلْغَفُورُ ٱلرَّحِيمُ ﴿٥﴾
وَٱلَّذِينَ ٱتَّخَذُوا۟ مِن دُونِهِۦٓ أَوْلِيَآءَ

---

to dispose of the affairs of all people at all places and that he comes to their help and answers their supplications. So is the phenomenon of regarding some people as having the mandate to bid and to forbid, to regard some people as having the authority to declare some things to be lawful and others unlawful, being sure that people will follow their commands in disregard of God as though they were invested with God's authority. These blasphemous acts are so outrageous that there should be no wonder if the sky were to rend apart. (Almost the same point is made in *Sūrah Maryam* 19: 88-91.)

4. Angels are outraged at the blasphemous utterances of earth's rebellious residents. They find it altogether incredible that anyone could be considered to be God's co-sharer in His Godhead and Sovereign authority. They find it beyond comprehension that anyone should sing hymns of and lavish praises on any other than God, the Great Benefactor of all. They are ablaze with the graveness of the offence committed on earth, fearing that it will provoke God's wrath. They, therefore, over and again implore God's mercy for the dwellers of the earth who have forgotten themselves and their God. They pray that they be spared God's punishment and be granted respite to mend their ways.

5. God is Most Forbearing and Most Merciful and is inclined to overlook and indulge those engrossed in unbelief, polytheism, atheism, sin and iniquity. As a result, they are granted respites that extend to years, and in the case of communities, to centuries. During this period they continue to receive sustenance, the acclaims of the world and such resplendent means of worldly adornment that make foolish people think that perhaps no God exists.

6. The word used is *awliyā'* (sing. *walī*) which is a very wide-ranging term in Arabic. Misguided people entertain many notions about and adopt

it is Allah Who oversees them; you are no guardian over them.[7]	ٱللَّهُ حَفِيظٌ عَلَيْهِمْ وَمَآ أَنتَ عَلَيْهِم بِوَكِيلٍ ۝٦

flawed attitudes towards their false deities. The Qur'ān brands these people as those who take others than God as their *awliyā'* or protectors.

A careful study of the Qur'ān yields the following connotations of the term *walī*: (i) He is the one who is generally followed and the ways, rituals and laws prescribed by him are commonly obeyed, (see *al-Nisā'* 4: 118-120 and *al-Ar'āf* 7: 3 and 27–30.) (ii) He is the one on whose guidance others rely, believing that he will direct them to the Straight Way and dissuade them from falsehood (*al-Baqarah* 2: 257; *Banī Isrā'īl* 17: 97; *al-Kahf* 18: 17 and 50 and *al-Jāthiyah* 45: 19). (iii) He is the one whom men take as their protector, irrespective of his deeds, and think that if there is a God and the Hereafter then that person will save them from punishment, (*al-Nisā'* 4: 123 and 173; *al-An'ām* 6: 51; *al-Ra'd* 13: 37; *al-'Ankabūt* 29: 22; *al-Aḥzāb* 33: 65 and *al-Zumar* 39: 3.) (iv) He is the one who is considered to help men in a supernatural manner, defending them against calamities, granting them livelihood, blessing them with children, and meeting their needs, (*Hūd*: 11: 20; *al-Ra'd* 13: 16 and *al-'Ankabūt* 29: 41.) At places the Qur'ān employs *walī* in one of the above meanings and at some places all the above-mentioned meanings are intended. In the verse under study all the above connotations of the term are implied; that is, reference is to the unbelievers who take others besides God as their patron and guardian.

7. 'God oversees them' means that He watches all of men's deeds and is preparing the scroll of their deeds and that it is for Him to call them to account. The Prophet (peace be on him) is not charged with taking the unbelievers to task. That the Prophet (peace be on him) is not a 'guardian over them' means that the fate of the unbelievers has not been left in the hands of the Prophet (peace be on him). He cannot just turn them into ashes, nor he could overthrow the dominance of those who do not accept his message, nor he could annihilate them. This, of course, does not at all imply that the Prophet (peace be on him) ever entertained such notions and what is said here is to remove such misperceptions.

Although the verse is addressed to the Prophet (peace be on him), its objective is to inform the unbelievers that the Prophet (peace be on him) makes no tall claims of the kind spouted by claimants of spiritual holiness and godliness in their own ranks. Such false beliefs are quite common in societies steeped in *Jāhilīyah* where their 'holinesses' are considered to have the power to instantly ruin the destiny of whosoever shows any

(7) And thus did We reveal this Arabic Qur'ān to you[8] that you may warn the people of the Mother of Cities (to wit, Makkah) and those who dwell around it;[9] and warn them of the Day of Gathering[10] concerning which there is no doubt: ▶

وَكَذَٰلِكَ أَوۡحَيۡنَآ إِلَيۡكَ قُرۡءَانًا عَرَبِيّٗا لِّتُنذِرَ أُمَّ ٱلۡقُرَىٰ وَمَنۡ حَوۡلَهَا وَتُنذِرَ يَوۡمَ ٱلۡجَمۡعِ لَا رَيۡبَ فِيهِۚ

disrespect to them. In fact, they are considered to have such power that even if someone were to show any lack of respect to their graves, or if there are any in whose mind a negative idea about them makes inroad, these divines are apt to destroy them. Baseless stories are spread by these holy persons themselves. As for the truly pious who do not lay any such claim, their names and their skeletal remains are used as capital by some of these worldly wise who circulate such stories. The public perception about a saintly figure, therefore, is that, being close to God, he can harm or benefit people. The Qur'ān strikes a blow at this false notion, telling the Prophet (peace be on him) that even though he has been blessed with Divine Revelation, the task assigned to him was no more than to direct mankind to the Straight Way. It is only God Who decides what man's fate is. Again, it is God's prerogative – and His alone – to punish or spare people in view of their deeds.

8. What was said at the outset is repeated here with greater force. The addressees are told that the Qur'ān is in their own tongue. They can directly approach it. On reflection they will realise that only the Lord of the universe can provide such perfect guidance.

9. The Prophet (peace be on him) is directed to warn those immersed in heedlessness. They should be told plainly and warned that their errors of thought and belief and the moral corruptions which have overtaken them and the flawed principles upon which their individual and national lives are operating, all are bound to lead to their perdition.

10. The Prophet (peace be on him) was also asked to impress on the unbelievers that their loss will not be confined to this-worldly life. What is more, they will soon be confronted with the Day of Judgement when

whereon some will be in Paradise, and some in the Blazing Fire.

(8) If Allah had so willed, He could have made them all a single community. But He admits whomsoever He pleases into His Mercy. As to those given to wrong-doing, they shall have none as protector or helper.[11] (9) (Are they so foolish that) they have chosen others rather than Allah as their protectors? Yet it is Allah Who is the Protector and Who resurrects the dead ▶

فَرِيقٌ فِى ٱلْجَنَّةِ وَفَرِيقٌ فِى ٱلسَّعِيرِ ۝٧ وَلَوْ
شَآءَ ٱللَّهُ لَجَعَلَهُمْ أُمَّةً وَٰحِدَةً وَلَٰكِن
يُدْخِلُ مَن يَشَآءُ فِى رَحْمَتِهِۦ ۚ وَٱلظَّٰلِمُونَ
مَا لَهُم مِّن وَلِىٍّ وَلَا نَصِيرٍ ۝٨ أَمِ ٱتَّخَذُوا۟
مِن دُونِهِۦٓ أَوْلِيَآءَ ۖ فَٱللَّهُ هُوَ ٱلْوَلِىُّ وَهُوَ
يُحْىِ ٱلْمَوْتَىٰ

God will gather together everyone and call them to account. If one failed to receive punishment in this world for one's misdeeds and errors, one cannot escape punishment in the Hereafter. Anyone who suffers in both this world and the Hereafter will indeed be an ill-fated person.

11. This point is made in the present context for the following three considerations:

(1) It aims at comforting and consoling the Prophet (peace be on him). He is directed not to grieve over the ignorance and error of the unbelievers. It is part of God's dispensation that man should exercise free will and choose between guidance and error. Had it not been a part of God's plan, there would have been no need to reveal Books and raise Messengers. With a single command God could direct everyone to follow the Straight Way and all mankind would have obeyed Him unquestioningly in the way rivers, mountains, trees, the earth, stones and animals do. (This truth is also enunciated in *al-An'ām* 6, nn. 23-5 and 71, *Towards Understanding the Qur'ān*, vol. II, pp. 228-9 and 262-3.)

(2) The verse is addressed to all those people who had mental reservations that if God indeed sought to guide mankind, there was hardly any need for revelation and Messengers. He could easily accomplish the same by creating everyone as a true believer. Another corollary of the same delusion was that since God has not done this, it means that He approves the different paths pursued by men. It is rather part of His will and hence the Prophet (peace be on him) should not object to it. The above misperception has been removed at several places in the Qur'ān. (Illustrative of this are the following passages: *al-An'ām* 6, nn. 80, 110 and 124-5, *Towards Understanding the Qur'ān*, vol. II, pp. 266-7, 280 and 288-9; *Yūnus* 10, n. 101, vol. IV, p. 68; *Hūd* 11, n. 116, vol. IV, pp. 140-1; and *al-Naḥl* 16, nn. 10 and 30-2, vol. IV, pp. 327-28.)

(3) The purpose of the verse is to explain to the believers that they will confront hardships and obstructions in the cause of faith. Some people fail to grasp the true nature of the free will granted by God and it is precisely as a result of this free will that men act differently. Again, there are some who are demoralised by the slow success and progress of faith. They look for miracles which could instantly change people's hearts. At times, some well-intentioned people tend to be over-zealous in serving the cause of their faith, thereby adopting injudicious means to effect reform. The Qur'ān also takes up this point elsewhere, (see *al-Ra'd* 13: 31 and *al-Naḥl* 16: 91-95.)

It is for the above considerations that the passage under discussion brings out these truths quite succinctly. It is asserted that God's vicegerency and admission to Paradise are not ordinary favours which may be bestowed upon every Tom, Dick and Harry. Rather, these represent the highest degree of felicity, for which even angels were not considered worthy. God has created man as a species with free will and has placed the vast resources of the earth at his disposal so that he may successfully pass the test to which he has been put, the test that will entitle him to enjoy God's mercy. No one can lay any special claim to His mercy. He showers it upon whom He wills. Nor can anyone force God to grant it. Only those who surrender themselves wholly to Him, who take Him as their only patron and repose all trust in Him, are helped and supported and enabled by God to pass the test and receive His mercy. However, the wrong-doers who turn away from Him and take others besides Him as their patrons are not succoured by Him. In any case, others do not have any knowledge, power or authority to act as man's patron.

and Who has power over everything.[12] (10) The judgement[13] on whatever you differ rests with Allah.[14] Such is Allah, ▸	وَهُوَ عَلَىٰ كُلِّ شَيْءٍ قَدِيرٌ ۝ وَمَا ٱخْتَلَفْتُمْ فِيهِ مِن شَيْءٍ فَحُكْمُهُۥٓ إِلَى ٱللَّهِ ۚ ذَٰلِكُمُ ٱللَّهُ

12. Patronship is not a matter of intuitive choice. Man cannot just take anyone or any thing as patron insofar as the latter cannot fulfil the expectations and act effectively as a patron. A true patron alone can help and assist mankind whereas others cannot render such service. As to the contention that God alone is the true Patron, one may appreciate this point with reference to the fact that God alone exercises control over man's life and death. It is He Who invests lifeless material with life. It is He alone Who can best discharge the role of a patron. It would be tantamount to ignorance, foolishness and self-destruction if someone were to take others as patrons besides God.

13. The whole paragraph from here to the end of verse 12 is a revelation from God, but the address is from the Prophet (peace be on him) rather than God. Through these words the Prophet (peace be on him) is directed to make this declaration on God's behalf. At times the Qur'ān specifically instructs the Prophet (peace be on him) to proclaim something while at other places it is implied and one learns about it from the context. In certain instances, while the discourse is God's it is expressed through the believers. *Sūrah al-Fātiḥah* best illustrates this. In other instances, such as *Maryam* 19: 64-65, those who articulate the discourse are angels.

14. This is a natural corollary of the fact that the universe is entirely God's and that He is also Sovereign and Lord for settling mutual differences among mankind here on earth. Those who think that this will happen only in the Hereafter are mistaken. For there is no evidence to establish the above proposition. Nor is God's role limited only to settling theological matters and questions of faith. The Qur'ānic declaration is general and categorical that judgement on disagreements between men rests with God. He is the King of the Day of Judgement as well as the Best of Judges in this world. He decides what represents truth in any dispute in matters of belief. Likewise, in legislative matters, His Word is final and clearly states what is good for man. He declares what is lawful and what

my Lord;[15] in Him I have put all my trust and to Him I always turn in devotion.[16] ▶	رَبِّي عَلَيْهِ تَوَكَّلْتُ وَإِلَيْهِ أُنِيبُ ﴿١٠﴾

is unlawful, what is desirable and what is undesirable, what is virtue and what is vice, what is good conduct and what is bad, and what are men's mutual rights and obligations. Again, it is He Who decides what is good and bad for man's social, cultural, political and economic life. The Qur'ān lays down the following laws in this context: 'If you were to dispute among yourselves about anything, refer it to God and the Messenger,' (*al-Nisā'* 4: 59). 'It does not behove a believer, male or female, that when God and His Messenger have decided an affair, they should exercise their choice,' (*al-Aḥzāb* 33: 36) and '(O people), follow what has been revealed to you from your Lord and follow no masters other than Him,' (*al-A'rāf* 7: 3).

The context of the verse points to another implicit meaning. It is not only God's legal right to settle mutual differences among men but, for all practical purposes, He distinguishes between truth and falsehood. As a result, those given to falsehood eventually meet their doom while the devotees of truth are elevated to great heights. People may feel that a Divine decision on such issues takes a very long time. However, the judgement is wholly God's. (This point reappears in verse 24 of this *sūrah*. It also features in the following verses: *al-Ra'd* 13: 17 and 40-41; *Ibrāhīm* 14: 18 and 23-27; *Banī Isrā'īl* 17: 86 and *al-Anbiyā'* 21: 18 and 44).

15. That God has the real authority to resolve disputes among people.

16. Here two acts are mentioned, one in the past tense and the other in the imperfect verbal form which conveys the sense of continuity. First, it is stated as follows in the past tense: '...in Him I have put all my trust'. This indicates that the believer decided that as long as he lives he will rely on God's assistance, God's guidance and God's protection and support and that he will depend on God's decision alone. This is followed by a statement in imperfect verb 'to Him I always turn in devotion.' What this implies is that the believer turns to God in whatever problems confront him in his life. When faced with any affliction, adversity or difficult problem he looks to none else but God from Whom He seeks assistance. When faced with a danger, it is God's refuge that he seeks, placing reliance on His protection. When faced with any problem that calls for solution he tries to find its solution in the Guidance that God has made available.

(11) The Originator of the heavens and the earth, He has appointed for you pairs of your own kind, and pairs also of cattle. Thus does He multiply you. Naught in the universe is like Him.[17] He is All-Hearing, All-Seeing.[18] (12) His are the keys of the heavens and the earth. He enlarges and straitens the sustenance of whomsoever He pleases. Surely He has knowledge of everything.[19]

فَاطِرُ ٱلسَّمَٰوَٰتِ وَٱلْأَرْضِ ۚ جَعَلَ لَكُم
مِّنْ أَنفُسِكُمْ أَزْوَٰجًا وَمِنَ ٱلْأَنْعَٰمِ
أَزْوَٰجًا ۖ يَذْرَؤُكُمْ فِيهِ ۚ لَيْسَ كَمِثْلِهِۦ شَىْءٌ ۖ وَهُوَ
ٱلسَّمِيعُ ٱلْبَصِيرُ ﴿١١﴾ لَهُۥ مَقَالِيدُ ٱلسَّمَٰوَٰتِ
وَٱلْأَرْضِ ۖ يَبْسُطُ ٱلرِّزْقَ لِمَن يَشَآءُ وَيَقْدِرُ ۚ
إِنَّهُۥ بِكُلِّ شَىْءٍ عَلِيمٌ ﴿١٢﴾

Also, if there is dispute with anyone, he looks up to God for its final resolution, fully trusting that His judgement will be right.

17. The actual words are لَيْسَ كَمِثْلِهِ شَيْءٌ ('naught in the universe is like Him'). There is nothing like God. Some Qur'ānic commentators and grammarians say that according to Arabic usage, the addition of *ka* before the word *mithl* is for idiomatic purposes and is aimed at giving force to the statement. This is a common practice in Arabic. For example, a poet employs it thus: وَقَتْلَى كَمِثْلِ جذُوعِ النَّخِيْلِ (They were dead like tracks of palm-dates), while another poet says: مَا إِنْ كَمِثْلِهِمِ فِي النَّاسِ مِنْ أَحَدٍ (There is none like them among people, not even one). (Ṭabarī, *Tafsīr*, comments on *Sūrah al-Shūrā* 42: 11.) Some others highlight the emphatic tone of the statement: what is here asserted is that it is simply out of the question that there will be any like God Himself. (Ṭabarī, *Tafsīr*, comments on *Sūrah al-Shūrā* 42: 11). If we were to accept for argument's sake that there was any that bore likeness to Him, nobody will be even similar to the one who bears likeness to God, let alone that he be like God Himself.

18. God listens to everyone and watches everything all the time.

19. These arguments vindicate that God alone is to be taken as the real patron and one should repose all trust only in Him. (For further details

(13) He has prescribed for you the religion which He enjoined upon Noah and which We revealed to you (O Muḥammad), and which We enjoined upon Abraham and Moses and Jesus, commanding: 'Establish this religion and do not split up regarding it.'[20] ▶

۞ شَرَعَ لَكُم مِّنَ ٱلدِّينِ مَا وَصَّىٰ بِهِۦ
نُوحًا وَٱلَّذِىٓ أَوْحَيْنَآ إِلَيْكَ وَمَا وَصَّيْنَا
بِهِۦٓ إِبْرَٰهِيمَ وَمُوسَىٰ وَعِيسَىٰٓ ۖ أَنْ أَقِيمُوا۟
ٱلدِّينَ وَلَا تَتَفَرَّقُوا۟ فِيهِ ۚ

---

see also, *al-Naml* 27, nn. 73-83, *Towards Understanding the Qur'ān*, vol. VII, pp. 171-9 and *al-Rūm* 30, nn. 25-31, vol. VIII, pp. 88-92.)

20. Here the statement that was made in passing earlier (see verse 3 above) is being elaborated. It is stated that the Prophet Muḥammad (peace be on him) is not the founder of any new religion. No Prophet ever laid the foundation of a new faith. Rather, each of them expounded the same faith on God's behalf. At the present, the same is being done by the Prophet Muḥammad (peace be on him).

In this context, mention is first made of the Prophet Noah (peace be on him), the first Messenger for the human race after the Flood. This is followed by mention of the Prophet Abraham (peace be on him), whom the Arabs looked upon as their patriarch. Next, reference is made to the Prophets Moses and Jesus (peace be on them), with whom Jews and Christians respectively associate themselves. In this verse a pointed reference is made to five Messengers. This does not mean that only those five were directed to preach the true faith. What is brought home is that all Prophets represent the same faith. To illustrate the point five outstanding Messengers have been mentioned by name.

It is through them that humanity received the best known codes of Divine Law. Since this verse throws ample light on faith and its objective, it should be grasped fully.

The Qur'ān here declares that 'He has prescribed for you [the religion] which He enjoined upon Noah...' The verb used is a derivative of *sharī'ah* which means to pave a way. As a term it stands for a way of life, a code of conduct and a set of laws. It is closely associated with legislation. This law making on God's part is the logical outcome of the fundamental truths enunciated in verses 9 and 10 above. According to them, God is the Lord of everything in the universe and the true Guardian of mankind and it is for Him to settle the differences found among men. Again, it is for Him to lay down a code of life for them.

The expression used here is مِنَ الدِّيْنِ, which Shāh Walī Allāh interprets as 'ordained for you as *ā'īn* (constitution)'. God's religion thus stands out as the constitution for all mankind. On studying this in conjunction with our definition of *dīn* (see *Sūrah al-Zumar* 39, n. 3 above), one may readily understand that faith signifies one's surrender and obedience to the laws of the One whom one looks upon as one's Sovereign. Used in the sense of a way, it stands for the way which one is obligated to follow. The verse, thus, declares that God's laws are to be obeyed by men. So what the Qur'ān presents as religion is not a set of recommendations or sermons or exhortations. Rather, it is God's law for His servants. Anyone who does not abide by it commits a rebellion against God and indulges in rejection of God's Lordship and of man's subservience to Him.

It is also pointed out that the same law and guidance that were conferred upon the Prophets Noah, Abraham and Moses (peace be on them) are now bestowed upon the Prophet Muḥammad (peace be on him). Implicit in it are the following points: (i) Rather than send His law from time to time to each and every individual directly, whenever God deems it necessary He appoints someone as His Messenger and entrusts him with the task of conveying His Law to people. (ii) This legislation has been identical all along because God did not prescribe several faiths; instead, He prescribed a single faith from the very beginning. (iii) It is an essential part of man's faith that besides accepting God's Sovereignty and Lordship he should also believe in His Messengers through whom the Law has been communicated, and to believe in Revelation of which the Law is an integral part. Reason and logic too require the same for man will be inclined to abide by that Law alone which he believes to be authentically from God.

This is followed by the observation that the Prophets were endowed with Law based on religious faith with the emphatic directive أَنْ أَقِيمُوا الدِّيْنَ. 'And establish this religion.' Shāh Walī Allāh has translated it as we have done. Shāh Rafī' al-Dīn and Shāh 'Abd al-Qādir have translated it as: 'And maintain the religion [by keeping it operative].' Both translators are correct for *iqāmāt al-dīn* means both: to establish religion and maintain it in that state. As for the Prophets, they are required to look after both tasks. Their first task is to establish the true religion whenever it was not in an established state and to maintain it in that state after it has been established. It is obvious that something can be maintained only after it has been established, or else effort has to be made first to establish it. Once this has been achieved, every effort will be needed to ensure that it will continue to be operative.

Here, however, we are faced with two questions: (i) What is meant by establishing faith? (ii) What is meant by faith which is to be established and maintained? It is easy to grasp the idea of establishing or putting in place a physical or material object. However, when the same directive is related to something abstract, it signifies its implementation, the bringing of it in vogue and enforcing it. For example, when we say that someone established his rule, it does not mean that he merely called people to accept his rule. Rather, it means that he made the people of that land subservient to his rule; he organised all affairs of the land in a way that only his command would reign supreme. By the same token, when we talk about the establishment of a legal system, it means that judges and courts are put in place and are engaged in the dispensation of justice. It does not refer to a mere discourse on that legal system on which praise is theoretically heaped in order to convince people of its excellence. Likewise, when the Qur'ān bids that Prayer be established, this is not confined only to calling people to Prayer. Rather, it signifies that one should not only offer Prayers while fulfilling all of its conditions, but should also devise a system which promotes the observance of regular Prayers among the believers. There should be mosques, arrangements for congregational Prayers, including Friday Prayer, and *adhān* at the appointed hours. Imāms and preachers should be appointed and all this should make people habituated to going to mosques on time for Prayers.

In the light of the above explanation, it should not be hard to understand that when the Prophets were asked to establish and maintain faith, their obligation was not confined to their personal lives. Nor was their role restricted only to preaching in order to convince people of the truth of Prayers. On the contrary, the purpose behind His command was that the believers should follow the faith in their lives as a whole and this should go on perpetually. Preaching is, no doubt, an initial but essential stage without which the next stage cannot be reached. Yet it is evident that preaching is not an end in itself. The goal is the establishment and maintenance of faith, of which preaching is only a means. Preaching cannot be regarded as the only objective of the Prophets' mission.

Let us now turn to the other question: what is meant by faith? It was noted that faith has been common to all the Prophets. On the other hand, their *sharī'ahs* vary from one another. As stated in the Qur'ān itself: 'For each of you We have appointed a Law and a way of life' (*al-Mā'idah* 5: 48.) Some people have, however, misconstrued the faith prescribed by God to be confined only to belief in monotheism, the Hereafter, the Scriptures and Messengership, without any regard for implementing the *sharī'ah* laws. At most, they include in faith some broad moral principles which permeate all *sharī'ahs*. This is a very superficial view of faith which is premised on a superficial view of the unity of all faiths and the diversity of *sharī'ahs*.

If this misconception is not removed, it might culminate into divorcing the *sharī'ah* from faith or repeating the mistake committed earlier by St. Paul in expounding the concept of a faith divorced from law. His mistake misled the Christian community. For it led them to believe that *sharī'ah* and faith are two separate entities and that believers are obliged only to embrace faith and have nothing to do with the *sharī'ah*. If this notion is accepted by Muslims, as it was done by Christians, they too will disregard the *sharī'ah* and will simply abide by the articles of faith and some broad moral principles.

Instead of making such speculations on the theoretical plane of Islam about faith and its requisites, let us turn to the Qur'ān itself to find out whether it is concerned only with articles of faith and some broad moral principles or whether it is concerned with the commands of the *sharī'ah* as well. The Qur'ān speaks of the following as constituents of faith:

(1) 'Yet all that they had been commanded was that they serve God with utter sincerity, devoting themselves exclusively to Him, and that they establish Prayer and pay *Zakāh*. That is the Right Faith,' (*al-Bayyinah* 98: 5.)

It is clear from the above that Prayer and *Zakāh* are ineluctable parts of faith, though their forms and commands have varied in several *sharī'ahs*. For it is nobody's contention that all the earlier *sharī'ahs* too prescribed the same forms, postures, components, *rak'ahs*, direction, timing and other rules of Prayer as laid down by Islam. Nor can it be proved that the same rates of *Zakāh* and its system of distribution obtained before the advent of the Prophet (peace be on him). Notwithstanding the variations in the *sharī'ah*, God reckons these two items – Prayer and *Zakāh* – as essential components of faith.

(2) 'Forbidden to you are carrion, blood, the flesh of swine, the animal slaughtered in any name other than Allah's, the animal which has either been strangled, killed by blows, or has died of fall or by goring or by being devoured by a beast of prey – unless it be that which you yourselves might have slaughtered while it was still alive – and forbidden to you also is that which was slaughtered at the altars. You are also forbidden to seek knowledge of your fate by divining arrows. All these are sinful acts. This day the unbelievers have fully despaired of your religion. Do not fear them; but fear Me. This day I have perfected for you your religion', (*al-Mā'idah* 5: 3.)

(3) 'Fight against those who do not believe in Allah and the Last Day – even though they were given the scriptures, and who do not hold as unlawful that which Allah and His Messenger

have declared to be unlawful, and who do not follow the true religion', (*al-Tawbah* 9: 29.)

(4) 'Those who fornicate – whether female or male – flog each one of them with a hundred lashes. And let not tenderness for them deter you from what pertains to God's religion, if you do truly believe in Allah and the Last Day', (*al-Nūr* 24: 2.)

'He [Prophet Joseph] had no right, according to the *religion of the king* [emphasis added] (i.e. the law of Egypt), to take his brother...' (*Yūsuf* 12: 76).

It emerges from the Prophet Joseph's story that criminal law is a part of faith. If one abides by the criminal law laid down by God, one is to be taken to be a follower of Divine faith. By the same token, if one observes the law of a king, one will be regarded as the devotee of that king. The above passages present the commands of the *sharī'ah* as synonymous with faith. On a little reflection one will note that men's acts which incur punishment in Hellfire relate to the domain of faith, as for example, illicit sex, usury, killing a believer, usurping the belongings of an orphan, devouring someone's possessions while resorting to falsehood, sodomy and committing unfair practices in business and trade, of which the Prophet Shu'ayb's community in particular was guilty. For one of the objectives of faith is to protect man from God's punishment and Hellfire. Moreover, there are many other *sharī'ah* commands which are an intrinsic part of faith. This because their violation entails eternal perdition in Hellfire. For example, the law of inheritance is followed by this dire warning: 'And he who disobeys Allah and His Messenger and transgresses the bounds set by Him – him shall Allah cause to enter the Fire. There he will abide. A humiliating chastisement awaits him', (*al-Nisā'* 4: 14.) The same holds true of some other Divine commands which lay down the unlawfulness of sexual relations with one's mother, sister and daughter and prohibit wine, theft, gambling and false testimony. If these commands are not reckoned as parts of faith, it would imply that they are superfluous and, as such, need not be enforced. By the same token, those commands which God declares as religious duties, for example fasting and *Ḥajj*, cannot be excluded from the establishment of faith. It cannot be argued that fasting is not compulsory as this 30-day fast was not part of the earlier *sharī'ahs* or that Pilgrimage to the Ka'bah was incumbent only on the progeny of Ishmael.

One, thus, realises that the *sharī'ah* is a constituent of faith and establishing faith involves the enforcement of the *sharī'ah* as a whole. That God has prescribed the *sharī'ah* for each community should not give rise to the misperception that since a *sharī'ah* was meant for each community, and the directive was to establish that particular faith, the command for establishing faith does not include the instruction to enforce the *sharī'ah*.

A study of this verse in its broader context makes one realise that the *sharī'ah* prescribed by God for each community represents the faith for that community and it was obligatory for the respective Prophets to establish it. While functioning as a Prophet, Muḥammad (peace be on him) was granted the *sharī'ah* which stands out as the Divine faith and its enforcement is synonymous with establishing faith. As to the differences in the *sharī'ah*s prescribed for different communities, this does not imply that these were at variance with one another. Instead, local colour and condition accounted for some minor differences. Take Prayers and fasting, which are parts of faith, offering them in a particular form or at the appointed days is not part of the same assignment. It will be rather correct to hold that every Messenger and his community were obliged to offer Prayers and fasting in the particular mode in which they were directed to perform them and it was a part of their duty to establish faith. Now, the duty of establishing faith involves that fasting and Prayer be observed in the manner prescribed by the Islamic *Sharī'ah*. The same holds true for other *sharī'ah* commands as well.

On studying the Qur'ān carefully it clearly emerges that the Qur'ān does not envision that believers will lead their lives in subservience to unbelievers and to an unbelieving order. Rather, the Qur'ān seeks to establish an order of its own liking, urging believers to exert themselves in making the true faith prevail in ideological, moral, cultural, legal and political spheres. It entrusts them with a programme of reform in human life much of which can become operational only if believers hold the reins of power and authority. Significantly, the purpose of sending down the Qur'ān is: '(O Messenger), We have revealed to you this Book with the Truth so that you may judge people in accordance with what Allah has shown you,' (*al-Nisā'* 4: 105.)

The Qur'ānic commands on the collection and distribution of *Zakāh* presuppose the existence of the state that will implement these commands by collecting and distributing it (*al-Tawbah* 9: 60 and 103.) The Qur'ānic denunciation of usury (*al-Baqarah*, verses 2: 275 and 279) can be put into practice only if the reins of power in a land are in the hands of believers. The Qur'ānic command to charge blood money from those guilty of homicide (*al-Baqarah* 2: 178), to amputate the hand of those guilty of theft (*al-Mā'idah* 5: 38), to award the punishments laid down by the *sharī'ah* for illicit sex and *qadhf* (*al-Nūr* 24: 2 and 4) are obviously not based on the assumption that believers will enforce these commands as the functionaries of an unbelieving state and as subjects of the unbelievers' rule. Nor has the Qur'ānic command to fight against unbelievers (*al-Baqhrah* 2: 90-216) been issued on the assumption that they will fight unbelievers as soldiers of an unbelieving state's army. Likewise, the command for levying *jizyah* on and assuming protection of the People of the Book (*al-Tawbah* 9: 29) is not premised on the proposition that Muslims will do so as subjects of unbelievers. These commands are not confined to the Madīnan *sūrahs*. One can discern even in Makkan *sūrahs* a blueprint for the dominance of faith rather than of unbelief, or of Muslims living as *dhimmīs*. (For further details see *Banī Isrā'īl* 17, nn. 89, 99 and 101, *Towards Understanding the Qur'ān*, vol. VI, pp. 62-3, 67-8; *al-Qaṣaṣ* 28: 104-5; *al-Rūm* 30, nn. 1-3, vol. VIII, pp. 73-5; *al-Ṣāffāt* 37, nn. 93-4, vol. IX, pp. 324-32; Introduction to *Sūrah Ṣād* (*Sūrah* 38 and n. 12 above.)

What illustrates the above point best is the Prophet's own conduct spanning over 23 years. It is common knowledge that he brought Arabia under his control both by preaching and the sword. He also established a state which was run according to detailed *sharī'ah* norms. The *sharī'ah* embraced every aspect of life, from articles of belief to acts of worship, personal conduct, collective morality, culture and civilisation, society, economy, politics, law, and war and peace.

By so doing, the Prophet (peace be on him) was following the same directive of establishing faith which was also given to all other Prophets. If this proposition is not accepted, its logical implication would be to believe that while the Prophet's mandate was limited only to preaching articles of faith and some broad moral principles, he exceeded his mandated limits and set up a state, with elaborate laws, which were either at variance with the common denominator of the *sharī'ahs* granted to earlier Prophets or were an addition to them. Alternatively, it amounts to charging God with having deviated from His categorically stated position in this *sūrah* (see verse 13), asking His Final Messenger to accomplish things over and above what is implied by establishing faith. Furthermore, in contravention of His earlier decree, He issued another proclamation as well, declaring: 'Today I have completed for you your religion', (*al-Mā'idah* 5: 3). May God protect us from such pernicious thoughts. Can there be any other interpretation of 'establishing faith' than the two mentioned by us, an interpretation that retains the concept of 'establishing faith' and precludes God and His Last Prophet from the allegations mentioned above?

The directive to establish faith is followed by another directive: that believers should not fall prey to dissensions in faith. What dissension in faith actually means is innovation in faith, which is undesirable. If one insists that faith is contingent upon following an innovation for which there is no justification, thus causing a schism between those who accept the innovation and those who don't. This innovation can have a variety of forms. It might consist of adding to *dīn* something extraneous

What you are calling to is very hard upon those who associate others with Allah in His Divinity. Allah chooses for Himself whomsoever He pleases and guides to Himself whoever penitently turns to Him.[21]	كَبُرَ عَلَى ٱلْمُشْرِكِينَ مَا تَدْعُوهُمْ إِلَيْهِ ٱللَّهُ يَجْتَبِيٓ إِلَيْهِ مَن يَشَآءُ وَيَهْدِيٓ إِلَيْهِ مَن يُنِيبُ ﴿١٣﴾

to it. It may consist of interpolating into faith what did not exist in the original faith. Or it may consist of deleting something that was part of the original faith. Or the fundamentals of faith may be twisted to invent a new set of beliefs and rites. Or it may represent a sheer distortion of faith by relegating the basics of faith to its margins or by exalting what was at most desirable to the level of an obligation, rather quintessential, in the communities of earlier Prophets. Gradually, these sects turned into separate religions, so distinct from one another that their adherents fail to notice any common ground between them. These dissensions are totally different from the perfectly legitimate and genuine differences of opinion found among *'ulamā'* in their efforts to elaborate and decode religious commands and to derive their inferences. Their differences are within the limits sanctioned by the syntax, grammar and usage of the Qur'ānic text. (For a detailed discussion on this topic, see *al-Baqarah* 2, n. 230, *Towards Understanding the Qur'ān*, vol. I, pp. 165-6; *Āl 'Imrān* 3, nn. 16-17, vol. I, p. 242; *al-Nisā'* 4, nn. 211-16, vol. II, pp. 116-17; *al-Mā'idah* 5, n. 101, vol. II, pp. 181-5; *al-An'ām* 6, n. 141, vol. II, pp. 297-8; *al-Naḥl* 16, nn. 117-21, vol. IV, pp. 372-5; *al-Anbiyā'* 21: 92-7; *al-Ḥajj* 22, nn. 114-17, vol. VI, pp. 64-5; *al-Mu'minūn* 23, nn. 43-5, vol. VI, pp. 102-4; *al-Qaṣaṣ* 28, nn. 72-4, vol. VII, pp. 228-32; and *al-Rūm* 30, nn. 50-1, vol. VIII, pp. 101-3.)

21. This reiterates the truth stated in verses 8-9 of this *sūrah*, one which we have explained in n. 11. Although the Prophet (peace be on him) expounds before the unbelievers the Straight Way of faith, they resent it. Yet there are some members of the same community who turn to God and He guides them. It is open to everyone to choose guidance or error. However, God makes only the pious incline towards faith. Those who shun faith are not compelled by God to embrace it.

(14) They did not split up except after knowledge had come to them,[22] and then only because they wished to commit excesses against each other.[23] Had your Lord not already decreed that judgement would be made later at an appointed time, the matter between them would surely have been decided once and for all.[24] Indeed those who were later made the heirs of the Book ▶

وَمَا تَفَرَّقُوٓاْ إِلَّا مِنۢ بَعۡدِ مَا جَآءَهُمُ ٱلۡعِلۡمُ
بَغۡيَۢا بَيۡنَهُمۡۚ وَلَوۡلَا كَلِمَةٞ سَبَقَتۡ مِن رَّبِّكَ
إِلَىٰٓ أَجَلٖ مُّسَمّٗى لَّقُضِيَ بَيۡنَهُمۡۚ وَإِنَّ ٱلَّذِينَ
أُورِثُواْ ٱلۡكِتَٰبَ

22. These differences arose after God had endowed people with knowledge. They are responsible for the dissensions insofar as they deviated from clear and explicit commands of the *sharī'ah* and invented false practices which led to the emergence of various sects.

23. They were not prompted by any good intention in sowing seeds of dissension. Their motives were to exhibit innovativeness, to do something novel and different from others and to amass wealth. The ambitious realised that as long as people obey the One True God and one Messenger and follow one Scripture and one way of life, they themselves will not be able to achieve any personal glory. They will fail to rally others around their holy personages. Nor will they be able to duly fleece them. Prompted by this realisation, they opted for innovating beliefs, philosophies, and ways of life and rituals and outlooks on life. It misled many into following false paths, and to driving them away from the Straight Way. Their polemics culminated in bitter conflicts which were aggravated by political and economic clashes. All of this ultimately resulted in violence and bloodshed which besmirched the annals of human history.

24. God has the power to decimate those who had concocted false doctrines to misguide people. However, He has deferred His final decision until the Day of Judgement. For, if the matter had been decided in the world, the test to which man has been put would be rendered meaningless.

are in disquieting doubt about it.[25]

(15) (This being so, O Muḥammad), call people to the same religion and be steadfast about it as you were commanded, and do not follow their desires,[26] and say (to them): ▶

مِنۢ بَعۡدِهِمۡ لَفِي شَكّٖ مِّنۡهُ مُرِيبٖ ﴿١٤﴾ فَلِذَٰلِكَ
فَٱدۡعُۖ وَٱسۡتَقِمۡ كَمَآ أُمِرۡتَۖ وَلَا تَتَّبِعۡ
أَهۡوَآءَهُمۡۖ وَقُلۡ

25. After a Prophet died and his immediate followers faded out, that Prophet's community often exhibited uncertainty about the authenticity and purity of their Scripture. They could not claim with full strength of conviction that their scripture had remained safe from corruption. This holds true of the Torah and the Gospel. These Scriptures were not faithfully transmitted to the subsequent generations in their pristine forms. God's Word was mingled with man's such as what one finds in exegetical comments, historical narratives, verbal traditions and juristic rulings. The translation of the Scripture came in such great vogue that the original scripture was virtually lost from sight; only the translations remained. The sources which transmitted the Scripture were not duly maintained with the result that the scripture lost its historical authority, so that it has become difficult to claim that the text that people have in their hands is the one that truly goes back to Moses or Jesus (peace be on them). Moreover, the clergy had from time to time introduced complex and confounding theories pertaining to theology and metaphysics, philosophy and law, physics, psychology and social life which enmeshed people's attention, causing them to lose track of the Straight Way of truth. Since God's Word was not available in its original form, people could not draw upon an infallible source which could enable them to distinguish truth from falsehood.

26. The Prophet (peace be on him) is directed here not to make any compromise in matters of faith in order to placate the unbelievers. Islam has no room for their superstitions and prejudices. The Prophet (peace be on him) is asked not to try to win them over by pandering to their errors. Those inclined to embrace faith should accept the unadulterated faith as revealed by God. Otherwise, those keen on stumbling into Hellfire are free to choose that path. Divine faith cannot be tailored to the whims and

'I believe in the Book Allah has sent down.[27] I have been commanded to establish justice among you.[28] Allah is our Lord and your Lord. We have our deeds and you have your deeds.[29] ▶

ءَامَنتُ بِمَآ أَنزَلَ ٱللَّهُ مِن كِتَٰبٍ ۖ وَأُمِرْتُ
لِأَعْدِلَ بَيْنَكُمُ ۖ ٱللَّهُ رَبُّنَا وَرَبُّكُمْ ۖ لَنَآ أَعْمَٰلُنَا
وَلَكُمْ أَعْمَٰلُكُمْ ۖ

fancies of people. If they want success and felicity, they should change themselves in accordance with the dictates of faith.

27. A true believer recognises that all of God's Books are true. He does not treat them differently, believing in a part of it and rejecting its other parts. As for the Prophet Muḥammad (peace be on him), he affirms that all the Books revealed by God are equally truthful.

28. This pervasive statement covers several meanings: (i) The Prophet (peace be on him) is required to act with perfect justice. He therefore, cannot be swayed by any bias be it for or against any particular group of people. For him, all people are equal and he is required to treat them alike. He supports only truth, even if it be with those quite alien to him. By the same token, he is opposed to falsehood and error, irrespective of who commits it, even if they be his own kith and kin. (ii) The truth preached by him has a universal import and is applicable to all whether rich or poor, noble or commoner, friend or foe. The same standards of truth and falsehood apply to all. The lawful and the unlawful are likewise binding on one and all. These laws make no allowance even for the Prophet (peace be on him). (iii) The Prophet's assignment consists in establishing justice. It is his responsibility to extirpate the imbalance and injustice found in the lives of people and in their society. (iv) This also had a fourth meaning which became evident after the *Hijrah* to Madīnah. This consisted of affirming that the Prophet (peace be on him) was the *qāḍī* appointed by God to dispense justice.

29. Everyone is responsible for his deeds. The reward due to a pious person cannot reach a wicked person. By the same token, a pious person will not be punished for the misdeeds of a sinner. Everyone is accountable for his own deeds. The same truth features in *al-Baqarah* 2: 139; *Yūnus* 10: 41; *Hūd* 11: 35 and *al-Qaṣaṣ* 28: 55.

There is no contention between us and you.[30] Allah will bring us all together. To Him all are destined to return.'

(16) Those who contend concerning Allah (after His call has been responded to),[31] their contention is absolutely void in the sight of their Lord. Allah's wrath is upon them and a grievous chastisement awaits them.

(17) Allah it is Who sent down this Book with the Truth and the Balance.[32] And what would make you know that the Hour (of Judgement) ▸

لَا حُجَّةَ بَيْنَنَا وَبَيْنَكُمُ ۖ ٱللَّهُ يَجْمَعُ بَيْنَنَا ۖ وَإِلَيْهِ
ٱلْمَصِيرُ ﴿١٥﴾ وَٱلَّذِينَ يُحَآجُّونَ فِى ٱللَّهِ مِنۢ
بَعْدِ مَا ٱسْتُجِيبَ لَهُۥ حُجَّتُهُمْ دَاحِضَةٌ
عِندَ رَبِّهِمْ وَعَلَيْهِمْ غَضَبٌ وَلَهُمْ عَذَابٌ
شَدِيدٌ ﴿١٦﴾ ٱللَّهُ ٱلَّذِىٓ أَنزَلَ ٱلْكِتَٰبَ
بِٱلْحَقِّ وَٱلْمِيزَانَ ۗ وَمَا يُدْرِيكَ لَعَلَّ ٱلسَّاعَةَ

---

30. The Prophet (peace be on him) preaches truth in a convincing manner. It is pointless quarrelling with him for he was not available for wrangling with those who are out to pick a quarrel.

31. Reference is to the situation which then prevailed in Makkah. As the Makkan unbelievers came to know of someone's acceptance of Islam, they took to persecuting him. As a result, he was under constant pressure from his people everywhere, both at home and outside. He was teased and persecuted in a hundred different ways until he disassociated himself from the Prophet (peace be on him) and reverted to *Jāhilīyah.*

32. 'Balance' here signifies the *sharī'ah* which distinguishes between truth and falsehood, between justice and wrong-doing and between good and bad. The Prophet (peace be on him) is obliged to act with perfect justice. Both the Qur'ān and the *sharī'ah* stand out as a means to give effect to justice.

has drawn near?[33] (18) Those who do not believe in it seek to hasten its coming. But those who believe (in it) hold it in dread and know that the Hour (of Judgement) is bound to come. Lo, those who dispute concerning the coming of the Hour are gone far in error.

(19) Allah is Most Gentle to His servants[34] and grants sustenance to whomsoever He pleases.[35] He is All-Strong, Most Mighty.[36] (20) Whoever seeks the harvest of the Hereafter, ▶

قَرِيبٌ ﴿١٧﴾ يَسْتَعْجِلُ بِهَا ٱلَّذِينَ لَا يُؤْمِنُونَ
بِهَا ۖ وَٱلَّذِينَ ءَامَنُوا۟ مُشْفِقُونَ مِنْهَا وَيَعْلَمُونَ
أَنَّهَا ٱلْحَقُّ ۗ أَلَآ إِنَّ ٱلَّذِينَ يُمَارُونَ فِى
ٱلسَّاعَةِ لَفِى ضَلَـٰلٍۭ بَعِيدٍ ﴿١٨﴾ ٱللَّهُ لَطِيفٌۢ
بِعِبَادِهِۦ يَرْزُقُ مَن يَشَآءُ ۖ وَهُوَ ٱلْقَوِىُّ
ٱلْعَزِيزُ ﴿١٩﴾ مَن كَانَ يُرِيدُ حَرْثَ ٱلْـَٔاخِرَةِ

33. The Makkan unbelievers should mend their ways at the earliest. They should not take the Last Day as a far-off, remote event. For one cannot say with certainty whether one will even survive until the next moment. At any time one could breathe one's last breath.

34. *Laṭīf* suggests that God is full of compassion, affection and favour towards His servants. Furthermore, He caters for all of their needs. It is worth clarifying that the above treatment is not exclusively for believers. His sustenance is showered without distinction upon all, believers and unbelievers alike.

35. God, however, does not grant His favours in equal measure to all individuals, which might seem to be a requirement of His being 'Most Gentle'. Rather, He grants something to one and denies that to others, and also what He grants to them is not of the same measure.

36. God's entire system of bounties is self-subsistent. No one has the power to change it or to extract something for himself or prevent anyone from receiving what God apportions for him.

We shall increase for him his harvest, and whoever seeks the harvest of this world, We shall give him thereof; but he will have no share in the Hereafter.[37]	نَزِدۡ لَهُۥ فِي حَرۡثِهِۦۖ وَمَن كَانَ يُرِيدُ حَرۡثَ ٱلدُّنۡيَا نُؤۡتِهِۦ مِنۡهَا وَمَا لَهُۥ فِي ٱلۡأٓخِرَةِ مِن نَّصِيبٍ ٢٠

37. The preceding verses draw attention to two facts which all of us observe all the time: first, that God's bounties are universal; second, that His system of granting bounties to human beings does not follow a strictly uniform and invariable pattern. As we observe, some are granted more than others. The present verse also conveys another significant point. In the first place, there are numerous differences between the sustenance provided to people. Over and above that, there is also qualitative difference between the sustenance provided to those who seek the Hereafter, which is of one kind, while that provided to those who seek only the good of this world is of another kind.

This is a very important fact which should be fully grasped so as to assist one in determining one's own attitude.

Those who strive for this world or for the Hereafter are likened to a farmer who works hard for a rich harvest. However, there is a world of difference between the intent and objective and general attitude of those who work for the harvest of the Hereafter and those who are concerned only with worldly gains. Accordingly, God has laid down that the result of their efforts will also be different. This despite the fact that the locale of their activity is the same – the world. As regards those who seek the harvest of the Hereafter, it has not been said that they will be denied worldly gains. They are bound to get their share of worldly goods, be it little or substantial. This, because all are God's creatures and are hence entitled to His universal munificence that is shared by those who are good as well as those who are otherwise. God, moreover, gives them the glad tiding of rewards in the Hereafter. They will draw greater reward: 'We shall increase for him his harvest.' The more one works for the Hereafter, the more opportunities one gets for doing good, and in fact, the easier it is to do good. As one resolves to have recourse only to legitimate means to achieve good objectives, one is granted manifold increase in his means. One is not forced to resort to unfair means. Above all, one will be rewarded amply in the Hereafter where God may increase one's reward many fold.

(21) Do they have any associates (of Allah) who have laid down for them a way pertaining to faith which Allah did not sanction?[38] But for the fact that a decree had already been made, the matter between them would have been ▶

أَمْ لَهُمْ شُرَكَٰٓؤُا۟ شَرَعُوا۟ لَهُم مِّنَ ٱلدِّينِ مَا لَمْ يَأْذَنۢ بِهِ ٱللَّهُ ۚ وَلَوْلَا كَلِمَةُ ٱلْفَصْلِ لَقُضِىَ

As for those who are not concerned about the Hereafter and strive only for worldly goods, God announces to them the following: (i) notwithstanding a person's exertion, he cannot get all worldly goods. He will get only a share of those goods apportioned for him by God. (ii) He will receive only in this life what is destined for him, but will not receive anything in the Afterlife.

38. *Shurakā'* does not denote in this context the associate gods whom the polytheists invoked, or those in whose names they made their offerings, or those to whom their rites of worship were devoted. The obvious reference here is to those fellow human beings regarded as associates in God's authority and sovereignty, to those who are generally obeyed, whose views and doctrines are faithfully followed, and whose standards are taken as norms. In religious, social, cultural, economic, legal and political life they are followed as if they constitute the *sharī'ah* which must be observed. This, however, is an alternate code of life, one which has been worked out in opposition to God's *sharī'ah*. In fact this represents a way of life opposed to Divine faith. It is tantamount to the same polytheism that consists in prostrating before someone other than the One True God or invoking anyone besides Him. (For further details see *al-Baqarah* 2: 172 and 256; *Āl 'Imrān* 3, n. 57, *Towards Understanding the Qur'ān,* vol. I, p. 262; *al-Nisā'* 4, n. 90, vol. II, pp. 52-3; *al-Mā'idah* 5, nn. 1-5, vol. II, pp. 126-9 and 188-9; *al-An'ām* 6: 118-21 and 136-7; *al-Tawbah* 9, n. 31, vol. III, p. 204; *Yūnus* 10, nn. 60-1, vol. IV, pp. 44-6; *Ibrāhīm* 14, nn. 30-2, vol. IV, pp. 265-7; *al-Naḥl* 16, nn. 14-16, vol. IV, pp. 371-2; *al-Kahf* 18: 52; *Maryam* 19, nn. 49-50, vol. V, p. 113; *al-Qaṣaṣ* 28, n. 86, vol. VII, pp. 239-40; *Saba'* 34, n. 63, vol. IX, pp. 197-8 and *Yā Sīn* 36, n. 53, vol. IX, pp. 268-9.)

decided once and for all.[39] Surely a grievous chastisement awaits the wrong-doers. (22) You will see the wrong-doers fearful of the consequence of their deeds which will certainly overtake them. But those who have faith and do good deeds will be in the meadows of the Gardens, wherein they shall have whatever they desire from their Lord; that is the great Bounty. (23) That is the Bounty of which Allah gives tidings to His servants who have faith and do good deeds. Tell them, (O Prophet): 'I do not ask you for any recompense for my work[40] except love towards kinsfolk.'[41] ▶

بَيْنَهُمْۗ وَإِنَّ ٱلظَّـٰلِمِينَ لَهُمْ عَذَابٌ أَلِيمٌ ﴿٢١﴾
تَرَى ٱلظَّـٰلِمِينَ مُشْفِقِينَ مِمَّا كَسَبُوا۟
وَهُوَ وَاقِعٌۢ بِهِمْۗ وَٱلَّذِينَ ءَامَنُوا۟ وَعَمِلُوا۟
ٱلصَّـٰلِحَـٰتِ فِى رَوْضَاتِ ٱلْجَنَّاتِۖ
لَهُم مَّا يَشَآءُونَ عِندَ رَبِّهِمْۚ ذَٰلِكَ هُوَ
ٱلْفَضْلُ ٱلْكَبِيرُ ﴿٢٢﴾ ذَٰلِكَ ٱلَّذِى يُبَشِّرُ
ٱللَّهُ عِبَادَهُ ٱلَّذِينَ ءَامَنُوا۟ وَعَمِلُوا۟
ٱلصَّـٰلِحَـٰتِۗ قُل لَّآ أَسْـَٔلُكُمْ عَلَيْهِ
أَجْرًا إِلَّا ٱلْمَوَدَّةَ فِى ٱلْقُرْبَىٰۗ

39. This is tantamount to an act of blasphemy towards God. Had God not preordained that the matter will be resolved on the Day of Judgement, God's scourge would have overtaken everyone who introduces a new religion on His earth. Likewise, those who prefer man-made isms to God's prescribed faith would also have been annihilated.

40. This refers to the Prophet's efforts to protect people from God's punishment and to make them worthy of admission to Paradise.

41. The Prophet (peace be on him) does not seek any worldly reward except 'love towards kinsfolk' (*qurbā*). This word, *qurbā*, has variously been interpreted by the Qur'ānic exegetes. Some consider it to mean ties of kinship. Accordingly, they take the verse to mean that the Prophet (peace be on him) does not seek any recompense for his mission. However, he

wants the Quraysh at least to give due consideration to his ties of kinship. What would have been appropriate for them was to accept the Prophet's call and join hands with him. However, the irony is that the Quraysh are more hostile to his mission than the rest of the Arabs. This is 'Abd Allāh ibn 'Abbās's interpretation which has been narrated by several chains of transmission by Aḥmad ibn Ḥanbal, *Musnad*; Bukhārī, *Kitāb Tafsīr al-Qur'ān, Bāb Qawlihi: 'Illā al-Mawaddah fī al-Qurbā'*; Muslim, *Kitāb al-Jihād wa al-Siyar, Bāb al-Nisā' al-Ghāziyāt Yurdakh lahunna wa lā Yusham*; Tirmidhī, *Kitāb Tafsīr al-Qur'ān 'an Rasūl Allāh Ṣallā Allāh 'alayhi wa Sallam*; Ṭabarī, *Tafsīr*, comments on *Sūrah al-Shūrā* 42: 23; al-Ṭabarānī, al-*Mu'jam al-Kabīr*, narrated by 'Abd Allāh ibn 'Abbās; al-Bayhaqī, *al-Sunan al-Kubrā, Kitāb al-Siyar, Bāb al-'Abīd wa al-Nisā' wa al-Ṣibyān Yaḥḍurūna al-Wuq'ah*; Ibn Sa'd, *Kitāb al-Ṭabaqāt al-Kubrā, Dhikr Man Intamā ilayhi Rasūl Allāh Ṣallā Allāh 'alayhi wa Sallam* and others. The same view is shared by Mujāhid. 'Ikrimah, Qatādah, al-Suddī, Abū Malik, 'Abd al-Raḥmān ibn Zayd, Ḍaḥḥāk, 'Aṭā' ibn Dīnār and other leading Qur'ānic scholars. (See also Ṭabarī, *Tafsīr*, comments on *Sūrah al-Shūrā* 42: 23.)

The other group of scholars, however, interprets *qurbā* in the sense of nearness. For them, the verse means: 'I do not seek any other reward for this mission except that you develop a desire to gain nearness with God,' (Ṭabarī, *Tafsīr*, comments on *Sūrah al-Shūrā* 42: 23.) In other words, their reform will constitute his wages. This is the view of al-Ḥasan al-Baṣrī, which, according to a report, is also endorsed by Qatādah. (Ṭabarī, *Tafsīr*, comments on *Sūrah al-Shūrā* 42: 23.) Al-Ṭabarānī attributes this to 'Abd Allāh ibn 'Abbās. Almost the same point is made in the Qur'ān as well: 'Say to them (O Muḥammad): "I ask of you no reward for my work. My only reward is that whosoever wills may follow the way leading to his Lord",' (*al-Furqān* 25: 57.)

Yet another group of scholars interprets the word *qurbā* to denote kinsfolk, and explains the verse to mean the following: the Prophet (peace be on him) declares that he seeks nothing in return for performing his mission except that he wants people to love his kinsfolk, (Ṭabarī, *Tafsīr*, comments on *Sūrah al-Shūrā* 42: 23.) For them, all the members of 'Abd al-Muṭṭalib's family were his relatives. Some, however, restrict *qurbā* only to 'Alī, Fāṭimah and their children. Sa'īd ibn Jubayr and 'Amr ibn Shu'ayb are credited with this view, (Ṭabarī, *Tafsīr*, comments on *Sūrah al-Shūrā* 42: 23.) Some reports ascribe the same view to 'Abd Allāh ibn 'Abbās and 'Alī ibn al-Ḥusayn, (Ṭabarī, *Tafsīr*, comments on *Sūrah al-Shūrā* 42: 23.)

Nonetheless, the above interpretation is not acceptable for many reasons. First of all, at the time of the revelation of this *sūrah* in Makkah, 'Fāṭimah was not yet 'Alī's wife, and obviously, therefore, they had no children. Furthermore, all members of 'Abd al-Muṭṭalib's family were not the Prophet's supporters. Some of them had openly joined the

Whoever does a good deed, We shall increase its merit for him. Surely Allah is Most Forgiving, Most Appreciative.[42]	وَمَن يَقْتَرِفْ حَسَنَةً نَّزِدْ لَهُۥ فِيهَا حُسْنًا ۚ إِنَّ ٱللَّهَ غَفُورٌ شَكُورٌ ﴿٢٣﴾

opposite camp. Abū Lahab's hostility towards the Prophet (peace be on him) was known to all. Moreover, 'Abd al-Muṭṭalib's family members alone did not represent the Prophet's kinsfolk. He was related to almost all the families of the Quraysh through his mother, his father and his wife, Khadījah. He had some of his sincere supporters who belonged to one or other of those families. Hence, the Prophet (peace be on him) could not have singled out 'Abd al-Muṭṭalib's family members as his relatives and asked that love and affection be shown to them. Furthermore, a Prophet addresses people from a very high pedestal and it is not quite consistent with his august office to ask people to show love and affection towards his kinsfolk. The Qur'ānic account of the Prophets clearly indicates that none of them ever asked any reward for their people on account of his mission. Rather, all of them declared that their wages rest with God alone. (*Yūnus* 10: 72; *Hūd* 11: 29 and 59 and *al-Shu'arā'* 26: 109, 127, 145, 164 and 180). In *Sūrah Yā Sīn*, a criterion has been given to test a Prophet's truthfulness and this is absolute selflessness (*Yā Sīn* 36: 21). At several places, the Qur'ān directs the Prophet Muḥammad (peace be on him) to declare that he is not after any reward for his work. (See *al-An'ām* 6: 90; *Yūsuf* 12: 104; *al-Mu'minūm* 23: 72; *al-Furqān* 25: 57; *Saba'* 34: 47; *Ṣād* 38: 86; *al-Ṭūr* 52: 40 and *al-Qalam* 68: 46.)

It is inconceivable that notwithstanding these instructions to the Prophet (peace be on him) he would ask for the kind of reward for his work mentioned above. Nor does this fit in with the context either. For the verse is addressed to the unbelievers, not to Muslims. The entire discourse is directed at them and the same continues in the verses that follow: The Prophet (peace be on him) could not obviously ask for any reward from his opponents. One expects some return only from those who appreciate one's work. The Makkan unbelievers did not endorse his mission at all and were in fact out to harm him, even mortally.

42. As distinct from those who are wilful culprits of disobedience, God treats those who try to follow the course of goodness as follows: (i) God makes them even better than they deserve by dint of their effort. (ii) He overlooks their lapses; and (iii) encourages them by amply rewarding them even for their modest achievements.

(24) Do they say: 'He has forged a lie against Allah?'[43] If Allah so wanted He could seal up your heart.[44] Allah blots out falsehood and confirms the truth by His Words.[45] He is well aware of all the secrets hidden in the breasts (of people).[46] (25) He it is Who accepts repentance from His servants and forgives sins and knows ▶

أَمْ يَقُولُونَ ٱفْتَرَىٰ عَلَى ٱللَّهِ كَذِبًا ۖ فَإِن يَشَإِ
ٱللَّهُ يَخْتِمْ عَلَىٰ قَلْبِكَ ۗ وَيَمْحُ ٱللَّهُ ٱلْبَٰطِلَ
وَيُحِقُّ ٱلْحَقَّ بِكَلِمَٰتِهِۦٓ ۚ إِنَّهُۥ عَلِيمٌۢ بِذَاتِ
ٱلصُّدُورِ ﴿٢٤﴾ وَهُوَ ٱلَّذِى يَقْبَلُ ٱلتَّوْبَةَ عَنْ
عِبَادِهِۦ وَيَعْفُوا۟ عَنِ ٱلسَّيِّـَٔاتِ وَيَعْلَمُ

---

43. The verse, couched in the interrogative form, is permeated with a strong note of reproach. The Makkan unbelievers were so brazen that they felt no qualm of conscience in accusing the Prophet (peace be on him) of having ascribed lies to God. They accused him of composing the Qur'ān himself and then falsely claiming that it was from God.

44. Such big lies are uttered only by those whose hearts are sealed. God could, if He so willed, include them in the same category. However, out of His mercy He has kept them in a category separate from them.

This rejoinder contains a strong satire against those who made false accusations against the Prophet (peace be on him). They are guilty of considering the Prophet (peace be on him) to be one of those who would resort to any falsehood for personal gain. Misled by the same notion, they charge him with inventing lies. However, as distinct from those whose hearts God had sealed, He was kind to them insofar as He did not seal their hearts.

45. It is part of Divine dispensation that falsehood does not flourish and that truth eventually triumphs. The Prophet (peace be on him) is, therefore, instructed not to pay any attention to the false charges levelled by the Makkan unbelievers. This storm of opposition will soon subside and the truth of the Prophet's teaching will become crystal clear.

46. God is well aware of all the allegations hurled against the Prophet (peace be on him). God also knows the motives behind the concerted effort to browbeat the Prophet (peace be on him).

all what you do,[47] (26) and answers the prayers of those who believe and do good deeds and bestows upon them even more out of His Bounty. As for those who deny (the Truth), a grievous chastisement awaits them.

(27) If Allah were to grant ample sustenance to His servants they would go about transgressing in the land. But He sends down in due measure whatever (sustenance) He wills. Surely He is Well-Aware and All-Seeing concerning matters that relate to His servants.[48] ▶

مَا تَفْعَلُونَ ﴿٢٥﴾ وَيَسْتَجِيبُ ٱلَّذِينَ ءَامَنُوا۟
وَعَمِلُوا۟ ٱلصَّٰلِحَٰتِ وَيَزِيدُهُم مِّن فَضْلِهِۦ ۚ
وَٱلْكَٰفِرُونَ لَهُمْ عَذَابٌ شَدِيدٌ ﴿٢٦﴾
۞ وَلَوْ بَسَطَ ٱللَّهُ ٱلرِّزْقَ لِعِبَادِهِۦ لَبَغَوْا۟ فِى
ٱلْأَرْضِ وَلَٰكِن يُنَزِّلُ بِقَدَرٍ مَّا يَشَآءُ ۚ إِنَّهُۥ
بِعِبَادِهِۦ خَبِيرٌۢ بَصِيرٌ ﴿٢٧﴾

---

47. The previous verse, which consisted of a stern warning to the unbelievers, is followed by the present verse which exhorts them to repent. The verse, thus, asks them by implication: why are you incurring God's further wrath by hurling absolutely false accusations against the Prophet (peace be on him)? However, since God is All-Pardoning, if they give up their misdeeds and repent, He will forgive them. This because repentance itself means man's feeling regretful at his misdeeds, coupled with a firm resolve to give them up and never repeat them. In fact true repentance also requires that one should make repairs for any harm that one might have caused any person. One is required to try one's best to make repairs, and where this is not possible, one should implore God's forgiveness and constantly strive to remove the dark spot from one's life-record by superogatory acts of goodness and charity. Let it be clear, however, that the word repentance can apply only to that act which is accompanied by a desire to please God. For abandoning any evil acts, if done for any other consideration, is not reckoned as repentance.

48. In view of the context in which this verse occurs, it seems to point out the basic reason of the rebellious stance of the Makkan unbelievers.

(28) He it is Who sends down the rain after they despair of it, spreading out His Mercy. He is the Protector, the Immensely Praiseworthy.[49] (29) And of His Signs is the creation of the heavens and the earth and the living creatures that He has spread out in them.[50] He has the power to bring them together when He so wills.[51] ▶

وَهُوَ ٱلَّذِى يُنَزِّلُ ٱلْغَيْثَ مِنۢ بَعْدِ مَا قَنَطُوا۟
وَيَنشُرُ رَحْمَتَهُۥ ۚ وَهُوَ ٱلْوَلِىُّ ٱلْحَمِيدُ ﴿٢٨﴾ وَمِنْ
ءَايَـٰتِهِۦ خَلْقُ ٱلسَّمَـٰوَٰتِ وَٱلْأَرْضِ
وَمَا بَثَّ فِيهِمَا مِن دَآبَّةٍ ۚ وَهُوَ عَلَىٰ جَمْعِهِمْ
إِذَا يَشَآءُ قَدِيرٌ ﴿٢٩﴾

Compared to the superpowers of the time – the Romans and the Persians – they counted for nothing. Were the Quraysh to be viewed in comparison with their neighbouring countries, they were a backward people engaged in petty trading. They were, no doubt, materially better off than the other tribes of Arabia. But this had made them so proud and arrogant that they were not prepared even to listen to the Prophet (peace be on him). The chiefs of their tribes considered it below their dignity even to consider the proposition of his being their guide, one whom they should follow. It is against this background that the Qur'ān points out that if God had thrown the doors of sustenance wide open for them – thanks to their pettiness – they would have totally lost their poise and balance. They are being granted sustenance only to that extent that will keep them within some reasonable limits. In substance, the same point is also made in the following verses: *al-Tawbah* 9: 68 and 70; *al-Kahf* 18: 32 and 42; *al-Qaṣaṣ* 28: 75 and 82; *al-Rūm* 30: 9; *Saba'* 34: 34 and 36 and *al-Mu'min* 40: 82 and 85.

49. Here *walī* signifies the Being Who looks after the needs of all His creatures, One Who has taken it upon Himself to meet all their needs.

50. That is, in both the heavens and the earth. This clearly indicates that life is not confined to earth, and that living beings are found on other planets as well.

51. God is capable of bringing His creatures back to life. In other words, in the same way that God has spread out His living creatures,

(30) Whatever misfortune befalls you is a consequence of your own deeds. But much of it He forgives.[52] (31) You cannot frustrate Him in the earth; you have no protector nor helper against Allah. (32) And of His Signs are the ships that sail in the sea like mountains. (33) If He so wills, He can cause the winds to become still so that they will remain ▶

وَمَآ أَصَٰبَكُم مِّن مُّصِيبَةٍ فَبِمَا كَسَبَتْ
أَيْدِيكُمْ وَيَعْفُوا۟ عَن كَثِيرٍ ۝٣٠ وَمَآ أَنتُم
بِمُعْجِزِينَ فِى ٱلْأَرْضِ ۖ وَمَا لَكُم مِّن
دُونِ ٱللَّهِ مِن وَلِىٍّ وَلَا نَصِيرٍ ۝٣١ وَمِنْ
ءَايَٰتِهِ ٱلْجَوَارِ فِى ٱلْبَحْرِ كَٱلْأَعْلَٰمِ ۝٣٢
إِن يَشَأْ يُسْكِنِ ٱلرِّيحَ فَيَظْلَلْنَ

He also has the power 'to bring them together'. In short, it is altogether wrong to think that those who were alive once cannot be brought back to life by the act of Resurrection.

52. Let it be clear that this Qur'ānic passage does not aim to explain the basic cause of all woes of mankind. What is said here is clearly addressed to those who were guilty of disbelief and disobedience in Makkah. They are being told that should God have taken them to task for their misdeeds, they would not have been left alive. They have, however, been afflicted with some calamities. (The allusion is presumably to the famine which had then overtaken the Makkans). These calamities stand out as a warning. They should realise their utter helplessness in face of God against Whom they had rebelled. Now, can those whom they take as their patrons and lords avail them if God's wrath strikes them?

As for true believers, they are governed by another set of Divine laws. They, too, encounter hardships and calamities. These, however, expiate their sins and lapses. The Prophet (peace be on him) said: 'As to the sorrow, grief, suffering and hardships afflicting a Muslim, even it be the pricking of a thorn, it serves as expiation for his lapses. God has devised this arrangement.' (Bukhārī, *Kitāb al-Marḍā, Bāb mā Jā'a fī Kaffārat al-Maraḍ* and Muslim, *Kitāb al-Birr wa al-Ṣilah wa al-Ādāb, Bāb Thawāb al-Mu'min fīmā Yuṣībuhu min Maraḍ aw Ḥuzn aw naḥw Dhālika ḥattā al-Shawkah Yushākuhā*.) As to the hardships which a believer faces in the cause of upholding the Word of God, these are means for his exaltation. There is no basis to assume that these are indicative of God's punishment for his sins.

motionless on its surface. Surely there are many Signs in this for those who are wont to be steadfast and give thanks.[53] (34) He may, while forgiving much of the sins of those that ride these ships, drown them on account of some of their misdeeds. (35) Then those who wrangle about Our Signs will come to know that there is no escape for them.[54]

رَوَاكِدَ عَلَىٰ ظَهْرِهِۦٓ ۚ إِنَّ فِى ذَٰلِكَ لَءَايَٰتٍ
لِّكُلِّ صَبَّارٍ شَكُورٍ ﴿٣٣﴾ أَوْ يُوبِقْهُنَّ
بِمَا كَسَبُوا۟ وَيَعْفُ عَن كَثِيرٍ ﴿٣٤﴾ وَيَعْلَمَ
ٱلَّذِينَ يُجَٰدِلُونَ فِىٓ ءَايَٰتِنَا مَا لَهُم
مِّن مَّحِيصٍ ﴿٣٥﴾

53. 'Those who are wont to be steadfast and give thanks' refers to those who exercise self-restraint and faithfully serve God both in the states of adversity and of prosperity; not to those who, by the very first flush of prosperity, lose their poise and allow themselves to forget their true position and become rebellious towards God and oppressive towards His creatures. Also, when they encounter adversity, they become utterly desperate and resort to all kinds of petty acts. Rather, it is, those 'who give thanks' to God, who attribute their success to Him, who never fail – no matter how high they ride on the crest of good fortune – to consider it all to be God's favour rather than the result of their inherent excellence. It is they who, when they find themselves in truly woeful conditions, their mind remains conscious of the blessings they have enjoyed rather than of the deprivations they may have suffered. Thus such people continue to thank God both in adversity and prosperity, and do so both by their tongues and from their hearts.

54. As part of their trade journeys, the Quraysh visited Abyssinia and the coastal regions of Africa. They undertook these voyages and crossed the turbulent Red Sea on sailing ships and boats. Now, the Red Sea is very hazardous for navigation, especially because it is often stormy and also abounds in submarineous rocks which imperil navigation. Thus, based on their experience, the Quraysh were in a good position to appreciate the state depicted here.

(36) That which has been given to you is only the wherewithal of the transient life of this world.[55] But that which is with Allah is better[56] and more enduring for those who believe and put their trust in their Lord;[57] ▶

فَمَآ أُوتِيتُم مِّن شَىْءٍ فَمَتَٰعُ ٱلْحَيَوٰةِ ٱلدُّنْيَا ۖ
وَمَا عِندَ ٱللَّهِ خَيْرٌ وَأَبْقَىٰ لِلَّذِينَ ءَامَنُوا۟ وَعَلَىٰ
رَبِّهِمْ يَتَوَكَّلُونَ ﴿٣٦﴾

---

55. What has been given to man is the 'wherewithal of transient life' rather than something that ought to puff him up with pride and cause him to exult. Thus, no matter how abundant the riches of the world available to a person, they are still meagre and transient. At the most, he will avail it for a number of years and will then leave it behind and go ahead empty-handed. Practically speaking, a man is able to avail only a tiny portion of his wealth while most of the time it only adorns account books and ledgers. How wise is it to exult at possessing such wealth for a person who understands the reality and true worth of this wealth and, for that matter, of the world itself?

56. By contrast, the bounties of the Hereafter are of an excellent nature, both qualitatively and quantitatively. Furthermore, they are not ephemeral but everlasting.

57. To repose trust in God is stated here as an essential requisite of faith as well as a necessary condition of success in the Hereafter. 'Reposing trust in God' means the following: (i) That one should completely confide in God's Guidance and be fully cognizant that knowledge about Reality, the principles of morality, the prescribed limits of what is lawful and what is unlawful, and the rules laid down to order and regulate human life are based on truth and lead to man's success and felicity. (ii) Instead of trusting one's own ability and competence and resources or of any others than God, one should rely on God and be fully persuaded of the truth that success depends wholly upon God's help and support, which one can earn only by observing God's laws and by keeping one's eyes firmly fixed on seeking God's pleasure and working within the limits laid down by Him. (iii) Likewise, one should have firm faith in God's promises made to those who believe and do good and devote themselves to the cause of Truth rather than falsehood. While reposing faith in these promises, believers should spurn any gain which might accrue from

(37) who eschew grave sins and shameful deeds,[58] and whenever they are angry, forgive;[59] (38) who obey their Lord[60] and establish Prayer; who conduct their affairs by consultation,[61] ▶

وَٱلَّذِينَ يَجْتَنِبُونَ كَبَٰٓئِرَ ٱلْإِثْمِ وَٱلْفَوَٰحِشَ وَإِذَا مَا غَضِبُوا۟ هُمْ يَغْفِرُونَ ﴿٣٧﴾ وَٱلَّذِينَ ٱسْتَجَابُوا۟ لِرَبِّهِمْ وَأَقَامُوا۟ ٱلصَّلَوٰةَ وَأَمْرُهُمْ شُورَىٰ بَيْنَهُمْ

following wrong paths. By the same token, they should patiently bear all losses and hardships which they may have to face in consequence of upholding the Truth. Without such trust in God, one cannot obtain the glorious rewards which God has promised to believers.

58. For further details see, *al-Nisā'* 4, nn. 53-4, *Towards Understanding the Qur'ān*,vol. II, pp. 32-5; *al-An'ām* 6, nn. 130-1, vol. II, pp. 291-2; *al-Naḥl* 16, n. 89, vol. IV, pp. 358-9; and *al-Najm* 53: 32.

59. Believers are not easily enraged and irritated; rather, they exercise restraint and are cool-minded. They are not revengeful either; rather, they overlook the excesses committed by others and keep good control over their anger. This, according to the Qur'ān, is one of the best traits of a human being, (*Āl 'Imrān* 3: 134.) It is projected as one of the main reasons for the Prophet's resounding success, (*Āl 'Imrān* 3: 159.) 'Ā'ishah relates that: 'The Prophet (peace be on him) never took revenge on personal grounds. He enforced punishment only when some Divine command was violated.' (Bukhārī, *Kitāb al-Ādāb, Bāb Qawl al-Nabī Ṣallā Allāh 'alayhi wa Sallam: 'Yassirū wa lā Tuassirū' wa Kāna Yuḥibb al-Takhfīf wa al-Yusr 'alā al-Nās;* and Muslim, *Kitāb al-Faḍā'il, Bāb Mubā'adatihi Ṣallā Allāh 'alayhi wa Sallam li al-Āthām wa Ikhtiyārihi min al-Mubāḥ Ashalahu wa Intiqāmihi li Allāh 'ind Intihāk Ḥurumātih*).

60. They respond wholeheartedly to God's call and are forthwith ready to attend to the tasks to which He invites them.

61. That the believers establish Prayers and conduct their affairs through consultation is highlighted as one of their excellent traits. The directive to conduct their affairs through consultation also occurs in *Āl 'Imrān* (3: 159). Little wonder, then, that mutual consultation is an important characteristic of Islamic polity. It only betrays a person's affinity to Ignorance (*jāhilīyah*) if he were to insist on deciding collective

issues without taking others into confidence. In fact, it also amounts to an infraction of the norm laid down by God. On studying why Islam places such emphasis on mutual consultation, the following three points stand out:

(1) If one arbitrarily decides something which concerns others, it is tantamount to committing excesses against them and no one has the right to act high-handedly in matters of common interest. Justice requires that all persons concerned with the matter should be consulted while taking a decision. If the issue relates to a very large number of people, their representatives should be taken into confidence.

(2) Any person who acts arbitrarily on public issues and disdainfully disregards others does so either to serve his personal interests or out of arrogance. Both these traits are morally reprehensible. A true believer cannot possess either of them. For he is not so selfish as to usurp others' rights in order to appropriate for himself unlawful gains. Nor is he so arrogant as to consider himself all-knowing and all-wise.

(3) It is a huge responsibility to adjudge others' interests. A God-fearing person realises the tremendous burden of His accountability to God. At times, he is deterred by this thought from accepting positions of responsibility. However, those negligent of God and the Hereafter have the audacity to take up any assignment. A God-conscious person who is all along cognizant of the Hereafter is bound to consult those who have an interest in the decision making of a question, or at least consult their representatives. For this may help in arriving at a sound and just decision. Even if an inadvertent mistake is committed, any specific individual cannot be faulted on that count.

These three considerations underlie the Islamic teachings with regard to mutual consultation as a requirement of Islam's broader ethical code of conduct. Any deviation from this norm is a major moral flaw which Islam does not condone.

The Islamic way of life presupposes mutual consultation at every level, both minor and major. Domestic issues should be decided together by husband and wife, and as children come of age, they should also be consulted. Family matters may be best resolved by taking into consideration the opinion of all adults. As for issues concerning a tribe or professional fraternity or town, or city, if all relevant people cannot be consulted, their representatives should settle matters in an acceptable manner.

The affairs of the state should be decided by the head of the state who should be appointed by the consent of all. He should draw upon the suggestions of truly representative advisors. He should hold office only for as long as he enjoys the confidence of his people. An honest, pious person cannot aspire or try to cling to his office if he forfeits without having the confidence of the public. Nor can he ever resort to fraudulent practices to keep occupying his office by force and coerce people into pledging their allegiance to him. He should not pick advisors who simply suit him. Rather, they should be independently minded, sincere people who are trusted by others. Only a dishonest person has recourse to unfair means. He may put up a façade of mutual consultation while he acts totally against its spirit. By so doing, he tries to deceive both God and the public. Needless to add, God cannot be deceived. Nor can the public be so misguided that they will fail to discern his misappropriations or accept him at his face value.

In terms of its nature and essence, the Qur'ānic directive for mutual consultation calls for the following: (i) People should enjoy full freedom of expression in matters concerning their rights and interests. They should be fully informed as regards how their affairs are decided. People should also be free to check the performance of those who hold the reins of responsibility and to admonish them if they commit lapses. They should also be authorised to replace their rulers if the latter do not mend their ways. It is the height of injustice and deceit to gag and coerce people and keep them in the dark. Such malpractices are grossly contrary to the spirit of mutual consultation. (ii) People entrusted with running collective affairs should be appointed with the consent of the people. Their consent should be free and independent. Any public consent, if secured fraudulently or forcibly or if it is bought by money, is no consent at all. Anyone who uses any of those unfair means is not fit to be the head of the state. Only he who is selected willingly by the public is entitled to this position. (iii) That the ruler should appoint only those people to advise him who enjoy public confidence. Those who appropriate this position for themselves by coercion, money, falsehood, deceit or misguiding people cannot be called their representatives. (iv) That those who are consulted should express their views to the best of their knowledge and in consonance with their conscience. They should be free to state their views clearly. If they are compelled into giving opinions which are against their conscience owing to any pressure, fear or incentive or because of group identity, it amounts to treachery, which runs counter to the underlying spirit of mutual consultation. (v) That the opinion arrived at by consensus or majority vote of the consultative assembly should be accepted. For, if one acts in total disregard of the consultation offered,

and spend out of what We have bestowed upon them;[62] (39) who, when a wrong is done to them, seek its redress.[63] ▶

وَمِمَّا رَزَقْنَٰهُمْ يُنفِقُونَ ۝٣٨ وَٱلَّذِينَ إِذَآ أَصَابَهُمُ ٱلْبَغْىُ هُمْ يَنتَصِرُونَ ۝٣٩

---

it renders the whole process useless. The Qur'ān categorically states that mutual consultation should be the basis of running public affairs. The consensus or majority view should, therefore, be the deciding factor. God not only directs Muslims that consultation be carried out in their affairs, but we find this as an observation about Muslim communal life that their mutual affairs are settled by consultation. It is, therefore, necessary that the suggestions enjoying public support be carried out.

It should be clear that the above mechanism of consultation is not characterised by absolute power and authority in terms of deciding the affairs of the Muslim community. Consultation is confined to the limits fixed by God's Law. The standing principle is that it is God Who decides matters on which Muslims have disagreements. Muslims are, therefore, obliged to turn, in the first place, to God and His Messenger in all their affairs. Going by this important proviso, it should be clearly understood that Muslims may carry out consultation after ascertaining the thrust and implications of a Divine command. However, they cannot overrule or alter what has already been decided by God and His Messenger.

62. This carries the following three meanings: (i) That they spend out of the sustenance granted to them by God; that they do not turn to unlawful earnings to meet their expenses. (ii) That they do not hoard the sustenance bestowed on them by God; rather, they feel no inhibition in spending it. (iii) That they also spend of what is granted to them in God's cause. They do not keep it exclusively for their own use.

The Qur'ān brands only lawful, wholesome sustenance as that which is bestowed by God. What is grabbed unlawfully does not represent the sustenance bestowed upon a person by God. Moreover, the sustenance bestowed by God should be expended, rather than stingily retained for one's strictly personal use. The Qur'ānic directive to spend also covers one's expenditure in the cause of God. Those who spend along the above lines will receive ample reward in the Hereafter for spending out of what God had bestowed on them.

63. This is also another excellent quality of believers: they are not easy prey for tyrants and oppressors. If they are tender-hearted and

(40) The recompense of evil[64] is evil the like of it.[65] But he who forgives and makes amends, his reward lies with Allah.[66] Surely He does not love the wrong-doers.[67] ▸

وَجَزَٰٓؤُاْ سَيِّئَةٍ سَيِّئَةٌ مِّثْلُهَا ۖ فَمَنْ عَفَا وَأَصْلَحَ فَأَجْرُهُۥ عَلَى ٱللَّهِ ۚ إِنَّهُۥ لَا يُحِبُّ ٱلظَّـٰلِمِينَ ﴿٤٠﴾

---

of forgiving disposition, then this is not because of their weakness for they have not been trained to live with the abject meekness of hermits and world-renouncing recluses. Such is their character that if those who are weaker than them commit an excess against them, they are likely to gracefully wink at it. On the contrary, if a power-drunk and arrogant person engages in high-handedness, they are wont to stand up and resist and prove their mettle. For the proud and the haughty, believers have proved a hard nut to crack.

64. From here on till verse 43 the import of the preceding verse is elaborated.

65. This is the first basic rule that must be observed in taking revenge: whereby a person may not exceed the extent of wrong done to him.

66. This is the second rule that ought to be taken into account: while one is entitled to take revenge against the wrong-doer, it is better to pardon him wherever this can bring about reform. Now, since pardoning another person mortifies a person's own feelings, God consecrates a reward for him because he suppressed his own feelings for the reform of evil-doers.

67. This warning alludes to a third rule: while taking revenge a person should be careful lest he become a tyrant himself. It is not permissible to exceed the original wrong in extracting revenge. For example, one may slap only once in retaliation for one slap. One is not permitted to go beyond the hurt sustained by oneself. Likewise, it is not permissible to commit a sin by way of revenge for the sin committed against oneself. For example, if a wicked person kills someone's son, the father is not authorised to kill the son of that person by way of revenge. Nor is one allowed to rape the daughter or sister of a rapist to take revenge for that kind of wrong.

(41) There is no blame against him who avenges himself after he has been wronged. (42) Blame attaches only to those who subject people to wrong and commit excesses on earth. A painful chastisement awaits them. (43) But he who patiently endures and forgives, that is a conduct of great resolve.[68]

(44) He whom Allah lets go astray, none after Him can be his protector.[69] You will see that when the wrong-doers observe ▶

وَلَمَنِ ٱنتَصَرَ بَعْدَ ظُلْمِهِۦ فَأُو۟لَـٰٓئِكَ مَا عَلَيْهِم
مِّن سَبِيلٍ ﴿٤١﴾ إِنَّمَا ٱلسَّبِيلُ عَلَى ٱلَّذِينَ
يَظْلِمُونَ ٱلنَّاسَ وَيَبْغُونَ فِى ٱلْأَرْضِ بِغَيْرِ
ٱلْحَقِّ ۚ أُو۟لَـٰٓئِكَ لَهُمْ عَذَابٌ أَلِيمٌ ﴿٤٢﴾ وَلَمَن
صَبَرَ وَغَفَرَ إِنَّ ذَٰلِكَ لَمِنْ عَزْمِ ٱلْأُمُورِ ﴿٤٣﴾
وَمَن يُضْلِلِ ٱللَّهُ فَمَا لَهُۥ مِن وَلِىٍّ مِّنۢ بَعْدِهِۦ ۗ
وَتَرَى ٱلظَّـٰلِمِينَ لَمَّا رَأَوُا۟

---

68. It is pertinent to clarify that all these qualities of believers characterised the conduct of the Prophet's Companions. The Makkan unbelievers saw all this at first hand. God, thus, instructs the Makkan unbelievers that if they have received some wealth from God for their ephemeral life, that should not cause them to be unduly puffed up and lose their heads. They should also bear in mind that that is not true wealth. True wealth consists of those good qualities and characteristics which the Qur'ān has cultivated in believers who belong to their own community.

69. God has revealed an excellent Book to guide people, which effectively instructs them in truth and directs them to the Straight Way. He also raised a Prophet of no less a stature and illustrious character than Muḥammad (peace be on him) the like of whom they had never seen before. Furthermore, God showed the results of the Prophet's instruction and training in the excellent lives and conduct of the Prophet's Companions. If the unbelievers continued to disregard God's guidance despite all this, then they were free to persist in error, for evidently they did not want to reform themselves. If God slams the door on someone to receive guidance, who can guide them to the Straight Way?

the chastisement, they will exclaim: 'Is there any way to go back?'[70] (45) You shall see them, as they are brought face to face with the chastisement, in a state of abject humiliation, looking with a furtive glance.[71] But the believers will say: 'Surely the true losers are they who lose themselves and their kindred on the Day of Resurrection.' Lo, the wrong-doers will be in an enduring torment. (46) They shall have no protectors to help them against Allah. For he whom Allah causes to go astray will have no way to save himself.

(47) Accept the command of your Lord before there comes a Day from Allah ▶

ٱلْعَذَابَ يَقُولُونَ هَلْ إِلَىٰ مَرَدٍّ مِّن سَبِيلٍ ﴿٤٤﴾
وَتَرَىٰهُمْ يُعْرَضُونَ عَلَيْهَا خَٰشِعِينَ مِنَ ٱلذُّلِّ
يَنظُرُونَ مِن طَرْفٍ خَفِيٍّ ۗ وَقَالَ ٱلَّذِينَ
ءَامَنُوٓا۟ إِنَّ ٱلْخَٰسِرِينَ ٱلَّذِينَ خَسِرُوٓا۟
أَنفُسَهُمْ وَأَهْلِيهِمْ يَوْمَ ٱلْقِيَٰمَةِ ۗ أَلَآ إِنَّ
ٱلظَّٰلِمِينَ فِى عَذَابٍ مُّقِيمٍ ﴿٤٥﴾ وَمَا كَانَ
لَهُم مِّنْ أَوْلِيَآءَ يَنصُرُونَهُم مِّن دُونِ ٱللَّهِ ۗ
وَمَن يُضْلِلِ ٱللَّهُ فَمَا لَهُۥ مِن سَبِيلٍ ﴿٤٦﴾
ٱسْتَجِيبُوا۟ لِرَبِّكُم مِّن قَبْلِ أَن يَأْتِىَ يَوْمٌ

---

70. That is, when it is possible for them to return to the Straight Way, they refuse to pay heed. However, after God's judgement has been finally issued for enforcement, they would very much like to have another opportunity to repent and reform themselves.

71. It is part of human nature that on being confronted with a dreadful spectacle, which poses a serious threat to oneself, one first closes one's eyes for one is unable to observe the dreadful object overtaking one. At most, one casts a glance over the terrifying object. The Qur'ān depicts the same condition of unbelievers when they will be on their way to Hellfire.

that cannot be averted.[72] On that Day there shall be no shelter for you, and none may change your predicament.[73] (48) (O Prophet), if they turn away from the Truth, know that We did not send you to them as their overseer.[74] Your task is only to convey (the Message). Indeed when We give man a taste of Our Mercy, he exults in it. But if any misfortune afflicts them on account of their deeds, man is utterly ungrateful.[75]

لَا مَرَدَّ لَهُۥ مِنَ ٱللَّهِ ۚ مَا لَكُم مِّن مَّلْجَإٍ
يَوْمَئِذٍ وَمَا لَكُم مِّن نَّكِيرٍ ﴿٤٧﴾ فَإِنْ
أَعْرَضُوا۟ فَمَآ أَرْسَلْنَـٰكَ عَلَيْهِمْ حَفِيظًا ۖ إِنْ
عَلَيْكَ إِلَّا ٱلْبَلَـٰغُ ۗ وَإِنَّآ إِذَآ أَذَقْنَا ٱلْإِنسَـٰنَ
مِنَّا رَحْمَةً فَرِحَ بِهَا ۖ وَإِن تُصِبْهُمْ سَيِّئَةٌۢ
بِمَا قَدَّمَتْ أَيْدِيهِمْ فَإِنَّ ٱلْإِنسَـٰنَ كَفُورٌ ﴿٤٨﴾

---

72. That is, God will neither avert that Day nor anyone else has the power to do so.

73. This is open to other meanings as well: (i) The unbelievers will not be able to deny any of their misdeeds. (ii) Also it will not be possible for them to hide by disguising themselves. (iii) They will not be in a position to lodge any protest or show any resentment against the treatment meted out to them. (iv) It will be beyond them to change the condition in which they are placed.

74. The Prophet (peace be on him) is not required to force the unbelievers into following the Straight Way, nor will he be taken to task for their sins.

75. 'Man' here refers to those mean and arrogant people who cannot gracefully carry the bounties they have received from God. When they are admonished to follow the Straight Way, they simply refuse to pay heed. However, when they are punished for their misdeeds, they bemoan and curse themselves and forget all the bounties that had earlier been showered upon them. They fail to realise that their plight is because of their misdeeds. They do not, however, take any lesson from their adverse

(49) The dominion of the heavens and the earth belongs to Allah.[76] He creates whatever He pleases. He grants females to whomever He pleases and males to whomever He pleases, (50) or grants them a mix of males and females, and causes whomever He pleases to be barren. He is All-Knowing, All-Powerful.[77]

لِّلَّهِ مُلْكُ ٱلسَّمَٰوَٰتِ وَٱلْأَرْضِ ۚ يَخْلُقُ
مَا يَشَآءُ ۚ يَهَبُ لِمَن يَشَآءُ إِنَٰثًا وَيَهَبُ لِمَن
يَشَآءُ ٱلذُّكُورَ ﴿٤٩﴾ أَوْ يُزَوِّجُهُمْ ذُكْرَانًا
وَإِنَٰثًا ۖ وَيَجْعَلُ مَن يَشَآءُ عَقِيمًا ۚ إِنَّهُۥ
عَلِيمٌ قَدِيرٌ ﴿٥٠﴾

---

or favourable circumstances.

It is evident from the context that the discourse is directed to the Makkan unbelievers, though they are not addressed directly. Rather, some general observations are made about human conduct and the causes of human weaknesses are identified. This provides one with a highly useful lesson about the wisdom that ought to accompany preaching: The weaknesses of the addressees should not be directly attacked. Only some general comments should be made so that they are not antagonised. These comments should spark off their good sense and rouse them to engage in soul-searching.

76. If the unbelievers refuse to take any lesson, that does not change facts. The dominion of the earth and the heavens does not belong to any earthly king or tyrant; it belongs to God. Those who rebel against Him can achieve no victory. Nor can those whom the unbelievers foolishly invest with Divinity rescue them.

77. This is a manifest proof of God's absolute authority and power. No human being, however great, is able to have children of his choice, let alone grant them to others. The one whom God has made barren cannot bear a child despite the best medical advice and treatment. Likewise, he who has been granted only daughters cannot have a son. The same holds true for the parents of sons who cannot have a daughter on their own. Man is utterly helpless in this regard. It is hard to ascertain whether an expecting mother will deliver a son or daughter. It is the height of

(51) It is not given to any human being[78] that Allah should speak to him except through revelation,[79] or from behind a veil,[80] or that a messenger (i.e., an angel) be sent to him who reveals to him by Allah's leave whatever He wishes.[81] ▶

۞ وَمَا كَانَ لِبَشَرٍ أَن يُكَلِّمَهُ ٱللَّهُ إِلَّا وَحْيًا
أَوْ مِن وَرَآئِ حِجَابٍ أَوْ يُرْسِلَ رَسُولًا
فَيُوحِيَ بِإِذْنِهِۦ مَا يَشَآءُ ۚ

---

foolishness on one's part to lay claim to Divinity or to credit anyone else with Divinity in the face of these evident truths. Those guilty of such foolishness will face dire consequences. Their unbelief and polytheism cannot even slightly alter the reality.

78. The theme broached at the opening of the *sūrah* is resumed in the concluding part. It is helpful, therefore, to rehearse the opening verses and their explanatory notes.

79. *Waḥy* here signifies inspiration or putting an idea or feeling in someone's heart, or making him observe a truth in a state of sleep. An example of this is the vision shown to the Prophets Abraham and Joseph (peace be on them) in their dreams as stated in *Sūrah*s *Yūsuf* 12: 4 and 100, and *al-Ṣāffāt* 37: 102.

80. One hears some voice, though one is unable to observe the caller. This happened to the Prophet Moses (peace be on him). He heard someone calling out from a tree yet he could not see the caller. (*Ṭā Hā* 20: 11-48; *al-Naml* 27: 8-12 and *al-Qaṣaṣ* 28: 30-35.)

81. This is the conventional mode of revelation, which accounts for the transmission of Heavenly Books to Prophets. Some people tend to misinterpret the verse to mean that when God sends a Prophet, the latter conveys His message by His command. However, the wording of the verse itself indicates the fallacy of the above interpretation. The Prophets' preaching cannot be equated with revelation. Such an interpretation is also not endorsed by Arabic idiom. *Waḥy* connotes a secret as distinct from open communication. *Waḥy* can be equated with Prophets' preaching only by those who are totally ignorant of Arabic idiom and syntax.

He is All-High, Most Wise.[82] (52) Even so We revealed to you, (O Prophet), a spirit by Our command.[83] (Before that) you knew neither what the Book ▶

إِنَّهُۥ عَلِىٌّ حَكِيمٌ ۝٥١ وَكَذَٰلِكَ أَوْحَيْنَآ إِلَيْكَ رُوحًا مِّنْ أَمْرِنَا ۚ مَا كُنتَ تَدْرِى مَا ٱلْكِتَٰبُ

82. God is far too exalted and hallowed to speak face-to-face with a human being. Moreover, He also has the power to resort to alternatives of direct means of communication with man.

83. 'Even so' does not necessarily mean that the last-mentioned communication of God's guidance was the only one, but includes all the three modes mentioned above. As for *rūḥ*, it denotes the message conveyed to the Prophet (peace be on him) through revelation. Both the Qur'ān and *Ḥadīth* testify that the Prophet (peace be on him) received revelation in all the above three modes: (i) There are *aḥādīth* that mention 'Ā'ishah as narrating that revelation to the Prophet (peace be on him) commenced with true dreams, (Bukhārī, *Kayfa Kāna Bad' al-Waḥy ilā Rasūl Allāh Ṣallā Allāh 'alayhi wa Sallam* ... and Muslim, *Kitāb al-Īmān, Bāb Bad' al-Waḥy ilā Rasūl Allāh Ṣallā Allāh 'alayhi wa Sallam.*) This lasted for some years. *Aḥādīth* recount many such dreams of the Prophet (peace be on him) in which he received some good tidings or directives. The Qur'ān also specifically mentions a dream that was shown to the Prophet (peace be on him), (*al-Fatḥ* 48: 27.) The Prophet (peace be on him) stated in several *aḥādīth* that he was inspired or instructed or commanded or prohibited on different occasions. All these are illustrative of this type of revelation. *Ḥadīth qudsī* belongs to the same category. (ii) On the occasion of his Night Journey the Prophet (peace be on him) was favoured with another mode of revelation. Several authentic *aḥādīth* narrate the dialogue between God and the Prophet (peace be on him) regarding the number of obligatory Prayers, (Bukhārī, *Kitāb al-Ṣalāh, Bāb Kayfa Furiḍat al-Ṣalāh fī al-Isrā'.*) One, thus, learns that the Prophet (peace be on him) was granted the same honour as was conferred earlier upon the Prophet Moses (peace be on him) on Mount Sinai when God spoke to him directly. (iii) The Qur'ān clearly states that revelation was conveyed to the Prophet (peace be on him) through the agency of Gabriel, (*al-Baqarah* 2: 97 and *al-Shu'arā'* 26: 192-5.)

nor what the faith was.[84] But We made that spirit a light whereby We guide those of Our servants whom We please to the Right Way. Surely you are directing people to the Right Way, (53) the Way of Allah, to Whom belongs the dominion of all that is in the heavens and the earth. Lo, it is to Allah that all things ultimately revert.[85]

وَلَا ٱلۡإِيمَٰنُ وَلَٰكِن جَعَلۡنَٰهُ نُورٗا نَّهۡدِي
بِهِۦ مَن نَّشَآءُ مِنۡ عِبَادِنَاۚ وَإِنَّكَ لَتَهۡدِيٓ إِلَىٰ
صِرَٰطٖ مُّسۡتَقِيمٖ ﴿٥٢﴾ صِرَٰطِ ٱللَّهِ ٱلَّذِي لَهُۥ
مَا فِي ٱلسَّمَٰوَٰتِ وَمَا فِي ٱلۡأَرۡضِۗ
أَلَآ إِلَى ٱللَّهِ تَصِيرُ ٱلۡأُمُورُ ﴿٥٣﴾

---

84. Prior to assuming the Prophetic office it had never occurred to the Prophet (peace be on him) that the Book would be granted to him. In fact, he had no inkling about the previous Books and their contents. Likewise, notwithstanding his belief in God, he did not have a clear idea of the articles of faith before he was appointed to the Prophetic office. He was also unaware of belief in angels, Prophethood, Heavenly Books and the Hereafter. The Makkan unbelievers were cognizant of all this. No Makkan could dare say that the Prophet (peace be on him) had ever even discussed the issue of faith before his designation to Prophetic office. An aspirant for this office would not have behaved in this fashion: of displaying complete unawareness of these subjects and then, out of the blue, presenting remarkable and highly cogent discourses on them.

85. This serves as the final warning to the Makkan unbelievers. Their rejection of the Prophet (peace be on him) cannot be taken lightly. Their unbelief is in God's knowledge and so is all else that is happening. He will pronounce His judgement regarding the fate of all.

Sūrah 43

Al-Zukhruf

(Ornaments)

(Makkan Period)

Title

The title is derived from verse 35 of this *sūrah*, wherein the word *al-zukhruf* (ornaments) occurs.

Period of Revelation

We have no authentic traditions indicating the time when the *sūrah* was revealed. On studying its contents, it appears, however, that it was revealed around the same time as *Sūrahs al-Mu'min*, *Ḥā Mīm al-Sajdah* and *al-Shūrā*. All of them seem to belong to one and the same series of *sūrahs* that were revealed at a time when the Makkan unbelievers were after the Prophet's blood. In secret meetings, they hatched conspiracies about the possible ways to eliminate him. In fact, an attempt on the Prophet's life had already been made; verses 79-80 clearly indicate this.

Subject Matter and Themes

The *sūrah* strongly debunks the foolish beliefs and superstitions to which the Quraysh, and the Arabs as a whole for that matter, adamantly clung to. Effectively and convincingly it brings into sharp relief the utter irrationality of such beliefs and superstitions. All this is done in such a manner as prompts all sensible people to reflect on the follies which they continue to hold on to. At that time, however, the Quraysh were hell-bent on eliminating the one person who was showing them the way out of their error and ignorance.

The *sūrah* opens by making it clear that the unbelievers' mischief-making will not interrupt the Qur'ān's revelation. Indeed, such opposition never prevented God from sending His Messengers and revealing His Scriptures. On the contrary, in the past, He destroyed all wrong-doers who obstructed the spread of His Guidance, and He will presently do the same. This statement is repeated later on in verses 41-43 and in verses 79-80. While addressing the Prophet (peace be on him) those who were hell bent on spilling his blood are sternly told that regardless of what happens to the Prophet (peace be on him), God will punish the miscreants. It is also made clear to them that if they act against the Prophet (peace be on him), God will act against them and decisively so.

This is followed by an account of the erroneous way of life cherished by the unbelievers accompanied by the arguments which they proffered against the Prophet (peace be on him).

These unbelievers, in any case, recognised that God was the Creator of the heavens and the earth and of everyone, including themselves and their deities. Yet still, they also recognised that God was the source of all the bounties from which they benefited. Yet still they insisted on associating others as partners with Him. They took God's creatures to be His children, and these included daughters whom they otherwise considered to be a matter of disgrace.

Likewise, they declared angels to be goddesses. Furthermore, their idols took feminine form and were even dressed in female clothing and jewellery. These they worshipped, held them to be God's daughters and invoked for help and support. It was quite obvious, however, that they had no basis to say with certainty anything about these angels' gender.

When these people were asked to give up their ignorant fancies, they argued that such idol-worship was part of their fate. They also argued that if their ways were unacceptable to God, they could not have indulged in polytheism in the first place. The fact, however, is that the Scriptures are the best means to ascertain what pleases God and what displeases Him. They should not, therefore, cite happenings in the world to prove their contention. This because everything ultimately happens by God's Will [even though not all of it pleases God]. Theft, robbery, illicit sex and all sorts of sins are committed every day and all happens by God's Will. Yet, if this argument is accepted, would it not then legitimate and justify all such misdeeds?

The unbelievers' main argument in support of polytheism was that it had come down from their ancestors, and this, for them, was sufficiently weighty. They also took great pride in being the Prophet Abraham's descendants. Abraham (peace be on him), however, had altogether rejected blind conformity to ancestral faith. If the Makkans were keen on following in the footsteps of their ancestors, they should better emulate the example set by their great forefathers, the Prophets Abraham and Ishmael (peace be on them.) Both had renounced their ancestral faith because it was flawed, and in so doing left their hearth and home. Strangely enough, shunning this aspect of the example set by Abraham and Ishmael, they chose to follow the ways of the most ignorant and foolish of their ancestors.

When they were asked whether any Prophet or Scripture had taught that others besides God should be worshipped, they cited the example of the Christians. They argued that the Christians took Jesus, son of Mary, as the Son of God and worshipped him. By so doing, they mixed the teachings of a Prophet with the practices of his people, for the Prophet Jesus (peace be on him) had never laid any claim to Divinity. Nor did he ever direct his followers to serve and worship him. His teaching was the same as that of every other Prophet: that God alone is his Lord and the Lord of all and that all should worship Him and Him alone. The unbelievers were disinclined to accept the Prophet Muḥammad (peace be on him) as

God's Messenger because he neither enjoyed wealth nor political authority, nor did he command social awe and prestige. They also contended that if God had to appoint a Prophet, He would have appointed a distinctively privileged person from Makkah and Ṭā'if. It was exactly on the same grounds that Pharaoh had earlier belittled the Prophet Moses' (peace be on him) claim. Pharaoh's contention was that if God, the King of the heavens, had indeed sent His emissary to him, the King on earth, he should have worn bracelets of gold and should have been escorted by a retinue of angels. Pharaoh also boasted of his rule over the Egyptian kingdom, including the River Nile. In short, he dismissed the Prophet Moses (peace be on him) as too lowly and resourceless to be a match for him.

Thus all false notions cherished by the unbelievers were refuted, one by one, on the basis of weighty, reasoned arguments. It is unequivocally stated in the concluding parts of the *sūrah* that God does not have any child. Nor are there several gods, the god of the heavens being separate from and independent of the god of earth. Nor is there any intercessor who can save the unbelievers from God's punishment. God alone is the Supreme Lord, while all others are His servants. No one has any share in His Divine attributes or authority. Only those who are themselves truthful can intercede with God on behalf of those who have adhered to the truth.

In the name of Allah, the Most Merciful, the Most Compassionate.

(1) *Ḥā. Mīm.* (2) By the Clear Book; (3) verily We have made it an Arabic Qur'ān that you may understand.[1] (4) Indeed it is transcribed in the Original Book[2] ▶

بِسۡمِ ٱللَّهِ ٱلرَّحۡمَٰنِ ٱلرَّحِيمِ

حمٓ ١ وَٱلۡكِتَٰبِ ٱلۡمُبِينِ ٢ إِنَّا
جَعَلۡنَٰهُ قُرۡءَٰنًا عَرَبِيّٗا لَّعَلَّكُمۡ تَعۡقِلُونَ ٣
وَإِنَّهُۥ فِيٓ أُمِّ ٱلۡكِتَٰبِ

---

1. The *sūrah* opens with an oath in the name of the Qur'ān, asserting that God, rather than the Prophet Muḥammad (peace be on him), is the Author of this Qur'ān. It is further emphasised that the Qur'ān is a clear Book. The pointed reference to this particular feature of the Qur'ān underlines that the unbelievers themselves should study this open, clear Book. They are invited to study the Qur'ān and reflect upon its contents, its teachings and its stylistic features, which unmistakably prove that no one other than God could have authored it.

That the Qur'ān is in Arabic carries the following two main lessons for the Makkans: (i) It is not in any foreign tongue; instead, it is delivered in their own language. They, therefore, can have no difficulty in evaluating its worth. Had it been in some other language, they could have come up with the excuse of incomprehension. However, no such excuse is now admissible as the Qur'ān is presented in their own language. They are thoroughly familiar with its diction and syntax. The meaning of the Qur'ānic text is, therefore, quite clear to them. They are also fully in a position to decide whether it could be the product of the Prophet Muḥammad's or of any other Arab's mind. (ii) The Qur'ān has been sent down in Arabic because the Arabs were its immediate addressees. Naturally, they can best understand a message sent to them in that language. If one disregards this obvious reason for the choice of Arabic as the language of the Qur'ān and insists that it is the product of the Prophet's mind because Arabic happens to be his mother tongue, then one is guilty of committing a grave offence. (For further details concerning this point see *Ḥā Mīm al-Sajdah* 41: 44 and n. 54 above.)

2. The expression *Umm al-Kitāb* ('Original Book') is used for the Qur'ān because it is the source of all Heavenly Books sent down through the ages

with Us; sublime and full of wisdom.[3] (5) Should We divert this Good Counsel from you because you are a people ▶	لَدَيْنَا لَعَلِيٌّ حَكِيمٌ ۝ أَفَنَضْرِبُ عَنكُمُ ٱلذِّكْرَ صَفْحًا أَن كُنتُمْ قَوْمًا

to various Prophets. In *Sūrah al-Burūj* (*Sūrah* 85: 23) it is termed as one inscribed on a 'well-guarded tablet' (*lawḥ maḥfūẓ*) and, hence, is immune to any tampering. That the Qur'ān is called *Umm al-Kitāb* signifies that while God sent down many Scriptures for different nations in various periods and in different languages, all of these have the same message, and all Scriptures embody the same faith. All of them articulate the same truth, lay down the same standards of good and evil and the same principles of morality and culture. What explains this is that they have a common root. If they differ, they differ only in wording. Their meaning is the same, one that is preserved in 'the well-guarded tablet'. Whenever a Prophet was sent, a particular text was transmitted to him in a certain language, one that would blend well with the conditions and tenor of that people. Had God decided to raise the Prophet Muḥammad (peace be on him) among a people other than the Arabs, He would have revealed to him the Book in the language of that particular people. Likewise, the circumstantial setting, style and context of each revealed Book might be different. However, its essential teachings would necessarily be the same. This idea is expressed in the Qur'ān thus:

> Indeed this is a revelation from the Lord of the Universe, which the truthful spirit has carried down to your heart that you might become one of those who warn (others on behalf of Allah), (a revelation) in clear Arabic language, (a revelation) embodied in the scriptures of the ancients. (*Al-Shu'arā'* 26: 192-6. For further details see *al-Shu'arā'* 26, nn. 119-21, *Towards Understanding the Qur'ān,* vol. VII, pp. 113-14.)

3. This qualifies both the Qur'ān and *Umm al-Kitāb*. As pointed out earlier, the latter is the source of the former. Ignorant people may not appreciate the greatness of the Qur'ān and may refuse to draw upon its teachings. However, anyone who finds fault with it betrays his own meanness. The disrespect shown to the Qur'ān will not lower its exalted status. Nor can any criticism becloud its glory. The statement that it is 'sublime and full of wisdom' underscores the lofty position of the Book

immersed in extravagance?[4] (6) How many a Prophet did We send to the earlier peoples! (7) Yet never did a Prophet come to them but they mocked him.[5] (8) We utterly destroyed them although they were greater in might than these. ▶

مُّسْرِفِينَ ۝ وَكَمْ أَرْسَلْنَا مِن نَّبِيٍّ فِى
ٱلْأَوَّلِينَ ۝ وَمَا يَأْتِيهِم مِّن نَّبِيٍّ إِلَّا كَانُوا۟
بِهِۦ يَسْتَهْزِءُونَ ۝ فَأَهْلَكْنَآ أَشَدَّ
مِنْهُم بَطْشًا

which stands out for its excellent teachings, its inimitable stylistic features and its superb wisdom. It is also sublime because of the incomparable stature of its Author. Therefore, it cannot be discredited by anyone. Later, in verse 44 of this *sūrah* the Arabs in general and the Quraysh in particular are told that the revelation of the Qur'ān has provided them with a golden opportunity. If they miss this, they will have to render an account to God for their failure. (For further details see also n. 39 below.)

4. This brief statement narrates the whole account of the Prophet's mission up to that point in time. On reading this verse we get the following picture of the situation: for centuries, a people had remained steeped in error and ignorance. Then, God in His mercy, turned His attention to them and raised a remarkable leader from among themselves. Moreover, He revealed His Own Word in order to bring them out of darkness to light so that they may liberate themselves from ignorance and superstition and be led to the truth. However, the Quraysh resorted to opposition, hostility and mischief-making in response to the Qur'ānic call for reform. With the passage of time, their hostility to the Prophet (peace be on him) intensified and they even plotted to assassinate him. They are now told in categorical terms that the reform effort would not be abandoned just because of their folly. The Qur'ān's opponents will not be allowed to persist in their degeneration. God's mercy to mankind does not sanction this. They should rather think of the dire consequences of their spurning God's favour and of their clinging to falsehood in preference to truth.

5. Had the folly of opponents been a deterrent in raising Prophets and revealing Heavenly Books, no Prophet would have been raised nor any Heavenly Book revealed.

The examples of ancient peoples have gone before.[6]

(9) Yet if you were to ask them: 'Who created the heavens and the earth?' they will certainly say: 'The All-Mighty, the All-Knowing has created them.' (10) He it is Who made this earth for you a cradle[7] ▶

وَمَضَىٰ مَثَلُ ٱلْأَوَّلِينَ ۝٨ وَلَئِن سَأَلْتَهُم
مَّنْ خَلَقَ ٱلسَّمَٰوَٰتِ وَٱلْأَرْضَ لَيَقُولُنَّ
خَلَقَهُنَّ ٱلْعَزِيزُ ٱلْعَلِيمُ ۝٩ ٱلَّذِى جَعَلَ
لَكُمُ ٱلْأَرْضَ مَهْدًا

6. The misconduct and opposition of a few people cannot prevent the whole of mankind from benefiting from Prophethood and Scriptures. On the contrary, those intoxicated with falsehood, who ridiculed the Prophets, were eventually destroyed. When God's scourge overwhelmed them, they were crushed like insects and this notwithstanding their redoubtable might and resources. If this happened with those much mightier than the Quraysh chiefs, how then do they think that they will be able to withstand God's scourge?

7. God has provided man with an excellent resting place, the earth. In this verse the earth has been likened to a cradle because of the comfort it provides to man,. It is a marvel of God's power that He has made the earth like a cradle for man, even though this planet hangs in the space and revolves at the speed of 1,000 miles per hour on its axis which, in turn, moves at a pace of 66,600 miles per hour. Inside its depths is such ferocious fire that can melt even rocks. At times, man witnesses its fury when volcanic eruptions take place. Yet the earth is so level and tranquil that man soundly sleeps on it and does not feel even the slightest jerk arising out of the phenomenal speed of its movement. Nor does it ever occur to him that he inhabits a body that is suspended in the void and that he is hanging by it with his head upside down. He traverses it day and night without feeling any unease. Man is on a vessel which is in an exceedingly fast motion, faster than a bullet. Despite all this man digs and ploughs on earth in order to extract his sustenance from it. Then, there are moments when a light earthquake jolts him and makes him realise just how immensely merciful God is to him by having made the earth, which is nothing short of a monster, subservient to him. (For further details see *al-Naml* 27, n. 74 *Towards Understanding the Qur'ān,* vol. VII, pp. 172-3.)

and made in it pathways for you[8] that you may find the way to your destination;[9] (11) He Who sent down water from the sky in a determined measure,[10] and thereby We revived a dead land: likewise will you be ▶

وَجَعَلَ لَكُمْ فِيهَا سُبُلًا لَّعَلَّكُمْ
تَهْتَدُونَ ۝ وَالَّذِي نَزَّلَ مِنَ السَّمَاءِ مَاءً
بِقَدَرٍ فَأَنشَرْنَا بِهِۦ بَلْدَةً مَّيْتًا كَذَٰلِكَ

---

8. God has made natural passes through the mountains. He has also made rivers and other paths across the plains as well as other regions on the earth's surface. These have been instrumental in the movement and settlement of human beings in different territories. Had the mountain ranges been like a solid wall without any passes, there could not be any river or spring, and man would have been more or less confined to the region he was born in. Another of God's favour is that He has not made all the regions of the earth alike. Rather, He has established distinct landmarks which help man recognise one region from another. These features are also very helpful in man's movement. One appreciates this favour all the more when one travels across a desert which does not have any noteworthy landmarks for hundreds of miles and one can easily lose his way.

9. This observation carries the following two meanings: (i) man may find his way, in a physical sense, with the help of these natural paths and landmarks; and (ii) by observing God's consummate artistry, man should be directed to the Straight Way. For this should make him cognizant of the ultimate reality and that the universe is not an outcome of fortuitous factors. Nor is it the creation of a multiplicity of gods. Rather, it is the handiwork of the All-Wise Lord, Who has devised an amazing system with an eye on the multifarious needs of all His creatures. He has invested each region with distinct characteristics, as a result of which man can easily distinguish one geographic area from another.

10. God has apportioned a certain measure of rainfall for every region. This average rainfall has continued down the millennia at an almost consistent level for each region. There are no wild or wide variations in it. Moreover, rainfall is spread throughout the year in such a way that larger chunks of land benefit from it and become fertile. Again, out of His infinite wisdom God has excluded some regions from rainfall,

raised up (from the earth)[11] – (12) He Who created these pairs,[12] all of them, and provided you ships and cattle on which you ride, (13) so that when you are mounted upon them you may remember the bounty of your Lord, and say: ▶

تُخْرَجُونَ ﴿١١﴾ وَٱلَّذِى خَلَقَ ٱلْأَزْوَٰجَ كُلَّهَا
وَجَعَلَ لَكُم مِّنَ ٱلْفُلْكِ وَٱلْأَنْعَٰمِ
مَا تَرْكَبُونَ ﴿١٢﴾ لِتَسْتَوُۥا عَلَىٰ ظُهُورِهِۦ ثُمَّ
تَذْكُرُوا۟ نِعْمَةَ رَبِّكُمْ إِذَا ٱسْتَوَيْتُمْ
عَلَيْهِ وَتَقُولُوا۟

as a result of which they have become vast deserts. Some regions are occasionally afflicted with famine while others are faced with heavy downpour, culminating in floods. All this has been done with a view to making man appreciate what a great blessing regular, consistent rainfall is. Furthermore, it reminds man that it is the All-Powerful God Who has accomplished all this and His decisions cannot be altered by anyone. No one can change this average rainfall or alter rainfall's distribution. Nor can anyone withhold the rising storm or cause the clouds to pour down rain. It is God Who sends rainfall at different times and to different regions in a way that enables man to raise crops. (For further details see *al-Ḥijr* 15, nn. 13-14, *Towards Understanding the Qur'ān*, vol. IV, pp. 286-7; and *al-Mu'minūn* 23, n. 17, vol. VI, p. 90.)

11. That rain contributes to vegetative life is referred to as a proof of two things: (i) it points to God's omnipotence and wisdom, which are at work everywhere; and (ii) it also points to the Afterlife which is both possible and imminent. (For further details see *al-Naḥl* 16, n. 54, *Towards Understanding the Qur'ān*, vol. IV, p. 340; *al-Ḥajj* 22, n. 9, vol. VI, pp. 9-11; *al-Naml* 27: 73 ; *al-Rūm* 30, nn. 25 and 35, vol. VIII, pp. 88 and 95; *Fāṭir* 35, n. 19, vol. IX, pp. 210-11 and *Yā Sīn* 36, n. 29, vol. IX, pp. 256-7.)

12. This refers not only to human pairs but also to the masculine and the feminine among animals and plants. There are innumerable objects in the universe which exist in pairs. Their union leads to the appearance of new life forms. If man reflects on the design, interrelationship and numerous forms of the interaction of these pairs and their results, he is bound to recognise that the universe has been created by the One Supreme Creator and Designer Who controls its affairs. Only a fool would deny the central role of the Creator behind this vast spectacle. Nor is there any room left for attributing all this to several gods.

'Glory be to Him Who has subjected this to Us whereas we did not have the strength to subdue it.[13] ▶	سُبۡحَٰنَ ٱلَّذِي سَخَّرَ لَنَا هَٰذَا وَمَا كُنَّا لَهُۥ مُقۡرِنِينَ ١٣

13. Of all creatures of the world, God has granted man alone the ability to sail boats and ships and utilise animals for transportation. This ability was not given merely so that human beings may put themselves aboard these vessels, as though they were sacks of merchandise, and never think of the Creator Who enabled them to sail such ships across vast oceans. Likewise, God has created animals some of which, notwithstanding their huge size and awesome strength, have been made subservient to man so that he may comfortably ride and use them for transportation. Those who benefit from these favours, but who fail to appreciate that the source of it all is God, only show that their hearts have become dead and their intellects and consciences are bereft of all sensitivity. In contrast, those endowed with a living heart and a sensitive conscience are filled with gratitude to God whenever they make use of such means of transportation. They are bound to be overwhelmed with gratitude and cry out how glorious is God Who has made these objects subservient to them. Glory be to God that anyone should share with Him His essence, attributes and authority. Glory be to God that He should be devoid of the power to singularly govern His Divine Realm and require the assistance of any associate gods. Glory be to God that one should associate any others with Him to share the thanks owed exclusively to Him.

The words of the Prophet's prayers which, according to 'Abd Allāh ibn 'Umar, he recited, whenever he mounted an animal, brings out in full, the true import of the verse. He said *Allāhu Akbar* three times and then prayed: 'O God, I earnestly implore You to grant me piety and virtue and enable me to do those deeds during this journey that will please You. O God, facilitate our journey and make us overcome its expanse. O God, You are our Companion of the journey and the caretaker of our family. O God, be our journey's Companion and look after our family in our absence'. (Aḥmad ibn Ḥanbal, *Musnad*, narrated by 'Abd Allāh ibn 'Umar; Muslim, *Kitāb al-Ḥajj, Bāb mā Yaqūl idhā Rakiba ilā Safar al-Ḥajj wa Ghayrih*; Abū Dā'ūd, *Kitāb al-Jihād, Bāb mā Yaqūl al-Rajul idhā Sāfar*; Nasā'ī, *al-Sunan al-Kubrā, Kitāb 'Amal al-Yawm wa al-Laylah, Bāb mā Yaqūl idhā Aqbala min al- Safar*; Dārimī, *Kitāb al-Isti'dhān, Bāb fī al-Du'ā' idhā Sāfara wa idhā Qadim*; and Tirmidhī, *Kitāb al-Da'awāt 'an Rasūl Allāh Sallā Allāh 'alayhi wa Sallam, Bāb mā Yaqūl idhā Rakib al-Nāqah*.)

(14) It is to our Lord that we shall eventually return."[14]	وَإِنَّآ إِلَىٰ رَبِّنَا لَمُنقَلِبُونَ ﴿١٤﴾

'Alī recounts that once while travelling, the Prophet (peace be on him) put his foot in the saddle and recited *Bismillāh*... After mounting the animal, he recited the *al-Zukhruf* 43: 13-14 and then said each of the following thrice: *Al-ḥamdu li Allāh* and *Allāhu Akbar*. Then he recited the verse: *Subḥān al-ladhī sakhkhara lanā hadhā*... Then he said: 'Glory to You. There is no God but You. I have subjected myself to wrong [that is, I have committed sins]. So forgive me.' At that point he laughed. When I asked him as to why he laughed, he replied: 'When a servant of God says: "O Lord! Forgive me," it pleases Him much and He says: "This servant of Mine knows that there is none but Me to grant forgiveness."' (Aḥmad ibn Ḥanbal, *Musnad*, narrated by 'Alī ibn Abī Ṭalib; Abū Dā'ūd, *Kitāb al-Jihād, Bāb mā Yaqul Idhā Rakib*, Tirmidhī, *Kitāb al-Da'awāt 'an Rasūl Allāh Ṣallā Allāh 'alayhi wa Sallam, Bāb mā Yaqūl idhā Rakiba al-Nāqah* and Nasā'ī, *al-Sunan al-Kubrā, Kitāb 'Amal al-Yawm wa al-Laylah, Bāb mā Yaqūl idhā Waḍa'a Rijlahu fī al-Rikāb*.)

Abū Mijlaz narrates: 'Once when I mounted an animal I recited the verse *Subhān al-ladhī sakhkhara lanā hadhā*... Ḥasan asked me whether I had received any instruction to do so. He then told me that I should first thank God for having guided us to Islam, for having sent the Prophet Muḥammad (peace be on him), and for having admitted us to the best community that has been raised for God's creatures. This should be followed by the recitation of the above verse'. (Ṭabarī, *Tafsīr*, comments on *Sūrah al-Zukhruf* 43: 13 and al-Jaṣṣāṣ, *Aḥkām al-Qur'ān*, comments on *Sūrah al-Zukhruf* 43: 13.)

14. While undertaking a journey one should also recall one's final journey. While travelling in or on a vehicle there is a chance that one may meet with some accident, which may make it one's final journey. It is, therefore, all the more important that one should always travel with the consciousness of returning to God rather than without it.

Let us reflect over the moral consequences of this directive to remember God while going out. He who sets out with the realisation of his return to, and accountability before God is not likely to indulge in any wrongdoing or injustice. With thoughts of the Hereafter in mind, he is unlikely to visit a prostitute, imbibe intoxicating drinks or visit a gambling house. In like manner, a civil servant is not likely to commit any dishonesty or excess when he reaches his work place after having recited this prayer. Can a solider, who utters these words, shed the blood

(15) Yet they have made some of His servants a part of Him.[15] Indeed man is most evidently thankless.

(16) Has Allah taken for Himself daughters out of those whom He creates and has chosen you to have sons? (17) (They believe so although when) any of them is given tidings of the birth of a female child the like of which he assigns to the Merciful One, his countenance darkens and he is choked with grief.[16] ▶

وَجَعَلُوا۟ لَهُۥ مِنْ عِبَادِهِۦ جُزْءًا ۚ إِنَّ ٱلْإِنسَـٰنَ
لَكَفُورٌ مُّبِينٌ ﴿١٥﴾ أَمِ ٱتَّخَذَ مِمَّا يَخْلُقُ
بَنَاتٍ وَأَصْفَىٰكُم بِٱلْبَنِينَ ﴿١٦﴾ وَإِذَا بُشِّرَ
أَحَدُهُم بِمَا ضَرَبَ لِلرَّحْمَـٰنِ مَثَلًا ظَلَّ
وَجْهُهُۥ مُسْوَدًّا وَهُوَ كَظِيمٌ ﴿١٧﴾

---

of innocents? The practice of reciting such prayers can indeed serve as a deterrent against misdeed and sin.

15. 'Yet they have made some of His servants a part of Him.' This refers to the belief about any human that he is God's son or daughter. Children represent the species of their parents and are a part of their father. Accordingly, when someone is taken as God's son or daughter, it amounts to associating him or her with God. Also to make someone a part of God implies that we invest them with attributes and powers that belong specifically to God. This amounts to ascribing Divinity and Lordship to a fellow creature, whereas they belong exclusively to God.

16. This verse fully lays bare the absurdity of the Arabian polytheists' position. These polytheists considered angels to be God's daughters. Their idols also took feminine form: these were the goddesses they worshipped. God berates them for setting up others as equals with Him. They commit this outrageous act while they know all too well that God alone is the Creator of the heavens and the earth. It is He Who has made the earth a comfortable place for them to live on. It is He Who sends down rain for them and has placed animals and cattle at their disposal.

(18) Do they assign to Allah one who grows up amidst ornaments and is not well-versed in the art of disputation?[17]

أَوَمَن يُنَشَّؤُاْ فِي ٱلۡحِلۡيَةِ وَهُوَ فِي ٱلۡخِصَامِ غَيۡرُ مُبِينٖ ١٨

Despite this they take others as objects of their worship even though they know these to be created beings. Furthermore, these polytheists are guilty of ascribing even Divine attributes to created beings. They also ascribe daughters to God whereas they resent even their births and regard them as dishonourable for themselves. They not only have the audacity to invest these deities with God's attributes but also made them a part of His essence by declaring them to be His children.

17. In other words, they allocate those that are weak and delicate to God and monopolise their claim over sons who are apt to act bravely.

This verse implies the permission of women's use of ornaments for women. Such accessories are natural for women as is evident from a variety of *aḥādīth*. Imām Aḥmad, Abū Dā'ūd and Nasā'ī have narrated from 'Alī: 'While holding silk in one of his hands and gold in the other, the Prophet (peace be on him) declared: "It is forbidden for the male members of my community to use both of these."' (Aḥmad ibn Ḥanbal, narrated by 'Alī ibn Abī Ṭālib, Abū Dā'ūd, *Kitāb al-Libās, Bāb fī al-Ḥarīr li al-Nisā'*; and Nasā'ī, *Kitāb al-Zīnah, Bāb Taḥrim al-Dhahab 'alā al-Rijāl.*) Likewise, Tirmidhī and Nasā'ī narrate a tradition from Abū Mūsā al-Ash'arī that the Prophet (peace be on him) allowed the use of silk and gold for the females of his community while he prohibited their use for males. (Tirmidhī, *Kitāb al-Libās 'an Rasūl Allāh Ṣallā Allāh 'alayhi wa Sallam, Bab mā Jā'a fī al-Ḥarīr wa al-Dhahab*; Nasā'ī, *Kitāb al-Zīnah, Bāb Taḥrim al-Dhahab 'alā al-Rijāl.*) While discussing this juristic issue Abū Bakr al-Jaṣṣāṣ cites the following tradition in his *Aḥkām al-Qur'ān*: According to 'Ā'ishah, 'Once Usāmah, son of Zayd ibn Ḥārithah, sustained an injury and started bleeding. The Prophet (peace be on him) loved him like his own son. In order to keep Usāmah in good humour, he kept telling the crying boy: "Had you been our daughter, we would have given you ornaments and dressed you in silk."' Abū Mūsā al-Ash'arī says: 'The Prophet (peace be on him) declared: "It is forbidden for the male members of my community to use ornaments and silken cloth, while it is lawful for females."'

'Amr ibn al-'Āṣ relates that two women who wore gold bracelets called on the Prophet (peace be on him). He asked them: 'Would you

(19) They claim that angels, who are Allah's chosen servants,[18] are females. Did they witness how their bodies are constituted?[19] Their testimony shall be written and they shall be called to account.

(20) They say: 'Had the Merciful One so willed, we would never have ▶

وَجَعَلُوا۟ ٱلْمَلَـٰٓئِكَةَ ٱلَّذِينَ هُمْ عِبَـٰدُ
ٱلرَّحْمَـٰنِ إِنَـٰثًا ۚ أَشَهِدُوا۟ خَلْقَهُمْ ۚ سَتُكْتَبُ
شَهَـٰدَتُهُمْ وَيُسْـَٔلُونَ ﴿١٩﴾ وَقَالُوا۟ لَوْ شَآءَ
ٱلرَّحْمَـٰنُ مَا عَبَدْنَـٰهُم ۗ

like God to replace these with bracelets of fire?' When they replied in the negative, he directed them as follows: 'Fulfil your obligation and pay *zakāh* on these'. 'Ā'ishah points out that as long as *zakāh* is paid, there is nothing wrong with wearing ornaments. Caliph 'Umar also issued the following directive to his governor, Abū Mūsā al-Ash'arī: 'Ask all Muslim women under your jurisdiction to pay *zakāh* on their ornaments.' Imām Abū Ḥanīfah narrated the following tradition on the authority of 'Amr ibn Dīnār whereby 'Ā'ishah had given over gold ornaments to her sisters and 'Abd Allāh ibn 'Umar had likewise given them over to his daughters. (Jaṣṣāṣ, *Aḥkam al-Qur'ān*, comments on *Sūrah al-Zukhruf* 43: 18.)

After citing all these traditions Abū Bakr al-Jaṣṣās writes: 'The traditions that have come down from the Prophet (peace be on him) as regards the lawfulness of gold and silk [for women] are more numerous than those about their unlawfulness. The present verse is also indicative of their lawfulness. Moreover, the practice of the *ummah* from the time of the Prophet (peace be on him) and his Companions to our own time [that is, the end of the fourth century of the *Hijrah*] has been the same and no one objects to this. Any objection to such matters on the basis of an isolated tradition is not acceptable.' (Jaṣṣāṣ, *Aḥkām al-Qur'ān*, comments on *Sūrah al-Zukhruf* 43: 18.)

18. The angels are beyond belonging to one gender or the other. This point comes out sharply from the wording of the verse.

19. This might alternatively be translated as follows: 'Were they present when they were born?'

worshipped these deities.'[20] But they have no knowledge of the matter and are simply conjecturing. (21) Or did We bestow upon them a Book before on whose authority they are holding on (to angel-worship)?[21] (22) Nay; they simply claim: ▶

مَّا لَهُم بِذَٰلِكَ مِنْ عِلْمٍ ۖ إِنْ هُمْ
إِلَّا يَخْرُصُونَ ﴿٢٠﴾ أَمْ ءَاتَيْنَٰهُمْ كِتَٰبًا مِّن
قَبْلِهِۦ فَهُم بِهِۦ مُسْتَمْسِكُونَ ﴿٢١﴾ بَلْ قَالُوٓا۟

20. They justified their error, pleading that had it not been God's will, He would not have let them indulge in worshipping others besides Him. All misguided people down the ages have resorted to this argument. Their contention has been that if they took to worshipping the angels it was because God let them do so. In other words, they have been engaged in this practice for centuries, yet they have still not been punished by God. This, they argue, proves that this practice does not carry God's disapproval.

21. In their ignorance they believed that all that actually happened in the world carried God's approval. Hence their polytheism too enjoyed His approval. Had this line of argument been sound, then not only would polytheism but also theft, robbery, bribery, fornication, violation of oaths and several other evils that are rampant among us would also be considered permissible. Nevertheless, no one claims such behaviour to be good and lawful. Had the logic of the polytheists been sound, even these misdeeds should be considered as good and lawful. However, the fact is that all that happens in the world is not indicative of God's approval or disapproval, of His pleasure or displeasure. These are determined in the light of the Scriptures sent down to Messengers, which declare what is approved and what is disapproved by God. In the Scriptures, God Himself declares which beliefs, deeds and morals are pleasing to Him and those which incur His displeasure. Hence, if the polytheists have any Scriptural evidence to prove that angels should be worshipped along with God, they should produce it. (For further details, see *al-An'ām* 6, nn. 71, 80, 110 and 124-5; *Towards Understanding the Qur'ān*, vol. II, pp. 262-3, 266-7, 280 and 288-9; *al-A'rāf* 7, nn. 17-18, vol. III, p. 18; *Yūnus* 10: 101; *Hūd* 11: 116; *al-Ra'd* 13: 49; *al-Naḥl* 16: 10, 30-2 and 94-5; *al-Zumar* 39: 20 and *al-Shūrā* 42, n. 11 above)

'We found our forefathers on a way, and we continue to find guidance in their footsteps.'[22] (23) And thus it is: whenever We sent any warner to a city its affluent ones said: 'We found our forefathers on a way and we continue to follow in their footsteps.'[23] (24) Each Prophet asked them: 'Will you do so even if we were ▶

إِنَّا وَجَدْنَآ ءَابَآءَنَا عَلَىٰٓ أُمَّةٍ وَإِنَّا عَلَىٰٓ ءَاثَٰرِهِم
مُّهْتَدُونَ ﴿٢٢﴾ وَكَذَٰلِكَ مَآ أَرْسَلْنَا مِن
قَبْلِكَ فِى قَرْيَةٍ مِّن نَّذِيرٍ إِلَّا قَالَ مُتْرَفُوهَآ
إِنَّا وَجَدْنَآ ءَابَآءَنَا عَلَىٰٓ أُمَّةٍ وَإِنَّا عَلَىٰٓ
ءَاثَٰرِهِم مُّقْتَدُونَ ﴿٢٣﴾ ۞ قَٰلَ أَوَلَوْ

---

22. Inevitably, the polytheists could not produce any Scriptural evidence in support of their beliefs and practices. Their only argument was that they followed what had come down from their ancestors. Accordingly, they took angels as goddesses.

23. It is worth considering why is it that the affluent in every nation have opposed the Prophets and preferred to cling to their ancestral faith? Why are they are always in the forefront of the opponents of Truth and seek to maintain the entrenched *Jāhilīyah* of the day? Again, why is it that they are always instrumental in misleading people and in provoking them to come forth with mischief in opposition to God's Prophets? The following reasons account for this: (i) The affluent are too engrossed in their worldly pleasures to be concerned with the far-fetched task of distinguishing between truth and falsehood. Their mental sloth and cynical disinterest with questions of right and wrong push them towards conservatism so that they become supporters of the *status quo ante*. (ii) Their interests are deeply interwoven with the existing order. Their acquaintance with the current system of life makes them fear that if there is any change their dominance will be undermined and it will no longer be possible for them to act in contravention of the law or to acquire unlawful earnings. (For further details, see *al-An'ām* 6, n. 91, *Towards Understanding the Qur'ān,* Vol. II, p. 272; *al-A'rāf* 7, nn. 46, 53, 58, 74, 88 and 92, Vol. III, pp. 36-37, 43, 46-47, 56-57, 66-67 and 70-71; *Hūd* 11, nn. 31-32 and 41, Vol. IV, pp. 93, 99, 100; *Banū Isrā'īl* 17, n. 18, Vol. V, p. 31; *al-Mu'minūn* 23, nn. 26-27, 35 and 59, Vol. VI, pp. 92-94, 97 and 110; *Saba'* 34, n. 54, Vol. IX, p. 193.)

to show you a way better than the way of your forefathers?' They answered: 'We disbelieve in the religion with which you have been sent.' (25) Then We exacted retribution from them. So do consider the end of those who gave the lie (to the Prophets).

(26) Call to mind when Abraham said to his father and his people: [24] 'I totally disown all whom you serve (27) except the One Who created me; and, behold, it is He Who will direct me to the Right Way.'[25] (28) And Abraham left behind this word[26] ▶

جِئۡتُكُم بِأَهۡدَىٰ مِمَّا وَجَدتُّمۡ عَلَيۡهِ ءَابَآءَكُمۡۖ
قَالُوٓاْ إِنَّا بِمَآ أُرۡسِلۡتُم بِهِۦ كَٰفِرُونَ ٢٤
فَٱنتَقَمۡنَا مِنۡهُمۡۖ فَٱنظُرۡ كَيۡفَ كَانَ عَٰقِبَةُ
ٱلۡمُكَذِّبِينَ ٢٥ وَإِذۡ قَالَ إِبۡرَٰهِيمُ لِأَبِيهِ
وَقَوۡمِهِۦٓ إِنَّنِي بَرَآءٞ مِّمَّا تَعۡبُدُونَ ٢٦
إِلَّا ٱلَّذِي فَطَرَنِي فَإِنَّهُۥ سَيَهۡدِينِ ٢٧
وَجَعَلَهَا كَلِمَةَۢ بَاقِيَةٗ

24. For a detailed discussion, see *al-Baqarah* 2: 124-33, *Towards Understanding the Qur'ān,* vol. I, pp. 111-15; *al-An'ām* 6, nn. 50-5, vol. II, pp. 245-53; *Ibrāhīm* 14, nn. 46-53, vol. IV, pp. 272-5; *Maryam* 19, nn. 26-7, vol. V, pp. 160-1; *al-Anbiyā'* 21, nn. 54-66, vol. V, pp. 272-81; *al-Shu'arā'* 26, nn. 50-62, vol. VII, pp. 74-80; *al-'Ankabūt* 29, nn. 26-46, vol. VIII, pp. 21-30; *al-Ṣāffāt* 37: 83-100 and nn. 44-55, vol. IX, pp. 296-300.

25. Thus the Prophet Abraham (peace be on him) not only stated his belief, but also adduced an argument in support of it. The reason he disassociated himself from his ancestral deities was that they had neither created him nor provided him with the guidance he needed. Likewise, the reason for his being wholly devoted to the One True God was that He alone is the Creator, Who can and does guide man to the Straight Way.

26. In other words, none other than God deserves to be worshipped.

to endure among his posterity so that they may return to it.[27] (29) (Even when they began worshipping others than Allah We did not destroy them) but bestowed sustenance on them and on their forefathers until there came to them the Truth and a Messenger who clearly expounded things to them.[28] ▶

فِي عَقِبِهِۦ لَعَلَّهُمۡ يَرۡجِعُونَ ۝٢٨ بَلۡ مَتَّعۡتُ
هَٰٓؤُلَآءِ وَءَابَآءَهُمۡ حَتَّىٰ جَآءَهُمُ ٱلۡحَقُّ
وَرَسُولٞ مُّبِينٞ ۝٢٩

---

27. Whenever they deviated from the Straight Way this 'word' would be there to bring them back to it. This event is especially recounted to expose the disbelieving Quraysh's irrational attitude. It was also recounted to put them to shame. For if they wanted to follow in the footsteps of their ancestors they should have chosen the role models of the Prophets Abraham and Ishmael (peace be on them). It is a pity that they chose instead the examples of their worst ancestors. It is pertinent to point out that the very basis of the Quraysh's pre-eminence was their descendency from Abraham and Ishmael (peace be on them) as also their custodianship of the Ka'bah, built by Abraham and Ishmael. The Quraysh should have followed those Prophets rather than those of their forefathers who were immersed in ignorance, those who had abandoned the way of the Prophets Abraham and Ishmael (peace be on them) and had adopted polytheism from the idol-worshippers of the lands around them. Moreover, by mentioning this error another error of those people is also laid bare: had blind imitation of ancestors, without distinguishing between good and evil, been right, the Prophet Abraham (peace be on him) would himself have done so. The fact, however, is that he told his people that he could not follow their beliefs which were based on ignorance, beliefs because of which they had abandoned their Creator and made imaginary beings, who had not created them, their deities.

28. The Qur'ānic expression *rasūl mubīn* can also signify that a Messenger whose Messengership was self-evident had appeared on the

(30) And when the Truth came to them they said: 'This is just sorcery[29] and we reject it.'

(31) They say: 'Why was this Qur'ān not sent down upon some great man from the two (main) cities?'[30] (32) Is it they who distribute the Mercy of your Lord? It is We Who have distributed their livelihood among them in the life of this world, and have raised some above ▶

وَلَمَّا جَآءَهُمُ ٱلْحَقُّ قَالُوا۟ هَٰذَا سِحْرٌ وَإِنَّا
بِهِۦ كَٰفِرُونَ ﴿٣٠﴾ وَقَالُوا۟ لَوْلَا نُزِّلَ هَٰذَا
ٱلْقُرْءَانُ عَلَىٰ رَجُلٍ مِّنَ ٱلْقَرْيَتَيْنِ عَظِيمٍ ﴿٣١﴾
أَهُمْ يَقْسِمُونَ رَحْمَتَ رَبِّكَ ۚ نَحْنُ قَسَمْنَا بَيْنَهُم
مَّعِيشَتَهُمْ فِى ٱلْحَيَوٰةِ ٱلدُّنْيَا ۚ وَرَفَعْنَا بَعْضَهُمْ

---

scene. His illustrious life, both before and after assuming Messengership, demonstrates that he is beyond doubt a true Messenger of God.

29. For further details, see *al-Anbiyā'* 21, n. 5, *Towards Understanding the Qur'ān*, vol. V, pp. 250-2; *Ṣād* 38, n. 5 above.

30. The two cities mean Makkah and Ṭā'if. The unbelievers contended that were God to send a Messenger, He would have chosen a leading person from either of these two main cities. On the contrary, he who was appointed to this office was an orphan, devoid of both wealth and worldly glory. As a youth, he had earned his livelihood as a shepherd. Later, he engaged in trading and in this regard he drew upon the capital of his wife. Nor was he a tribal chief. Such eminent Makkan chiefs as Walīd ibn al-Mughīrah and 'Utbah ibn Rabī'ah were, in their opinion, better suited for this position. Likewise, leading figures such as 'Urwah ibn Mas'ūd, Ḥabīb ibn 'Amr, Kinānah ibn 'Abd 'Amr and Ibn 'Abd Yālīl flourished in Ṭā'if. Initially, they were not even prepared to consider that a fellow human being could be God's Messenger.

The Qur'ān, however, refuted their baseless contentions by stressing that all along it is humans who have been God's Messengers, as it is they alone who can serve as guides to their fellow human beings. It is also affirmed that these Messengers did not abruptly descend from the

others in rank that some of them may harness others to their service.[31] Your Lord's Mercy is better than all ▶	فَوْقَ بَعْضٍ دَرَجَٰتٍ لِّيَتَّخِذَ بَعْضُهُم بَعْضًا سُخْرِيًّا ۗ وَرَحْمَتُ رَبِّكَ خَيْرٌ

sky. Rather, they were born like other humans and were brought up in their respective communities; they too walked about in the markets and enjoyed family lives and needed food and drink to sustain them. (See *al-Naḥl* 16: 43; *Banū Isrā'īl* 17: 94-95; *Yūsuf* 12: 109, *al-Furqān* 25: 7 and 20, *al-Anbiyā'* 21: 7-8 and *al-Ra'd* 13: 38.) In response to the Qur'ānic argument the unbelievers said that some prominent person who commanded a large band of followers among them and inspired awe in such people should have been made God's Messenger. According to their view, Muḥammad ibn 'Abd Allāh (peace be on him), was not suited for that office.

31. This is the Qur'ānic response to their objection. Here, a number of important points are succinctly brought out:

(1) It is God's right to decide to whom He grants a portion of His Mercy and to whom He does not. If this is not the case, one might ask, is it the prerogative of humans to decide who should receive a certain portion of God's Mercy and who should not? (God's Mercy here signifies that universal, encompassing Mercy in which everyone necessarily has a share.)

(2) Let alone designation to God's Messengership, even the bestowal of daily sustenance lies in God's Hand. It is God Who causes the birth of humans of all types: beautiful and ugly, strong and weak, those with a sweet and others with an offensive voice, the intelligent and the dull-witted, and the rich and the poor. He grants some a retentive memory and makes others prone to forgetfulness. He grants some sound limbs and makes others crippled from birth. He causes some to be born among a developed and others among a backward people. No one other than God has any role in deciding such matters about human beings. They are, therefore, bound to live with the characteristics with which they were born. Again, it is God Who bestows on people sustenance, power, honour, fame, wealth and political authority. No one can interfere in God's decisions on these matters. Those whom God causes to rise can never suffer a fall because of the machinations of others.

the treasures that they hoard.[32] (33) Were it not that all mankind would become a single community (and follow the same way), We would have provided ▶	مِّمَّا يَجْمَعُونَ ﴿٣٢﴾ وَلَوْلَآ أَن يَكُونَ ٱلنَّاسُ أُمَّةً وَٰحِدَةً لَّجَعَلْنَا

As for those about whom God decides that they shall encounter a fall, none can ever avert this. For all human efforts ultimately prove in vain against God's decisions.

In a realm so exclusively and firmly in God's control, it seems that some people like to arrogate to themselves the right to decide on God's behalf on a matter so vital as to who should be appointed His Messenger.

(3) God does not bestow all endowments upon a single individual. One notes a striking difference between various people in this regard. Some are granted a particular endowment while others do not share this. As a result, human beings are interdependent. Given this, they should not foolishly think that an elite of their community, which has already been given political power and worldly glory, should also be endowed with the office of God's Messengership. Their demand to combine all excellent qualities and privileges in one single person cannot be entertained. Likewise, there is nothing odd in the fact that some people have not received a combination of excellence in intellect, knowledge, wealth, physical attractiveness, power and prestige.

32. God's Mercy here specifically means the Mercy of Messengership.

The Qur'ān here clearly points out that the Quraysh chiefs, whom the Makkans respected for their affluence and exalted rank, are unworthy of the august office of Messengership. Compared to other positions, there is a different criterion for appointing people to the elevated office of God's Messengership, for this is an office that requires the highest qualities. It is not for every powerful tribal chief or opulent tycoon to hold such august office. The contrary view held by the Quraysh simply shows how very low the standards they had set up for appointment to God's Messengership were or else they would not have thought of their chiefs in this regard. As for God, they should not expect Him to follow such an unwise course.

for all those who disbelieve in the Merciful One silver roofs for their houses, and (silver) stairs on which to go up, (34) and (silver) doors to their houses, and couches (of silver) upon which they would recline; (35) or that they be made of gold.[33] Surely all this is only the enjoyment of the life of the world. But (true prosperity) in the Hereafter with Your Lord is only for the God-fearing.

(36) He who is negligent to remember the Merciful One,[34] to him We assign a satan as his boon companion, (37) and these satans hinder them from the Right Path, while he still reckons himself to be ▶

لِمَن يَكْفُرُ بِٱلرَّحْمَٰنِ لِبُيُوتِهِمْ سُقُفًا مِّن فِضَّةٍ
وَمَعَارِجَ عَلَيْهَا يَظْهَرُونَ ﴿٣٣﴾ وَلِبُيُوتِهِمْ أَبْوَٰبًا
وَسُرُرًا عَلَيْهَا يَتَّكِـُٔونَ ﴿٣٤﴾ وَزُخْرُفًا وَإِن
كُلُّ ذَٰلِكَ لَمَّا مَتَٰعُ ٱلْحَيَوٰةِ ٱلدُّنْيَا وَٱلْءَاخِرَةُ
عِندَ رَبِّكَ لِلْمُتَّقِينَ ﴿٣٥﴾ وَمَن يَعْشُ عَن
ذِكْرِ ٱلرَّحْمَٰنِ نُقَيِّضْ لَهُۥ شَيْطَٰنًا فَهُوَ لَهُۥ
قَرِينٌ ﴿٣٦﴾ وَإِنَّهُمْ لَيَصُدُّونَهُمْ عَنِ ٱلسَّبِيلِ
وَيَحْسَبُونَ أَنَّهُم

33. For the Prophet's detractors, wealth represented the very zenith of all bounties, the climax of all that deserves to be cherished. God, however, attaches scant importance to it. Had it not been feared that men would be drawn towards unbelief, God would have granted all unbelievers houses of gold and silver. Wealth is no index of a person's moral or spiritual excellence. This is evident from the fact that many wicked people, whose rotten stench engulfs a whole society, are wealthy. Hence, it is foolish to regard wealth as a sign of someone's greatness.

34. *Dhikr al-Raḥmān* has a wide-ranging significance. Apart from its literal meaning, 'remembrance of God,' it also signifies 'exhortation' from God as well as the Qur'ān.

rightly-guided. (38) But when he comes to Us, he will say (to his satan): 'Would that there had been between me and you the distance as between the East and the West. How evil a companion you were!' (39) (He will then be told): 'Today it will not benefit you the least that after your wrong-doing you and your satans now share the chastisement.'[35]

(40) Can you, (O Prophet), then make the deaf hear, or direct to the Right Way the blind or one lost in manifest error?[36] (41) We shall inflict retribution on them, whether We take you away from the world (before We do that), (42) or make you see the end that ▶

مُّهْتَدُونَ ﴿٣٧﴾ حَتَّىٰٓ إِذَا جَآءَنَا قَالَ يَٰلَيْتَ
بَيْنِى وَبَيْنَكَ بُعْدَ ٱلْمَشْرِقَيْنِ فَبِئْسَ ٱلْقَرِينُ ﴿٣٨﴾
وَلَن يَنفَعَكُمُ ٱلْيَوْمَ إِذ ظَّلَمْتُمْ أَنَّكُمْ فِى
ٱلْعَذَابِ مُشْتَرِكُونَ ﴿٣٩﴾ أَفَأَنتَ تُسْمِعُ ٱلصُّمَّ
أَوْ تَهْدِى ٱلْعُمْىَ وَمَن كَانَ فِى ضَلَٰلٍ
مُّبِينٍ ﴿٤٠﴾ فَإِمَّا نَذْهَبَنَّ بِكَ فَإِنَّا مِنْهُم
مُّنتَقِمُونَ ﴿٤١﴾ أَوْ نُرِيَنَّكَ

35. That is, there should be no cause for consolation in the fact that those who led them astray are being chastised. This because those who succumbed to misguidance, and not only those who led them astray, will be chastised.

36. The Prophet (peace be on him) is directed to focus his attention on those who are disposed to pay heed to the Truth and who are not blind to it. He should better not waste his time and energy on trying to guide those that are spiritually and morally blind and deaf. Nor should he consume himself with grief for his kith and kin who are averse to following the Right Way and thereby invite God's punishment on themselves.

We had promised them, for We have full power over them.[37] (43) So hold fast to what has been revealed to you. Surely you are on the Straight Way.[38] (44) Verily it is a great source of eminence for you and your people, and soon you will be called to account concerning that.[39] ▶

ٱلَّذِى وَعَدْنَـٰهُمْ فَإِنَّا عَلَيْهِم مُّقْتَدِرُونَ ﴿٤٢﴾
فَٱسْتَمْسِكْ بِٱلَّذِىٓ أُوحِىَ إِلَيْكَ ۖ
إِنَّكَ عَلَىٰ صِرَٰطٍ مُّسْتَقِيمٍ ﴿٤٣﴾ وَإِنَّهُۥ لَذِكْرٌ
لَّكَ وَلِقَوْمِكَ ۖ وَسَوْفَ تُسْـَٔلُونَ ﴿٤٤﴾

---

37. In order to understand this it is necessary to bear in mind the actual context in which it was said. The Makkan unbelievers regarded the Prophet (peace be on him) as a nuisance. They thought that once he was removed from the scene, they would enjoy peace and tranquillity. Thanks to this misgiving, they constantly deliberated among themselves as to how they could get rid of him. They believed that if they could do only this, then, things would be fine thereafter. At this point, God turns His attention away from the unbelievers and addresses the Prophet (peace be on him), impressing upon him that his presence or absence in Makkah makes little difference. He will witness their grievous doom if he is alive at the time when they are afflicted by it. However, if he dies before this, the evil ones will still encounter their doom even if after the lapse of some time. What is beyond any doubt is that the unbelievers have incurred God's wrath and that they cannot escape being seized by it.

38. The Prophet (peace be on him) should not unduly concern himself with questions about when those who resort to dishonest and oppressive measures in opposing the Truth will be punished, nor with what kind of punishment will be meted out to them. Nor should he bother himself about whether Islam will flourish during his own lifetime or thereafter. Instead, he should be satisfied with the fact that he is following the Right Way. He should, therefore, carry out his duty without being excessively concerned about its outcome. He should leave it to God to bring the unbelievers to disgrace during his lifetime or, if He so wishes, at a later date.

39. The highest honour imaginable for a man is that God should choose him to be His Prophet and reveal His Book to him. By the same

(45) Ask all Our Messengers whom We sent before you whether We had appointed any deities beside the Merciful One to be worshipped.[40]

(46) Indeed We[41] sent Moses with ▶

وَسْـَٔلْ مَنْ أَرْسَلْنَا مِن قَبْلِكَ مِن رُّسُلِنَآ أَجَعَلْنَا مِن دُونِ ٱلرَّحْمَـٰنِ ءَالِهَةً يُعْبَدُونَ ﴿٤٥﴾ وَلَقَدْ أَرْسَلْنَا مُوسَىٰ

token, it is the good fortune of a people that a Prophet is born among them and the honour of conveying God's message is thereby conferred upon them. If the Quraysh and the rest of the Arabs fail to appreciate this honour, they will be held accountable for it in due course.

40. To ask 'all Our Messengers' means to refer to the Books revealed to them. The Qur'ānic directive that disputes should be referred to God and His Messenger (see *al-Nisā'* 4: 59), is obviously not to be taken literally. What it rather means is that all disputes should be resolved in the light of the Book of God and the *Sunnah* of the Prophet (peace be on him). Likewise, to ask the earlier Messengers does not mean literally to go to those Messengers (who, in any case, are no longer alive) and pose questions to them. What is rather meant is to consult those Messengers' teachings. In other words, let people go and explore if any of the earlier Messengers had ever taught people to worship any other than the One True God.

41. The Prophet Moses' story is related at this juncture because of the following three considerations: (i) Whenever God raises any of His Prophets in a country and among a people, He thereby makes it possible for them to benefit from that opportunity. This grace was also granted to the Arabs by raising the Prophet Muḥammad (peace be on him) among them. However, if they refuse to believe in him, as Pharaoh and his people did with regard to the Prophet Moses (peace be on him), they will meet the fate of Pharaoh's people and become an example of God's punishment to others. (ii) Pharaoh exulted on account of his arrogance, the pride of his royal power and his grandeur and wealth. He belittled Moses, treating him as an object of contempt. In like manner, the unbelieving Quraysh now look down upon the Prophet Muḥammad (peace be on him), considering him insignificant as compared to their haughty chiefs.

Our Signs[42] to Pharaoh and his nobles. He told them: 'I am a Messenger of the Lord of the Universe.' (47) Yet when he brought forth Clear Signs from Us, then lo, they burst into laughter. (48) Every Sign that We showed them was greater than its predecessor; and then We seized them with Our chastisement so that they may return (to the Right Way).[43] ▶

بِـَٔايَـٰتِنَآ إِلَىٰ فِرْعَوْنَ وَمَلَإِي۟هِۦ فَقَالَ إِنِّى
رَسُولُ رَبِّ ٱلْعَـٰلَمِينَ ﴿٤٦﴾ فَلَمَّا جَآءَهُم
بِـَٔايَـٰتِنَآ إِذَا هُم مِّنْهَا يَضْحَكُونَ ﴿٤٧﴾ وَمَا
نُرِيهِم مِّنْ ءَايَةٍ إِلَّا هِىَ أَكْبَرُ مِنْ أُخْتِهَا ۖ
وَأَخَذْنَـٰهُم بِٱلْعَذَابِ لَعَلَّهُمْ يَرْجِعُونَ ﴿٤٨﴾

However, God's judgement is different, which makes it quite clear who is truly contemptible: the Prophets or their detractors? (iii) To mock God's signs and to demonstrate arrogance at His warnings is not a jocular matter, but rather one of grave consequence, which costs people dear. If they learn no lesson from those who committed this mistake and suffered in the past, they are then bound to face the same grievous fate of those punished by God for such misdeeds.

42. This refers to those miracles of the Prophet Moses (peace be on him) – the rod and the shining hand – with which he initially encountered Pharaoh's court. (For further details, see *al-A'rāf* 7, nn. 87-89, *Towards Understanding the Qur'ān,* vol. III, pp. 65-7; *Ṭā Hā* 20, nn. 12-13 and 29-30, vol. V, pp. 186-7, 196-8; *al-Shu'arā'* 26, nn. 26-9, vol. VII, pp. 63-5; *al-Naml* 27, n. 16, vol. VII, p. 143; *al-Qaṣaṣ* 28, nn. 44-5, vol. VII, p. 217.)

43. This refers to the miraculous signs which God later showed them through the Prophet Moses (peace be on him). They are as follows:

(1) Pharaoh's magicians were publicly defeated in the tournament and God's Prophet prevailed. Once defeated, these magicians embraced the faith. (For details, *al-A'rāf* 7, nn. 88-92, *Towards Understanding the Qur'ān,* vol. III, pp. 66-71; *Ṭā Hā* 20, nn. 30-50, vol. V, pp. 197-205; *al-Shu'arā'* 26, nn. 29-40, vol. VII, pp. 64-70.)

(2) Exactly as forewarned by the Prophet Moses (peace be on him), Egypt was overtaken by a severe famine, one which ended only when Moses prayed to God for its end.

(3) Moses' other predictions also came true. For the whole of Egypt was successively afflicted by a series of heavy downpours, hailstorms and thunder and lightning which destroyed towns and crops. Once again, these natural calamities came to an end only as a result of Moses' prayer to God.

(4) As foretold by Moses, swarms of locusts hung over the entire country. When Moses prayed to God, this disaster ended.

(5) In accord with Moses' prediction, lice and bugs infested the whole country, putting men and animals to enormous inconvenience. Worse, these pests destroyed food stores. The Egyptians beseeched the Prophet Moses (peace be on him) to pray to God to bring an end to these.

(6) As Moses had warned, every nook and corner of Egypt was infested with frogs. This great nuisance for the Egyptians only ended after Moses' prayer.

(7) As foretold by Moses, the Egyptians were facing a scourge of blood. Well water, springs, canals and pools all turned into blood. As a result, fish died and water supplies came to a standstill, for a whole week drinking water becoming too foul to use. It was only after Moses prayed to God that they were delivered from this scourge and clean drinking water became available to them. (For further details, see *al-A'rāf* 7, nn. 94-6, *Towards Understanding the Qur'ān,* vol. III, pp. 72-3; *al-Naml* 27, nn. 16-17, vol. VII, pp. 143-4; *al-Mu'min* 40, n. 37 above.)

The Biblical account of these inflictions features in *Exodus* (Chs. 7-10 and 12.) However, this represents no more than a mixture of fact and fantasy, for it relates that the punishment of blood was matched on the same scale by the magicians. However, the magicians failed to produce lice, thereby admitting that only God could do this. Incredibly enough, the Bible relates that when frogs infested Egypt, the magicians produced frogs as well. Yet Pharaoh requested the Prophet Moses (peace be on him) to pray to God to bring that scourge to an end. Had the magicians been capable of producing frogs, then surely it is the magicians themselves who should have been asked to drive the frogs away. How could the Egyptians distinguish between the frogs brought about by God and the ones by the magicians? The same question arises about blood. How could it be established as to which water had been turned into blood by God and which by the magicians? All this proves that the Bible is not God's

(49) (Whenever they faced an affliction) they would say: 'O magician, pray for us to your Lord according to your station with Him. We shall certainly be guided to the Right Way.' (50) But lo, each time We removed Our affliction from them, they would go back on their word.[44] ▶

وَقَالُوا۟ يَـٰٓأَيُّهَ ٱلسَّاحِرُ ٱدْعُ لَنَا رَبَّكَ بِمَا عَهِدَ
عِندَكَ إِنَّنَا لَمُهْتَدُونَ ﴿٤٩﴾ فَلَمَّا كَشَفْنَا عَنْهُمُ
ٱلْعَذَابَ إِذَا هُمْ يَنكُثُونَ ﴿٥٠﴾

unadulterated Word. Rather, later writers have interpolated many of their own fanciful notions into it. Worse, doing so, they clearly lacked even the common sense and mental maturity needed for skilful fabrication.

44. As for the obstinacy betrayed by Pharaoh and his people, this is best illustrated by their conduct. Even when they were confronted with God's scourge and asked the Prophet Moses (peace be on him) to pray that it be brought to an end and they be spared, they addressed him as a magician rather than as a Prophet. These people were aware of the true nature of magic. They also realised that a magician could not accomplish what was done by the Prophet Moses (peace be on him). What a magician can do, at most, is that on a very limited scale, he might make some people think that water has turned into blood or frogs have appeared from nowhere or that locusts are pouncing on them. This, when in reality, nothing of the sort actually happens. Magicians' tricks are confined to a particular place. Water does not actually change into blood. Nor do frogs or locusts or any other creatures appear. These are only imaginary and those present at a magic show understand this quite well. As for the incidence of a nationwide famine, or the turning of all water reservoirs into blood or infestations of lice, frogs and locusts stretching over a territory covering thousands of square miles, these have never been performed by any magician. Nor is it possible for them to do so. Had such magicians and their skills really existed, kings would not have needed armies nor would they have needed to wage wars. With their magicians' expertise, they could have conquered the whole world. Rather, had magicians been so accomplished, they would not have served kings; they would have installed themselves as kings.

(51) And Pharaoh proclaimed among his people: [45] 'My people, do I not have dominion over Egypt, and are these streams not flowing beneath me? ▶

وَنَادَىٰ فِرْعَوْنُ فِى قَوْمِهِۦ قَالَ يَٰقَوْمِ
أَلَيْسَ لِى مُلْكُ مِصْرَ وَهَٰذِهِ ٱلْأَنْهَٰرُ
تَجْرِى مِن تَحْتِىٓ ۖ

Some Qur'ānic scholars find it difficult to explain why Pharaoh and his courtiers addressed the Prophet Moses (peace be on him) as a magician. As those courtiers were in distress, they should have spoken highly of him. In order to resolve this issue, some scholars have said that by calling Moses a magician they did not intend to offend him, for being a magician was considered honourable in the then Egyptian society. (Zamakhsharī, *al-Kashshāf*, comments on *Sūrah al-Zukhruf* 43: 49.)

This interpretation, however, is not correct. At other places too in the Qur'ānic account Pharaoh dismisses Moses as a magician. In so branding him, the note of contempt is too conspicuous to be missed. Pharaoh, too, regarded magic as something false and in branding Moses a magician he rejected his claim to be a Prophet.

As to why the Prophet Moses (peace be on him) acceded to Pharaoh's and his courtiers' request even when they addressed him disparagingly as a magician, all this was part and parcel of clinching God's argument against them. That they requested the Prophet Moses (peace be on him) to pray to God to avert the scourge shows that they inwardly recognised what the source and reason of their afflictions was. Yet they addressed Moses as a magician and broke their promise to mend their ways once the scourges had come to an end. By doing so they did no harm to the Prophet Moses (peace be on him.) Rather, the case against them became stronger and eventually they were obliterated. They knew all too well that magic could not be behind the scourges that had afflicted them. Rather, they perceived them as signs from the Lord of the universe. Yet, as the Qur'ān states, they lied about this: 'They denied those signs out of iniquity and arrogance, although their hearts were convinced of their truth' (*al-Naml* 27: 14).

45. Pharaoh made this proclamation through his chiefs and heralds who announced it throughout all parts of his kingdom. These were the only means of mass communication available to him for he had no access to a state-controlled press, to sycophantic news agencies or to official

Can't you see?[46] (52) Am I better or this contemptible[47] man who is scarcely able to express himself?[48] (53) Why were bracelets of gold not bestowed upon him? Why did a retinue of angels ▶

أَفَلَا تُبْصِرُونَ ﴿٥١﴾ أَمْ أَنَا۠ خَيْرٌ مِّنْ هَٰذَا
ٱلَّذِى هُوَ مَهِينٌ وَلَا يَكَادُ يُبِينُ ﴿٥٢﴾ فَلَوْلَآ
أُلْقِىَ عَلَيْهِ أَسْوِرَةٌ مِّن ذَهَبٍ أَوْ جَآءَ
مَعَهُ ٱلْمَلَٰٓئِكَةُ

information media and government controlled radio like those of today which specialise in 'manufacturing' news.

46. Pharaoh's response betrays his panic. The series of miracles presented by the Prophet Moses (peace be on him) had shaken the Egyptians. They were becoming skeptical about their gods. It is worth reminding ourselves that Pharaoh ruled over them in his capacity as the incarnation of gods. Even after realising the gravity of the situation, Pharaoh insisted on his claim to both kingship and godhead. He boasted that there was prosperity in his realm precisely because of his rule. Likewise, he claimed that all works of development had been carried out by the royal family, his family. In view of this, people should pay no heed to Moses (peace be on him).

47. That is, the Prophet Moses (peace be on him) who possessed neither wealth, nor power nor authority. The same point was raised by the unbelieving Quraysh about the Prophet Muḥammad (peace be on him).

48. Some Qur'ānic commentators are of the view that what Pharaoh refers to is the Prophet Moses' stammering. (Qurṭabī, *al-Jāmi' li Aḥkām al-Qur'ān*, comments on *Sūrah al-Zukhruf* 43: 52.) We have noted in *Sūrah Ṭā Hā* that when Moses (peace be on him) was designated a Prophet, he requested that God loosen the knot of his tongue so that people might more easily comprehend his message. This, along with his other requests, was granted. (See *Ṭā Hā* 20: 27-36.) Some of Moses' speeches, as recorded in the Qur'ān, fully demonstrate his eloquence and fluency. So Pharaoh's objection did not refer, contrary to some Qur'ānic exegetes' view, to Moses' stammering. Rather, Pharaoh complained that Moses' message was incoherent; in other words, he was simply unable to grasp it.

not accompany him as attendants?'[49]

(54) He incited his people to levity and they obeyed him. Surely they were an iniquitous people.[50] ▶

مُقْتَرِنِينَ ﴿٥٣﴾ فَٱسْتَخَفَّ قَوْمَهُۥ فَأَطَاعُوهُ ۚ
إِنَّهُمْ كَانُوا۟ قَوْمًا فَـٰسِقِينَ ﴿٥٤﴾

---

49. At that time, when anyone was elevated to high public office, he received from the king a robe and gold bracelets, and also a posse of guards and pageboys. This was designed to evoke awe and reverence both for the holder of the public office and for the king who had appointed him. Pharaoh argued that had Moses (peace be on him) been a genuine Prophet, he should have been dressed exquisitely and accompanied by a retinue of angels. He could not accept an ordinary person as Moses, with only a rod in his hand, as the Messenger of the Lord of the universe.

50. A significant truth is stated here: when a person seeks to assert his authority, he resorts to all conceivable means from bribery to oppressing those who refuse to be cowed down, and to openly buying people's loyalty. Whether he verbally says so or not, his conduct is based on the assumption that the intellectual and moral calibre of the people concerned is very low and that he can drive them in whichever direction he wants. Once he is installed in power, his misdeeds come out into the open. Iniquitous people are prone to surrender themselves to him for they are not concerned with the fine distinctions between truth and falsehood. Their only concern is their own selfish interest. Accordingly, they reconcile themselves with any tyrant and put up with the disgrace to which he subjects them. These people prove by their very conduct that the wicked tyrant's low estimate of them was pretty correct: they are indeed as he had thought them to be.

The main cause of these people's succumbing to humiliation is that they are iniquitous. Given this propensity, they are least concerned to find out what is right as distinct from what is wrong, what is just as distinct from unjust, what is honest as distinct from dishonest, and whether truthfulness and honesty and magnanimity are to be valued or falsehood, dishonesty and pettiness. As a result, what really counts are one's own personal interests and for their sake such people are always ready to cooperate with anyone, no matter how evil he might be. They thus yield to any tyrant, accept all possible falsehood and are prepared to suppress every voice that rises in support of the truth.

(55) So when they incurred Our wrath, We exacted retribution from them, and drowned them all, (56) and made them a thing of the past and an example for those who would come after them.[51]

(57) No sooner the example of the son of Mary was mentioned than, lo and behold, your people raised a clamour (58) and said: 'Who is better, our deities or he?'[52] They said so only out of contentiousness. They are a disputatious people. ▶

فَلَمَّآ ءَاسَفُونَا ٱنتَقَمْنَا مِنْهُمْ فَأَغْرَقْنَٰهُمْ
أَجْمَعِينَ ﴿٥٥﴾ فَجَعَلْنَٰهُمْ سَلَفًا وَمَثَلًا
لِّلْءَاخِرِينَ ﴿٥٦﴾ ۞ وَلَمَّا ضُرِبَ ٱبْنُ مَرْيَمَ
مَثَلًا إِذَا قَوْمُكَ مِنْهُ يَصِدُّونَ ﴿٥٧﴾
وَقَالُوٓا۟ ءَأَٰلِهَتُنَا خَيْرٌ أَمْ هُوَ ۚ مَا ضَرَبُوهُ لَكَ
إِلَّا جَدَلًۢا ۚ بَلْ هُمْ قَوْمٌ خَصِمُونَ ﴿٥٨﴾

51. Those who fail to learn any lesson from the tragic end met by Pharaoh's people and who follow in their footsteps will meet the same grievous end. Moreover, they will also serve as an example for those who are able to take heed.

52. It was said earlier in verse 45: 'Ask all Our Messengers whom We sent before you whether We had appointed any deities beside the Merciful One to be worshipped'. As this point was made to the Makkans, 'Abd Allāh ibn Ziba'rī posed the question: 'The Christians who regard Jesus, son of Mary, as God, do they worship him or not? If they do, what is wrong if the Makkans worship their own idols?' On hearing this the crowd of unbelievers burst into laughter and, raising boisterous slogans and mockingly insisting for a satisfactory answer to this question if there was any. (Zamakhsharī, *al-Kashshāf*, comments on *Sūrah al-Zukhruf* 43: 57.)

Here, the continuity of the revelation was not interrupted to answer the objections raised. However, after completing the issue at hand, attention was paid to the interlocutors' objections.

It is pertinent to note that this incident has been variously reported in works of *tafsīr*, and hence there are disagreements about the matter.

(59) He was no more than a servant (of Ours), one upon whom We bestowed Our favours and whom We made an example[53] (of Our infinite power) for the Children of Israel. (60) If We had so willed We could have made some of you into angels[54] to become your successors on earth. ▶

إِنۡ هُوَ إِلَّا عَبۡدٌ أَنۡعَمۡنَا عَلَيۡهِ وَجَعَلۡنَٰهُ
مَثَلٗا لِّبَنِيٓ إِسۡرَٰٓءِيلَ ٥٩ وَلَوۡ نَشَآءُ لَجَعَلۡنَا
مِنكُم مَّلَٰٓئِكَةٗ فِي ٱلۡأَرۡضِ يَخۡلُفُونَ ٦٠

However, reflection over the content of the revelation and the relevant traditions about the incident convince us that the view we have expressed above is correct.

53. That the Prophet Jesus (peace be on him) was an example (of God's infinite power) is a reference to Jesus' birth without a father and the bestowal upon him of miracles which had not been bestowed upon anyone either before or after him. He would make a bird of clay, breathe into it and it would become a living bird. He would give sight to those born blind. He would cure lepers. He would even raise the dead back to life.

The purpose of what is said here is to emphasise that despite Jesus' extraordinary birth and the miracles granted to him, it was wrong to consider him as anything other than God's creature and servant. As for worshipping him, that is absolutely out of the question. He was no more than a servant of God upon whom He had bestowed extraordinary favours, making him an example of His infinite power. (For further details, see *Āl 'Imrān* 3, nn. 42-4, *Towards Understanding the Qur'ān*, vol. I, pp. 251-4; *al-Nisā'* 4, n. 190, vol. II, p. 105; *al-Mā'idah* 5, nn. 40, 46 and 125-6, vol. II, pp. 149, 152-3 and 203; *Maryam* 19, nn. 15-22, vol. V, pp. 152-7; *al-Anbiyā'* 21, nn. 88-90, vol. V, pp. 294-5; *al-Mu'minūn* 23, n. 43, vol. VI, pp. 101-2.)

54. Alternatively, this can be translated as follows: '...make some of you give birth to angels.'

(61) Verily he (i.e., Jesus) is a portent of the Hour.[55] So be in no doubt concerning it and follow Me. This is the Straight Way. ▶	وَإِنَّهُۥ لَعِلْمٌ لِّلسَّاعَةِ فَلَا تَمْتَرُنَّ بِهَا وَٱتَّبِعُونِ هَٰذَا صِرَٰطٌ مُّسْتَقِيمٌ ﴿٦١﴾

55. This may also be translated to mean that it is a source of knowledge about the Hour. This naturally raises the question about identifying the source. For al-Ḥasan al-Baṣrī and Sa'īd ibn Jubayr, the reference is to the Qur'ān. (Qurṭubī, *al-Jāmi' li Aḥkām al-Qur'ān*, comments on *Sūrah al-Zukhruf* 43: 61.) In other words, by studying the Qur'ān one can learn about the Hour. However, this interpretation is not borne out by the context. The verse does not contain any clue or hint which would link it with the Qur'ān.

As for other exegetes, they are unanimous in their view that the allusion here is to Jesus, son of Mary. (Ṭabarī, *Tafsīr*, comments on *Sūrah al-Zukhruf* 43: 61.) This fits in with the context. Yet one is still faced with the question as to the sense in which Jesus is to be taken as a portent of the Hour or as a means of knowing it. In the opinion of many exegetes, namely 'Abd Allāh ibn 'Abbās, 'Ikrimah, Qatādah, Suddī, Ḍaḥḥāk, Abū al-'Āliyah and Abū Mālik, the reference is to the Second Coming of the Prophet Jesus (peace be on him), which is foretold in several *aḥādīth*. The verse, therefore, means that when Jesus reappears, this will indicate the approach of the Last Day. (Ṭabarī, *Tafsīr,* comments on *Sūrah al-Zukhruf* 43: 61.)

It is, however, hard to agree with these scholars that the verse speaks of the Second Coming of the Prophet Jesus (peace be on him). Besides, this view is also not supported by the latter part of the verse. Jesus' Second Coming may serve as the portent of the Last Day only for the people present at that time. It could not serve this purpose for the Makkan unbelievers. In view of this, the directive to them: 'So be in no doubt concerning it' does not say much.

We are, therefore, inclined to endorse the interpretation of those exegetes who are of the opinion that the reference here is to Jesus' miraculous birth and his extraordinary miracle-making which stand out as proofs in support of the possibility of the Last Day. (Biqā'ī, *Naẓm al-Ḍurar*, comments on *Sūrah al-Zukhruf* 43: 61.) What is being said here is that God, Who can cause the birth of a person without a father and Whose servant can breathe life into a bird of clay and revive the dead, can easily resurrect the Makkan unbelievers and, for that matter, all dead people.

(62) Let not Satan hinder you (from believing in the Hour),[56] for surely he is your open enemy. (63) When Jesus came with Clear Signs and said: 'I have brought wisdom to you that I may make plain to you some of the things you differ about. So fear Allah and follow me. (64) Allah is my Lord and your Lord; therefore, serve Him. That is the Straight Way.'[57] (65) Then the factions fell apart among themselves.[58] So woe to the wrong-doers ▶

وَلَا يَصُدَّنَّكُمُ ٱلشَّيْطَٰنُ ۖ إِنَّهُۥ لَكُمْ
عَدُوٌّ مُّبِينٌ ﴿٦٢﴾ وَلَمَّا جَآءَ عِيسَىٰ بِٱلْبَيِّنَٰتِ
قَالَ قَدْ جِئْتُكُم بِٱلْحِكْمَةِ وَلِأُبَيِّنَ لَكُم
بَعْضَ ٱلَّذِى تَخْتَلِفُونَ فِيهِ ۖ فَٱتَّقُوا۟ ٱللَّهَ
وَأَطِيعُونِ ﴿٦٣﴾ إِنَّ ٱللَّهَ هُوَ رَبِّى
وَرَبُّكُمْ فَٱعْبُدُوهُ ۚ هَٰذَا صِرَٰطٌ مُّسْتَقِيمٌ ﴿٦٤﴾
فَٱخْتَلَفَ ٱلْأَحْزَابُ مِنۢ بَيْنِهِمْ ۖ فَوَيْلٌ
لِّلَّذِينَ ظَلَمُوا۟

56. Satan incites man to disbelieve in the Last Day.

57. Notwithstanding the Christians' flawed concepts, the Prophet Jesus (peace be on him) never claimed to be God or His Son, nor did he ever ask people to worship him. His message was exactly the same as that of the Prophet Muḥammad (peace be on him) and all other Prophets. (For further details, see *Āl 'Imrān* 3, nn. 45-8, *Towards Understanding the Qur'ān,* vol. I, pp. 254-6; *al-Nisā'* 4, nn. 213 and 217-18, vol. II, pp. 116-17 and 119; *al-Mā'idah* 5, nn. 100 and 130, vol. II, pp. 180-1 and 206-7; *Maryam* 19, nn. 21-3, vol. V, pp. 156-8.)

58. Some of those who opposed Jesus went to such extremes as to accuse him of being an illegitimate child and made concerted efforts towards his crucifixion. On the other hand, some of those whose faith in him exceeded all reasonable limits made him into God's son. Jesus' 'godhead' proved to be a highly complex issue which caused the Christians to split into countless sects. (For further details, see *al-Nisā'* 4, nn. 211-16, *Towards Understanding the Qur'ān,* vol. II, pp. 116-19; *al-Mā'idah* 5, nn. 39-40, 101 and 130, vol. II, pp. 148-9, 181-5 and 206-7.)

from the chastisement of a grievous Day.

(66) Are they awaiting anything other than the Last Hour that it should suddenly come upon them without their even perceiving it? (67) On that Day even bosom friends shall become enemies to one another, all except the God-fearing.[59] (68) (It will be said to them): 'My servants, today you have nothing to fear or regret, (69) you who believed in Our Signs and had surrendered yourselves (to Us)! (70) Enter Paradise joyfully, both you and your spouses.'[60] (71) Platters and cups of gold shall be passed around them, ▶

مِنۡ عَذَابِ يَوۡمٍ أَلِيمٍ ﴿٦٥﴾ هَلۡ يَنظُرُونَ
إِلَّا ٱلسَّاعَةَ أَن تَأۡتِيَهُم بَغۡتَةً وَهُمۡ
لَا يَشۡعُرُونَ ﴿٦٦﴾ ٱلۡأَخِلَّآءُ يَوۡمَئِذِۭ بَعۡضُهُمۡ
لِبَعۡضٍ عَدُوٌّ إِلَّا ٱلۡمُتَّقِينَ ﴿٦٧﴾ يَٰعِبَادِ
لَا خَوۡفٌ عَلَيۡكُمُ ٱلۡيَوۡمَ وَلَآ أَنتُمۡ
تَحۡزَنُونَ ﴿٦٨﴾ ٱلَّذِينَ ءَامَنُواْ بِـَٔايَٰتِنَا وَكَانُواْ
مُسۡلِمِينَ ﴿٦٩﴾ ٱدۡخُلُواْ ٱلۡجَنَّةَ أَنتُمۡ
وَأَزۡوَٰجُكُمۡ تُحۡبَرُونَ ﴿٧٠﴾ يُطَافُ عَلَيۡهِم
بِصِحَافٖ مِّن ذَهَبٖ وَأَكۡوَابٖۖ

59. Only those friendships that are rooted in Godliness and righteousness will remain intact in the Hereafter. All other friendships will turn into bitter hostility. Those who are presently cooperating in acts of wickedness and error will blame each other on the Day of Judgement so as to obtain their own exoneration. This point occurs recurrently in the Qur'ān. Hence, one should think very carefully and then decide whom to make his friend in this life. In choosing friends one should give serious thought as to whose friendship will be truly beneficial or harmful.

60. *Azwāj* is used to denote both wives and close companions and friends. This comprehensive word is deliberately employed here to convey both meanings. In other words, true believers will be accompanied by believing wives and believing companions.

and there shall be all that they might desire and all that their eyes might delight in. (They shall be told): 'Herein shall you abide for ever. (72) Such is the Paradise that you shall inherit by virtue of your good deeds in the life of the world. (73) Herein you will have abundant fruits of which you will eat.' (74) But the evil-doers shall abide in the torment of Hell. (75) Never will their torment be lightened for them. They shall remain in utter despair. (76) It is not We Who wronged them; rather, it is they who wronged themselves. (77) They shall call out: 'O Mālik,[61] let your Lord put an end to us.' He will reply: 'You must stay on in it. (78) We brought you the Truth; but to the truth most of you were averse.'[62]

وَفِيهَا مَا تَشْتَهِيهِ ٱلْأَنفُسُ وَتَلَذُّ ٱلْأَعْيُنُ ۖ وَأَنتُمْ
فِيهَا خَٰلِدُونَ ﴿٧١﴾ وَتِلْكَ ٱلْجَنَّةُ ٱلَّتِىٓ
أُورِثْتُمُوهَا بِمَا كُنتُمْ تَعْمَلُونَ ﴿٧٢﴾ لَكُمْ
فِيهَا فَٰكِهَةٌ كَثِيرَةٌ مِّنْهَا تَأْكُلُونَ ﴿٧٣﴾ إِنَّ
ٱلْمُجْرِمِينَ فِى عَذَابِ جَهَنَّمَ خَٰلِدُونَ ﴿٧٤﴾
لَا يُفَتَّرُ عَنْهُمْ وَهُمْ فِيهِ مُبْلِسُونَ ﴿٧٥﴾
وَمَا ظَلَمْنَٰهُمْ وَلَٰكِن كَانُوا۟ هُمُ
ٱلظَّٰلِمِينَ ﴿٧٦﴾ وَنَادَوْا۟ يَٰمَٰلِكُ لِيَقْضِ
عَلَيْنَا رَبُّكَ ۖ قَالَ إِنَّكُم مَّٰكِثُونَ ﴿٧٧﴾ لَقَدْ
جِئْنَٰكُم بِٱلْحَقِّ وَلَٰكِنَّ أَكْثَرَكُمْ
لِلْحَقِّ كَٰرِهُونَ ﴿٧٨﴾

---

61. That is, the angel in charge of Hell.

62. The truth was clearly put before the unbelievers. However, they preferred falsehood. Why should they weep and cry when they are confronted in the Hereafter by the dire consequences of their wrong choices? It is likely that this observation is made by the angel in charge of Hell. Likewise, it is possible that the angel's statement ends with:

(79) Have they contrived some scheme?[63] If so, We too will contrive a scheme. (80) Or do they think that We do not hear their secret talks and their whispering counsels? Yes, indeed We do and Our messengers (i.e., angels) are with them, writing.

(81) Say: 'If the Merciful One had a son, I would have been the first one to worship him.'[64] (82) Exalted be the Lord of the heavens and the earth, the Lord of the Throne, above what they attribute to Him. (83) So leave them alone to indulge in their vanities and to frolic about until they ▶

أَمْ أَبْرَمُوٓا۟ أَمْرًا فَإِنَّا مُبْرِمُونَ ﴿٧٩﴾ أَمْ
يَحْسَبُونَ أَنَّا لَا نَسْمَعُ سِرَّهُمْ وَنَجْوَىٰهُم ۚ بَلَىٰ
وَرُسُلُنَا لَدَيْهِمْ يَكْتُبُونَ ﴿٨٠﴾ قُلْ إِن كَانَ
لِلرَّحْمَـٰنِ وَلَدٌ فَأَنَا۠ أَوَّلُ ٱلْعَـٰبِدِينَ ﴿٨١﴾
سُبْحَـٰنَ رَبِّ ٱلسَّمَـٰوَٰتِ وَٱلْأَرْضِ
رَبِّ ٱلْعَرْشِ عَمَّا يَصِفُونَ ﴿٨٢﴾ فَذَرْهُمْ
يَخُوضُوا۟ وَيَلْعَبُوا۟ حَتَّىٰ

'You must stay on in it' and what follows thereafter is an addition by God Himself. In the first case, the Hell-keeper's statement is akin to a government officer's use of 'we' whereby he means that the government did this or issued such and such order.

63. This refers to the conspiracies hatched by the Quraysh chiefs against the Prophet (peace be on him.)

64. The Prophet's denial of anyone being God's son and his refusal to worship those whom the misguided ones worshipped is not on account of any stubbornness on his part. His attitude is rather based on the fact that God has neither any son nor any daughter and that the notions people held in this regard were contrary to reality. Had it been otherwise, he would have been in the forefront of those who worship gods besides the One True God.

encounter that Day of theirs against which they have been warned.

(84) He it is Who is God in the heavens and the earth. He is the Most Wise, the All-Knowing.[65] (85) Blessed is He Who has dominion over the heavens and the earth and all that is between them.[66] With Him is the knowledge of the Hour; and to Him you shall all be sent back.[67]

(86) Those whom they call upon, instead of Allah have no power of intercession, except such that testify to the truth based on knowledge.[68]

يَلْـٰقُوا۟ يَوْمَهُمُ ٱلَّذِى يُوعَدُونَ ﴿٨٣﴾ وَهُوَ
ٱلَّذِى فِى ٱلسَّمَآءِ إِلَـٰهٌ وَفِى ٱلْأَرْضِ إِلَـٰهٌ ۚ
وَهُوَ ٱلْحَكِيمُ ٱلْعَلِيمُ ﴿٨٤﴾ وَتَبَارَكَ ٱلَّذِى لَهُۥ
مُلْكُ ٱلسَّمَـٰوَٰتِ وَٱلْأَرْضِ وَمَا بَيْنَهُمَا
وَعِندَهُۥ عِلْمُ ٱلسَّاعَةِ وَإِلَيْهِ تُرْجَعُونَ ﴿٨٥﴾
وَلَا يَمْلِكُ ٱلَّذِينَ يَدْعُونَ مِن دُونِهِ
ٱلشَّفَـٰعَةَ إِلَّا مَن شَهِدَ بِٱلْحَقِّ وَهُمْ
يَعْلَمُونَ ﴿٨٦﴾

---

65. God is the Lord of the heavens and the earth, there being no separate gods of the heavens and the earth. God's wisdom embraces the whole universe and His knowledge encompasses everything.

66. God is far too exalted to have any partner. All those who exist in the heavens and the earth, be they Prophets, saints, angels, jinns, spirits, stars or planets are all His creation and are bound in service and obedience to Him. It is simply impossible for them to possess any of God's attributes or any of His powers or have any share in His Divinity.

67. Notwithstanding the unbelievers' deification of a host of beings, they will have to confront the One True God after their deaths. Thereafter, they will have to render their accounts in God's court of justice.

68. This observation encompasses several ideas:

(87) If you were to ask them: 'Who created them?' they will surely say: 'Allah.'[69] ▶	وَلَئِن سَأَلْتَهُم مَّنْ خَلَقَهُمْ لَيَقُولُنَّ ٱللَّهُ

(1) Only those who testify to truth out of knowledge will be able to intercede. Those who are taken by men as gods will not be able to do so. As for those who are misguided, they will appear in the Hereafter as culprits.
(2) The ones who intercede will be able to do so only with regard to those who had consciously testified to the truth. They will not recommend anyone who had rejected the truth. They will not be authorised to do so even for those who uttered without thinking: 'I testify that there is no god besides God,' yet who kept serving and worshipping others than the One True God.
(3) Those who claim that their idols enjoy such power and authority that they will secure the deliverance of everyone, irrespective of their beliefs and deeds, are in gross error. No one enjoys such power. If anyone claims to have such absolute power of intercession, he should produce proof of the same. Since no one is authorised to do so, it is the height of ignorance and self-deception to entertain such a baseless notion.

The verse also lays down two important principles: (a) A testimony to truth without knowledge may be acceptable in this life. However, God does not admit it. Anyone who utters the Islamic creedal statement testifying to the Oneness of God and the Messengership of the Prophet Muḥammad (peace be on him), will be considered a Muslim in this life unless he publicly indulges in acts of unbelief. However, God will reckon only those as true believers who consciously recognise the implications and pre-requisites of their faith and of Islam's basic creedal statement. (b) Knowledge is central to evidence. Without knowledge, one's testimony will not be admitted. This truth comes out from the Prophet's observation which he made while addressing a witness: 'If you have witnessed this happening as you see the sun, you may go ahead with your testimony. Otherwise, you should not'. (Jaṣṣāṣ, *Aḥkām al-Qur'ān*, comments on *Sūrah al-Zukhruf* 43: 86.)

69. This verse is open to two meanings: (i) If the unbelievers are asked: who is their Creator, they say that God is their Creator. (ii) If they are asked: who is the Creator of their deities, they still say that the Creator of their deities is God.

Whence are they, then, being led astray? (88) We call to witness the cry of the Messenger: 'O Lord, these are a people not wont to believe!'[70]

(89) Indulge them, (O Prophet), and say to them: 'Peace to you.'[71] For soon they shall come to know.

فَأَنَّىٰ يُؤْفَكُونَ ﴿٨٧﴾ وَقِيلِهِۦ يَٰرَبِّ إِنَّ
هَٰٓؤُلَآءِ قَوْمٌ لَّا يُؤْمِنُونَ ﴿٨٨﴾ فَٱصْفَحْ عَنْهُمْ
وَقُلْ سَلَٰمٌ ۚ فَسَوْفَ يَعْلَمُونَ ﴿٨٩﴾

---

70. This is one of the most difficult verses of the Qur'ān since it involves a difficult question of syntax. This concerns the meaning of the *wa* preceding *qīlihi* and its relationship with the preceding verses. Though several opinions have been expressed, none seems to me fully satisfactory. (See Zamakhsharī, *al-Kashshāf*, comments on *Sūrah al-Zukhruf* 43: 88). In my opinion, the soundest view is that which is implicit in Shāh 'Abd al-Qādir's translation of the verse. According to him, *wa* here is not used as a conjunctive but rather in the sense of an oath and is related to *fa annā yu'fakūn* and the pronoun in the word *qīlihi* refers to the Prophet (peace be on him).

This is also borne out by verse 88 of the *sūrah*. The Prophet (peace be on him) observes that the unbelievers refuse to believe. In light of the above, the verse means: 'I swear by this statement of the Prophet (peace be on him): "O Lord, these are a people not wont to believe"'; that is, they are so deluded that although they acknowledge God alone to be the Creator of their deities, nonetheless they still insist on worshipping creatures other than the Creator.

The purpose of swearing by this saying of the Prophet (peace be on him) is to underscore those people's attitude. It clearly shows that they are utterly stubborn and that their foolishness is evident from their own admission. Such an obviously unreasonable attitude can only be adopted by those who have clearly decided not to believe. In other words, the Prophet's words about their strong disposition against belief are quite true.

71. The believers should not react to their opponents' harsh words or the scornful and mocking statements by cursing them or hurling harsh words back at them. Instead, they should simply greet them with 'peace' and part from their company.

Sūrah 44

Al-Dukhān

(Smoke)

(Makkan Period)

Title

Since the word *al-dukhān,* meaning smoke, occurs in verse 10 of the *sūrah,* it is known by this title.

Period of Revelation

There is no clear indication in authentic traditions as to the precise time of the *sūrah*'s revelation. Internal evidence provided by the *sūrah*'s contents, however, indicates that it was revealed during the same time as when *al-Zukhruf* and other *sūrah*s belonging to this group were revealed. This *sūrah,* however, was revealed relatively later than the other *sūrah*s of the group.

As regards the *sūrah*'s historical background, the following points are noteworthy. When the hostility of the unbelieving Makkans reached its climax, the Prophet (peace be on him) prayed to God to aid him by afflicting the Quraysh with a famine similar to that which had broken out in the days of the Prophet Joseph (peace be on him.) The Prophet (peace be on him) did so hoping that the famine would open the unbelievers' hearts to Truth and possibly prompt them to turn to God. It was expected that in their hour of severest distress they might become receptive to admonition. As for the Prophet's prayer, God accepted it and a severe famine overtook the Makkans. Eventually, some Makkan chiefs, including Abū Sufyān, as stated in a tradition narrated by 'Abd Allāh ibn Mas'ūd, called on the Prophet (peace be on him) and implored him to pray to God to deliver the people, his own people, from this calamity. It was in these circumstances that this *sūrah* was revealed. (Ṭabarī, *Tafsīr*, comments on *Sūrah al-Dukhān* 44: 10.)

Subject Matter and Themes

The introduction to the *sūrah*, which aims to instruct and warn the Makkan unbelievers, was comprised of the following crucial points:

(1) In the first place, the people of Makkah were told that they had a very flawed notion about the Qur'ān. They were totally wrong in considering it to be the product of a human mind, whereas, in fact, it contains every evidence that it is the Word of God.

(2) They are also mistaken as regards the worth of the Qur'ān since they consider its revelation nothing short of a calamity. The fact, however, is that the Qur'ān was revealed at a highly blessed moment when God, out of sheer mercy, decided to raise His Messenger and send His Book for the guidance of the people of Makkah in the first instance.

(3) They were also mistaken in believing that they would be able to vanquish God's Messenger and overwhelm His Book. The advent of the Messenger and the sending down of the Book happened at that particular moment when God decides the fate of a people. God's decisions are not half-baked or tentative so that people might arbitrarily abrogate them. Since God's decrees are fully backed by knowledge and wisdom, they cannot and do not contain any imperfection or flaw. God's decrees are final since He

is also All-Seeing, All-Knowing, and All-Wise. It would be no joke to trifle with these decrees.

(4) The Makkan unbelievers themselves regard God as the Lord and Sustainer of the whole universe. They, nevertheless, also take others besides God as objects of devotion and worship. They have no solid argument to justify their stance. Their only plea is that this practice has come down to them from their ancestors of yore. Yet if someone recognises that God alone is the Lord and Sustainer of the universe, and that He alone grants life and causes death, it would not even occur to him that there could be any deity other than the One True God. The unbelievers' plea was that they had found their ancestors worshipping other deities and hence, they felt they should hold on to this. However, given that their ancestors had committed a folly, what good reason could there be for clinging to such irrationality?

(5) Since God is the Lord and Sustainer of human beings this not only requires that He provide for their physical and material needs, but also that He provide for their guidance. It is for this reason that God has raised His Messengers and sent His Books.

These introductory observations are followed by an account of the famine which afflicted Makkah at that time. As we have stated above, God caused a famine to break out at the Prophet's asking. The Prophet (peace be on him) had asked God for it in the hope that such adversity might shake the unbelievers out of their arrogance whereafter they might heed words of admonition. Indeed, even diehard unbelievers were seen exclaiming at that difficult hour that if God were to deliver them from this famine, they would embrace faith.

In this regard, the Prophet (peace be on him) is virtually told that these afflictions will hardly prompt unbelievers to mend their ways. They had refused to listen to God's Messenger whose words and deeds fully demonstrated the genuineness of his claim to Messengership. So how can a famine shake such obstinate people out of their stupor? The unbelievers are categorically told that their promise to embrace faith after they were rescued from the famine was absolutely hollow. The famine will, nonetheless, be ended in order to further test them. It is apparent, however, that they are incapable of drawing the right lessons from such incidents as their deliverance from famine. In other words, it is unlikely that they will take any lesson from it. It will hardly rouse unbelievers out of their negligence. It appears they are heading steadily towards their doom. What they perhaps need is not a mild jolt of misfortune but rather a shake-up of catastrophic proportions.

In this connection, reference is made to Pharaoh and his people. They were also subjected to the same kind of test that the unbelieving Quraysh were then facing and an outstanding Messenger, Moses (peace be on him), was sent to them. Despite the fact that they witnessed a number of miracles, they still did not give up their adamant opposition to the Truth. They even set about conspiring to assassinate God's Messenger. The result was that Pharaoh and his people encountered a massive catastrophe, one that has become a lesson for all times.

This is followed by a discourse on the Hereafter, a belief that was vehemently rejected by the Makkan unbelievers. Their contention was that they had never seen anyone rise from the grave. If the Prophet's assertion about the Hereafter was true, they said, he should bring their ancestors back to life before their very eyes. In this connection, two arguments were succinctly adduced to counter them and to reinforce belief in the Hereafter. First, it was pointed out that rejection of the Hereafter has always had a destructive effect on human morality. Secondly, that the universe itself is not a meaningless sport. On the contrary, its working is characterised by perfect wisdom arising from the fact that it was devised by the All-Wise God. As to the plea that the Prophet (peace be on him) should bring their ancestors back to life, it was pointed out that God has preordained the Day of Resurrection when all the dead will be brought back to life whereafter God will call all of them to account. Each of them, then, should better worry about his own salvation for no one will be able to help or support anyone else on the Day of Judgement.

After facing God's judgement, all who are found guilty will meet a terrible end and those declared successful will be showered with God's rewards. By way of conclusion it is pointed out that the Qur'ān has been sent down in their own tongue and in a clear, simple style such that it is easy for them to understand it. If they still refuse to take heed, they should just wait a little while until the ultimate reality becomes manifest to them in all its starkness.

In the name of Allah, the Most Merciful, the Most Compassionate.

بِسۡمِ ٱللَّهِ ٱلرَّحۡمَٰنِ ٱلرَّحِيمِ

(1) *Ḥā. Mīm.* (2) By the Clear Book. (3) We revealed it on a Blessed Night, for We were intent on warning;[1] (4) (We revealed it on the Night) wherein ▶

حمٓ ﴿١﴾ وَٱلۡكِتَٰبِ ٱلۡمُبِينِ ﴿٢﴾ إِنَّآ
أَنزَلۡنَٰهُ فِي لَيۡلَةٖ مُّبَٰرَكَةٍۚ إِنَّا كُنَّا
مُنذِرِينَ ﴿٣﴾ فِيهَا

1. As to the oath here concerning the 'Clear Book', this has already been explained by us in *Sūrah al-Zukhruf*. (See *Sūrah* 43, n. 1 above.) It is emphasised that it is God, and not the Prophet Muḥammad (peace be on him), Who has authored the Qur'ān. This truth does not stand in need of any external proof. The Qur'ān itself sufficiently proves this. An additional observation made here is that the Qur'ān was sent down on a blessed night. It was an auspicious moment for mankind when God decided to send this Book in order to awaken and arouse those immersed in heedlessness. Some of those who have no awareness of what is good from what is bad consider this Book to be a sheer misfortune that has struck them. Such people are eager to somehow get rid of its fetters. The fact, however, remains that it was a highly blessed moment for all mankind when God decided to send this Book so as to shake people out of their negligence.

According to some Qur'ānic commentators, the word 'night' in the verse has to be understood literally. In other words, the phenomenon of the Qur'ān's revelation commenced on that particular night. Others take it to mean that the whole of the Qur'ān was transmitted on that night from *Umm al-Kitāb* and entrusted to the angels who were charged with bringing it down to the Prophet (peace be on him.) It was, however, transmitted to the Prophet (peace be on him) piecemeal, as and when needed, over a period of 23 years. (Zamakhsharī, *al-Kashshāf*, comments on *Sūrah al-Dukhān* 44: 3.) As to what truly happened on that occasion, God knows best.

Some scholars are of the opinion that reference here is made to the blessed night which has been called *Laylat al-Qadr* in *Sūrah al-Qadr (Sūrah* 97.) It is further clarified in the Qur'ān that it was a Ramaḍān night (see *al-Baqarah* 2: 185).

every matter is wisely[2] determined[3] (5) by Our command. Verily, We were set to send a Messenger (6) as a Mercy from your Lord.[4] Surely He is All-Hearing, ▶

يُفۡرَقُ كُلُّ أَمۡرٍ حَكِيمٍ ﴿٤﴾ أَمۡرًا مِّنۡ عِندِنَآۚ
إِنَّا كُنَّا مُرۡسِلِينَ ﴿٥﴾ رَحۡمَةً مِّن رَّبِّكَۚ إِنَّهُۥ
هُوَ ٱلسَّمِيعُ

2. Use of the expression *amr ḥakīm* in the verse signifies two things: (i) that God's commands are characterised by wisdom, admitting of no lapse or imperfection; and (ii) that those commands are so well-conceived and solid that none has the power to alter them.

3. The same point is made in *Sūrah al-Qadr (Sūrah* 97), where it is stated that angels and Gabriel descend with the permission of their Lord with all kinds of decrees *(Sūrah al-Qadr* 97: 4.) One, thus, learns that on that particular night God decides the fates of individuals and communities and passes on His decrees to the angels for execution.

Among exegetes, 'Ikrimah strongly holds the view that this alludes to the night of 15th Sha'bān because some *aḥādīth* say as much about that night. (Ṭabarī, *Tafsīr,* comments on *Sūrah al-Dukhān* 44: 4.) However, 'Abd Allāh ibn 'Abbās, 'Abd Allāh ibn 'Umar, Mujāhid, Qatādah, al-Ḥasan al-Baṣrī, Sa'īd ibn Jubayr, Ibn Zayd, Abū Mālik, Ḍaḥḥāk and several other Qur'ānic scholars identify it with the *laylat al-qadr* of Ramaḍān on the grounds that this is what the Qur'ān itself says. (Ṭabarī, *Tafsīr,* comments on *Sūrah al-Dukhān* 44: 3-4.) It is evident that when something is explicitly stated in the Qur'ān, one cannot hold a variant opinion on the basis of solitary traditions. According to Ibn Kathīr, 'Uthmān ibn Muḥammad's report which Imām al-Zuhrī has related that God decrees on that night all matters from Sha'bān of one year till the next is only a *mursal* tradition, and such traditions cannot be taken into account when we find them opposed to clear texts. (Ibn Kathīr, *Tafsīr,* comments on *Sūrah al-Dukhān* 44: 3.) 'According to Abū Bakr ibn al-'Arabī, no *ḥadīth* concerning the excellence of the night of 15th Sha'bān nor about the fact that the fate of people is decided on that night is reliable and hence no attention need be paid to such traditions', (Ibn al-'Arabī, *Aḥkām al-Qur'ān*, comments on *Sūrah al-Dukhān* 44: 3.)

4. It was not only a part of God's Wisdom but also of His Mercy and Compassion to send a Messenger along with a Book to mankind. Being the Lord of mankind, God is bound to guide them by providing them

All-Seeing,[5] (7) the Lord of the heavens and the earth and of all that is between them: if you would only have sure faith.[6] (8) There is no god but He:[7] He gives life and causes death.[8] ▶

ٱلْعَلِيمُ ﴿٦﴾ رَبِّ ٱلسَّمَٰوَٰتِ وَٱلْأَرْضِ
وَمَا بَيْنَهُمَآ ۖ إِن كُنتُم مُّوقِنِينَ ﴿٧﴾ لَآ إِلَٰهَ
إِلَّا هُوَ يُحْىِۦ وَيُمِيتُ ۖ

---

with sound knowledge. He caters not only to the sustenance of man's body but also his soul. The knowledge imparted by God helps man distinguish truth from falsehood so that he may not be lost in darkness and keep groping about in it.

5. These two attributes of God are specifically mentioned in this context in order to draw man's attention to the fact that He alone can guide him to the Straight Way. This because God alone encompasses all facts. Were a single human being or all human beings taken together to decide what should be the way of life for mankind there is no guarantee that their decisions would be sound or correct. The reason is that even the totality of human beings would be short of becoming All-Hearing and All-Seeing as each of them separately is not all-hearing and all-seeing. Human beings cannot encompass all facts, which is a prerequisite for deciding what is the appropriate way of life for mankind. God alone has the knowledge needed for this for He is All-Hearing and All-Knowing. Thus, only He can lay down what constitutes true guidance as distinguished from error, and what is good as distinct from evil.

6. The Arabs recognised God to be the Lord (that is, the Owner and Provider) of the universe as a whole and of every part of it. They are, therefore, told that if they truly believe in this, they should also recognise that it is part of God's mercy and wisdom that He should raise Messengers and send Books for mankind's guidance. Being the Lord of human beings, God is bound to guide them and they, being His servants, are expected to follow His guidance and to willingly surrender themselves to His commands.

7. That is, the true deity to whom every kind of service and worship is exclusively due.

8. This proves that neither is there nor can there be any deity besides the One True God. It defies common sense and logic that man should

He is your Lord and the Lord of your forefathers of yore.[9] (9) (But the fact is, they lack certainty) and frolic about in doubt.[10]

(10) So watch for the Day when the sky will come down with a pall of smoke, (11) enveloping people. ▶

رَبُّكُمْ وَرَبُّ ءَابَآئِكُمُ ٱلْأَوَّلِينَ ﴿٨﴾ بَلْ هُمْ
فِى شَكٍّ يَلْعَبُونَ ﴿٩﴾ فَٱرْتَقِبْ يَوْمَ تَأْتِى
ٱلسَّمَآءُ بِدُخَانٍ مُّبِينٍ ﴿١٠﴾ يَغْشَى ٱلنَّاسَ ۖ

---

serve and worship others while God alone has brought him into being by putting life into lifeless material. It is He alone Who decides when to grant life to someone and when to bring it to an end.

9. Implicit in this is the subtle message that God is the Lord of their ancestors as well. Their ancestors had done no good in worshipping others besides Him. What is appropriate now is that they should no longer follow in the footsteps of their misguided ancestors. In the first instance, their ancestors should have served the One True Lord. Now, it is the duty of their descendants to abandon the polytheism of their forefathers and turn to God alone, for He alone is their Lord.

10. Here an important truth is succinctly stated: even the hearts of atheists and polytheists occasionally tell them that their position contains some basic flaw, be it one or another. An atheist might also be quite diehard in denying the existence of God. Nevertheless, there are moments when he realises the astounding order of the universe, which embraces everything from an atom to vast galaxies and from a blade of grass to the creation of human beings. This is so replete with wisdom and purposefulness that it could never have been there had there been no wise Creator behind it. The same also holds true for the diehard polytheist. It is occasionally evident to him in the depths of his heart that there is no justification to associate his deities with God. This inner voice of his heart, however, does not always lead the atheist to affirm belief in God or the polytheist to affirm the oneness of the Deity. At the same time this realisation prevents them from being fully satisfied with their atheism or polytheism. The religious position of atheists and polytheists is essentially one based on doubt and uncertainty rather than on conviction and faith.

That will be a grievous scourge. (12) (People will then say): 'Our Lord, remove this scourge from us; we shall believe.' (13) But how will they take heed? Such are they that a Messenger came to them clearly expounding the Truth,[11] ▶

هَٰذَا عَذَابٌ أَلِيمٌ ﴿١١﴾ رَّبَّنَا ٱكْشِفْ
عَنَّا ٱلْعَذَابَ إِنَّا مُؤْمِنُونَ ﴿١٢﴾ أَنَّىٰ لَهُمُ
ٱلذِّكْرَىٰ وَقَدْ جَآءَهُمْ رَسُولٌ مُّبِينٌ ﴿١٣﴾

This raises the question: why does their inner dissatisfaction with atheism or polytheism not lead them to embrace faith? Why do they not undertake a quest for truth which would lead them to firm faith? Explanation as to why it is so lies in the fact that such people do not take the issue of faith with the necessary seriousness. Their only interest lies in this world and in its benefits and pleasures. They, therefore, devote themselves wholly to worldly pursuits. For them, the issue of faith is, at most, something peripheral and to which they pay no serious attention. As for religious rituals, they observe them as a part of their socio-cultural etiquettes. They are not truly keen, doctrinally speaking, as regards their polytheism or atheism. The issue of truth or of deviation from it in matters of religious belief does not seriously bother them. As a result, they are not concerned with what the consequences of having sound beliefs are, or alternatively, of deviant ones. It is worldly acquisitions and worldly pleasures that they truly care for and for the sake of which they devote their physical and mental energy. As for religious belief and practice, they are for them a source of mental amusement. Hence, they hardly devote any time to serious reflection over them. Religious rites are also performed because of the amusement they provide. If they engage in discussions about matters like atheism, they do so for the sake of mental recreation. No one is ready to spare a few precious moments from his worldly pursuits to seriously pause and consider whether he is following the truth or has turned away from it, and if that is the case, what the consequences of his deviation are.

11. The Prophet (peace be on him) is here called *rasūl mubīn*. This expression could mean two things: (i) that his superb morals and manners, his unblemished conduct and his excellent achievements proved beyond every shadow of doubt that he was God's true Messenger; and (ii) that he expounds the Truth making it unequivocally clear.

(14) yet they turned away from him and said: 'This is a well-tutored madman.'[12] (15) Yet We will hold the scourge back for a while, (but no sooner than We will do so) you will revert to your old ways. (16) The Day when We shall seize them with a mighty seizing, that will be the Day on which We shall inflict upon you full retribution.[13]

ثُمَّ تَوَلَّوْا۟ عَنْهُ وَقَالُوا۟ مُعَلَّمٌ مَّجْنُونٌ ﴿١٤﴾ إِنَّا كَاشِفُوا۟ ٱلْعَذَابِ قَلِيلًا ۚ إِنَّكُمْ عَآئِدُونَ ﴿١٥﴾ يَوْمَ نَبْطِشُ ٱلْبَطْشَةَ ٱلْكُبْرَىٰٓ إِنَّا مُنتَقِمُونَ ﴿١٦﴾

12. The unbelievers tried to undermine the Prophet's position by saying on his behalf that he himself was a man of quite ordinary abilities and that the Qur'ān was the result of the assistance he received from some very sharp-witted people who composed its verses. They considered the Prophet (peace be on him) to be a simpleton, as mediocre, someone who only rehearsed to his people the verses he had been taught by others. They portrayed him as the one who had become the target of popular tirade and hostility while the true authors of the Qur'ān smugly and gleefully watched events as they unfolded. Such people were in the habit of dismissing serious matters and then tossing comical remarks about the same. They neither took note of the brilliant reasoning enshrined in the Qur'ān, nor did they take into account the unparalleled moral stature of the Prophet (peace be on him). Nor did they realise that the allegations his opponents commonly made against him were nothing more than rubbish. It is obvious that had others been forging the Qur'ānic verses and passing them on to the Prophet (peace be on him) for onward transmission, he could not have kept this hidden from the likes of people like Khīdijah, Abū Bakr, 'Alī and Zayd ibn Ḥārithah and the other early Muslims who were extremely close to him and were virtually always around him. Moreover, how did it happen that these people were ardently devoted to the Prophet (peace be on him)? Had some other people been passing on religious teachings to him, then surely they would have been among his foremost opponents.

13. Qur'ānic commentators, including some Companions, are fairly divided as regards the import of these verses. Masrūq, a disciple of 'Abd

Allāh ibn Mas'ūd, says: 'Once we found an orator speaking in a mosque at Kūfah. He recited verse 10 of *Sūrah al-Dukhān* and explained it by saying that it speaks of the smoke which will appear on the Last Day that will render all unbelievers and hypocrites blind and deaf. As for believers, they will only be slightly affected by it as they have been stricken by the common cold.' When we later related this to Ibn Mas'ūd, he was shocked. He said to us: 'An ignorant person should better consult those who know. When the Quraysh grew in their opposition to Islam, the Prophet (peace be on him) prayed to God to aid him by causing a famine similar to the one which took place in the days of the Prophet Joseph (peace be on him). As a result of his prayer, there took place a severe famine which forced the Makkans to subsist on bones, skin and carcasses. This calamity affected all such that when anyone turned his gaze upwards at this time, all he could see was smoke.' Eventually, Abū Sufyān approached the Prophet (peace be on him), invoked ties of kinship, and pleaded that he should pray to God to bring an end to the famine from which his people were starving. During those days the Quraysh openly said that if this scourge ended, they would embrace faith. The present verses refer to this.

As to the statement that 'We shall seize them with a mighty seizing' (verse 16), it refers to the affliction that seized the unbelievers on the occasion of the Battle of Badr. Aḥmad ibn Ḥanbal, Bukhārī, Tirmidhī, Nasā'ī, Ibn Jarīr al-Ṭabārī and Ibn Abī Ḥātim have narrated Masrūq's traditions with several chains. (Aḥmad ibn Ḥanbal, *Musnad*, narrated by 'Abd Allāh ibn Mas'ūd; Bukhārī, *Kitāb al-Jumu'ah, Bāb Du'ā' al-Nabī Ṣallā Allāh 'alayhi wa Sallam Ij'alhā 'alayhim Sinīn ka Sinīn Yūsuf*; Tirmidhī, *Kitāb Tafsīr al-Qur'ān 'an Rasūl Allāh Ṣallā Allāh 'alayhi wa Sallam, Bāb wa min Sūrah al-Dukhān*; Nasā'ī, *al-Sunan al-Kubrā, Kitāb al-Tafsīr, Bāb Sūrah al-Dukhān Qawluhu Ta'ālā Yawm Ta'tī al-Samā' bi Dukhān Mubīn*; Ṭabarī,*Tafsīr*, comments on *Sūrah al-Dukhān* 44: 10.) Apart from Masrūq, Ibrāhīm al-Nakha'ī, Qatādah, 'Āṣim and 'Āmir also endorse that 'Abd Allāh ibn Mas'ūd offered the above interpretation. (Ṭabarī, *Tafsīr*, comments on *Sūrah al-Dukhān* 44: 10) His interpretation also enjoys the support of the following Successors: Mujāhid, Qatādah, Abū al-'Āliyah, Muqātil, Ḍaḥḥāk and 'Aṭīyah al-'Awfī, (Ṭabarī, *Tafsīr*, comments on *Sūrah al-Dukhān* 44: 10.)

Conversely, 'Alī, 'Abd Allāh ibn 'Umar and 'Abd Allāh ibn 'Abbās maintain that these verses refer to a time close to the Last Day. (Qurṭubī, *al-Jāmi' li Aḥkām al-Qur'ān*, comments on *Sūrah al-Dukhān* 44: 10.) A smoke will then envelope the whole earth. This interpretation is further reinforced by the traditions narrated on the Prophet's authority. Ḥudhayfah ibn Usayd al-Ghifārī states: 'Once while we were discussing the Last Day, the Prophet (peace be on him) joined us. He informed us of its following ten signs which will appear in quick succession, and which will mark the approach of the Last Day: the sun rising in the west, the smoke, the beast, the appearance of Gog and Magog, the descent of Jesus son of Mary, the caving of the earth in the east, in the west and in the Arabian Peninsula, and the breaking out of a fire in Aden which will drive people along.' (Muslim, *Kitāb al-Fitan wa Ashrāṭ al-Sā'ah, Bāb fī al-Āyāt al-Latī Takūn qabl al-Sā'ah.*) This is reinforced by Abū Mālik al-Ash'arī's tradition cited by Ibn Jarīr al-Ṭabarī and al-Ṭabarānī. (Ṭabarī, *Tafsīr,* comments on *Sūrah al-Dukhān* 44: 10; Ṭabarī Ṭabarānī, *al-Mu'jam al-Kabīr,* narrated by Abū Mālik al-Ash'arī) Abū Sa'īd al-Khudrī's tradition, recounted by Ibn Abī Ḥātim, makes the same point. (Ibn Abī Ḥātim, *Tafsīr,* comments on *Sūrah al-Dukhān* 44: 10.) These traditions state that the Prophet (peace be on him) spoke of the smoke as a sign of the Last Day. He also said that believers will be affected lightly by this smoke, in the same way as one suffers from a common cold. Conversely, the smoke will totally overwhelm the unbelievers.

On closely studying these verses one can reconcile these two interpretations. As to the version offered by 'Abd Allāh ibn Mas'ūd, it is true that the Prophet's prayer had led to famine in Makkah which had greatly mortified the unbelievers. They had then requested that he pray to God to bring an end to it. The Qur'ān alludes to the same at several places. (See *al-An'ām* 6, n. 29, *Towards Understanding the Qur'ān,* vol. II, pp. 231-3; *al-A'rāf* 7, n. 77, vol. III, pp. 59-60; *Yūnus* 10, nn. 14, 15 and 29, vol. IV, pp. 14-16 and 26-7; *al-Mu'minūn* 23, n. 72, vol. VI, 116-17.) It appears that all these verses refer to one and the same matter. What is described did happen during the Prophet's days and the signs of the Hereafter have nothing to do with it. 'Abd Allāh ibn Mas'ūd's interpretation, therefore, seems to be in order. However, that part of his statement which says that the smoke appeared during the Prophet's time is not correct. This is neither borne out by the Qur'ānic text nor by *aḥādīth*. The Qur'ān pointedly mentions that the smoke will overwhelm mankind and the Makkan unbelievers are asked to wait for that day. In other words, the thrust of the passage is that if they do not take any heed from the Prophet's preaching, or from the note of warning served by the famine, they should better wait for the Last Day. The truth will then dawn upon them. For the smoke is one of the signs of the Last Day.

This point is mentioned in several *aḥādīth* as well. It is somewhat surprising, therefore, that some Qur'ānic scholars supported Ibn Mas'ūd's view in totality whilst others rejected it in totality. Actually, his view is partly sound and partly incorrect.

(17) Indeed before that We subjected the Pharaonites to the same test. A noble Messenger came to them[14] (18) (and said): [15] 'Deliver to me Allah's servants.[16] I am a trustworthy Messenger to you,[17] (19) and do not exalt ▶

۞ وَلَقَدْ فَتَنَّا قَبْلَهُمْ قَوْمَ فِرْعَوْنَ وَجَآءَهُمْ
رَسُولٌ كَرِيمٌ ﴿١٧﴾ أَنْ أَدُّوٓا۟ إِلَىَّ عِبَادَ ٱللَّهِ ۖ
إِنِّى لَكُمْ رَسُولٌ أَمِينٌ ﴿١٨﴾ وَأَن لَّا تَعْلُوا۟

---

14. When the expression *karīm* is used with regard to a fellow human being, it signifies his excellent conduct and admirable traits. It is not, however, used for an ordinary person.

15. It needs to be understood at the very outset that the Prophet Moses' observations, which are recounted here, do not form part of a single discourse. Rather, he made these observations over a period of time on different occasions while addressing Pharaoh and his courtiers. A summary of his speeches directed at them is stated in the present passage. (For a detailed study, see *al-A'rāf* 7: 103-37, nn. 83-97, *Towards Understanding the Qur'ān*, vol. III, pp. 63-73; *Yūnus* 10: 75-92, nn. 72-93, vol. IV, pp. 54-64; *Ṭā Ḥā* 20: 47-76, nn. 18a-52, vol. V, pp. 190-206; *al-Shu'arā'* 26: 10-66, nn. 7-49, vol. VII, pp. 55-74; *al-Naml* 27: 7-14, nn. 8-17, vol. VII, pp. 138-44; *al-Qaṣaṣ* 28, nn. 46-56, vol. VII, pp. 217-22; *al-Mu'min* 40: 23-46, and *al-Zukhruf* 43: 48-56, along with their explanatory notes above.)

16. The Prophet Moses (peace be on him) demanded that Pharaoh deliver the Children of Israel to him. This demand is also mentioned in *al-A'rāf* 7: 105; *Ṭā Hā* 20: 47, and *al-Shu'arā'* 26: 17. 'Abd Allāh ibn 'Abbās, however, offers the following alternative rendering: 'O servants of Allah! Fulfil your obligations to me'. In other words, he asked them to believe in him and follow the guidance he had communicated to them. (Ṭabarī, *Tafsīr,* comments on *Sūrah al-Dukhān* 44: 10.) The assertion that he was a trustworthy Messenger for them is in keeping with this latter interpretation.

17. Moses is a trustworthy Messenger insofar as he does not mix up any extraneous thing with revelation. He is also not prompted by any selfish motive or interest in fabricating commands and then ascribing them to God; he only faithfully conveys what God communicates to him through revelation. It is worth clarifying that the Prophet Moses

yourselves in defiance of Allah. I have come to you with a clear authority (as a Messenger).[18] (20) I have taken refuge with my Lord and your Lord lest you should attack me with stones. (21) But if you do not believe what I say, leave me alone (and desist from laying hands on me).'[19] ▶

عَلَى ٱللَّهِ إِنِّىٓ ءَاتِيكُم بِسُلْطَٰنٍ مُّبِينٍ ﴿١٩﴾
وَإِنِّى عُذْتُ بِرَبِّى وَرَبِّكُمْ أَن تَرْجُمُونِ ﴿٢٠﴾
وَإِن لَّمْ تُؤْمِنُوا۟ لِى فَٱعْتَزِلُونِ ﴿٢١﴾

(peace be on him) made these observations at a time when he commenced preaching his message.

18. This means that their defiance of the Prophet (peace be on him) was, in fact, defiance of God. This because his teachings which irked them were from God rather than from him, teachings which he related in his capacity as God's Messenger. As for their doubt about whether Moses (peace be on him) was a genuine Messenger, he presented a series of miracles which conclusively proved that he certainly was a Messenger of God. Indeed, he presented not one but a whole series of miracles commencing from the time of his appearance in Pharaoh's court. When they rejected one miracle, he came to them with another. (For details, see *al-Zukhruf* 43, nn. 42-3 above.)

19. This relates to the period when Pharaoh adamantly rejected the Prophet Moses' miracles. However, the Egyptians, both the elites and the commoners, were greatly impressed by these miracles, which posed a serious threat to Pharaoh. In sheer desperation, Pharaoh spoke disparagingly about the Prophet Moses (peace be on him) (as mentioned in *al-Zukhruf* 43: 51-3.) As Pharaoh grew more alarmed, he began to plot Moses' assassination. On learning about Pharaoh's impious designs, the Prophet Moses (peace be on him) remarked: 'I have taken refuge with my Lord and your Lord against everyone who waxes arrogant and does not believe in the Day of Reckoning,' (*al-Mu'min* 40: 27.) Pharaoh's panic is also graphically described in *al-Zukhruf* 43: 51 and 53, (see also *al-Zukhruf* 43, nn. 45-9), in speaking of his taking refuge with God, the Prophet Moses (peace be on him) made it clear to Pharaoh and his entourage that they

(22) Then he called upon his Lord: 'These are a criminal people.'[20] (23) (He was told): 'Set out with My servants by night[21] for you will certainly be pursued.[22] (24) And leave the sea behind you as calm as ever. Surely they are an army that is doomed to be drowned.'[23] ▶

فَدَعَا رَبَّهُۥٓ أَنَّ هَٰٓؤُلَآءِ قَوْمٌ مُّجْرِمُونَ ﴿٢٢﴾
فَأَسْرِ بِعِبَادِى لَيْلًا إِنَّكُم مُّتَّبَعُونَ ﴿٢٣﴾
وَٱتْرُكِ ٱلْبَحْرَ رَهْوًا ۖ إِنَّهُمْ جُندٌ مُّغْرَقُونَ ﴿٢٤﴾

---

could not harm him. Rather, it was in their own interests not to launch any violent offensive against him. They may, if they so choose, disregard his message. However, if they tried to assassinate him, they would face terrible consequences of the same.

20. This constitutes the Prophet Moses' last and final submission to God. He clearly declared that Pharaoh's people were diehard criminals who did not deserve any further forbearance or respite. This amounted to saying that the time had come for God to make a final decision about them.

21. This refers to all believers, regardless of whether they were Israelites or the Copts who had become Muslims during the period commencing from the Prophet Joseph's time to the advent of the Prophet Moses (peace be on him) or the Egyptians who had embraced faith after witnessing the miracles performed by the Prophet Moses (peace be on him). (For further details, see *Yūsuf* 12, n. 68, *Towards Understanding the Qur'ān,* vol. IV, pp. 205-6.)

22. This was the preliminary directive to migrate that was given to the Prophet Moses (peace be on him.) For further details, see *Ṭā Hā* 20, n. 53, *Towards Understanding the Qur'ān,* vol. V, pp. 206-7; *al-Shu'arā'* 26: 52-66, nn. 39-47, vol. VII, pp. 68-73.

23. This command was issued when the Prophet Moses (peace be on him) had crossed the sea along with his followers. He wanted to strike his rod again so that Pharaoh's pursuing army might not be able to cross the sea. He was, however, asked not to do so and to let Pharaoh and

(25) How many gardens did they leave behind, and how many fountains (26) and sown fields and splendid mansions, (27) and the life of ease in which they took delight! (28) Thus it was; and We made another people inherit all that.[24] (29) Then neither the sky shed tears over them nor the earth.[25] They were granted no respite. ▶

كَمْ تَرَكُوا۟ مِن جَنَّٰتٍ وَعُيُونٍ ﴿٢٥﴾
وَزُرُوعٍ وَمَقَامٍ كَرِيمٍ ﴿٢٦﴾ وَنَعْمَةٍ كَانُوا۟ فِيهَا
فَٰكِهِينَ ﴿٢٧﴾ كَذَٰلِكَ ۖ وَأَوْرَثْنَٰهَا قَوْمًا
ءَاخَرِينَ ﴿٢٨﴾ فَمَا بَكَتْ عَلَيْهِمُ ٱلسَّمَآءُ
وَٱلْأَرْضُ وَمَا كَانُوا۟ مُنظَرِينَ ﴿٢٩﴾

---

his army enter the dry passage created in the sea, for then they would be drowned soon thereafter. (For further details, see *Ṭā Hā* 20, nn. 53-4, *Towards Understanding the Qur'ān,*vol. V, pp. 206-7; *al-Shu'arā'* 26, n. 47, vol. VII, pp. 72-3.)

24. According to al-Ḥasan al-Baṣrī, the reference here is to the Children of Israel whom God made to inherit Egypt after the destruction of Pharaoh's people. According to Qatādah, however, the reference is to another people who were settled in Egypt after the Pharaonites were destroyed. Since it is not recorded in any historical source that the Children of Israel ever returned to Egypt after the exodus, the later Qur'ānic exegetes have remained divided on this point. (Ālūsī, *Rūḥ al-Ma'ānī,* comments on *Sūrah al-Dukhān* 44: 28.) (For a detailed discussion, see *al-Shu'arā'* 26, n. 45, *Towards Understanding the Qur'ān,* vol. VII, pp. 71-2.)

25. When Pharaoh and his people were rulers, they exulted in their power and glory. They were also magnified and eulogised by their courtiers. Their sycophantic entourage projected them as the high and mighty ones who had done numberless favours to all. However, when they were destroyed, no one lamented their destruction. Rather, people were relieved at these tyrants' fall. Since Pharaoh had not treated anyone kindly, no one mourned his drowning. Since he did not care to please God, those in the heavenly realm too did not mourn the disaster that had overtaken him. As long as God had granted them respite, they abused it

(30) Thus did We deliver the Children of Israel from the humiliating chastisement, (31) from Pharaoh[26] who was most prominent among the prodigals.[27] (32) We knowingly exalted them (i.e., the Children of Israel) above other peoples of the world[28] (33) and bestowed upon them the Signs wherein lay an evident test for them.[29]

وَلَقَدۡ نَجَّيۡنَا بَنِيٓ إِسۡرَٰٓءِيلَ مِنَ ٱلۡعَذَابِ
ٱلۡمُهِينِ ٣٠ مِن فِرۡعَوۡنَۚ إِنَّهُۥ كَانَ عَالِيٗا مِّنَ
ٱلۡمُسۡرِفِينَ ٣١ وَلَقَدِ ٱخۡتَرۡنَٰهُمۡ عَلَىٰ عِلۡمٍ
عَلَى ٱلۡعَٰلَمِينَ ٣٢ وَءَاتَيۡنَٰهُم مِّنَ ٱلۡأٓيَٰتِ
مَا فِيهِ بَلَٰٓؤٞاْ مُّبِينٌ ٣٣

---

to exploit and oppress their fellow beings. When their crimes exceeded all limits, they were cast aside like a heap of rubbish.

26. Pharaoh himself was the source of their disgrace. It was on account of him that his people were subjected to a series of disasters.

27. The statement about Pharaoh that 'he was the most prodigal among the prodigals' contains a subtle taunt at the Quraysh chiefs. Insofar as exceeding the appropriate limits of creatureliness is concerned, Pharaoh was a mighty emperor who impudently lay claim to Divinity. Ultimately, he was destroyed. The Quraysh chiefs stand no chance whatsoever of remaining unscathed if God's scourge strikes them. As we know, the stature of the Quraysh bore no comparison to that of Pharaoh and his people.

28. God knew the weaknesses and strengths of the Children of Israel. They were the best people available at that time to shoulder the responsibility of preaching His message.

29. For details, see *al-Baqarah* 2: 49-73, nn. 64-85, vol. I, pp. 73-84; *al-Nisā'* 4: 153-61, nn. 182-99, *Towards Understanding the Qur'ān,* vol. II, pp. 103-11; *al-Mā'idah* 5: 20-6, nn. 42-7, vol. II, pp. 150-3; *al-A'rāf* 7: 137-71, nn. 97-132, vol. III, pp. 73-96 and *Ṭā Hā* 20: 80-98, nn. 56-74, vol. V, pp. 210-22.

(34) Indeed these people say: (35) 'This is our first and only death, and we shall never be raised again.[30] (36) Bring back to us our fathers if you are truthful.'[31] (37) Are these better or the people of Tubba',[32] and those who went before them? We destroyed them for they ▶

إِنَّ هَٰٓؤُلَآءِ لَيَقُولُونَ ﴿٣٤﴾ إِنْ هِىَ
إِلَّا مَوْتَتُنَا ٱلْأُولَىٰ وَمَا نَحْنُ بِمُنشَرِينَ ﴿٣٥﴾
فَأْتُوا۟ بِـَٔابَآئِنَآ إِن كُنتُمْ صَٰدِقِينَ ﴿٣٦﴾
أَهُمْ خَيْرٌ أَمْ قَوْمُ تُبَّعٍ وَٱلَّذِينَ مِن قَبْلِهِمْ
أَهْلَكْنَٰهُمْ إِنَّهُمْ

---

30. The unbelievers thought that death would mark the end of their existence for they did not believe in the Afterlife. Use of the expression 'first death', however, does not necessarily mean that they believed that another death would take place in the future. When we say someone has had their first child this does not necessarily mean that they will have a second one. What it rather implies is the negation of the birth of any child before the present one.

31. The argument underlying their rejection of the Hereafter was that they had never seen anyone from among the dead come back to life. They, therefore, said to the Prophet (peace be on him) that if human beings were going to return to life, he should bring back their deceased ancestors from their graves so that they might affirm that there is a second life. They regarded this as a weighty argument in support of their standpoint on the question of life after death. In fact, however, it holds no water. For the Prophet (peace be on him) had never claimed that the dead would be brought back to life *in this world*. Nor had any Muslim contended that *he would resurrect the dead*.

32. Tubba' was the title of the Ḥimyarite kings. These kings represented a branch of the people of Saba'. (Tubba' seems to be a title similar to the titles Caesar, Chosroes and Pharaoh.) In 115 B.C. the Tubba' established their rule over Saba' and reigned supreme there till 300 C.E. They were acclaimed for centuries all over Arabia for their greatness. (For further details, see *Saba'* 34, n. 37, *Towards Understanding the Qur'ān*, vol. IX, pp. 178-83.)

were a criminal people.[33] (38) It was not in idle sport that We created the heavens and the earth and all that is between them. (39) We did not create them except in Truth.[34] But most of them do not know. ▶

كَانُوا۟ مُجْرِمِينَ ﴿٣٧﴾ وَمَا خَلَقْنَا ٱلسَّمَـٰوَٰتِ وَٱلْأَرْضَ وَمَا بَيْنَهُمَا لَـٰعِبِينَ ﴿٣٨﴾ مَا خَلَقْنَـٰهُمَآ إِلَّا بِٱلْحَقِّ وَلَـٰكِنَّ أَكْثَرَهُمْ لَا يَعْلَمُونَ ﴿٣٩﴾

33. This constitutes the first rejoinder to the unbelievers' objection. In essence, it says that if a person, a group of people or a nation rejects the idea of the Hereafter, then this inevitably gives rise to immoral behaviour. This because disbelief in the Hereafter has a definitely adverse effect on human morality. History bears out that those who rejected the Hereafter were eventually destroyed.

There remains the question posed by the Qur'ān: 'Are those better or the people of Tubba' and those who went before them?' It should be realised that in terms of material prosperity, greatness and glory the Quraysh were way behind the people of Tubba', Saba' or Pharaoh and several other peoples. Notwithstanding this, the affluence and worldly glory of these peoples could not avert the evil consequences of their moral degeneration. Thus, in view of man's historical record, the Makkan unbelievers, with their meagre resources, stood no chance of survival. (For further details, see *Saba'* 34, nn. 25 and 36, *Towards Understanding the Qur'ān,* vol. IX, pp. 173-4, 178.)

34. This is the second rejoinder to the unbelievers' objection. The fact is that whoever denies the Afterlife and Divine recompense considers this universe no more than sport and play, and its Creator no more than a silly child. Accordingly, he thinks that life will come to naught after he did whatever he liked during his lifespan and that he will face no consequences for his deeds. The fact, however, is that the universe has been brought into existence by the All-Wise Creator and such a Creator cannot be expected to indulge in something altogether vain and purposeless. The Qur'ān adduces this argument at several places. (See *al-An'ām* 6, n. 46, *Towards Understanding the Qur'ān,* vol. II, pp. 243-4; *Yūnus* 10, n. 10-11, vol. IV, pp. 9-11; *al-Anbiyā'* 21, nn. 15-17, vol. V, pp. 257- 8; *al-Mu'minūn* 23, nn. 101-2, vol. VI, pp. 128-9; *al-Rūm* 30, n. 4-10, vol. VIII, pp. 75-9.)

(40) The Day of Final Decision is the appointed time for all;[35] (41) the Day when a friend shall be of no avail to his friend[36] nor shall they be helped, (42) except those to whom Allah shows mercy. He is the Most Mighty, the Most Compassionate.[37]

إِنَّ يَوْمَ ٱلْفَصْلِ مِيقَـٰتُهُمْ أَجْمَعِينَ ﴿٤٠﴾ يَوْمَ لَا يُغْنِى مَوْلًى عَن مَّوْلًى شَيْـًٔا وَلَا هُمْ يُنصَرُونَ ﴿٤١﴾ إِلَّا مَن رَّحِمَ ٱللَّهُ ۚ إِنَّهُۥ هُوَ ٱلْعَزِيزُ ٱلرَّحِيمُ ﴿٤٢﴾

35. This is said in answer to the unbelievers' demand: 'Bring back to us our fathers if you are truthful.' In response they are told that the Afterlife is far more grave a matter than an entertaining public show whereby the dead are taken out of their graves and brought back to life and put on public display. The Lord of the universe has preordained the Day of Resurrection. On that Day, everyone will be brought back to life and be made to stand before God Who will thereafter pronounce His judgement about them. All this will happen on that appointed Day, irrespective of whether anyone accepts the reality of that Day or not. However, if people do accept it, this is in their own interest for it will help them prepare for that great event. Conversely, they will end up as utter losers. This because they will have wasted the opportunity that has been granted to them. They wallowed in the wrong belief that this worldly life is all that there is. They mistakenly believe that after a person dies all things will end and he will face no consequences for his good or bad deeds.

36. *Mawlā* denotes a supporter or guardian who comes to someone's aid or support out of consideration for his relationship with that person, be it one of kinship, friendship or any other.

37. This vividly depicts the state of affairs obtaining on the Day of Judgement. No one's help or support will be effective in rescuing a culprit or lightening his punishment. On that Day, God alone will exercise all power and authority and no one will be able to prevent Him from enforcing His judgement. Also, no one will have the power to prevail upon Him. It will be God's exclusive discretion to spare someone from punishment or to award him a light punishment out of His mercy. True, since God is Most Merciful, mercy will be the hallmark of His judgement.

(43) The tree of al-
Zaqqūm[38] (44) shall be the
food of the sinful. (45) Like
dregs of oil,[39] it will boil in
their bellies (46) like boiling
water. (47) 'Seize him and
drag him to the middle of
the Blazing Fire, (48) then
pour boiling water over
his head as chastisement.
(49) Taste this, you are a
person mighty and noble!
(50) This is what you used
to doubt.'

(51) Verily the God-
fearing shall be in a secure
place[40] (52) amidst gardens
and springs. ▶

إِنَّ شَجَرَتَ ٱلزَّقُّومِ ﴿٤٣﴾ طَعَامُ ٱلْأَثِيمِ ﴿٤٤﴾
كَٱلْمُهْلِ يَغْلِى فِى ٱلْبُطُونِ ﴿٤٥﴾ كَغَلْىِ
ٱلْحَمِيمِ ﴿٤٦﴾ خُذُوهُ فَٱعْتِلُوهُ إِلَىٰ سَوَآءِ
ٱلْجَحِيمِ ﴿٤٧﴾ ثُمَّ صُبُّوا۟ فَوْقَ رَأْسِهِۦ مِنْ
عَذَابِ ٱلْحَمِيمِ ﴿٤٨﴾ ذُقْ إِنَّكَ أَنتَ ٱلْعَزِيزُ
ٱلْكَرِيمُ ﴿٤٩﴾ إِنَّ هَٰذَا مَا كُنتُم بِهِۦ
تَمْتَرُونَ ﴿٥٠﴾ إِنَّ ٱلْمُتَّقِينَ فِى مَقَامٍ أَمِينٍ ﴿٥١﴾
فِى جَنَّٰتٍ وَعُيُونٍ ﴿٥٢﴾

Nonetheless, God's judgement will be strictly enforced. This is followed by an account of those who will be pronounced guilty on the Day of Judgement. In contrast, those who feared God during their lives and shunned disobedience of Him will be granted abundant reward.

38. For a detailed note on *zaqqūm* see *al-Ṣāffāt* 37, n. 34, *Towards Understanding the Qur'ān,* vol. IX, p. 293.

39. The word *al-muhl* carries the following meanings: molten metal, pus, blood, molten tar-coal and dregs of oil or lava. (al-Rāzī, *al-Tafsīr al-Kabīr,* comments on *Sūrah al-Dukhān* 44: 43) It appears that the juice of the *zaqqūm* tree will be like dregs of oil.

40. Quite different will be the state of the God-fearing who will be in a 'secure place' which will be characterised by perfect peace and tranquillity and will be free of sorrow, grief, worry, fear, danger, hardship and suffering. The Prophet (peace be on him) said: 'The inmates of Paradise will be told that they will always enjoy sound health and will never fall ill.

(53) Attired in silk and brocade,[41] they shall be arrayed face to face. (54) Thus shall it be: and We shall espouse them to fair, wide-eyed maidens.[42] (55) While resting in security, they shall call for all kinds of fruit.[43] (56) They shall not taste death except the death in this world. And Allah will save them from the chastisement of Hell (57) as a favour from your Lord.[44] That is the great triumph.

يَلْبَسُونَ مِن سُندُسٍ وَإِسْتَبْرَقٍ
مُّتَقَٰبِلِينَ ﴿٥٣﴾ كَذَٰلِكَ وَزَوَّجْنَٰهُم بِحُورٍ
عِينٍ ﴿٥٤﴾ يَدْعُونَ فِيهَا بِكُلِّ فَٰكِهَةٍ
ءَامِنِينَ ﴿٥٥﴾ لَا يَذُوقُونَ فِيهَا ٱلْمَوْتَ
إِلَّا ٱلْمَوْتَةَ ٱلْأُولَىٰ ۖ وَوَقَىٰهُمْ عَذَابَ
ٱلْجَحِيمِ ﴿٥٦﴾ فَضْلًا مِّن رَّبِّكَ ۚ ذَٰلِكَ هُوَ
ٱلْفَوْزُ ٱلْعَظِيمُ ﴿٥٧﴾

Likewise, they will live for ever and will never die. They will enjoy eternal prosperity and will never be afflicted with any adversity. They will enjoy eternal youth and will never grow old'. (Muslim, *Kitāb al-Jannah wa Ṣifah Na'īmihā wa Ahlihā, Bāb fī Dawām Na'īm Ahl al-Jannah*).

41. *Sundus* and *istabraq* respectively denote fine and thick silken fabric.

42. *Ḥūr* is the plural form of *ḥawrā'* and signifies in Arabic a fair-complexioned woman. As for *'īn*, it is the plural form of *'aynā'* and is used to describe women with large eyes. (For further details, see *al-Ṣāffāt* 37, nn. 28-9, *Towards Understanding the Qur'ān*, vol. IX, p. 291.)

43. The inmates of Paradise will be free to obtain whatever they wish. They will ask their attendants to provide them with whatever they want and the same will be immediately be brought to them. Even in one's own home, one cannot freely get all one wants for one has to pay and arrange for it. In Paradise, however, people will be free to have anything on an unlimited scale. Nor will there be any chance that supplies will be exhausted.

44. Two points contained within the verse are noteworthy: (i) After an account of the bounties of Paradise, deliverance from Hell is

(58) (O Prophet), We have made this Book easy in your tongue so that they may take heed. (59) Wait, then; they too are waiting.[45]

فَإِنَّمَا يَسَّرْنَـٰهُ بِلِسَانِكَ لَعَلَّهُمْ يَتَذَكَّرُونَ ﴿٥٨﴾ فَٱرْتَقِبْ إِنَّهُم مُّرْتَقِبُونَ ﴿٥٩﴾

specifically mentioned. It is obvious that one values the reward of one's obedience more when one comes to know the punishment of disobedience. This also gives one the additional satisfaction of having avoided a terrible punishment. (ii) God ascribes to His grace that some people will enter Paradise and will, thus, be safe from the Hellfire. This is stated so as to bring home to them the truth that no one can attain success unless they are aided by God's grace. It is an altogether different point that one will be rewarded for one's good deeds. Let it be realised that one is inspired to do good only by God's grace. Moreover, even the best deed is not absolutely free from imperfection. God, out of His grace, accepts man's efforts and confers rewards upon him. Were God to take man strictly to account, no one would be able to enter Paradise by dint of his good deeds alone. An observation made by the Prophet (peace be on him) further amplifies this point: 'Do good deeds to the best of your ability. However, know that no one will be admitted to Paradise only on the basis of his record of deeds'. When those who were present asked the Prophet (peace be on him) whether that applied to him as well, he replied: 'Yes, I too will not enter Paradise by dint of my deeds unless God covers me with His Mercy. Only God's Mercy will help me gain entry into it.' (Ibn Kathīr, *Tafsīr*, comments on *Sūrah al-Dukhān* 44: 57.)

45. If the people concerned refuse to pay any heed to admonition, they should look forward to the doom that will overtake them. Likewise, the Prophet's adversaries too should wait and see how resplendent the finale of his mission will be.

Sūrah 45

Al-Jāthiyah

(Kneeling)

(Makkan Period)

Title

Since the word *al-jāthiyah,* (kneeling), occurs in verse 28 of this *sūrah,* it is known by this title.

Period of Revelation

It appears from the contents of the *sūrah* that it must have been revealed immediately after *Sūrah al-Dukhān*. The subject matter of the two *sūrahs* is so closely related that they can be regarded as twins.

Subject Matter and Themes

The main theme of this *sūrah* is to remove the unbelievers' doubts and answer their objections regarding monotheism and the Hereafter and to send them a note of warning as regards their attitude to Islam.

The *sūrah* opens with presenting evidence for monotheism. In this regard, it mentions man's own existence and the innumerable signs spread all over from heaven to earth: they are told that they can observe the proofs of monotheism that they deny, wherever they look. If one looks around with open eyes and is straight in one's thinking then the variety of wild animals, the alternation of day and night, rainfall and the vegetation to which it gives rise, the winds and man's own creation, all provide persuasive proof of the fact that this universe is neither without God nor has a multiplicity of gods. Rather, the universe is the handiwork of a single Creator Who alone regulates and governs it. However, if we are talking of someone who has sworn to disbelieve or has made up his mind to remain immersed in doubt, then this is a very different case. Nothing can lead that person to the treasure of belief. Later in the *sūrah* (see verses 12 ff.), man is told that all the things he benefits from in this world and the innumerable objects and forces of this universe that serve his interests are not there automatically, nor have they been provided by any of his gods and goddesses. Rather, all these have been provided by the One True God and harnessed to man's service. The rationality of every person who adopts straight thinking will cry out that it is the One True God Who is man's Benefactor and He alone deserves to be thanked.

Thereafter, the Makkan unbelievers are severely reproached for their obstinacy and arrogance, their mocking attitude and their obstinate clinging to the unbelief with which they greeted the Qur'ānic call. They are emphatically told that the Qur'ān has come down with the same bounty that was bestowed earlier on the Children of Israel, the bounty thanks to which they enjoyed excellence over all other nations in the world. However, they demonstrated ingratitude and caused the teachings of their faith to be lost in schism and dissension. Now, the same bounty is being offered to the Makkans. It is a guideline that directs man to the Straight Way of true faith. Those who reject this will court disaster. Only those who accept it and become God-fearing will merit God's clemency and support. In this regard the Prophet's followers are instructed to act with patience and forbearance towards those who were subjecting them to mean and horrid treatment. If they patiently bear with their persecution, God will avenge on their behalf and will reward them for their patience.

This is followed by the discussion of the unbelievers' flawed notions about the Hereafter. Their mistaken belief that there is no Afterlife is forcefully refuted. The unbelievers thought that death is the terminal point and that the soul does not exist. They ruled out resurrection. They even had the audacity to challenge the Prophet (peace be on him) to revive their ancestors to prove the truth of the Hereafter. In response to their objections, the Qur'ān presents the following arguments in quick succession: First, their rejection of the Hereafter is not based on any definite knowledge. They dismiss it whimsically. What is the basis of their contention that there is no Afterlife? How can they assert that souls are not seized and simply perish at death? Their objection rests, at most, on their observation that they have not witnessed any of the dead rising from their graves. Is this sufficient evidence for rejecting Resurrection? If one does not know, see or hear about a thing, does this necessarily mean that it does not exist?

Furthermore, it is against the dictates of reason and justice that those who are good and those who are evil, the obedient and the rebellious, the oppressor and the oppressed should meet the same end. Reason and justice demand that they must be recompensed in accordance with their deeds. Victims should be redressed while wrong-doers should be punished. Those entertaining such notions as the non-existence of Resurrection have a very faulty concept of the universe. Furthermore, those who are evil naturally try to avoid the dire consequences of their misdeeds. However, Divine dispensation is not haphazard. It is a perfect scheme of things in which those who are evil are bound to suffer punishment and the pious are bound to be rewarded. All cannot be treated alike.

Rejection of the Hereafter is also morally flawed. Only those who give fresh rein to their unbridled desires deny the Hereafter. Once they opt for this view, they become morally degenerate, and as a consequence, are unable to benefit from God's guidance. God emphasises that since man does not bring about his own life and is dependent upon Him for it, he also cannot bring upon himself death. It is God Who also causes his death. There will be the Day of Reckoning when all men will be gathered simultaneously. They will then see with their own eyes that they appear before God and their record of deeds is presented, testifying to all that they did. It is then that they will realise the gravity of their error in having rejected and mocked belief in the Hereafter.

In the name of Allah, the Most Merciful, the Most Compassionate.

بِسۡمِ ٱللَّهِ ٱلرَّحۡمَٰنِ ٱلرَّحِيمِ

(1) *Ḥā. Mīm.* (2) This Book is a revelation from the Most Mighty, the Most Wise.[1]

(3) Behold, for those who believe[2] there are (myriad) Signs in the heavens and the earth ▶

حمٓ ﴿١﴾ تَنزِيلُ ٱلۡكِتَٰبِ مِنَ ٱللَّهِ
ٱلۡعَزِيزِ ٱلۡحَكِيمِ ﴿٢﴾ إِنَّ فِي ٱلسَّمَٰوَٰتِ
وَٱلۡأَرۡضِ لَأٓيَٰتٖ لِّلۡمُؤۡمِنِينَ ﴿٣﴾

1. This serves as a short prelude to the *sūrah* which alerts the addressees to the following two truths: (i) The Qur'ān is not a product of the Prophet's mind. Rather, it is being sent down to him by God. (ii) God Who has been revealing the Qur'ān is Most Mighty and Most Wise. Since He is Most Mighty, one should not dare to defy Him. Moreover, God has perfect wisdom. This requires man to faithfully observe all His commands. His wisdom rules out any lapse or mistake in His commands.

2. The manner in which the main theme is treated after this prelude makes it evident that the Makkan unbelievers' objections to the Prophet's teachings underlie the main discourse. These unbelievers contended that they could not abandon their venerated gods only because of a single person's call to do so. In response, they are told that the truth of Islam is endorsed by the signs scattered all over the universe. On reflection, they can note these signs even in their own selves and in the universe at large. It is beyond any shadow of doubt that the whole universe is the creation of the One True God, Who alone owns it, holds its reins and regulates it.

The unbelievers contended that their deities were partners in God's Divinity. The Qur'ān, on the contrary, emphatically tells them that there is no deity other than the One True God. The signs spread across the cosmos underscore the truth of monotheism and refute polytheism. As to the Qur'ānic assertion that these signs are for believers signifies that though they are meant for everyone, they actually guide only believers to sound results. For those lost in negligence and error the existence of these signs is immaterial. For they live like animals, oblivious to all truth. An insensitive person cannot, of course, feel or take note of anything.

(4) and in your own creation; and in the animals which He spreads out over the earth too there are Signs for those endowed with sure faith;[3] (5) and in the succession of night and day,[4] ▶

وَفِى خَلْقِكُمْ وَمَا يَبُثُّ مِن دَآبَّةٍ ءَايَـٰتٌ
لِّقَوْمٍ يُوقِنُونَ ﴿٤﴾ وَٱخْتِلَـٰفِ ٱلَّيْلِ وَٱلنَّهَارِ

---

3. As to those bent upon denying the truth or those who prefer to be mired in skepticism, they are beyond redemption. However, as for those who do not have such closed minds and who reflect on their own births, on their bodies, on the immense variety of species of animals scattered on earth, they will perceive the signs which will lead them to believe in God's Oneness. (For further details, see also *al-An'am* 6, nn. 25-27, *Towards Understanding the Qur'ān,* vol. II, pp. 229-30; *al-Naḥl* 16, nn. 6-8, vol. IV, pp. 313-14; *al-Ḥajj* 22, nn. 5-9, vol. VI, pp. 7-11; *al-Mu'minūn* 23, nn. 12-13, vol. VI, pp. 87-8; *al-Furqān* 25, n. 69, vol. VII, p. 33; *al-Shu'arā'* 26, nn. 57-9, vol. VII, pp. 77-8; *al-Naml* 27, nn. 80-1, vol. VII, pp. 174-6; *al-Rūm* 30, nn. 25-32 and 79, vol. VIII, pp. 88-93 and 114; *al-Sajdah* 32, nn. 14-18, vol. VIII, pp. 163-6; *Yā Sīn* 36: 71-3; *al-Zumar* 39: 6 and *al-Mu'min* 40, nn. 97-8 and 110 above.)

4. The alternation of day and night stands out as one of God's signs in the sense that this alternation happens regularly. It is a sign insofar as day is bright whereas night is dark. Moreover, it is also a sign insofar as the duration of day keeps gradually receding until it equals the duration of night. Then again day's duration begins to increase and night's duration gradually recedes until the duration of the two becomes equal. The variations between night and day and the wisdom underlying these variations indicate that only One True God is the Creator, Master and Ruler of the sun, the earth and all beings on earth. God also controls the sun and the moon. All this indicates as well that His control over day and night is characterised by immense wisdom. For He has put in place unalterable laws which have made the earth a fitting habitat for numerous life forms. (For further details, see *Yūnus* 10, n. 65, *Towards Understanding the Qur'ān,* vol. IV, pp. 48-50; *al-Naml* 27, n. 104, vol. VII, pp. 187-8; *al-Qaṣaṣ* 28, n. 92, vol. VII, p. 243; *Luqmān* 31: 29 and n. 50, vol. VIII, p. 144; *Yā Sīn* 36: 37 and n. 32, vol. IX, pp. 258-9.)

and in the provision[5] that Allah sends down from the sky wherewith He gives life to the earth after it had been lifeless,[6] and in the change of the winds: [7] (in all these) there are Signs for people who use reason. (6) These are Allah's Signs that We rehearse to you in Truth. In what kind of discourse ▶

وَمَآ أَنزَلَ ٱللَّهُ مِنَ ٱلسَّمَآءِ مِن رِّزْقٍ فَأَحْيَا
بِهِ ٱلْأَرْضَ بَعْدَ مَوْتِهَا وَتَصْرِيفِ ٱلرِّيَٰحِ
ءَايَٰتٌ لِّقَوْمٍ يَعْقِلُونَ ۝٥ تِلْكَ ءَايَٰتُ
ٱللَّهِ نَتْلُوهَا عَلَيْكَ بِٱلْحَقِّ ۖ فَبِأَيِّ حَدِيثٍۭ

5. Sustenance, in this context, signifies rainfall, a point clarified in the next verse.

6. For further elaboration, see *al-Mu'minūn* 23, n. 17, *Towards Understanding the Qur'ān*, vol. VI, p. 90; *al-Furqān* 25, nn. 62-5, vol. VII, pp. 30-1; *al-Shu'arā'* 26, n. 5, vol. VII, p. 55; *al-Naml* 27, n. 73-4, vol. VII, pp. 171-3; *al-Rūm* 30, n. 35-73, vol. VIII, pp. 95-112 and *Yā Sīn* 36, nn. 26-31, vol. IX, pp. 255-8.

7. The reference here is to the movement of the winds in different regions and on earth in different seasons which results in climatic changes. God has provided air in such manner that it caters for the breathing of all creatures. The air around the earth also saves mankind from many calamities. Moreover, air is not restricted or uniform; it veers from hot to cold and from slow to gusty. At times it turns into storms. Sometimes it brings rain and at others, it drives away clouds. Moreover, the movement of the winds is not haphazard; this phenomenon is governed by a particular law which is characterised by order and purpose, indicating the perfect wisdom of the One Who devised this arrangement. The movement of winds is closely related with winter and summer which change with the revolution of the earth around the sun. Moreover, it has its direct bearing on seasonal changes and the distribution of rainfall. All these pieces of evidence clearly indicate that it was not the result of mere accident by some blind force of nature. Nor are there separate and independent regulators for the sun, the earth, winds, rainfall and the plant and animal kingdom. On the contrary, all of them have the same lord and master, the One True God Who is their Creator. Quite evidently,

after Allah and His Signs will they, then, believe?[8]

(7) Woe to every guilty impostor (8) who hears Allah's Signs being rehearsed to him, and yet persists in his pride, as though he had not heard it.[9] Announce to him, then, the tidings of a grievous chastisement. (9) Whenever he comes to know ▶

بَعْدَ ٱللَّهِ وَءَايَٰتِهِۦ يُؤْمِنُونَ ﴿٦﴾ وَيْلٌ
لِّكُلِّ أَفَّاكٍ أَثِيمٍ ﴿٧﴾ يَسْمَعُ ءَايَٰتِ ٱللَّهِ
تُتْلَىٰ عَلَيْهِ ثُمَّ يُصِرُّ مُسْتَكْبِرًا كَأَن لَّمْ يَسْمَعْهَا ۖ
فَبَشِّرْهُ بِعَذَابٍ أَلِيمٍ ﴿٨﴾ وَإِذَا عَلِمَ

---

all these elaborate arrangements have been made for a definite purpose by the All-Wise God.

8. If the unbelievers refuse to profess faith even in the face of these weighty proofs of God's existence and Oneness, nothing can direct them to accept faith. The Word of God is the final and ultimate source of guidance. All weighty arguments for persuading man to embrace faith are contained in it. One is free to reject them. However, this does not and cannot alter the ultimate reality.

9. There is a world of difference between he who studies God's signs with an unprejudiced mind and seriously reflects over them and he who rejects them out of hand because of his deeply entrenched prejudice. The former is not keen on clinging to unbelief. Rather, he is on a quest for truth and seeks to reach the point of total satisfaction. In such a case, some other signs may convince him of the Divine truth at a later date. In comparison, the latter is not moved by any sign. This because he has made up his mind not to believe. While the former is expected to embrace faith sooner or later, the latter group can never accept faith. These latter display the following three characteristics: (i) They are given to lies, hence truth does not appeal to them. (ii) They are given to wickedness. Therefore, they strongly resent those teachings that place moral restrictions upon them. (iii) They suffer from the delusion that they know everything, hence they do not need any guidance. Misled by these false notions, they do not pay any attention to God's signs.

anything of Our Signs, he makes them an object of jest.[10] For such there awaits a humiliating chastisement. (10) Hell is behind them.[11] Their worldly earnings shall not avail them, nor those whom they took as protectors instead of Allah.[12] An awesome chastisement lies in store for them.

مِنْ ءَايَٰتِنَا شَيْـًٔا ٱتَّخَذَهَا هُزُوًا ۚ أُو۟لَٰٓئِكَ
لَهُمْ عَذَابٌ مُّهِينٌ ﴿٩﴾ مِّن وَرَآئِهِمْ
جَهَنَّمُ ۖ وَلَا يُغْنِى عَنْهُم مَّا كَسَبُوا۟ شَيْـًٔا
وَلَا مَا ٱتَّخَذُوا۟ مِن دُونِ ٱللَّهِ أَوْلِيَآءَ ۖ وَلَهُمْ
عَذَابٌ عَظِيمٌ ﴿١٠﴾

---

10. Not only do unbelievers mock a particular sign of God, but they are prone to dismissing all signs of God with contempt. For example, on coming to know some Qur'ānic statement, they first seek to find some crookedness in it in order to reduce it to a butt of ridicule. They are also given to mocking the Prophet (peace be on him) and the Qur'ān and never fail to play up what they consider to be the outlandish and ridiculous contents of the Qur'ān.

11. *Warā'* in Arabic applies to everything that is not visible, whether it is behind or in front of someone. Therefore, part of the verse may be translated thus: 'Hell is behind them'. Taken in the former sense, the verse means that they are on their way to Hell, without realising that they will soon land themselves in it. In its latter sense, it signifies that they disregard the Hereafter and are engrossed in mischief-making, without realising that Hell is after them.

12. *Walī* is open to the following two meanings: (i) Such gods and goddesses, and living and dead leaders, about whom the polytheists believe have the power to rescue them so that they will not be punished by God, no matter how they conduct themselves. This because they believe that the intervention and intercession of their patrons will enable them to attain deliverance. (ii) This verse warns the unbelievers who unquestioningly obey and would do anything to please their tribal chiefs, leaders and rulers, even at the expense of displeasing God. They are warned that when their attitude lands them in Hell, their patrons will fail to come forward to save and defend them. (For further details, see *al-Shūrā* 42, n.6 above.)

(11) This (Qur'ān) is the true guidance. Those who deny the Signs of their Lord shall suffer the torment of a woeful scourge.

(12) Allah it is Who has subjected the sea to you so that ships may sail upon it at His bidding[13] and you may seek of His Bounty and give thanks to Him.[14] (13) He has subjected to you all that is in the heavens and the earth,[15] all being from Him.[16] Verily there are Signs in this for those who reflect.[17]

هَٰذَا هُدًى ۖ وَالَّذِينَ كَفَرُوا بِآيَاتِ
رَبِّهِمْ لَهُمْ عَذَابٌ مِّن رِّجْزٍ أَلِيمٌ ﴿١١﴾ ۞ اللَّهُ
الَّذِي سَخَّرَ لَكُمُ الْبَحْرَ لِتَجْرِيَ الْفُلْكُ
فِيهِ بِأَمْرِهِ وَلِتَبْتَغُوا مِن فَضْلِهِ وَلَعَلَّكُمْ
تَشْكُرُونَ ﴿١٢﴾ وَسَخَّرَ لَكُم مَّا فِي
السَّمَاوَاتِ وَمَا فِي الْأَرْضِ جَمِيعًا مِّنْهُ ۚ
إِنَّ فِي ذَٰلِكَ لَآيَاتٍ لِّقَوْمٍ يَتَفَكَّرُونَ ﴿١٣﴾

---

13. For a detailed account, see *Banū Isrā'īl* 17, n. 83, vol. V, p. 60; *al-Rūm* 30, n. 69, *Towards Understanding the Qur'ān,* vol. VIII, p. 111; *Luqmān* 31, n. 55, vol. VIII, p. 145; *al-Mu'min* 40, n. 111 and *al-Shūrā* 42, n. 54 above.

14. That is, God's subjection of the sea for man is in order that he may earn a wholesome livelihood by sea-trade, fishing, pearl diving, shipping and other means.

15. For details, see *Ibrāhīm* 14, n. 44, *Towards Understanding the Qur'ān,* vol. IV, pp. 271-2; and *Luqmān* 31, n. 35, vol. VIII, pp. 138-9.

16. This has the following two meanings: (i) God's bestowal of bounties is not akin to the award of some favour by earthly kings. The latter give out of what they receive from their subjects. On the contrary, God has created all the bounties in the universe out of which He grants to man what He pleases. (ii) God does not have any partner in the creation of these bounties or in making them subservient to man. God alone is their Creator and it is He Who has conferred these upon man.

17. For those who reflect there are major signs in God's yoking the objects of nature to serve man's purposes. These signs underscore that

(14) (O Prophet), tell the believers to indulge those who have no fear of any evil days coming upon them from Allah[18] so that Allah may Himself requite them for their deeds.[19] ▶	قُل لِّلَّذِينَ ءَامَنُوا۟ يَغْفِرُوا۟ لِلَّذِينَ لَا يَرْجُونَ أَيَّامَ ٱللَّهِ لِيَجْزِىَ قَوْمًۢا بِمَا كَانُوا۟ يَكْسِبُونَ ١٤

the One True God is the Creator, Master, Regulator and Disposer of all objects in the universe. He has bound all these to His laws. His power and wisdom account for making all these objects useful for man's life, economy, comfort, culture and civilisation. God alone, therefore, merits all thanks and gratitude. None besides Him has any role in the creation of these objects or in subjugating them for man's service.

18. Literally, it may be translated thus: 'Those who do not expect Allah's days.' However, in Arabic idiom, it signifies momentous, historic days. For example the expression *Ayyām al-'Arab* stands for the eventful days and major battles among the Arab tribes which have been recorded in memory for centuries. The verse alludes to inauspicious days when a people are afflicted with God's scourge. They are destroyed in punishment for their misdeeds. In keeping with the same, the verse has been translated thus: 'Those who have no fear of any evil days coming upon them from Allah.'

19. Qur'ānic exegetes offer two interpretations of this verse, both of which are admissible in the light of the wording: (i) The believers are asked to 'indulge' the excesses committed by the wrong-doers so that God may reward them for their perseverance, forbearance and gentleness and for their enduring persecution in His cause. (Zamakhsharī, *al-Kashshāf*, comments on *Sūrah al-Jāthiyah* 45: 14.) (ii) The believers should 'indulge' the wrong-doers so that God may fully avenge on their behalf. (Ṭabarī, *Tafsīr*, comments on *Sūrah al-Jāthiyah* 45: 14.)

Some scholars take this verse as abrogated, holding that this command was valid whilst the Muslims were not permitted to fight. When they were granted this permission, the above command was abrogated. (Ṭabarī, *Tafsīr*, comments on *Sūrah Jāthiyah* 45: 14.) However, this claim of abrogation is not supported by the Qur'ānic text. Since the believers are directed to 'indulge' these wrong-doers, the message is that they should not retaliate against them, notwithstanding their capacity to do so.

(15) Whoever acts righteously, does so to his own good; and whoever commits an evil will suffer its consequence. All of you will then be sent back to your Lord.

(16) Indeed We endowed the Children of Israel with the Book and Wisdom[20] and Prophethood, and provided them with good things as sustenance, and exalted them above the peoples ▶

مَنْ عَمِلَ صَٰلِحًا فَلِنَفْسِهِۦ ۖ وَمَنْ أَسَآءَ
فَعَلَيْهَا ۖ ثُمَّ إِلَىٰ رَبِّكُمْ تُرْجَعُونَ ﴿١٥﴾ وَلَقَدْ
ءَاتَيْنَا بَنِىٓ إِسْرَٰٓءِيلَ ٱلْكِتَٰبَ وَٱلْحُكْمَ
وَٱلنُّبُوَّةَ وَرَزَقْنَٰهُم مِّنَ ٱلطَّيِّبَٰتِ وَفَضَّلْنَٰهُمْ

This is despite the fact that the unbelievers, being fearless of God, had transgressed all limits of morality and decency. This directive is not discordant with the Qur'ānic permission to Muslims to go to war. Yes, war is to be waged as and when the Muslim state has a valid reason to declare war against an unbelieving people. The above directive, however, relates to the believers' encounter in one way or another with the unbelievers in which the latter resort to hurting Muslims by all possible means. The objective of the directive is that Muslims should not stoop to the unbelievers' low level. They should not quarrel with them or repay them in their own coin. They may defend their position as long as it is possible to do so within the bounds of civility. However, if the unbelievers misbehave, they should observe silence and refer the matter to God. If Muslims confront them in disregard of the norms of civility, God will leave them on their own to take them on. However, if they 'indulge' God, He will deal with the wrong-doers and reward the victims for their forbearance.

20. *Ḥukm* signifies: (i) knowledge and understanding of both the Book and faith; (ii) the ability to work in accordance with the purport of the Book; and (iii) the ability to decide matters. (Zamakhsharī, comments on *Sūrah al-Jāthiyah* 45: 16.)

of the whole world.[21] (17) We gave them clear directions in matters pertaining to religion. Yet they differed among themselves (not out of ignorance but) after knowledge had come to them; and they did so out of the desire to commit excesses against one another.[22] On the Day of Resurrection Allah will judge among them regarding what they had differed. (18) And then We set you, (O Prophet), on a clear high road in religious matters.[23] So follow that and do not follow the desires ▶

عَلَى ٱلْعَٰلَمِينَ ﴿١٦﴾ وَءَاتَيْنَٰهُم بَيِّنَٰتٍ مِّنَ
ٱلْأَمْرِ ۖ فَمَا ٱخْتَلَفُوٓا۟ إِلَّا مِنۢ بَعْدِ مَا جَآءَهُمُ
ٱلْعِلْمُ بَغْيًۢا بَيْنَهُمْ ۚ إِنَّ رَبَّكَ يَقْضِى بَيْنَهُمْ يَوْمَ
ٱلْقِيَٰمَةِ فِيمَا كَانُوا۟ فِيهِ يَخْتَلِفُونَ ﴿١٧﴾ ثُمَّ
جَعَلْنَٰكَ عَلَىٰ شَرِيعَةٍ مِّنَ ٱلْأَمْرِ فَٱتَّبِعْهَا
وَلَا تَتَّبِعْ أَهْوَآءَ ٱلَّذِينَ

21. This does not mean that they were granted excellence over others for ever. Of all the nations found then, God chose the Children of Israel for this assignment. It was their task to uphold the Word of God and champion Godliness.

22. For details, see *al-Baqarah* 2, n. 230, *Towards Understanding the Qur'ān,* vol. I, pp. 165-6; *Āl 'Imrān* 3, n. 17, vol. I, p. 242 and *al-Shūrā* 42, nn. 22-3.

23. This means that the task entrusted earlier to the Children of Israel is now transferred to the Prophet [and his followers]. Notwithstanding their knowledge of faith, the former had caused dissensions out of selfish motives. They had divided themselves into many sects. As a result, they were unable to invite others to the Way of God. Now, Muslims are charged with the same responsibility. They are required to take up the assignment which the Children of Israel had abandoned. (For further details, see *al-Shūrā* 42: 13-15 and nn. 20-6 above.)

of those who do not know. (19) Surely they will be of no avail to you against Allah.[24] Indeed the wrong-doers are friends of each other, whereas Allah is the friend of the God-fearing. (20) These are the lights of discernment for people and guidance and mercy for those endowed with sure faith.[25]

(21) Do the evil-doers imagine that We shall make them equal to those who believe[26] and do good, making their lives and deaths alike? How vile is their judgement![27] ▶

لَا يَعْلَمُونَ ﴿١٨﴾ إِنَّهُمْ لَن يُغْنُوا عَنكَ مِنَ اللَّهِ
شَيْئًا وَإِنَّ الظَّالِمِينَ بَعْضُهُمْ أَوْلِيَاءُ بَعْضٍ
وَاللَّهُ وَلِيُّ الْمُتَّقِينَ ﴿١٩﴾ هَٰذَا بَصَائِرُ
لِلنَّاسِ وَهُدًى وَرَحْمَةٌ لِّقَوْمٍ يُوقِنُونَ ﴿٢٠﴾
أَمْ حَسِبَ الَّذِينَ اجْتَرَحُوا السَّيِّئَاتِ
أَن نَّجْعَلَهُمْ كَالَّذِينَ آمَنُوا وَعَمِلُوا
الصَّالِحَاتِ سَوَاءً مَّحْيَاهُمْ وَمَمَاتُهُمْ
سَاءَ مَا يَحْكُمُونَ ﴿٢١﴾

---

24. If the believers alter the Divine faith in order to placate the unbelievers, they too will not escape God's punishment.

25. This Book and this *Sharī'ah* provide light to all mankind which enables them to distinguish between truth and falsehood. However, only those who believe in their veracity are actually able to derive any guidance. For such people it is a great blessing and mercy.

26. The discourse on monotheism concludes here and is followed by a discussion of the Hereafter.

27. This is a moral argument in support of belief in the Hereafter. Since good and evil radically differ from each other, it is essential that the upright and the wicked should not meet the same end. Rather, the upright should be rewarded for their good deeds and the wicked punished for their misdeeds. Should there be no Hereafter, morals would lose their meaning and relevance. In fact, in such an event one might even ascribe injustice to God. Those given to evil doing naturally oppose the idea

(22) Allah created the heavens and the earth in Truth[28] that each person may be requited for his deeds. They shall not be wronged.[29]

وَخَلَقَ ٱللَّهُ ٱلسَّمَـٰوَٰتِ وَٱلْأَرْضَ بِٱلْحَقِّ
وَلِتُجْزَىٰ كُلُّ نَفْسٍۭ بِمَا كَسَبَتْ وَهُمْ
لَا يُظْلَمُونَ ﴿٢٢﴾

of recompense in the Hereafter. They do so because it puts restraint on their unbridled ways. However, God, Who is Wise and Just, cannot be expected to treat the upright and the wicked alike. He will certainly take into account how people spent their lives and how some abused the faculties granted to them. For, the upright abide by the moral code, faithfully discharge their obligations, avoid unlawful gains and suffer losses on account of their commitment to truth and honesty. As opposed to this, the wicked gratify their base desires, refuse to serve God, usurp what belongs to others and unlawfully appropriate for themselves all that they can. If these two groups have not been alike in their conduct in life, they should not be treated alike after death. If they are treated alike, it would be tantamount to injustice in God's realm. (For further details, see *Yūnus* 10, nn. 9-10, *Towards Understanding the Qur'ān*, vol. IV, pp. 8-10; *Hūd* 11, n. 105, vol. IV, p. 133; *al-Nahl* 16, n. 35, vol. IV, pp. 329-30; *al-Ḥajj* 22, n. 9, vol. VI, pp. 9-11; *al-Naml* 27, n. 86, vol.VII, pp. 180-1; al-*Rūm* 30, nn. 6-8, vol. VIII, pp. 76-9; and *Ṣād* 38: 28 and n. 30 above.)

28. God has not created the heavens and the earth as a sport. Rather, their creation is animated by perfect wisdom and a sense of purpose. It is, therefore, inconceivable that the upright and the wicked will be reduced to dust after death and that there will be no Afterlife in which they will be recompensed proportionate to their good and bad deeds. Those who properly utilised the faculties and resources bestowed upon them by God in doing good should be rewarded. On the contrary, those who misused these and perpetrated mischief must be punished. (For further details, see *al-An'ām* 6, n. 46, vol. II, pp. 243-4; *Yūnus* 10, n. 11, *Towards Understanding the Qur'ān*, vol. IV, pp. 10-11; *Ibrāhīm* 14, n. 26, vol. IV, p. 263; *al-Naḥl* 16, n. 6, vol. IV, p. 313; *al-'Ankabūt* 29, n. 75, vol. VIII, p. 40; *al-Rūm* 30, n. 6, vol. VIII, pp. 76-8.)

29. The meaning of this verse is quite clear in the present context: if the upright are not rewarded for their good conduct and the wrong-doers are not punished for their wrongs and if the wrongs of the victims

(23) Did you ever consider the case of him who took his desire as his god,[30] and then Allah caused him to go astray despite knowledge,[31] ▸	أَفَرَءَيْتَ مَنِ ٱتَّخَذَ إِلَـٰهَهُۥ هَوَىٰهُ وَأَضَلَّهُ ٱللَّهُ عَلَىٰ عِلْمٍ

are not redressed this would amount to injustice. Such injustice is out of the question with regard to God's realm. Likewise, the other form of injustice is that an upright person is rewarded less than what he deserves or a wicked person is punished more than what his wickedness warrants. This is also inconceivable with regard to God.

30. To take one's desires as one's god means that one fully becomes the slave of one's desires. Such a person does whatever yields pleasure, irrespective of the fact that it is forbidden by God. Likewise, he will not do what is prescribed by God as an obligatory duty if he doesn't want to do it. If someone behaves as described above, he is the servant of his unbridled desires, no matter whether he verbally calls them his god or not and whether he worships them as idols or not. This because such an attitude amounts to treating his desires as deities. In the case of such behaviour, one cannot deny committing idolatry on the technical grounds that one had not verbally declared any of one's desires to be one's lord or that one had not literally prostrated before them.

This is how distinguished Qur'ānic scholars have understood this verse. In the words of Ibn Jarīr al-Ṭabarī: 'This person has made his base self his deity. He does all that his base self asks for. In so doing, he fails to observe the limits of the lawful and the unlawful laid down by God'. (Ṭabarī, *Tafsīr*, comments on *Sūrah al-Jāthiyah* 45: 23.) According to Abū Bakr al-Jaṣṣāṣ: 'Such a person obeys the promptings of his base self so religiously as one should serve God.' (Jaṣṣaṣ, *Aḥkām al-Qur'ān*, comments on *Sūrah al-Jāthiyah* 45: 23.) Zamakhsharī offers the following interpretation: 'He is led by his base self and follows it blindly. In other words, he looks after his self with a devotion that one consecrates to God.' (Zamakhsharī, *al-Kashshāf*, comments on *Sūrah al-Jāthiyah* 45: 23.) (For further details, see *al-Furqān* 25, n. 56, *Towards Understanding the Qur'ān*, vol. VII, pp. 27-8; *Saba'* 34, n. 63, vol. IX, pp. 197-8; *Yā Sīn* 36, n. 53, vol. IX, pp. 268-9; *al-Shūrā* 42, n. 38 above.)

31. This is open to more than one meaning. It may mean that notwithstanding that person's knowledge, God directed him to error

and sealed his hearing and his heart, and cast a veil over his sight?[32] Who, after Allah, can direct him to the Right Way? Will you not take heed?[33]	وَخَتَمَ عَلَىٰ سَمْعِهِۦ وَقَلْبِهِۦ وَجَعَلَ عَلَىٰ بَصَرِهِۦ غِشَـٰوَةً فَمَن يَهْدِيهِ مِنۢ بَعْدِ ٱللَّهِ ۚ أَفَلَا تَذَكَّرُونَ ﴿٢٣﴾

for he was a slave of his own desires. Or, it might mean that in view of God's knowledge that one deifies one's desires, God pushes him into error and misguidance.

32. God's causing some people to go astray and His sealing of their hearing and His casting a veil over their sight has been explained by us. For details, see *al-Baqarah* 2, nn. 10 and 16, *Towards Understanding the Qur'ān*, vol. I, pp. 48-9, 51; *al-An'ām* 6, nn. 17 and 28, vol. II, pp. 223-4, 231; *al-A'rāf* 7, nn. 80-1, vol. III, p. 62; *al-Tawbah* 9, n. 89, vol. III, p. 239; *Yūnus* 10, n. 71, vol. IV, pp. 53-4; *al-Ra'd* 13, n. 44, vol. IV, pp. 239-40; *Ibrāhīm* 14, n. 40, vol. IV, p. 270; *al-Naḥl* 16: 107-8; *Banū Isrā'īl* 17, n. 51, *Towards Understanding the Qur'ān*, vol. V, pp. 47-8; *al-Rūm* 30, n. 84, vol. VIII, p. 116; *Fāṭir* 35, nn. 16-17, vol. IX, pp. 212-14; and *al-Mu'min* 40, n. 54 above.

33. It becomes evident from the context of the verse that those who are bent on unbridled gratification of their desires are none else than those that deny the Hereafter. Such people look upon the idea of the Hereafter as so many shackles and fetters upon their freedom. Once they deny the Hereafter, they become even more engrossed in gratifying their desires and wander about in error, committing all conceivable misdeeds. They feel no scruples in usurping what belongs to others. Since they are given to committing injustices and excesses, even the fear of the law does not deter them from evil-doing. They also tend to disregard the incidents that should serve as lessons for them. Lost in self-complacency, they feel satisfied with their conduct even when it is evil. They pay no heed to any admonition. An argument that generally dissuades people from doing evil is misconstrued by them as an incentive for committing further evil. They look for any pretext to justify their unbridled freedom. As a result, rather than being concerned with doing good, their hearts and minds are given wholly to the gratification of desire. This proves beyond any shadow of doubt that denial of the Hereafter is fatal for morality. What can restrain and keep man under control is his belief in accountability to God for his

(24) They say: 'There is no life other than our present worldly life: herein we live and we die, and it is only (the passage of) time that destroys us.' Yet the fact is that they know nothing about this and are only conjecturing.[34] (25) And when Our Clear Signs are rehearsed to them,[35] their only contention is: 'Bring back to us our fathers if you are truthful.'[36] ▶

وَقَالُوا۟ مَا هِىَ إِلَّا حَيَاتُنَا ٱلدُّنْيَا نَمُوتُ
وَنَحْيَا وَمَا يُهْلِكُنَآ إِلَّا ٱلدَّهْرُ ۚ وَمَا لَهُم
بِذَٰلِكَ مِنْ عِلْمٍ ۖ إِنْ هُمْ إِلَّا يَظُنُّونَ ﴿٢٤﴾
وَإِذَا تُتْلَىٰ عَلَيْهِمْ ءَايَـٰتُنَا بَيِّنَـٰتٍ مَّا كَانَ
حُجَّتَهُمْ إِلَّآ أَن قَالُوا۟ ٱئْتُوا۟ بِـَٔابَآئِنَآ إِن
كُنتُمْ صَـٰدِقِينَ ﴿٢٥﴾

deeds. Even a learned person, who is devoid of this consciousness, is apt to behave like a brute.

34. The unbelievers do not have any definite source of knowledge that categorically informs them that there is no Afterlife. Likewise, they are not on sure ground in holding that the human soul is not seized by God's command and that man simply dies in the course of time. These ideas are simply their speculations. They may, at most, claim that they do not know whether there is an Afterlife or not. However, they have no grounds to rule it out categorically. By the same token, they cannot claim with certainty that the human soul is not seized by God and that man dies as a result of a mechanical process. Since both options exist, the unbelievers are not justified in dismissing one altogether and insisting only on the other. In fact, in so doing, they are swayed by their own biases. Far from basing their view on any weighty argument, it is their desire that there should not be any Afterlife. In other words, it is their wishful thinking which prompts them to deny the reality of the Hereafter.

35. That is, those signs which provide weighty arguments in support of the Hereafter. These prove that both justice and common sense demand that there should be an Afterlife. For, in its absence the present order loses its meaning.

36. The unbelievers refused to believe in resurrection. They insisted that the Hereafter can be affirmed only if they see with their own eyes

(26) Tell them, (O Prophet): 'It is Allah Who gives you life and then causes you to die,[37] and He it is Who will then bring all of you together on the Day of Resurrection, a Day regarding which there can be no doubt.[38] Yet most people do not know.'[39] (27) Allah's is the kingdom of the heavens and the earth,[40] and on the Day when the Hour (of Resurrection) shall come to pass, ▶

قُلِ ٱللَّهُ يُحْيِيكُمْ ثُمَّ يُمِيتُكُمْ ثُمَّ يَجْمَعُكُمْ
إِلَىٰ يَوْمِ ٱلْقِيَـٰمَةِ لَا رَيْبَ فِيهِ وَلَـٰكِنَّ
أَكْثَرَ ٱلنَّاسِ لَا يَعْلَمُونَ ﴿٢٦﴾ وَلِلَّهِ مُلْكُ
ٱلسَّمَـٰوَٰتِ وَٱلْأَرْضِ ۚ وَيَوْمَ تَقُومُ ٱلسَّاعَةُ

---

the dead rising from their graves. If this did not happen, they were not prepared to believe in resurrection. However, the fact remains that they were never told that the dead will rise from their graves *in this world*. Rather, the Qur'ānic doctrine is that it is on the Day of Judgement that God will resurrect all mankind and recompense them.

37. This is a rejoinder to their fallacious notion that the death of humans is caused simply by the passage of time. They are told that life and death are not a chance happening. It is God Who grants life to people and it is He who seizes their soul.

38. This is said in response to the demand to resurrect their ancestors. It is pointed out that it is not a few individuals who will be brought back to life. Rather, on the Day of Judgement, all humans will be resurrected.

39. Their ignorance and myopic vision account for their denial of the Hereafter. This doctrine is neither novel nor bizarre. On the contrary, its absence is unthinkable. Anyone who studies the workings of the universe and his own existence will realise that the Hereafter is imminent.

40. Were we to keep in mind the context of the discourse, it becomes quite evident that, since God exercises control over the entire universe, He is doubtlessly capable of resurrecting the dead.

يَوْمَئِذٍ يَخْسَرُ ٱلْمُبْطِلُونَ ﴿٢٧﴾ وَتَرَىٰ كُلَّ أُمَّةٍ
جَاثِيَةً ۚ كُلُّ أُمَّةٍ تُدْعَىٰٓ إِلَىٰ كِتَٰبِهَا ٱلْيَوْمَ
تُجْزَوْنَ مَا كُنتُمْ تَعْمَلُونَ ﴿٢٨﴾ هَٰذَا كِتَٰبُنَا
يَنطِقُ عَلَيْكُم بِٱلْحَقِّ ۚ إِنَّا كُنَّا نَسْتَنسِخُ
مَا كُنتُمْ تَعْمَلُونَ ﴿٢٩﴾ فَأَمَّا ٱلَّذِينَ ءَامَنُوا۟
وَعَمِلُوا۟ ٱلصَّٰلِحَٰتِ فَيُدْخِلُهُمْ رَبُّهُمْ فِى
رَحْمَتِهِۦ ۚ ذَٰلِكَ هُوَ ٱلْفَوْزُ ٱلْمُبِينُ ﴿٣٠﴾ وَأَمَّا
ٱلَّذِينَ كَفَرُوٓا۟ أَفَلَمْ تَكُنْ ءَايَٰتِى تُتْلَىٰ عَلَيْكُمْ

the followers of falsehood shall be in utter loss.

(28) On that Day you shall see every people fallen on their knees.[41] Every people will be summoned to come forth and see its Record and will be told: 'Today you shall be requited for your deeds. (29) This is Our Record which bears witness against you with truth; We used to record all what you did.'[42] (30) As for those who believe and act righteously, their Lord shall admit them to His Mercy. That indeed is the manifest triumph. (31) But those who denied the Truth, they shall be told: 'Were My Signs not rehearsed to you? ▶

41. People will be filled with such awe and dread in the Grand Assembly on the Day of Judgement that they will give up their boasting and arrogance. They will surrender themselves, meekly and humbly, before God.

42. This does not necessarily mean putting something into writing. There are many other ways of recording human speech and action. It is hard to imagine what developments may take place here on earth in this field in the future. It is, therefore, not possible for man to ascertain how God gets each and every word and deed of man recorded, including his intentions and thoughts. Nor is it possible to say how this record of both individuals and communities will be presented on the Day of Judgement.

But you waxed proud[43] and became a guilty people.' (32) And when it was said to them: 'Surely Allah's promise is true, and there is no doubt regarding the Hour of Resurrection,' you were wont to say: 'We do not know what the Hour (of Resurrection) is. We are simply making conjectures and are not at all certain.'[44] (33) (On that Day) the evil of their deeds will become apparent[45] ▶

فَٱسۡتَكۡبَرۡتُمۡ وَكُنتُمۡ قَوۡمٗا مُّجۡرِمِينَ ٣١ وَإِذَا
قِيلَ إِنَّ وَعۡدَ ٱللَّهِ حَقّٞ وَٱلسَّاعَةُ لَا رَيۡبَ
فِيهَا قُلۡتُم مَّا نَدۡرِي مَا ٱلسَّاعَةُ إِن نَّظُنُّ
إِلَّا ظَنّٗا وَمَا نَحۡنُ بِمُسۡتَيۡقِنِينَ ٣٢ وَبَدَا لَهُمۡ
سَيِّـَٔاتُ مَا عَمِلُواْ

43. The unbelievers arrogantly consider it beneath their dignity to pledge their obedience to God. They suffer from the delusion that they are simply too exalted to serve and worship Him.

44. Verse 24 speaks of those who deny the Hereafter without any hesitation. Reference is made in this verse to those who do not believe in it, though they do not rule it out altogether. Apparently there is a big difference between the two groups. For the former rejects it altogether whereas the latter regards it as a remote possibility. However, both of them will meet the same fate, for the same moral consequences flow from rejecting the Hereafter. In either case, such people will be devoid of the consciousness about their accountability to God. This adversely affects their beliefs and actions. Only belief in the Hereafter enables man to adhere to the Straight Way. Any denial or reservation about the Hereafter renders man's attitude irresponsible and this culminates in his punishment and suffering in the Hereafter. Neither the unbelievers nor the sceptics can avoid Hellfire because their notions about the Hereafter are false.

45. They will realise in the Hereafter that their ways, habits, deeds and activities in which they took great pride were absolutely wrong. By considering themselves unanswerable they committed a fundamental error which vitiated their outlook on life.

to them and what they had mocked will encompass them, (34) and it will be said: 'We will forget you today as you forgot the meeting of this Day of yours. The Fire shall now be your abode, and you shall have none to come to your aid. (35) You reached this end because you made Allah's Signs an object of jest and the life of the world deluded you.' So they shall not be taken out of the Fire nor shall they be asked to make amends (and thus please their Lord).[46]

(36) So all praise be to Allah, the Lord of the heavens, the Lord of the earth, the Lord of the whole Universe. (37) His is the glory in the heavens and the earth. He is the Most Mighty, the Most Wise.

وَحَاقَ بِهِم مَّا كَانُوا۟ بِهِۦ يَسْتَهْزِءُونَ ﴿٣٣﴾ وَقِيلَ
ٱلْيَوْمَ نَنسَىٰكُمْ كَمَا نَسِيتُمْ لِقَآءَ يَوْمِكُمْ
هَٰذَا وَمَأْوَىٰكُمُ ٱلنَّارُ وَمَا لَكُم مِّن
نَّٰصِرِينَ ﴿٣٤﴾ ذَٰلِكُم بِأَنَّكُمُ ٱتَّخَذْتُمْ
ءَايَٰتِ ٱللَّهِ هُزُوًا وَغَرَّتْكُمُ ٱلْحَيَوٰةُ
ٱلدُّنْيَا ۚ فَٱلْيَوْمَ لَا يُخْرَجُونَ مِنْهَا وَلَا هُمْ
يُسْتَعْتَبُونَ ﴿٣٥﴾ فَلِلَّهِ ٱلْحَمْدُ رَبِّ ٱلسَّمَٰوَٰتِ
وَرَبِّ ٱلْأَرْضِ رَبِّ ٱلْعَٰلَمِينَ ﴿٣٦﴾ وَلَهُ
ٱلْكِبْرِيَآءُ فِى ٱلسَّمَٰوَٰتِ وَٱلْأَرْضِ ۖ
وَهُوَ ٱلْعَزِيزُ ٱلْحَكِيمُ ﴿٣٧﴾

46. This brings to mind the punishment which the master will award to his disobedient servants.

Sūrah 46

Al-Aḥqāf

(The Sand Dunes)

(Makkan Period)

Title

The title of the *sūrah* is derived from the word *al-aḥqāf*, meaning sand dunes, which occurs in verse 21.

Period of Revelation

Verses 29-32 relate an event which indicates that this *sūrah* was revealed in either the tenth or eleventh year of the Prophet's mission. These particular verses narrate that the jinn came, heard the Qur'ān and then went back to their abode. This incident, according to those reports of *Ḥadīth* and *Sīrah* on whose authenticity there is absolute agreement, took place when the Prophet was returning from Ṭā'if to Makkah, and had halted at Nakhlah, which is where this incident took place. According to all authentic historical reports, the Prophet's journey to Ṭā'if took place three years before *Hijrah*. Hence it is obvious that the *sūrah* was revealed either towards the end of the tenth or at the beginning of the eleventh year of his Prophethood.

Historical Background

The tenth year of the Prophet's mission was marked by severe hardships. For three years, all the clans of the Quraysh had imposed a total boycott on the Banū Hāshim and the Muslims. As a result, the Prophet (peace be on him) was confined, along with his Companions, to Shi'b Abī Ṭālib. The Quraysh had imposed such stringent sanctions that no food supplies could reach the Muslims. Indeed, it was only during the *Ḥajj* season that they could buy some provisions. However, when they did approach any trader, Abū Lahab would ask that person to charge the believers an exorbitant price, one which they could not afford. He then bought the item himself at that high price. He did this in order to win over the traders to his side. Given that this boycott continued for three long years, it inevitably and painfully hurt the Muslims and the Banū Ḥāshim. So much so that they were forced at times to subsist on grass and the leaves of trees.

When the boycott finally came to an end, the Prophet's uncle, Abū Ṭālib, who had been a source of great strength to him, died. Within another month, the Prophet's wife, Khadījah, also passed away. Since the beginning of his Prophethood, she had been a tremendous help and consolation for him. In view of these sorrowful events, the Prophet (peace be on him) referred to that year as the year of sorrow.

After the deaths of Khadījah and Abū Ṭālib, the Makkan unbelievers' temerity and hostility towards Islam reached new heights, this to the extent that they started flagrantly persecuting the Prophet (peace be on him). It was even hard for him to go out. Ibn Hishām relates that it was during this period that a wicked member of the Quraysh threw dirt at his head in broad daylight. Eventually, the Prophet (peace be on him) left for Ṭā'if in order to invite the Banū Thaqīf to Islam and if they refused to do so, to ask, at least, to let him carry out his mission there.

Since he could not afford a ride, he went all the way to Ṭā'if on foot. Some reports suggest that he had gone there alone, while others indicate that he was accompanied by Zayd ibn Ḥārithah. During his few days' stay there he called on all the leading people and chiefs of the town, one by one. However, the Ṭā'if chiefs refused to listen to him and asked him to leave town immediately. As he so left the town, the Thaqīf chiefs incited all the resident urchins to misbehave towards him. Let loose, they hurled abuses and showered stones on him. The Prophet (peace be on him) was so badly wounded that his shoes were filled with blood. He then sat down beside the wall of an orchard and prayed to God:

> O Allah! I complain to You of the feebleness of my strength and the slenderness of my resources and my humiliation in people's sight. O Most Merciful of the merciful! You are [especially] the Lord of the weak; You are my Lord as well. To whom are You entrusting me? To one who will be cruel and harsh towards me? Or are you entrusting my affairs to any close friend of mine? [Yet] if You are not displeased with me, I do not care. But the well-being You grant me is more commodious for me. I take Your shelter, invoking the light of Your Countenance that replaces darkness with brilliance and puts one's state on a sound footing in both this world and the Hereafter. I seek Your protection against Your anger or displeasure. I will keep seeking Your pleasure until such time that You are pleased with me. There is no power nor authority other than Yours. ('Abd al-Malik ibn Hishām, *al-Sīrah al-Nabawīyah*, Muṣṭafā al-Saqqā et al. eds., Beirut: Dār Iḥyā' al-Turāth al-'Arabī, n. d., vol. II, pp. 60-2.)

In this heartbroken state, as the Prophet (peace be on him) approached Qarn al-Manāzil, he noted clouds appearing in the sky. When he looked up, he found Gabriel there, who told him: 'God has noted the response of your people to your call. He has directed the angel of the mountains to see you. Order him as you please.' Then the angel of the mountains appeared and greeted the Prophet (peace be on him) and told him: 'If you tell me, I will make the mountains of both sides fall together on these people.' To this he replied: 'No! I rather hope that God will raise from their future generations those who would worship the One True God.'

(Bukhārī, *Kitāb Bad' al-Khalq, Bāb Dhikr al-Malā'ikah*; Muslim, *Kitāb al-Jihād wa al-Siyar, Bāb mā Laqiya al-Nabī min Adhā al-Mushrikīn wa al-Munāfiqīn* ; and Nasā'ī, *al-Sunan al-Kubrā, Kitāb al-Nu'ūt, Bāb al-Samī'*.)

The Prophet (peace be on him) stayed at Nakhlah for a few days. During those days, when he was once reciting the Qur'ān as part of his prayers, a group of jinn passed by. When they listened to the Qur'ān, they embraced faith and, upon their return to their abodes, started preaching Islam in their own ranks. God gave the Prophet (peace be on him) the glad tiding that while the members of his community were averse to his call, many jinn had accepted it and were preaching it among themselves.

Subject Matter and Themes

This was the backdrop in which this *sūrah* was revealed. On reading it in the above context one is not left with any doubt that the Qur'ān could be the product of the Prophet's mind. It is patently clear from the study of the *sūrah* that 'The revelation of this Book is from Allah, the Most Mighty, the Most Wise' (verse 1). This is evident from the fact that the *sūrah* does not show any trace of those feelings that naturally arise in a person who passes through such heart-rending circumstances. Had the Qur'ān been the Prophet Muḥammad's own composition, it would have reflected his distresses at the series of shocks, the volley of hardships and his heart-rending experiences in Ṭā'if. The supplication of the Prophet (peace be on him) quoted above reflects his innermost feelings. However, this *sūrah*, which belongs to the same period, displays no trace of such emotion.

The theme of the *sūrah* is to warn the unbelievers against the consequences of their errors. They were proud about clinging to their erroneous ways. Not only that, they were bent on condemning the Prophet (peace be on him), who was sincerely trying to wean them away from their errors. For them, life was no more than a mere sport and they did not regard themselves as answerable to anyone. They rejected monotheism altogether, for they firmly believed that their idols had a share in Divinity. Nor did they consider the Qur'ān to be the Word of God. They also held false and odd notions about Messengership, which they applied in judging the Prophet's claim. One of their assumptions was that since their chiefs had not accepted his call, it could not be true. They dismissed Islam simply on the grounds that it was professed by some immature youth, some poor people and slaves. For them the doctrines of the Day of Judgement, of an Afterlife and Divine recompense were absolutely meaningless. This *sūrah* briefly refutes all their fallacious notions, one after another. They are warned that if they reject the message of the Qur'ān and refuse to accept Muḥammad (peace be on him) as God's Messenger, they will suffer loss and destruction.

In the name of Allah, the Most Merciful, the Most Compassionate.

(1) *Ḥā. Mīm.* (2) The revelation of this Book is from Allah, the Most Mighty, the Most Wise.[1]

(3) We have created the heavens and the earth and all that is between them in Truth and for an appointed term.[2] But those who disbelieve have turned away from what they were warned against.[3]

بِسْمِ ٱللَّهِ ٱلرَّحْمَٰنِ ٱلرَّحِيمِ

حمٓ ۝١ تَنزِيلُ ٱلْكِتَٰبِ مِنَ ٱللَّهِ ٱلْعَزِيزِ
ٱلْحَكِيمِ ۝٢ مَا خَلَقْنَا ٱلسَّمَٰوَٰتِ وَٱلْأَرْضَ
وَمَا بَيْنَهُمَآ إِلَّا بِٱلْحَقِّ وَأَجَلٍ مُّسَمًّى ۚ وَٱلَّذِينَ
كَفَرُوا۟ عَمَّآ أُنذِرُوا۟ مُعْرِضُونَ ۝٣

1. For explanation, see *al-Zumar* 39, n. 1 above; *al-Jāthiyah* 45, n. 1 above and *al-Sajdah* 32, n. 1, *Towards Understanding the Qur'ān*, vol. VIII, pp. 156-7. All these are helpful in enabling one to better appreciate the spirit of this *sūrah*'s introduction.

2. For a detailed discussions, see *al-An'ām* 6, n. 46, *Towards Understanding the Qur'ān*, vol. II, pp. 243-4; *Yūnus* 10, n. 11, vol. IV, pp. 10-11; *Ibrāhim* 14, n. 26, vol. IV, p. 263; *al-Ḥijr* 15, n. 47, vol. IV, p. 301; *al-Naḥl* 16, n. 6, vol. IV, p. 313; *al-Anbiyā'* 21, nn. 15-17, vol. V, pp. 257-8; *al-Mu'minūn* 23, nn. 102-3, vol. VI, pp. 128-9; *al-'Ankabūt* 29, n. 75-6, vol. VIII, p. 40; *al-Rūm* 30, n. 6, vol. VIII, pp. 76-8; *Luqmān* 31, n. 51, vol. VIII, p. 144; *al-Dukhān* 44, n. 34 and *al-Jāthiyah* 45, n. 28 above.

3. The fact is that the working of the universe, rather than representing a purposeless sport, is characterised by perfect wisdom. Under such a scheme of things it is inevitable that the pious and the wicked, the wrong-doers and their victims are judged with perfect justice. The present order will not last for ever. It is time-bound; at a given moment it is bound to wither away. The time for God's Judgement which will follow this is also ordained. Whenever that time comes it will be inevitably held.

(4) Tell them, (O Prophet): 'Did you consider those whom you call upon beside Allah? Show me, which part of the earth they created? Or do they have any share in creating the heavens? Bring to me any Scripture earlier than this one, or any vestige of knowledge (in support of your belief) if you are truthful.'[4] ▶

قُلْ أَرَءَيْتُم مَّا تَدْعُونَ مِن دُونِ ٱللَّهِ أَرُونِى
مَاذَا خَلَقُوا۟ مِنَ ٱلْأَرْضِ أَمْ لَهُمْ شِرْكٌ
فِى ٱلسَّمَـٰوَٰتِ ۖ ٱئْتُونِى بِكِتَـٰبٍ مِّن قَبْلِ
هَـٰذَآ أَوْ أَثَـٰرَةٍ مِّنْ عِلْمٍ إِن كُنتُمْ
صَـٰدِقِينَ ﴿٤﴾

However, those who have refused to believe in God's message and His Book disregard these facts. They have altogether forgotten that on the Day of Judgement they will have to render an account of their deeds. They mistake the Prophet (peace be on him) as their enemy, because he informs and warns them about these truths. They misperceive this to be an act of the Prophet's ill-will towards them. On the contrary, the fact is that he does so out of goodwill. For he forewarns them against their imminent accountability and also explains sincerely what preparations they should make for the Day of Recompense.

For a better understanding of the following discourse, it should be borne in mind that man's fundamental error is that he entertains preconceived and biased notions about God. Taking this issue lightly and forming an opinion about this matter on the basis of some ancestral traditions is an act of colossal foolishness. This because it affects man's world view and his ultimate end. As a result of this false notion, man considers himself unanswerable to anyone. He suffers from the delusion that there is no Afterlife in which he will be taken to task. Or he thinks that his gods will rescue him in the Hereafter. This is what makes man act so casually and complacently in matters of faith. Little wonder, then, that he falls prey to absurd doctrines like atheism and polytheism, or opts for a blind and unthinking conformity to absurdities concocted by others.

4. Since this passage is directed to a polytheistic people, they are told that, for want of a sense of responsibility, they are blindly clinging to a highly irrational belief. Just consider this: they acknowledge God to be the Creator of the universe and believe, at the same time, that several other

(5) Who is farther strayed from the Right Path than he who calls upon others than Allah that cannot answer his call till the Day of Resurrection,[5] the while they are not ▶

وَمَنْ أَضَلُّ مِمَّن يَدْعُوا۟ مِن دُونِ ٱللَّهِ مَن لَّا يَسْتَجِيبُ لَهُۥٓ إِلَىٰ يَوْمِ ٱلْقِيَـٰمَةِ وَهُمْ

beings too are their deities. To them they address their supplications, it is to them that they call upon in moments of crisis, it is to them that they prostrate themselves, and it is to them that they make their offerings and sacrifices. They do so because of their false belief that those deities can make or mar their destinies. They are asked: what entitles those beings to Godhead? There can obviously be only two grounds for taking someone as a partner with God: (i) man may come to know from a dependable source of knowledge that others too have a share in the creation of the heavens and the earth; or (ii) God may have informed him that someone is His partner in Divinity. Since the polytheists cannot substantiate their contention in either of the above two respects their standpoint is patently baseless.

The verse makes a pointed reference to 'any Scripture earlier than this'. This means any Scripture revealed before the Qur'ān's revelation. As for the expression 'vestige of knowledge', this refers to the teachings of the earlier Prophets and righteous people, authentically transmitted by subsequent generations. Both these sources are absolutely free even from any suggestion of polytheism. Even if the above allusion is not taken to mean the earlier Scriptures and Prophets' teachings, no one can even otherwise point to anyone other than God as having created anything whatsoever. Likewise, no one can establish that any of the bounties on which man draws are provided by someone other than God.

5. By 'answering the call' is meant the action taken in response to the caller's calling rather than an answer received in writing. If one invokes these false gods, they are so utterly helpless that they cannot act at all on the call of the caller for they lack all power to act positively or negatively. (For further details see *al-Zumar* 39, n. 33.)

That these false gods cannot answer the call of the callers 'till the Day of Resurrection' means that as long as the present world lasts they will be unable to answer. However, when the Day of Reckoning arrives, these deities will become enemies of their devotees as is said in the verse that follows.

عَن دُعَآئِهِمْ غَٰفِلُونَ ۝٥ وَإِذَا حُشِرَ
ٱلنَّاسُ كَانُوا۟ لَهُمْ أَعْدَآءً وَكَانُوا۟ بِعِبَادَتِهِمْ
كَٰفِرِينَ ۝٦

even conscious that callers are calling upon them?[6] (6) When all human beings will be gathered together those who had been called upon will become the enemies to their votaries and will disown their worship.[7]

---

6. These false gods do not even hear the prayers addressed to them. They are even unaware that their devotees call upon them. Such false gods invoked by polytheists all over the world may be broadly categorised under the following three headings: (i) soulless creatures that are devoid of rational faculty; (ii) deceased saints and pious people; and (iii) the misguided people who put themselves and others on a deviant path. The gods belonging to the first category cannot obviously hear the prayers of their devotees. As for the second category consisting of those close to God, there are two reasons for their being unaware of the caller's calls. One, that they are in a state where such calls do not reach them. Two, God and His angels do not inform them that those whom they had always urged to turn only to God have degenerated to the point of calling upon them. Such information would greatly hurt them, and God does not want to put His pious servants to grief. As for the gods belonging to the third category, there are two reasons for their ignorance: (i) they are lodged with God as culprits and they cannot find out what goes on in this world; and (ii) God and His angels do not tell them that their mission has been flourishing in the world insofar as misguided people have taken them as gods. This because it would greatly please them and God does not want to make these wrong-doers feel happy.

It is pertinent to note in the above context that God conveys the greetings and prayers of people for His pious servants, as this pleases them. By the same token, He apprises the iniquitous of the curses and reproaches directed at them by people. According to a tradition, those unbelievers who were killed in the Battle of Badr were made to hear the Prophet's reproach for it would agonise them. However, any piece of information which grieves the pious or pleases the iniquitous is not conveyed to the relevant party. This throws some light on the issue of the dead persons' ability to hear.

7. All false gods will clearly declare that they had never asked those people to worship them. Furthermore, they will also say that they were not

(7) When Our Clear Messages are rehearsed to them, the unbelievers exclaim about the Truth when it came to them: 'This is plain sorcery.'[8] (8) Do they claim that the Messenger himself has fabricated it?[9] ▶

وَإِذَا تُتْلَىٰ عَلَيْهِمْ ءَايَٰتُنَا بَيِّنَٰتٍ قَالَ ٱلَّذِينَ
كَفَرُوا۟ لِلْحَقِّ لَمَّا جَآءَهُمْ هَٰذَا سِحْرٌ
مُّبِينٌ ۝٧ أَمْ يَقُولُونَ ٱفْتَرَىٰهُ ۖ

even aware that those people worshipped them. If they were entangled in such error, it was simply their own responsibility and they alone should suffer its consequence. As for the false gods themselves, they are not to blame for they did not contribute to such people's errors.

8. When the Qur'ānic verses were recited before the Makkan unbelievers, they did feel that the Word of God was much more elevated and lofty than the human word. Even their best poets, orators or litterateurs could not come close to the Qur'ān's unmatched eloquence and rhetorical force, its overpowering oration, its lofty themes and its heart-captivating style. Above all, the Prophet's own speech, although lucid and elegant, lacked the power and grandeur of the Qur'ān. Those who had known the Prophet (peace be on him) since childhood could note the tremendous difference between his own speech and the Word of God. It was inconceivable that someone who had lived in the midst of his people for a full 40 to 50 years could all of a sudden compose a work whose style had no resonance with his own speech. This was an unmistakable indication of the truth that the Qur'ān is the Word of God. However, since its detractors had made up their minds to cling to unbelief and not accept the Qur'ān to be God's revelation, they attributed the Qur'ān's glory and splendour to magic. (They branded the Qur'ān as magic in another sense as well, which is explained in *al-Anbiyā* 21, n. 5, *Towards Understanding the Qur'ān,* vol. V, pp. 250-2 and *Ṣād* 38, n. 5 above.)

9. The question posed here strongly suggests the quaintness of the Makkan unbelievers' position. The question amounts to saying: Are these people devoid of even a shred of shame that they are accusing the Prophet (peace be on him) of fabricating the Qur'ān despite every evidence that it could not be the product of his mind. That they dismissed the Qur'ān as magic itself reflected their admission that it was an extraordinary discourse, one beyond any human's capacity to compose.

(If so), tell them: 'If I have fabricated it, then you have no power to protect me from Allah's chastisement. He knows well the idle talk in which you indulge. He suffices as a witness between me and you.[10] He is Most Forgiving, Most Merciful.'[11]

(9) Tell them: 'I am not the first of the Messengers; and I do not know what shall be done with me or with you. I follow only what is revealed to me, ▶

قُلْ إِنِ ٱفْتَرَيْتُهُۥ فَلَا تَمْلِكُونَ لِى مِنَ ٱللَّهِ
شَيْـًٔا ۖ هُوَ أَعْلَمُ بِمَا تُفِيضُونَ فِيهِ ۖ كَفَىٰ بِهِۦ
شَهِيدًۢا بَيْنِى وَبَيْنَكُمْ ۖ وَهُوَ ٱلْغَفُورُ ٱلرَّحِيمُ ۝٨
قُلْ مَا كُنتُ بِدْعًا مِّنَ ٱلرُّسُلِ
وَمَآ أَدْرِى مَا يُفْعَلُ بِى وَلَا بِكُمْ ۖ إِنْ أَتَّبِعُ
إِلَّا مَا يُوحَىٰٓ إِلَىَّ

---

10. Since the unbelievers' allegations were utterly baseless and stemmed only from obstinacy, the Qur'ān does not adduce any arguments to refute them. It says only this much: that if the Prophet (peace be on him) is guilty of fabricating the Qur'ān and ascribing it to God, they cannot save him from God's punishment. However, if the case is otherwise, they will be severely punished for hurling baseless charges against him. The truth is not hidden from God. He suffices to adjudge between truth and falsehood. If a truthful person is rejected by the whole of mankind that is immaterial, for God will declare him to be true. They should, therefore, better think of their own ultimate ends, rather than indulge in this specious task.

11. In the context of the verse this observation conveys the following two meanings: (i) It is only owing to God's mercy and forgiveness that the unbelievers are alive. For they had brazenly rejected the Word of God as the Prophet's fabrication. Had He been merciless and impatient, He would have instantly decimated such blasphemous people. (ii) The wrong-doers are asked to give up their obstinacy. The gates of God's mercy are wide open for them. As for their past misdeeds, they will be forgiven if they repent and mend their ways.

and I am nothing but a plain warner.'[12] (10) Tell them, (O Prophet): 'Did you consider (what would be your end) if this Qur'ān were indeed from Allah ▸

وَمَآ أَنَا۠ إِلَّا نَذِيرٌ مُّبِينٌ ۝ قُلْ أَرَءَيْتُمْ إِن

كَانَ مِنْ عِندِ ٱللَّهِ

---

12. When the Prophet (peace be on him) presented himself as the Messenger of God, the Makkans took to raising all sorts of objections. They found it strange that he had a family, walked about the markets, ate and drank and led his life as an ordinary person. They failed to discern anything exceptional in him which could persuade them that he had been designated by God as His Messenger. Their assumption was that God's Messenger should have been escorted by an angel, who would attend upon him and proclaim him to be God's Messenger and instantly punish those who showed any disrespect towards him. It was beyond them how God could ask His Messenger to fend for himself in Makkah and be left to suffer all kinds of persecution. They thought that God should have, at least, provided him with a lofty palace and a flourishing garden. It should simply not have happened that when his wife's resources at times were exhausted, the Prophet (peace be on him) was forced to starve. Furthermore, it is on record that he did not have any ride or transport and had to travel to Ṭā'if on foot. The unbelievers asked him to come forth with miracles of all sorts and demanded that he should inform them of matters belonging to the Unseen. They thought a Messenger should be superhuman and in full knowledge of the Unseen. At his gesture, mountains should move and deserts turn into oases! He should be fully aware of the past as well as of the future. All that lies beyond human perception should be at his fingertips.

These points are taken up in this passage. The Prophet (peace be on him) is directed to tell his detractors that he is like other Messengers. His advent as a Messenger is not new in history. They know well the traits of a Messenger. For many Messengers had appeared before him and in this respect he is no different from them. He is also asked to tell them that he does not know what will happen either to him or to them tomorrow. Every Messenger had a family, subsisted on food and drink and lived like any other human being. No Messenger was ever escorted by an angel who announced his status and whipped his detractors. Nor was any Messenger ever granted palaces and gardens. Like him, the earlier Messengers too

and yet you rejected it?[13] And this even though a witness from the Children of Israel has testified to the like of it. But he believed, while you waxed arrogant.[14] Verily Allah does not guide such wrong-doers to the Right Way.'

(11) The unbelievers say to the believers: 'If there was any good in this Book, ▶

وَكَفَرْتُم بِهِۦ وَشَهِدَ شَاهِدٌ مِّنۢ بَنِىٓ إِسْرَٰٓءِيلَ
عَلَىٰ مِثْلِهِۦ فَـَٔامَنَ وَٱسْتَكْبَرْتُمْ ۖ إِنَّ ٱللَّهَ
لَا يَهْدِى ٱلْقَوْمَ ٱلظَّـٰلِمِينَ ۝ وَقَالَ ٱلَّذِينَ
كَفَرُوا۟ لِلَّذِينَ ءَامَنُوا۟ لَوْ كَانَ خَيْرًا

faced persecution. Never did any Messenger reveal a miracle on his own. None of them was omniscient. In view of this, they should not apply such an extraordinary yardstick for judging the Prophet's claim to be God's Messenger. He simply abides by the revelations sent down to him. In other words, he does not possess knowledge of the Unseen. He is not aware of his or their future. His knowledge is restricted to what is communicated to him by revelation. He never claimed to know anything beyond the knowledge imparted to him by God. Nor was such a claim made by any other Messenger. They should not expect him to inform them of their lost goods, or foretell whether a woman will give birth to a son or daughter, or predict whether a patient will survive or die. He is also directed to declare that he is only a clear warner. In other words, he does not have any share in Divinity which may enable him to produce the miracles they ask for. His assignment consists in presenting the Straight Way to people and in warning those who refuse to believe.

13. Almost the same occurs in *Ḥā Mīm al-Sajdah* 41: 52, n. 69 above.

14. Qur'ānic exegetes hold divergent views in identifying who the witness is. A large number of them believe that the allusion is to 'Abd Allāh ibn Salām, a leading Jewish scholar of Madīnah. He had embraced Islam after the Prophet's arrival there. Since this event took place in that city, some Qur'ānic commentators consider this verse to be Madīnan. Their view rests on Sa'd ibn Abī Waqqaṣ's report that the verse is related to 'Abd

Allāh ibn Salām. (Bukhārī, *Kitāb al-Manāqib, Bāb Manāqib 'Abd Allāh ibn Salām Raḍiya Allāh 'anh;* Muslim, *Kitāb al-Faḍā'il Bāb min Faḍā'il 'Abd Allāh ibn Salām Raḍiya Allāh 'anh;* Nasā'ī, *al-Sunan al-Kubrā, Kitāb al-Manāqib, Bāb 'Abd Allāh ibn Salām Raḍiya Allāh 'anh;* and Ṭabarī, *Tafsīr,* comments on *Sūrah al-Aḥqāf* 46: 10.) The above viewpoint is endorsed by Ibn 'Abbās, Mujāhid, Qatādah, Ḍaḥḥāk, Ibn Sīrīn, al-Ḥasan al-Baṣrī, Ibn Zayd and 'Awf ibn Mālik al-Ashja'ī. (Ṭabarī, *Tafsīr,* comments on *Sūrah al-Aḥqāf* 46: 10.) On the other hand, 'Ikrimah, Sha'bī and Masrūq contend that the verse could not be about 'Abd Allāh ibn Salām for the whole discourse is addressed to the Makkan unbelievers. This because the *sūrah* in its entirety was revealed in Makkah. (Suyūṭī, *al-Durr al-Manthūr,* comments on *Sūrah al-Aḥqāf* 46: 10.) Ibn Jarīr al-Ṭabarī shares the same view. He points out the Makkan context of the *sūrah,* as it addresses the Makkan polytheists both before and after this verse. It is hardly conceivable, therefore, that a Madīnan verse would be put in between Makkan verses. (Ṭabarī, *Tafsīr,* comments on *Sūrah al-Aḥqāf* 46: 10.) However, some Qur'ānic scholars do not discount Sa'd ibn Abī Waqqāṣ's report. For them, the verse is equally applicable to 'Abd Allāh ibn Salām's acceptance of Islam. Sa'd's allusion to 'Abd Allāh ibn Salām should be taken in this light. (Ṭabarī, *Tafsīr,* comments on *Sūrah al-Aḥqāf* 46: 10.)

The second interpretation appears more sound and plausible. Yet the question of the identity of 'the witness' remains to be determined. Some exegetes express the opinion that the allusion is to the Prophet Moses (peace be on him). (Ṭabarī, *Tafsīr,* comments on *Sūrah al-Aḥqāf* 46: 10.) However, this does not fit in with the later part of the verse which asserts: 'But he believed, while you waxed arrogant.'

The more plausible view, therefore, is that of Ibn Kathīr and Nīshāpūrī, that the reference is not to someone in particular. Rather, it holds true for an ordinary member of the Children of Israel. (Nīshāpūrī, *Tafsīr,* comments on *Sūrah al-Aḥqāf* 46: 10; Ibn Kathīr, *Tafsīr,* comments on *Sūrah al-Aḥqāf* 46: 10.) The point brought home is that the Qur'ānic teachings being presented to them are neither novel nor weird. They cannot, therefore, plead that they are unable to believe in something altogether novel in human history. This because the same teachings form part of the Torah and other Scriptures, which owe their origin to revelation, and they are held true by the common man. The common man also recognises that revelation is the source of these teachings. Therefore, they cannot put forward their ignorance of revelation as a pretext for their rejection. Rather, it is their pride, arrogance and haughtiness that mainly accounts for their unbelief.

مَا سَبَقُونَآ إِلَيۡهِۚ وَإِذۡ لَمۡ يَهۡتَدُواْ بِهِۦ فَسَيَقُولُونَ
هَٰذَآ إِفۡكٞ قَدِيمٞ ﴿١١﴾ وَمِن قَبۡلِهِۦ كِتَٰبُ
مُوسَىٰٓ إِمَامٗا وَرَحۡمَةٗۚ وَهَٰذَا كِتَٰبٞ
مُّصَدِّقٞ لِّسَانًا عَرَبِيّٗا لِّيُنذِرَ ٱلَّذِينَ ظَلَمُواْ
وَبُشۡرَىٰ لِلۡمُحۡسِنِينَ ﴿١٢﴾

others would not have beaten us to its acceptance.'[15] But since they have not been guided to it, they will certainly say: 'This is an old fabrication.'[16] (12) Yet before this the Book was revealed to Moses as a guide and a mercy. This Book, which confirms it, is in the Arabic tongue to warn the wrong-doers[17] and to give good tidings to those who do good. ▶

15. This is an argument employed by the Quraysh chiefs to provoke people against the Prophet (peace be on him.) Their contention was that if the Qur'ān represented the truth and the Prophet's call signified the Straight Way, their community chiefs and elites would have been the first ones to accept Islam. However, since Islam was accepted by some inexperienced youth, slaves and poor people and was rejected by mature, experienced leaders of the community known for their sagacity, they found it hard to believe in Islam. While resorting to this fallacious logic, they misled common people into thinking that there is something innately wrong with Islam, which accounted for its rejection by the tribal chiefs. Accordingly, so the logic went, they should also stay away from it.

16. The unbelievers consider themselves to be the criterion of truth and falsehood. They believe that what they reject is necessarily false. However, they cannot muster the courage to dismiss Islam as an altogether new fabrication and, therefore, brand it 'an old fabrication' for its teachings are identical with those of the earlier Messengers. In other words, all those people who have believed in these truths for thousands of years were also stupid and wisdom and sound judgement are the monopoly of these unbelievers.

17. The Prophet (peace be on him) warns all those who disbelieve in God and wrong themselves by worshipping others besides Him.

إِنَّ ٱلَّذِينَ قَالُوا۟ رَبُّنَا ٱللَّهُ ثُمَّ ٱسْتَقَـٰمُوا۟
فَلَا خَوْفٌ عَلَيْهِمْ وَلَا هُمْ يَحْزَنُونَ ﴿١٣﴾
أُو۟لَـٰٓئِكَ أَصْحَـٰبُ ٱلْجَنَّةِ خَـٰلِدِينَ
فِيهَا جَزَآءًۢ بِمَا كَانُوا۟ يَعْمَلُونَ ﴿١٤﴾ وَوَصَّيْنَا
ٱلْإِنسَـٰنَ بِوَٰلِدَيْهِ إِحْسَـٰنًا ۖ حَمَلَتْهُ أُمُّهُۥ
كُرْهًا وَوَضَعَتْهُ كُرْهًا ۖ وَحَمْلُهُۥ وَفِصَـٰلُهُۥ
ثَلَـٰثُونَ شَهْرًا ۚ

(13) Surely those who said: 'Our Lord is Allah' and then remained steadfast shall have nothing to fear nor to grieve.[18] (14) They are the people of Paradise. They shall remain in it forever as a reward for their deeds.

(15) We have enjoined man to be kind to his parents. In pain did his mother bear him and in pain did she give birth to him. The carrying of the child to his weaning is a period of thirty months.[19] ▶

18. For details see *Ḥā Mīm al-Sajdah* 41, nn. 33-5 above.

19. It is evident from the verse that while children should serve both parents, the mother has a greater right over her children insofar as she bears greater hardships for them. The same point is made in the *ḥadīth* which is narrated with slight variations by Bukhārī, *Kitāb al-Adab, Bāb Man al-Aḥaqq al-Nās bi Ḥusn al-Ṣuḥbah*; Muslim, *Kitāb al-Birr wa al-Ṣilah wa al-Ādāb, Bāb Birr al-Wālidayn wa Annahumā Aḥaqq bih*; Abū Dā'ūd, *Kitāb al-Adab, Bāb fī Birr al-Wālidayn*; Tirmidhī, *Kitāb al-Birr wa al-Ṣilah min Rasūl Allāh Ṣallā Allāh 'alayhi wa Sallam, Bāb mā Jā'a fī Birr al-Wālidayn*; Ibn Mājah, *Kitāb al-Adab, Bāb Birr al-Wālidayn*; and Aḥmad ibn Ḥanbal, *Musnad*, narrated by Abū Hurayrah; and Bukhārī, *al-Adab al-Mufrad, Bāb Birr al-Umm*. The *ḥadīth* is as follows: 'Once someone asked the Prophet (peace be on him) as to who is more entitled to his service? He replied: "Your mother". Then he asked as to who was next to her, he again replied, "Your mother". The same question was asked for the third time and the answer was the same. It was only on the fourth asking that the Prophet (peace be on him) said: "Your father".' The Prophet's observation amplifies the point made in this verse. For this, too, speaks of the three points special to one's mother: (i) she carries one in the womb with hardship; (ii) she

delivers one with much agony; and (iii) conception and weaning together take 30 months.

On reading this verse in conjunction with *Luqmān* 31: 14 and *al-Baqarah* 2: 233, one notes a legal point identified by 'Alī and 'Abd Allāh ibn 'Abbās during a legal case, and in view of which Caliph 'Uthmān changed his judgement. The tradition is as follows: During 'Uthmān's reign, someone married a woman of the Juhaynah tribe. She gave birth to a sound baby six months after marriage. The husband reported the case to the Caliph, who declared her an adultress and sentenced her to be stoned to death. 'Alī, however, contested his ruling and recited before him the following three Qur'ānic verses, one after the other:

(1) If they (i.e. the fathers) wish that the period of suckling for their children be completed, mothers may suckle their children for two whole years (*al-Baqarah* 2: 233).
(2) His mother bore him... and his weaning lasted two years, (*Luqmān* 31: 14.)
(3) The carrying of the child to his weaning is a period of thirty months, (*al-Aḥqāf* 46: 15.)

On deducting two years of suckling from the total period of 30 months, a pregnancy may only be of six months duration. So, such a woman cannot be branded an adulteress. On noting 'Alī's reasoning, 'Uthmān admitted his oversight and changed his judgement. According to a report, 'Alī's contention was also supported by Ibn 'Abbās, and it was then that 'Uthmān changed his judgement. (Ṭabarī, *Tafsīr*, comments on *Sūrah al-Zukhruf* 43: 81; Jaṣṣāṣ, *Aḥkām al-Qur'ān*, comments on *Sūrah al-Aḥqāf* 46: 15 and Ibn Kathīr, *Tafsīr*, comments on *Sūrah al-Aḥqāf* 46: 15.)

By studying these three Qur'ānic verses one learns the following legal points: (i) A woman who delivers a sound baby in less than six months of her marriage, provided that it is not via miscarriage but normal delivery, will be regarded as guilty of illicit sex. The baby will not be credited to her husband. (ii) A woman who delivers a baby after six months of marriage or more cannot be accused of adultery simply on the basis of delivery alone. Nor is her husband entitled to accuse her of that. The baby will be credited to her husband and she will not be punished. (iii) The maximum period of weaning is two years. If a baby takes the milk of a woman when he is above two years of age, she will not be considered as his foster mother. Accordingly, the legal commands embodied in *al-Nisā'* 4: 23 which relates to foster relationships will not apply. As a precautionary measure, Abū Ḥanīfah fixed the weaning period up to two-and-a-half years lest any mistake might be made in such a delicate matter as the prohibition

And when he is grown to full maturity and reaches the age of forty, he prays: 'My Lord, dispose me that I may give thanks for the bounty that You have bestowed upon me and my parents, and dispose me that I may do righteous deeds that would please You,[20] and also make my descendants righteous. I repent to You, and I am one of those who surrender themselves to You.' (16) Such are those from whom We accept their best deeds and whose evil deeds ▸

حَتَّىٰٓ إِذَا بَلَغَ أَشُدَّهُۥ وَبَلَغَ أَرۡبَعِينَ سَنَةٗ قَالَ
رَبِّ أَوۡزِعۡنِيٓ أَنۡ أَشۡكُرَ نِعۡمَتَكَ ٱلَّتِيٓ أَنۡعَمۡتَ
عَلَيَّ وَعَلَىٰ وَٰلِدَيَّ وَأَنۡ أَعۡمَلَ صَٰلِحٗا
تَرۡضَىٰهُ وَأَصۡلِحۡ لِي فِي ذُرِّيَّتِيٓۖ إِنِّي تُبۡتُ
إِلَيۡكَ وَإِنِّي مِنَ ٱلۡمُسۡلِمِينَ ﴿١٥﴾ أُوْلَٰٓئِكَ
ٱلَّذِينَ نَتَقَبَّلُ عَنۡهُمۡ أَحۡسَنَ مَا عَمِلُواْ

---

of a foster relationship. (For further details, see *Luqmān* 31, n. 23, *Towards Understanding the Qur'ān,* vol. VIII, pp. 133-4.)

It is pertinent to point out that the latest medical studies suggest that a baby takes at least 28 weeks inside its mother's womb to be born alive. In other words, it takes a little more than six and half months. Islamic law reduces the period by approximately another half a month. This because holding a woman guilty of adultery and depriving a baby of his family status is a serious matter. Accordingly, both the mother and the baby are granted maximum allowance. Moreover, no physician, judge and even the pregnant woman herself knows for sure the exact time of conception. This, therefore, calls for extending the legally stipulated period of pregnancy by a few days.

20. He prayed that he be granted the ability to perform those good deeds that are formally sound and in full accordance with God's Law so that they may also be accepted by God. For an action, however good it might be, cannot bring any good if it is not in conformity with God's Law. Likewise, if a person's good action is vitiated by impious intention such as the desire to show off virtuousness, pride or excessive worldliness, its reward will be reduced.

We overlook.[21] They will be among the people of Paradise in consonance with the true promise made to them. (17) But he who says to his parents: 'Fie on you! Do you threaten me that I shall be resurrected, although myriad generations have passed away before me (and not one of them was resurrected)?' The parents beseech Allah (and say to their child): 'Woe to you, have faith. Surely Allah's promise is true.' But he says: 'All this is nothing but fables of olden times.'

(18) It is against such that Allah's sentence (of punishment) has become due. They will join the communities of humans and *jinn* that have preceded them. Verily all of them will court utter loss.[22] ▶

وَنَتَجَاوَزُ عَن سَيِّـَٔاتِهِمْ فِىٓ أَصْحَٰبِ
ٱلْجَنَّةِ ۖ وَعْدَ ٱلصِّدْقِ ٱلَّذِى كَانُوا۟
يُوعَدُونَ ﴿١٦﴾ وَٱلَّذِى قَالَ لِوَٰلِدَيْهِ أُفٍّ
لَّكُمَآ أَتَعِدَانِنِىٓ أَنْ أُخْرَجَ وَقَدْ خَلَتِ
ٱلْقُرُونُ مِن قَبْلِى وَهُمَا يَسْتَغِيثَانِ ٱللَّهَ
وَيْلَكَ ءَامِنْ إِنَّ وَعْدَ ٱللَّهِ حَقٌّ فَيَقُولُ مَا
هَٰذَآ إِلَّآ أَسَٰطِيرُ ٱلْأَوَّلِينَ ﴿١٧﴾ أُو۟لَٰٓئِكَ
ٱلَّذِينَ حَقَّ عَلَيْهِمُ ٱلْقَوْلُ فِىٓ أُمَمٍ قَدْ خَلَتْ
مِن قَبْلِهِم مِّنَ ٱلْجِنِّ وَٱلْإِنسِ ۖ إِنَّهُمْ كَانُوا۟
خَٰسِرِينَ ﴿١٨﴾

---

21. One will earn one's rank in the Hereafter on the basis of one's best deeds and one will not be taken to task for one's minor lapses, weaknesses and mistakes. This is analogous to the case of a loyal servant whose efforts are appreciated by a gracious master who rewards him in recognition of his substantive achievements. With such a servant the employer is likely not to be pickish about minor failings.

22. Here, two different types of character appear on the scene. The addressees are asked to decide for themselves as to which of the two is better.

(19) Of these all have ranks according to their deeds so that Allah may fully recompense them for their deeds. They shall not be wronged.[23] (20) And on the Day when the unbelievers will be exposed to the Fire, they will be told: 'You have exhausted your share of the bounties in the life of the world, and you took your fill of enjoyments. So, degrading chastisement shall be yours on this Day for you waxed arrogant in the earth without justification and acted iniquitously.'[24]

وَلِكُلٍّ دَرَجَٰتٌ مِّمَّا عَمِلُواْ ۖ وَلِيُوَفِّيَهُمْ
أَعْمَٰلَهُمْ وَهُمْ لَا يُظْلَمُونَ ﴿١٩﴾ وَيَوْمَ
يُعْرَضُ ٱلَّذِينَ كَفَرُواْ عَلَى ٱلنَّارِ أَذْهَبْتُمْ
طَيِّبَٰتِكُمْ فِى حَيَاتِكُمُ ٱلدُّنْيَا وَٱسْتَمْتَعْتُم
بِهَا فَٱلْيَوْمَ تُجْزَوْنَ عَذَابَ ٱلْهُونِ
بِمَا كُنتُمْ تَسْتَكْبِرُونَ فِى ٱلْأَرْضِ بِغَيْرِ
ٱلْحَقِّ وَبِمَا كُنتُمْ تَفْسُقُونَ ﴿٢٠﴾

Since both these types were found at that time, it was not hard to identify them. The verse serves as a rejoinder to the Quraysh chiefs' contention that had acceptance of Islam been a good thing they would have superseded the youth and slaves in its acceptance. This rejoinder provides a mirror to all to see the characteristics of believers and unbelievers alike.

23. Neither the good deeds and sacrifices of the good will go to waste, nor will the wicked be punished more than their actual wickedness requires, nor will pious people be denied their due reward, nor will anyone receive less reward than he deserves for that too is a kind of injustice. If a wicked person goes unpunished, or is punished more than his wickedness, that too will be reckoned unjust.

24. The degrading chastisement they will receive will be a sequel to their arrogance. They thought very highly of themselves. They considered it beneath their dignity to profess belief in the Messenger and to join the company of poor, indigent Muslims in their faith. God will humiliate them in the Hereafter and their pride and arrogance will be reduced to dust.

(21) Recount to them the story of (Hūd), the brother of (the tribe of) 'Ād. Hūd warned his people beside the sand-dunes[25] – and there have been other warners before him and since his time – saying: 'Serve none but Allah. Verily I fear that the chastisement of an awesome day shall come upon you.' (22) They said: 'Have you come to us to turn us away from our gods? Then, bring upon us ▶

۞ وَاذْكُرْ أَخَا عَادٍ إِذْ أَنذَرَ قَوْمَهُۥ
بِالْأَحْقَافِ وَقَدْ خَلَتِ النُّذُرُ مِن بَيْنِ يَدَيْهِ
وَمِنْ خَلْفِهِۦٓ أَلَّا تَعْبُدُوٓا۟ إِلَّا اللَّهَ إِنِّىٓ
أَخَافُ عَلَيْكُمْ عَذَابَ يَوْمٍ عَظِيمٍ ﴿٢١﴾
قَالُوٓا۟ أَجِئْتَنَا لِتَأْفِكَنَا عَنْ ءَالِهَتِنَا فَأْتِنَا

---

25. Since the Quraysh chiefs thought very highly of themselves and boasted of their glory and affluence, the story of the people of 'Ād is related to them. The 'Ād were known in Arabia for their might and glory.

Aḥqāf is the plural form of *ḥiqf,* which literally means a sand dune. This was used as a special term for the empty quarter in the Arabian desert which to this day has remained unsuitable for habitation.

According to Ibn Isḥāq, the 'Ād were settled in the region extending from Oman to Yemen. (Ṭabarī, *Tafsīr,* comments on *Sūrah al-A'rāf* 7: 69). According to the Qur'ān, al-Aḥqāf was their homeland. They then moved out from their land and established control over neighbouring lands. At a place near Ḥaḍramawt, which is about 125 miles away from Mukallah in Yemen, there is a grave which people regard as that of the Prophet Hūd (peace be on him.) On 15 Sha'bān every year a religious festival is held there, attracting thousands of people from every nook and corner of Arabia. Although it is not conclusively established that what is believed to be the Prophet Hūd's grave is truly his, yet the pilgrims' visit and the attachment of the people of southern Arabia to it show that according to local traditions the place is associated with the 'Ād. Many ruins in the area are called the abode of the 'Ād by locals.

While looking today at al-Aḥqāf region, it is hard to believe that a mighty and glorious civilisation once flourished there. It is quite likely,

the scourge that you threaten us with. Do so if you are truthful.' (23) He replied: 'Allah alone knows about this.[26] I only convey to you the Message that I have been sent with. But I see that you are an ignorant people.'[27] (24) When they saw the scourge advancing towards their valleys, they said: ▶

بِمَا تَعِدُنَآ إِن كُنتَ مِنَ ٱلصَّٰدِقِينَ ﴿٢٢﴾
قَالَ إِنَّمَا ٱلْعِلْمُ عِندَ ٱللَّهِ وَأُبَلِّغُكُم مَّآ أُرْسِلْتُ
بِهِۦ وَلَٰكِنِّىٓ أَرَىٰكُمْ قَوْمًا تَجْهَلُونَ ﴿٢٣﴾
فَلَمَّا رَأَوْهُ عَارِضًا مُّسْتَقْبِلَ أَوْدِيَتِهِمْ قَالُوا۟

however, that this was a fertile region thousands of years ago and was later reduced to an arid desert as it appears today. Today, however, it is a huge desert and people can hardly muster the courage to penetrate its depths. In 1843, a Bavarian German soldier managed to reach its southern edge. He pointed out that if one looks at it from Ḥaḍramawt's northern plateau, the desert appears to be a one-thousand-feet-deep valley. The Arab bedouins are mortally afraid of this desert and are not prepared to go there at all. According to the above-mentioned traveller, no local person was willing to escort him there, so he went there alone. According to him, the sand is like fine powder and anything dropped into it sinks and is decomposed in no time. When he threw a plummet into the desert from a distance, it sank into it within five minutes and the end of the rope with which it was attached also decomposed. (For further details of the region, see the following: Harold Ingrams, *Arabia and the Isles*, London, 1964; R.H. Kiernan, *The Unveiling of Arabia*. London, 1937; and H. Philby, *The Empty Quarter*, London, 1933.)

26. God alone knows when His scourge will strike the unbelievers. The Messenger (peace be on him) is not authorised to decide the period of respite or the date of punishment.

27. Out of their ignorance, the unbelievers take the Prophet's warnings lightly and ask him in a jocular mood to expedite the punishment. They have absolutely no idea of the gravity and enormity of Divine punishment. Their misdeeds, however, will soon bring such punishment upon them.

'This is a cloud that will bring much rain to us.' 'By no means;[28] it is what you had sought to hasten – a wind-storm bearing a grievous chastisement (25) that will destroy everything by the command of its Lord.' Thereafter nothing was left to be seen except their dwellings. Thus do We requite the wrong-doers.[29] (26) We had established them firmly in a manner We have not established you.[30] We had given them ears and eyes and hearts. But nothing availed them – neither their ears, nor their eyes, nor their hearts, ▶

هَـٰذَا عَارِضٌ مُّمْطِرُنَا ۚ بَلْ هُوَ مَا ٱسْتَعْجَلْتُم
بِهِۦ ۖ رِيحٌ فِيهَا عَذَابٌ أَلِيمٌ ﴿٢٤﴾ تُدَمِّرُ كُلَّ شَىْءٍۭ
بِأَمْرِ رَبِّهَا فَأَصْبَحُوا۟ لَا يُرَىٰٓ إِلَّا مَسَـٰكِنُهُمْ ۚ
كَذَٰلِكَ نَجْزِى ٱلْقَوْمَ ٱلْمُجْرِمِينَ ﴿٢٥﴾ وَلَقَدْ
مَكَّنَّـٰهُمْ فِيمَآ إِن مَّكَّنَّـٰكُمْ فِيهِ وَجَعَلْنَا
لَهُمْ سَمْعًا وَأَبْصَـٰرًا وَأَفْـِٔدَةً فَمَآ أَغْنَىٰ
عَنْهُمْ سَمْعُهُمْ وَلَآ أَبْصَـٰرُهُمْ وَلَآ أَفْـِٔدَتُهُم

28. It is not specified who said so. It emerges from the context that the statement represents what the prevailing state of affairs practically told them. They thought that the clouds would provide them with water. However, in reality it was God's punishment that was rushing towards them, bent upon destroying them.

29. For a detailed account of the story of the people of 'Ād, see *al-A'rāf* 7, nn. 51-6, *Towards Understanding the Qur'ān,* vol. III, pp. 42-5; *Hūd* 11, nn. 54-65, vol. IV, pp. 108-11; *al-Mu'minūn* 23, nn. 34-7, vol. VI, pp. 96-9; *al-Shu'arā'* 26, nn. 88-94, vol. VII, pp. 91-4; *al-'Ankabūt* 29, nn. 65-6, vol. VIII, pp. 36-7; and *Ḥā Mīm al-Sajdah* 41, nn. 20-1 above.

30. The unbelieving Quraysh are no match for the 'Ād in their affluence, power, authority and might. Their authority is confined only to the city of Makkah whereas the 'Ād exercised control over very large chunks of territory.

for they denied the Signs of Allah.[31] Then what they had mocked at encompassed them.

(27) Surely We destroyed many a town around you. We sent Our Messages to them repeatedly and in diverse forms that they may eschew (their evil ways) and return (to Allah). (28) So why did those whom they had set up as gods apart from Allah, hoping that they would bring them nearer to Him, not come to their aid?[32] ▶

مِّن شَيْءٍ إِذْ كَانُوا۟ يَجْحَدُونَ بِـَٔايَـٰتِ
ٱللَّهِ وَحَاقَ بِهِم مَّا كَانُوا۟ بِهِۦ يَسْتَهْزِءُونَ ﴿٢٦﴾
وَلَقَدْ أَهْلَكْنَا مَا حَوْلَكُم مِّنَ ٱلْقُرَىٰ
وَصَرَّفْنَا ٱلْـَٔايَـٰتِ لَعَلَّهُمْ يَرْجِعُونَ ﴿٢٧﴾ فَلَوْلَا
نَصَرَهُمُ ٱلَّذِينَ ٱتَّخَذُوا۟ مِن دُونِ ٱللَّهِ
قُرْبَانًا ءَالِهَةًۢ ۖ

31. This states a significant truth: God's signs impart to man true understanding and insight. Thanks to this, man draws sound conclusions, takes proper decisions and thinks in the right way. However, when man refuses to recognise God's signs, he is unable to perceive truth notwithstanding his faculty of sight. Likewise, he does not heed any advice although he is able to hear. He misuses the powers and abilities of his mind and heart and draws false conclusions. Ultimately, he courts his own disaster.

32. When the polytheists developed their initial veneration of those personalities [that later became their deities], they took them as God's chosen servants. They thought they would gain His proximity through them. However, they gradually deified them, invoked them, addressed their supplications to them and imagined that they had the power to meet their needs. In order to guide them to the Straight Way, God first explained the matter to them with the help of His signs through His Messengers. However, as they insisted on their false ways and idolatry, God's punishment struck them and their false gods were incapable of coming to their rescue.

Instead, they failed them. This was the end of the lie they had fabricated and the false beliefs they had invented.

(29) And call to mind when We sent to you a party of the *jinn* that they may listen to the Qur'ān.[33] When they reached the place (where you were reciting the Qur'ān), they said to one another: 'Be silent (and listen).' And when the recitation ended, they went back to their people as warners. ▶

بَلْ ضَلُّوا۟ عَنْهُمْ ۚ وَذَٰلِكَ إِفْكُهُمْ وَمَا كَانُوا۟
يَفْتَرُونَ ﴿٢٨﴾ وَإِذْ صَرَفْنَآ إِلَيْكَ نَفَرًا مِّنَ
ٱلْجِنِّ يَسْتَمِعُونَ ٱلْقُرْءَانَ فَلَمَّا حَضَرُوهُ
قَالُوٓا۟ أَنصِتُوا۟ ۖ فَلَمَّا قُضِىَ وَلَّوْا۟ إِلَىٰ قَوْمِهِم
مُّنذِرِينَ ﴿٢٩﴾

33. All the reports about the circumstantial setting of this verse, narrated on the authority of 'Abd Allāh ibn Mas'ūd, Zubayr, 'Abd Allāh ibn 'Abbās, al-Ḥasan al-Baṣrī, Sa'īd ibn Jubayr, Zarr ibn Ḥubaysh, Mujāhīd and 'Ikrimah are unanimous on the point that the jinn appeared for the first time in the valley of Nakhlah. (Ṭabarī, *Tafsīr*, comments on *Sūrah al-A'rāf* 7: 69.) Ibn Isḥāq Abū Na'aym Iṣfahānī and Wāqidī state that it happened when the Prophet (peace be on him) was on his way back to Makkah from Ṭā'if. He stayed at Nakhlah and was reciting the Qur'ān during the *'Ishā'* or *Tahajjud* or *Fajr* Prayer when a group of jinn passed by. They stopped there to listen to his recitation. (Ibn Kathīr, *Tafsīr*, comments on *Sūrah al-Aḥqāf* 46: 29; Suyūṭī, *al-Durr al-Manthūr*, comments on *Sūrah al-Aḥqāf* 46: 29.) All the reports indicate that at that time the jinn did not physically appear before the Prophet (peace be on him). Nor did he note their presence. Later on, God informed him through revelation about their visit and their listening to the Qur'ān. (Ṭabarī, *Tafsīr*, comments on *Sūrah al-Aḥqāf* 46: 29.)

This happened either at al-Zaymah or at al-Sayl al-Kabīr, both of which are located in the Nakhlah Valley. Both abound in water and greenery. The visitors from Ṭā'if usually break their journey there.

(30) They said: 'Our people, We have heard a Scripture revealed after Moses, verifying the Scriptures revealed before it; it guides to the Truth and to the Straight Way.[34] (31) Our people, respond to the call of him who calls you to Allah and believe in him. Allah will forgive your sins and will protect you from a grievous chastisement.'[35] ▶

قَالُوا۟ يَـٰقَوْمَنَآ إِنَّا سَمِعْنَا كِتَـٰبًا أُنزِلَ مِنۢ
بَعْدِ مُوسَىٰ مُصَدِّقًا لِّمَا بَيْنَ يَدَيْهِ يَهْدِىٓ
إِلَى ٱلْحَقِّ وَإِلَىٰ طَرِيقٍ مُّسْتَقِيمٍ ﴿٣٠﴾
يَـٰقَوْمَنَآ أَجِيبُوا۟ دَاعِىَ ٱللَّهِ وَءَامِنُوا۟ بِهِۦ
يَغْفِرْ لَكُم مِّن ذُنُوبِكُمْ وَيُجِرْكُم مِّنْ
عَذَابٍ أَلِيمٍ ﴿٣١﴾

34. One thus learns that these jinn were already believers in the Prophet Moses (peace be on him) and the Scriptures. For, on listening to the Qur'ān, they readily recognised that its message was identical with that of the earlier Prophets. Accordingly, they decided to believe in the Qur'ān and its bearer, the Prophet Muḥammad (peace be on him).

35. Authentic traditions indicate that after this incident a series of delegations of the jinn called on the Prophet (peace be on him) and met him directly. Collation of the relevant *aḥādīth* indicates that at least six delegations visited Makkah before the Migration to Madīnah. 'Abd Allāh ibn Mas'ūd reports: 'Once the Prophet (peace be on him) did not turn up for the whole night which caused great concern. We feared that someone had attacked him. The next morning we saw him coming from the Ḥirā' cave. On being asked he told us that a jinn had invited him and he recited the Qur'ān before a whole group of them'. (Muslim, *Kitāb al-Ṣalāh, Bāb al-Jahr bi al-Qirā'ah fī al-Ṣubḥ wa al-Qirā'ah 'alā al-Jinn;* Aḥmad ibn Ḥanbal, narrated by 'Abd Allāh ibn Mas'ūd; and Tirmidhī, *Kitāb Tafsīr al-Qur'ān 'an Rasūl Allāh Ṣallā Allāh 'alayhi wa Sallam, Bāb wa min Sūrah al-Aḥqāf*). Abd Allāh ibn Mas'ūd narrates another tradition: 'Once the Prophet (peace be on him) told his Companions in Makkah: "Who among you will accompany me to meet the jinn?" I expressed my desire to accompany him. While we reached the upper region of Makkah, he drew a line and directed me not to cross it. He went beyond that and started reciting the Qur'ān. I saw many people surrounding him.' (Ṭabarī, *Tafsīr*, comments on *Sūrah al-Aḥqāf* 46: 29; Bayhaqī, *Dalā'il*

(32) And he who does not respond[36] to the one who calls to Allah will not be able to frustrate Him on earth, nor will they have anyone to protect them from Allah. Such people are in manifest error.

(33) Do they not see that Allah, Who created the heavens and the earth – and creating them did not wear Him out – has the power to bring the dead back to life? Why not! He certainly has the power over everything. (34) On the Day when the unbelievers will be brought within sight of the Fire, they will be asked: 'Is this not the Truth?' ▶

وَمَن لَّا يُجِبْ دَاعِيَ ٱللَّهِ فَلَيْسَ بِمُعْجِزٍ فِى
ٱلْأَرْضِ وَلَيْسَ لَهُۥ مِن دُونِهِۦٓ أَوْلِيَآءُ ۚ
أُو۟لَـٰٓئِكَ فِى ضَلَـٰلٍ مُّبِينٍ ﴿٣٢﴾ أَوَلَمْ يَرَوْا۟
أَنَّ ٱللَّهَ ٱلَّذِى خَلَقَ ٱلسَّمَـٰوَٰتِ وَٱلْأَرْضَ
وَلَمْ يَعْىَ بِخَلْقِهِنَّ بِقَـٰدِرٍ عَلَىٰٓ أَن يُحْـِۧىَ
ٱلْمَوْتَىٰ ۚ بَلَىٰٓ إِنَّهُۥ عَلَىٰ كُلِّ شَىْءٍ قَدِيرٌ ﴿٣٣﴾
وَيَوْمَ يُعْرَضُ ٱلَّذِينَ كَفَرُوا۟ عَلَى ٱلنَّارِ
أَلَيْسَ هَـٰذَا بِٱلْحَقِّ ۖ

al-Nubūwah, Jimā' Abwāb al-Mab'ath, Bāb Dhikr Islām al-Jinn wa mā Ẓahara fī Dhālika min Āyāt al-Muṣṭafā Ṣallā Allāh 'alayhi wa Sallam and; Abū Na'aym al-Iṣfahānī, *Dalā'il al-Nubūwah, Kitāb mā Ẓahara min al-Āyāt fī Makhrijihi ilā al-Madīnah wa fī al-Ṭarīq, Bāb Mā Ruwiya fī Iltiqā'ihim bi Rasūl Allāh Ṣallā Allāh 'alayhi wa Sallam.*)

On another occasion while 'Abd Allāh ibn Mas'ūd accompanied the Prophet (peace be on him), the latter decided a case involving the jinn at Ḥajūn, near Makkah. Many years after this incident, when 'Abd Allāh ibn Mas'ūd saw some people in Kūfah, he remarked that they resembled the jinn whom he had seen at Ḥajūn. (Ṭabarī, *Tafsīr*, comments on *Sūrah al-Aḥkāf* 46: 29.)

36. It is likely that this part of the verse is a statement made by the jinn. Or it might be a remark by God. The latter, however, seems more plausible.

and they will answer 'Yes, by Our Lord (this is the Truth).' Allah will say: 'Then suffer the chastisement as a requital for your disbelieving.'

(35) So bear with patience, (O Prophet), even as the Messengers endowed with firmness of resolve (before you) bore with patience, and do not be hasty in their regard.[37] The Day when they see what they had been warned against they will feel as though they had remained in the world no more than an hour of a day. (The Truth has been conveyed.) Will any, then, suffer perdition except those who disobey?

قَالُوا۟ بَلَىٰ وَرَبِّنَا ۚ قَالَ فَذُوقُوا۟ ٱلْعَذَابَ
بِمَا كُنتُمْ تَكْفُرُونَ ﴿٣٤﴾ فَٱصْبِرْ كَمَا صَبَرَ أُو۟لُوا۟
ٱلْعَزْمِ مِنَ ٱلرُّسُلِ وَلَا تَسْتَعْجِل لَّهُمْ ۚ كَأَنَّهُمْ
يَوْمَ يَرَوْنَ مَا يُوعَدُونَ لَمْ يَلْبَثُوٓا۟ إِلَّا سَاعَةً
مِّن نَّهَارٍۭ ۚ بَلَٰغٌ ۚ فَهَلْ يُهْلَكُ إِلَّا ٱلْقَوْمُ
ٱلْفَٰسِقُونَ ﴿٣٥﴾

37. The Prophet (peace be on him) is directed to bear, like other Messengers, with the indifference, opposition and resistance of his people. He should keep on working tirelessly for the cause of his mission. He should not expect people to embrace faith immediately or think that in case of their not believing God will send down His punishment upon them overnight.

Glossary of Terms

'Abd is used in Arabic as an antonym of the one who is free, hence denoting a slave, one who is in someone else's ownership. Man being a born creature of God is His *'abd*.

'Ābid is he who humbles himself before the Lord, surrendering and worshipping Him and obeying His commands.

Adhān is the Islamic call to congregational Prayer.

Ahl al-Dhimmah (or *Dhimmīs*) are the non-Muslim subjects of an Islamic state who have been guaranteed protection of their rights – life, property, honour and practice of their religion, etc.

Aḥqāf is the plural form of *ḥiqf*, which literally means a sand dune. It was used as a special term for the Empty Quarter in Arabia which, to this day, remains unsuitable for habitation.

'Aṣr, taken literally, means 'time, age, and epoch'; it also signifies 'afternoon'. The *'Aṣr* Prayer is one of the five obligatory Prayers and is performed after the time for the *Ẓuhr* Prayer ends, and before the time for the *Maghrib* Prayer begins. The time for the *Aṣr* Prayer is reckoned to start when the shadow of an object exceeds its size (and according to the Ḥanafī school, when the shadow of an object becomes double its size), and ends with sunset.

Awliyā', (sing. *walī*), has a wide range of connotation. A *walī* is: (1) he who is obeyed in all matters, (2) he in whose guidance someone has full faith, (3) he who is right and will save others from error and protect them from the evil consequences of their ill deeds in the world, and from the torment of God in the Hereafter, and (4) he about whom someone believes that he will come to his aid in worldly matters in supernatural ways.

Ayyām al-'Arab refer to the eventful days and major battles among Arab tribes which remained recorded in memory for centuries.

Barakah signifies growth and increase. The notions of elevation and greatness as well as of permanence and stability are also an essential part of the word's meaning.

Barzakh is an Arabicized form of the Persian word *pardah* (signifying a barrier). According to the Qur'ān, there presently exists a barrier between those who are dead and the present world. This barrier prevents the dead from returning to life and so they will stay in this state till the Day of Judgement. In technical Islamic usage, it signifies the stage beginning with one's death until Resurrection.

Basmalah is the abbreviated form of *Bi ism Allāh al-Raḥmān al-Raḥīm.*

Bayyināt signify the following: (i) the clear, distinct signs which attest that the Messenger had been raised by God; (ii) the weighty arguments which prove that the teachings of those Messengers were utterly true; and (iii) the valuable guidance about various issues of life that would convince every sensible person that a liar or selfish person could not have imparted the teachings that are so utterly true and morally so superb.

Dīn – the core meaning of *dīn* is obedience. As a Qur'ānic technical term, *dīn* refers to the way of life and the system of conduct based on recognising God as one's Sovereign and committing oneself to obey Him. According to Islam, true *dīn* consists of living in total submission to God, and the way to do so is to accept as binding the guidance communicated through God's Prophets and Messengers.

Dhū al-Aydī is a metaphor of authority in Arabic. Used in the Qur'ān with reference to the Prophet David (peace be on him), it stresses his power and authority. Indeed, it might refer to many aspects of his power. One aspect of it was that he had been endowed with exceptional physical prowess, which was demonstrated in his encounter with Goliath. It might also refer to his military and political might, which enabled him to inflict defeat upon the polytheistic communities of the neighbouring countries, as a result of which a vast Islamic state was established. This statement might also be an allusion to David's moral strength, which lay in his simple ascetic ways, despite being a king.

Fajr Prayer is the first Prayer of the day. Its time commences with dawn and lasts until sunrise.

Fiqh, which literally means 'understanding of a speaker's purpose from his speech', technically refers to the branch of learning concerned with the injunctions of the *Sharīʻah* relating to human actions, derived from their detailed evidences.

Ḥadīth: the word *ḥadīth* literally means communication or narration. In the Islamic context it has come to denote the record of what the Prophet (peace be on him) said, did, or tacitly approved. According to some scholars, the word *ḥadīth* also covers reports about the sayings and deeds, etc. of the Companions of the Prophet in addition to the Prophet himself. The whole body of Traditions is termed *Ḥadīth* and its science, *'Ilm al- Ḥadīth*.

Ḥadīth Qudsī is defined as the tradition whose words are from the Prophet but whose content comes from God through inspiration or a dream.

Ḥajj (major Pilgrimage) is one of the five pillars of Islam, a duty one is required to perform once during one's lifetime if one has the ability to do so. *Ḥajj* resembles *'Umrah* in some respects, but differs from it insofar as it can only be performed during certain specified dates of *Dhū al-Ḥijjah*. In addition to *ṭawāf* and *sa'y* (which are also required for *'Umrah*), there are a few other requirements but especially 'standing' (*wuqūf*) in 'Arafāt during the daytime on 9th of *Dhū al-Ḥijjah*. For details of the rules of *Ḥajj*, see the books of *Fiqh*.

Hijrah signifies migration from a land where a Muslim is unable to live according to the precepts of his faith to a land where it is possible for him to do so. The *hijrah par excellence* for Muslims is the *hijrah* of the Prophet (peace be on him) which not only provided him and his followers refuge from persecution, but also an opportunity to build a society and state according to the ideals of Islam.

Ḥīlah, (pl. *ḥiyal*), denotes a legal device to avoid some harm or to gain some legitimate benefit.

Ḥukm means authority. It signifies wisdom and understanding as well as the authority that is bestowed by God upon a Prophet or Messenger, which enables him to speak authoritatively.

'Ibādah is used in three meanings: (1) worship and adoration; (2) obedience and submission; and (3) service and subjection. The fundamental message of Islam is that man, as God's creature, should direct his *'ibādah* to Him in all the above-mentioned meanings, and associate none with Him in that act.

Iblīs literally means 'thoroughly disappointed; one in utter despair'. In Islamic terminology, it denotes the jinn who refused God's command to prostrate himself before Adam. After his fall from grace, he asked God to allow him a term during which he might mislead and tempt mankind to error. This was granted to him by God whereafter he became the chief promoter of evil and prompted Adam and Eve to disobey God's order. He is also called *al-Shayṭān* (Satan). He is, however, possessed of a specific personality and is not just an abstract force.

Ilḥād, religious deviation, heresy.

Imām signifies the leader, and in its highest form, refers to the head of the Islamic state. It is also used with reference to the founders of the different systems of theology and law in Islam. It is also applied to those who lead congregational Prayers.

Iqāmat al-Dīn means both to establish religion and maintain it in that state.

'Ishā' (Night) Prayer signifies one of the five obligatory Prayers, one that is performed after the night has set in and the red glow of sunset has disappeared. It may be performed until the commencement of the time of *Fajr* Prayer.

Jāhilīyah denotes all those world views and ways of life that are based on rejection or disregard of the heavenly guidance communicated to mankind through God's Prophets and Messengers; the attitude of treating human life – whether wholly or partly – as independent of God's directives.

Jihād means 'to strive, to exert to the utmost'. The words *jihād* and *mujāhid* imply the existence of forces of resistance against whom it is necessary to wage a struggle. Moreover, the usual stipulation in the Qur'ān that *jihād* should be *fī sabīl Allāh* (in the way of God) explains that these forces obstruct people from serving God and pursuing His good pleasure, and that it is necessary to engage in strife and struggle to overcome those forces. The term, however, embraces all kinds of striving aimed at making the Word of God supreme in human life and is not confined only to fighting and warfare. The Prophet (peace be on him) even regarded the striving to subdue one's self to the will of God as one of the forms of *jihād*.

Jinn are an independent species of creation about whom little is known except that, unlike man, who was created out of earth, the jinn were created out of fire. But like man, a Divine Message has also been addressed to them and they too have been endowed with the capacity, again like man, to choose between good and evil, between obedience and disobedience to God.

Ka'bah, literally cube, is a large cubic stone structure covered with a black cloth which stands in the centre of *al-Masjid al-Ḥarām*. It is the first structure erected for God's worship. Abraham and Ishmael are mentioned as its constructors. It is also known as *al-Bayt al-Ḥarām* and *al-Bayt al-'Atīq*. It marks the direction to which the Muslims should turn in their Prayers.

Kāfir signifies the person who denies or rejects the truth, i.e. one who disbelieves in the message of the Prophets.

Khalīfah or vicegerent is one who exercises the authority delegated to him by his principal. According to the Qur'ān, God appointed Adam, the first man, as His *khalīfah*.

Kufr's original meaning is 'to conceal'. This word has been variously used in the Qur'ān to denote: (1) the state of absolute lack of faith; (2) the rejection or denial of any of the essentials of Islam; (3) the attitude of ingratitude and thanklessness to God; and (4) the non-fulfilment of the basic requirements of faith. In the accepted technical sense, *kufr* consists of the rejection of the Divine Guidance communicated through the Prophets and Messengers of God, including that communicated through Muḥammad (peace be on him), God's last and final Prophet.

Laṭīf with respect to God suggests that He is full of compassion, affection and favour towards His servants. Furthermore, He caters for all of their needs.

Al-Lawḥ al-Maḥfūẓ, literally the Guarded Tablet; the repository of destiny (*al-qadr*).

Laylat al-Qadr, the Night of Power, refers to the night when the Qur'ān began to be revealed to the Prophet (peace be on him).

Maghrib Prayer is one of the five obligatory Prayers. The time for its performance begins with sunset and ends when the setting sun's red glow disappears from the horizon.

Mawlā denotes a supporter or guardian who comes to someone's aid or support out of consideration for his relationship with the other person, be it that of kinship, friendship or any other. It also refers to a slave, a freed slave and a person who frees his slave.

Mursal in *Ḥadīth* terminology refers to a tradition from the Prophet (peace be on him) which does not specifically mention any Companion (*Ṣaḥābī*) as the initial transmitter of the tradition, even though the tradition was narrated by a Successor (*Tābi'ī*) who refers to it as a saying or act of the Prophet.

Qadhf literally means to throw stones. Metaphorically it means to abuse. As an Islamic legal term, it means to accuse someone of *zinā* (unlawful sexual intercourse). In case one accuses someone of *zinā* and fails to support it by the required number of witnesses, the punishment laid down in Islamic Law is eighty lashes.

Rajīm denotes the one who is accursed or expelled. It is used for a person who falls from grace and who stands humiliated and disgraced. *Par excellence,* it applies to Iblīs.

Rak'ah, (pl. *raka'āt*), represents a unit of Prayer and consists of bending the torso from an upright position followed by two prostrations.

Rukū' means to bend the body, to bow. This bowing is one of the acts required in Islamic Prayer. Additionally, the same word denotes a certain unit in the Qur'ān. The whole Book, for the sake of the convenience of readers, is divided into thirty parts (*ajzā'*, sing. *juz'*), and each *juz'* consists of several *rukū'*s.

Sajdah means prostration, a posture of the *Ṣalāh* in which one puts one's forehead on the ground while the weight of the body rests on the knees. It is generally thought to be the most devout form of posture in worship.

Sayyi'āt, a synonym for evils or ills, is used to indicate the following: (i) erroneous beliefs, degenerate morals and evil deeds; (ii) the evil consequences of error and wickedness; and (iii) the calamities, sufferings and torment in this world or in *barzakh* or on the Day of Judgement.

Shukr means thankfulness. In Islam, it is a basic religious value. Man owes thanks to God for an infinite number of things. He owes thanks to God for all that he possesses – his life as well as all that makes his life pleasant, enjoyable and wholesome. And above all, man owes thanks to God for making available His Guidance, which can enable him to find his way to his salvation and felicity.

Sunnah signifies the normative life-pattern of the Prophet (peace be on him) as evident from his sayings, deeds and tacit approvals. In this regard *Sunnah* and *Ḥadīth* (*q.v.*) are cognate terms, but not quite identical. Stated succinctly, while *Sunnah* represents the Prophet's normative life-pattern, *Ḥadīth* is its record and repository.

Sūrah, literally a row or fence, refers to any of the 114 chapters of the Qur'ān.

Ṭāghūt literally denotes the one who exceeds legitimate limits. In Qur'ānic terminology it refers to the creature that exceeds the limits of his creatureliness and arrogates to himself godhead and lordship. In the negative scale of values, the first stage of man's error is *fisq* (i.e. disobeying God without necessarily denying that one should obey Him). The second stage is that of *kufr* (i.e. rejection of the very idea that one ought to obey God). The last stage is that man not only rebels against God but also imposes his rebellious will on others. All those who reach this stage are *ṭāghūt*.

Tahajjud is the Prayer offered in the last quarter of the night before the commencement of the time of *Fajr* Prayer. It is a supererogatory rather than an obligatory Prayer, but one that has been emphasised in the Qur'ān and in the *Ḥadīth* as meriting great reward from God.

Tawātur is a narration which is transmitted by people so many in number that their agreement on falsehood is, as a rule, inconceivable.

Ummah (literally 'collectivity', sharing the same origin or source) has been generally used in the Qur'ān to refer to those who receive the message of a Messenger of God, or happen to be living in an age when the teachings of that Messenger are extant.

Umm al-Kitāb variously refers to the Qur'ān, to *Sūrah al-Fātiḥah*, to verses basic or fundamental of established meaning (*āyāt muḥkamāt*) and to *al-Lawḥ al-Maḥfūẓ*. In some philosophical and mystical writings it also denotes the First Intellect (*al-'Aql al-Awwal*) which refers to the state of unity (*martabat al-waḥdah*).

Al-'Uzzā has been identified with Venus. However, it was given the form of an acacia tree and worshipped. It was the deity of the Ghaṭafān tribe.

Zaqqūm is the name of the tree that will grow in the depths of Hell and will be the sustenance of the inmates of Hell. It will boil in their intestines like scalding water.

Biographical Notes

'Abd Allāh ibn 'Abbās, see Biographical Notes, vol. I.

'Abd Allāh ibn 'Amr ibn al-'Āṣ, see Biographical Notes, vol. I.

'Abd Allāh ibn Mas'ūd, see Biographical Notes, vol. I.

'Abd Allāh ibn Salām ibn al-Ḥārith al-Isrā'īlī, d. 43 A.H./663 C.E., was a Companion of the Prophet (peace be on him). Originally a Jew, he embraced Islam after the Prophet's arrival in Madīnah. He accompanied 'Umar ibn al-Khaṭṭāb to Jerusalem after its conquest. He narrated 25 *aḥādīth* from the Prophet (peace be on him).

'Abd Allāh ibn 'Umar, see Biographical Notes, Abridged Version.

'Abd Allāh ibn al-Ziba'rā ibn Qays al-Qurashī, see Biographical Notes, vol. V.

'Abd al-Raḥmān ibn Zayd ibn Aslam al-'Umarī al-Madanī, d. 182 A.H./798-99 C.E., was a scholar of the Qur'ān. He wrote a *Tafsīr* and authored a book on *al-Nāsikh wa al-Mansūkh*.

'Abd al-Razzāq al-Ṣan'ānī, see Biographical Notes, vol. VII.

Abraham (Ibrāhīm), see Biographical Notes, vol. III.

Abū al-'Āliyah Rufay' ibn Mahrān al-Riyāḥī al-Baṣrī, d. 90 A.H./*c.* 709 C.E., a freed slave of a woman from Banū Riyāḥ ibn Yarbū', was a scholar of the Qur'ān.

Abū Bakr, 'Abd Allāh ibn 'Uthmān, see Biographical Notes, vol. I.

Abū al-Dardā', 'Uwaymir ibn Mālik, see Biographical Notes, vol. I.

Abū Ḥanīfah, al-Nu'mān ibn Thābit, see Biographical Notes, vol. I.

Abū Hurayrah, see Biographical Notes, vol. I.

Abū Jahl, 'Amr ibn Hishām ibn al-Mughīrah, see Biographical Notes, vol. I.

Abū Lahab, 'Abd al-'Uzzā ibn 'Abd al-Muṭṭalib ibn Hāshim, see Biographical Notes, vol. I.

Abū Mālik Ḥammād ibn Mālik al-Ashja'ī, d. 228 A.H./? C.E., was a scholar of *Ḥadīth*. He narrated *aḥādīth* from al-Awzā'ī, Sa'īd ibn Bashīr and Ismā'īl ibn 'Ayyāsh, etc.

Abū Mālik al-Ash'arī, d. 18 A.H./639 C.E., was a Companion of the Prophet (peace be on him). He came to Madīnah with the delegation of al-Ash'ariyīn via sea. He accompanied the Prophet (peace be on him) in several military campaigns and narrated *aḥādīth* from him.

Abū Mijliz, Lāḥiq ibn Ḥamīd al-Sadūsī, d. 100 A.H./718-19 C.E., was a Successor (*Tābi'ī*). He heard traditions from 'Umar ibn al-Khaṭṭāb, 'Abd Allāh ibn 'Abbās and Anas ibn Mālik among others. He settled in Marw and was made custodian of *Bayt al-Māl* there.

Abū Mūsā al-Ash'arī, 'Abd Allāh ibn Qays, see Biographical Notes, vol. I.

Abū Nu'aym, Aḥmad ibn 'Abd Allāh al-Aṣbahānī, d. 430 A.H/1038 C.E., was a historian and a distinguished scholar of *Ḥadīth*. He was born and died in Aṣbahān. His works include *Ḥilyat al-Awliyā'*, *Dalā'il al-Nubūwah*, *Ta'rīkh Aṣbahān* and *Ma'rifat al-Ṣaḥābah*.

Abū Sufyān, Ṣakhr ibn Ḥarb ibn Umayyah, see Biographical Notes, vol. I.

Abū Ṭālib, 'Abd Manāf ibn 'Abd al-Muṭṭalib, see Biographical Notes, vol. II.

Abū Yūsuf, Ya'qūb ibn Ibrāhīm, see Biographical Notes, vol. II.

'Ād, see Biographical Notes, vol. VIII.

Aḥmad ibn Ḥanbal, see Biographical Notes, Vol. I.

'Ā'ishah, see Biographical Notes, vol. I.

'Alī ibn Abī Ṭālib, see Biographical Notes, vol. I.

Al-Ālūsī, Maḥmūd ibn 'Abd Allāh al-Ḥusaynī, see Biographical Notes, vol. I.

'Amr ibn Dīnār al-Jumaḥī, d. 126 A.H./743 C.E., was a Makkan jurist. He was also a scholar of *Ḥadīth*.

'Amr ibn Shu'ayb ibn Muḥammad al-Sahmī, see Biographical Notes, vol. VII.

Anas ibn Mālik, see Biographical Notes, vol. I.

Al-'Āṣ ibn Wā'il al-Sahmī, see Biographical Notes, vol. VIII.

Al-Aswad ibn 'Abd al-Muṭṭalib ibn Asad ibn 'Abd al-'Uzzā ibn Quṣayy al-Qurashī al-Asadī, was a cousin of Khadījah bint Khuwaylid, a notable of Quraysh and an inveterate enemy of Islam. He lost two sons and one grandson in the Battle of Badr.

'Aṭā' ibn Dīnār al-Hudhalī, d. 126 A.H./744 C.E., was an Egyptian scholar of *Ḥadīth*. He also narrated a book on *Tafsīr* from Sa'īd ibn Jubayr. He died in Egypt.

'Awf ibn Mālik al-Ashja'ī al-Ghaṭafānī, d. 73 A.H./692 C.E., a Companion of the Prophet (peace be on him), was a brave chieftain. He held the flag of Banū Ashja' on the day of the conquest of Makkah. He narrated 67 *aḥādīth*.

Al-'Awfī, 'Aṭīyah ibn Sa'd ibn Junādah, see Biographical Notes, vol. V.

Al-Bazzār, Aḥmad ibn 'Amr ibn 'Abd al-Khāliq Abī Bakr, see Biographical Notes, vol. I.

Al-Bukhārī, Muḥammad ibn Ismā'īl, see Biographical Notes, vol. I.

Fāṭimah bint Muḥammad, see Biographical Notes, Abridged Version.

Ḥabīb ibn 'Amr ibn 'Umayr, belonged to Banū Thaqīf of Ṭā'if. He was the brother of Mas'ūd, Rabī'ah and 'Abd Yālīl, the sons of 'Amr ibn 'Umayr ibn 'Awf al-Thaqafī. According to a tradition the verse (2: 279) was revealed about Ḥabīb ibn 'Amr and his brothers. He was also the father of Abū Miḥjan al-Thaqafī (d. 30 A.H./650 C.E.), a Companion of the Prophet (peace be on him) and a great warrior.

Hāmān, see Biographical Notes, vol. VIII.

Ḥamzah ibn 'Abd al-Muṭṭalib, see Biographical Notes, vol. III.

Al-Ḥasan al-Baṣrī, see Biographical Notes, Abridged Version.

Hūd, see Biographical Notes, vol. III.

Ḥudhayfah ibn Usayd al-Ghifārī, see Biographical Notes, vol. V.

Ibn Abī Ḥātim, 'Abd al-Raḥmān, see Biographical Notes, vol. VIII.

Ibn Abī Shaybah, 'Abd Allāh ibn Muḥammad, see Biographical Notes, vol. VII.

Ibn al-'Arabī, Abū Bakr ibn Muḥammad ibn 'Abd Allāh, see Biographical Notes, vol. VIII.

Ibn 'Asākir, 'Alī ibn al-Ḥasan, d. 571 A.H./1176 C.E., was a famous Shāfi'ī jurist, traditionist, historian and traveller. He was a prolific writer. His works include *Ta'rīkh Dimashq al-Kabīr* and *Tabyīn Kadhib al-Muftarī fī mā Nusiba ilā Abī al-Ḥasan al-Ash'arī*.

Ibn Hishām, 'Abd al-Malik, see Biographical Notes, vol. I.

Ibn Isḥāq, Muḥammad, see Biographical Notes, vol. IV.

Ibn al-Jawzī, Abū al-Faraj 'Abd al-Raḥmān ibn 'Alī ibn Muḥammad, d. 597 A.H./1201 C.E., was a prolific writer and a distinguished scholar of *Ḥadīth* and History. He was also famous for his oratory. He wrote around 300 books. His works include *Manāqib 'Umar ibn 'Abd al-'Azīz, Talbīs Iblīs, Funūn al-Afnān, Ṣayd al-Khāṭir*, and *al-Ḍu'afā' wa al-Matrūkīn*.

Ibn Kathīr, Ismā'īl ibn 'Umar, see Biographical Notes, vol. I.

Ibn Mājah, Muḥammad ibn Yazīd, see Biographical Notes, vol. I.

Ibn Mardawayh, Aḥmad ibn Mūsā al-Aṣbahānī, d. 410 A.H./1019 C.E., was a distinguished scholar of the Qur'ān, *Ḥadīth* and History. His works include *al-Ta'rīkh, Tafsīr al-Qur'ān, Musnad* and *Mustakhraj*.

Ibn Sa'd, Muḥammad, see Biographical Notes, Abridged Version.

Ibn al-Sā'ib, Hishām ibn Muḥammad al-Kalbī, d. 204 A.H./819 C.E., was a prolific writer and scholar of History, genealogies of Arabs and *Ayyām al-'Arab*. He authored more than 150 books which include *Jamharat al-Ansāb, al-Aṣnām, Alqāb Quraysh*, and *Mā Kānat al-Jāhilīyah Taf'aluh wa Yuwāfiq Ḥukm al-Islām*, etc.

Ibn Sīrīn, Muḥammad, see Biographical Notes, Abridged Version.

Ibn Taymīyah, Taqī al-Dīn Aḥmad ibn 'Abd al-Ḥalīm, see Biographical Notes, vol. I.

Ibrāhīm, see Abraham.

Ibrāhīm al-Nakha'ī, see Biographical Notes, vol. I.

'Ikrimah ibn 'Abd Allāh al-Barbarī al-Madanī, see Biographical Notes, vol. VIII.

'Īsā, see Jesus.

Jābir ibn 'Abd Allāh, see Biographical Notes, vol. I.

Jābir ibn Zayd, see Biographical Notes, Abridged Version.

Ja'far al-Ṭayyār, see Biographical Notes, vol. IV.

Al-Jaṣṣāṣ, Aḥmad ibn 'Alī, see Biographical Notes, vol. I.

Jesus ('Īsā), see Biographical Notes, vol. VIII.

Khadījah bint Khuwaylid, see Biographical Notes, Abridged Version.

Al-Khaṭṭābī, Abū Sulaymān Ḥamd ibn Muḥammad, d. 388 A.H./998 C.E., was a jurist and traditionist. He was a descendant of Zayd ibn al-Khaṭṭāb, 'Umar ibn al-Khaṭṭāb's brother. His noted works include *Ma'ālim al-Sunan fī Sharḥ Sunan Abī Dā'ūd, Bayān I'jāz al-Qur'ān* and *Iṣlāḥ Ghalaṭ al-Muḥaddithīn*.

Al-Khudrī, Abū Sa'īd Sa'd ibn Mālik ibn Sinān al-Anṣārī, see Biographical Notes, Abridged Version.

Mālik ibn Anas, see Biographical Notes, vol. I.

Moses (Mūsā), see Biographical Notes, vol. VIII.

Masrūq ibn Ajda', 63 A.H./683 C.E., was a famous Successor. He was a Yemenite who came to Madīnah during the reign of Abū Bakr and settled in Kūfah. He fought on the side of 'Alī ibn Abī Ṭālib in the armed conflict after the martyrdom of 'Uthmān ibn 'Affān.

Mu'ādh ibn Jabal, see Biographical Notes, vol. I.

Mujāhid ibn Jabr, see Biographical Notes, vol. VIII.

Muqātil ibn Sulaymān, see Biographical Notes, vol. I.

Mūsā see Moses.

Muslim ibn al-Ḥajjāj al-Nīsābūrī, see Biographical Notes, vol. I.

Al-Nasā'ī, Aḥmad ibn 'Alī, see Biographical Notes, vol. I.

Naṣr ibn Aḥmad ibn Asad ibn Sāmān, d. 279 A.H./892 C.E., was the founder of the Samanid dynasty in Transoxiana. He belonged to a renowned Persian family of Khurāsān.

Al-Nīsābūrī, Niẓām al-Dīn al-Ḥasan ibn Muḥammad, see Biographical Notes, vol. IX.

Nūḥ see Noah.

Noah (Nūḥ), see Biographical Notes, vol. VIII.

Al-Nu'mān ibn Bashīr al-Khazrajī al-Anṣārī, d. 65 A.H./684 C.E., a Companion of the Prophet (peace be on him), was famous for his poetry and oratory. He was in the camp of Mu'āwiyah in the Battle of Ṣiffīn and was appointed the judge of Damascus. Mu'āwiyah also appointed him to the governorship of Yemen, Kūfah and then Ḥimṣ. However, after the death of Yazīd ibn Mu'āwiyah he joined the camp of 'Abd Allāh ibn al-Zubayr and was killed by Khālid ibn 'Alī al-Kulā'ī. He narrated 124 *aḥādīth*.

Qatādah ibn Di'āmah, see Biographical Notes, vol. VIII.

Al-Raqqāshī, Abū 'Amr Yazīd ibn Abān ibn 'Abd Allāh, d. 119 A.H./737 C.E., was a Successor (*Tābi'ī*). He lived in Baṣrah. He was a sermoniser (*qāṣṣ*) and was famous for his piety. However, questions were raised about his authority in *Ḥadīth*.

Al-Rāzī, Muḥammad ibn 'Umar Fakhr al-Dīn, see Biographical Notes, vol. III.

Sa'd ibn Abī Waqqāṣ, see Biographical Notes, vol. III.

Sa'īd ibn Jubayr, see Biographical Notes, vol. I.

Sa'īd ibn al-Musayyib, see Biographical Notes, vol. I.

Sa'īd ibn Sa'd ibn 'Ubādah al-Anṣārī, was a Companion of the Prophet (peace be on him) and a brother of Qays ibn Sa'd ibn 'Ubādah. 'Alī ibn Abī Ṭālib appointed him the governor of Yemen.

Salmān al-Fārisī, d. 36 A.H./656 C.E., was a famous Companion of the Prophet (peace be on him). Originally he belonged to the Magians of Aṣbahān. The story of his quest for and acceptance of Islam is well known. The Prophet (peace be on him) counted him among his own household. He advised Muslims to dig a trench around Madīnah to defend it on the occasion of the Battle of Trench. 'Alī ibn Abī Ṭālib appointed him the governor of al-Madā'in.

Al-Sha'bī, 'Āmir ibn Shuraḥbīl, see Biographical Notes, vol. II.

Al-Shāfi'ī, Muḥammad ibn Idrīs, see Biographical Notes, vol. I.

Shāh 'Abd al-Qādir, d. 1230 A.H./1815 C.E., was a son of Shāh Walī Allāh (*q.v.*). He was a scholar of *Fiqh* and *Ḥadīth*. He was the first person who translated the Qur'ān into idiomatic Urdu and named it *Mūḍiḥ al-Qur'ān*. This translation was completed in 1205/1791 and is considered a work of especially high standard in Urdu literature.

Shāh Rafī' al-Dīn, d. 1233 A.H./1817 C.E., a specialist in *Tafsīr* and *Ḥadīth*, was also a son of Shāh Walī Allāh (*q.v.*). His works include translation of and commentary on the Qur'ān. He was the younger brother of Shāh 'Abd al-'Azīz and the elder brother of Shāh 'Abd al-Qādir (*q.v.*) and Shāh 'Abd al-Ghanī. The whole family richly contributed to the reform of Indian Muslims.

Shāh Walī Allāh, see Biographical Notes, Abridged Version.

Shaybah ibn Rabī'ah ibn 'Abd Shams, d. 2 A.H./624 C.E., was one of the notables of Quraysh in *Jāhilīyah*. He fought against Muslims in the Battle of Badr and was killed.

Al-Shaybānī, Muḥammad ibn al-Ḥasan, see Biographical Notes, vol. II.

Shu'ayb, see Biographical Notes, vol. VIII.

Al-Suddī, Ismā'īl ibn 'Abd al-Raḥmān, see Biographical Notes, Abridged Version.

Al-Sulamī, Abū 'Abd al-Raḥmān 'Abd Allāh ibn Ḥabīb ibn Rabī'ah, d. 74 A.H./693 C.E., was a Successor (*Tābi'ī*). He was born during the life of the Prophet (peace be on him). He lived in Kūfah and taught the Qur'ān for forty years.

Al-Ṭabarānī, Sulaymān ibn Aḥmad ibn Ayyūb, see Biographical Notes, vol. VII.

Al-Ṭabarī, Muḥammad ibn Jarīr, see Biographical Notes, vol. I.

Thamūd, see Biographical Notes, vol. VIII.

Al-Tirmidhī, see Biographical Notes, vol. I.

'Umar ibn al-Khaṭṭāb, see Biographical Notes, vol. I.

Umayyah ibn Khalaf ibn Wahb, see Biographical Notes, vol. III.

'Uqbah ibn Abī Mu'ayṭ, see Biographical Notes, vol. I.

'Urwah ibn Mas'ūd al-Thaqafī, d. 9 A.H./630 C.E., was a famous Companion of the Prophet (peace be on him). He was well respected among his people in Ṭā'if. When he embraced Islam he asked the Prophet (peace be on him) to allow him to return to his people in order to preach Islam among them. The Prophet (peace be on him) replied: 'I am afraid they will kill you.' However, when he insisted, the Prophet allowed him to return. So he preached to his people to accept Islam and, as feared, was killed by them.

Usāmah ibn Zayd ibn Ḥārithah, see Biographical Notes, vol. VI.

'Utbah ibn Rabī'ah ibn 'Abd Shams, Abū al-Walīd, see Biographical Notes, vol. VI.

'Uthmān ibn 'Affān, see Biographical Notes, vol. I.

'Uthmān ibn Muḥammad ibn al-Mughīrah al-Akhnasī al-Ḥijāzī was a *Tabi' al-Tābi'ī*. He narrated from Sa'īd al-Maqbarī, Sa'īd ibn al-Musayyib and 'Abd al-Raḥmān ibn Hurmuz al-A'raj. 'Abd Allāh ibn Ja'far al-Makhzūmī, Muḥammad ibn 'Amr ibn 'Alqamah and al-Zuhrī narrated from him.

Al-Walīd ibn al-Mughīrah, see Biographical Notes, vol. VIII.

Al-Wāqidī, Muḥammad ibn 'Umar, see Biographical Notes, vol. I.

Al-Zamakhsharī, Maḥmūd ibn Muḥammad ibn Aḥmad, see Biographical Notes, vol. IV.

Zirr ibn Ḥubaysh al-Asadī, d. 83 A.H./702 C.E., was a *Tābi'ī*. He lived in the eras of both *Jāhilīyah* and Islam, but could not meet the Prophet (peace be on him). He was a scholar of the Qur'ān.

Zayd ibn Ḥārithah ibn Sharāḥīl (or Shuraḥbīl) al-Kalbī, see Biographical Notes, Abridged Version.

Zayn al-'Ābidīn, 'Alī ibn al-Ḥusayn ibn 'Alī ibn Abī Ṭālib, d. 94 A.H./712 C.E., was famous for his knowledge, forbearance and piety. He is also called 'Alī al-Aṣghar ('Alī the younger) to distinguish him from his elder brother, 'Alī al-Akbar ('Alī the elder), who was martyred in Karbalā' with his father. He is the fourth of the twelve imāms of Imāmī Shī'īs. He was born and died in Madīnah.

Al-Zubayr ibn al-'Awwām ibn Khuwaylid, see Biographical Notes, vol. III.

Zufar ibn al-Hudhayl, see Biographical Notes, vol. II.

Al-Zuhrī, Muḥammad ibn Muslim ibn Shihāb, see Biographical Notes, vol. I.

Zayn al-'Ābidīn, 'Alī ibn al-Ḥusayn ibn 'Alī ibn Abī Ṭālib, d. 94 A.H./712 C.E., was famous for his knowledge, forbearance and piety. He is also called 'Alī al-Aṣghar ('Alī the younger) to distinguish him from his elder brother 'Alī al-Akbar ('Alī the elder) who was martyred in Karbalā' with his father. He is the fourth of the twelve Imāms of Imāmī Shī'is. He was born and died in Madīnah.

Al-Zubayr ibn al-'Awwām ibn Khuwaylid, see Biographical Notes, vol. [illegible]

Zufar ibn al-Hudhayl, see Biographical Notes, vol. II.

Al-Zuhrī, Muḥammad ibn Muslim ibn Shihāb, see Biographical Notes, vol. I.

Bibliography

Abū Dā'ūd, Sulaymān ibn al-Ash'ath al-Sijistānī, *al-Sunan*.

Al-Ālūsī, Maḥmūd ibn 'Abd Allāh al-Ḥusaynī, *Rūḥ al-Ma'ānī*.

Al-Baghawī, 'Abd Allāh ibn Muḥammad Abī al-Qāsim, *Ma'ālim al-Tanzīl*.

Al-Bayhaqī, Abū Bakr Aḥmad ibn al-Ḥusayn ibn 'Alī, *Dalā'il al-Nubūwah*.

———, *al-Sunan al-Kubrā*.

Al-Bazzār, Aḥmad ibn 'Amr ibn 'Abd al-Khāliq, *Musnad*.

Al-Biqā'ī, Burhān al-Dīn Ibrāhīm ibn 'Umar, *Naẓm al-Durar fī Tanāsub al-Āyāt wa al-Suwar*.

Al-Bukhārī, Muḥammad ibn Ismā'īl, *al-Adab al-Mufrad*.

———, *al-Jāmi' al-Ṣaḥīḥ*.

———, *Kitāb al-Ta'rīkh*.

Al-Dārimī, Abū Muḥammad 'Abd Allāh ibn 'Abd al-Raḥmān, *al-Sunan*.

Al-Fattanī, Muḥammad Ṭāhir, *Tadhkirat al-Mawḍū'āt*.

Al-Ḥaṣkafī, Muḥammad 'Alā' al-Dīn, *al-Durr al-Mukhtār*.

Heller, Bernhard, 'Mūsā,' in Martijin Theodoor Houtsma *et al.* eds, *E. J. Brill's First Encyclopaedia of Islam 1913-1936*, Leiden-New York, E. J. Brill, 1987.

The Holy Bible, Revised Standard Edition, New York, 1952.

Ibn 'Abbās, 'Abd Allāh, *Tanwīr al-Miqbās min Tafsīr ibn 'Abbās.*

Ibn Abī Shaybah, 'Abd Allāh, *al-Muṣannaf.*

Ibn al-'Arabī, Abū Bakr, *Aḥkām al-Qur'ān.*

Ibn Ḥanbal, Aḥmad, *Musnad.*

Ibn Hishām, 'Abd al-Malik, *al-Sīrah al-Nabawīyah*, eds. Muṣṭafā al-Saqqā et al., Beirut, Dār Iḥyā' al-Turāth al-'Arabī, n.d.

Ibn Isḥāq, *The Life of Muḥammad*, tr. and notes by A. Guillaume, 6th impression, Karachi, Oxford University Press, 1980.

Ibn Kathīr, Ismā'īl ibn 'Umar, *al-Bidāyah wa al-Nihāyah.*

———, *Tafsīr.*

Ibn Mājah, Muḥammad ibn Yazīd, *al-Sunan.*

Ibn Manẓūr, Mukram, *Lisān al-'Arab.*

Ibn Sa'd, Muḥammad, *al-Ṭabaqāt Al-Kubrā.*

Ibn Taymīyah, Taqī al-Dīn Aḥmad ibn 'Abd al-Ḥalīm, *Kitāb Minhāj al-Sunnah al-Nabawīyah fī Naqd Kalām al-Shī'ah wa al-Qadarīyah*, Būlāq, al-Maṭba'ah al-Kubrā al-Amīrīyah, 1322 AH.

Ingrams, H., *Arabia and the Isles*, London, 1964.

Al-Iṣfahānī, Abū Nu'aym Aḥmad ibn 'Abd Allāh, *Dalā'il al-Nubūwah.*

Al-Jaṣṣāṣ, Aḥmad ibn 'Alī, *Ahkām al-Qur'ān.*

Al-Khaṭṭābī, Ḥamd ibn Muḥammad, *Ma'ālim al-Sunan.*

Kiernan, R. H., *The Unveiling of Arabia*, London, 1937.

Mawdūdī, Sayyid Abul A'lā, *Rasā'il-o Masā'il*, Lahore, Islamic Publications Limited, n.d.

———, *Tafhīmāt* (Urdu), 17th ed., Lahore, Islamic Publications (Pvt.) Ltd., 1995.

Al-Nasā'ī, Aḥmad ibn 'Alī, *al-Sunan.*

———, Aḥmad ibn 'Alī, *al-Sunan al-Kubrā.*

Al-Nīsābūrī, Muslim ibn al-Ḥajjāj, *al-Ṣaḥīḥ*.

Al-Nīsābūrī, Niẓām al-Dīn al-Ḥasan ibn Muḥammad, *Gharā'ib al-Qur'ān wa Raghā'ib al-Furqān*.

Parvaiz, Ghulām Aḥmad, *Niẓām-i Rabūbīyat* Karachi, Idārah-i Ṭulū'-i Islām, 1954.

Philby, H., *The Empty Quarter*, London, 1933.

Al-Qurṭubī, Muḥammad ibn Aḥmad, *al-Jāmi' li Aḥkām al-Qur'ān*.

Al-Rāzī, 'Abd al-Raḥmān ibn Abī Ḥātim, *Tafsīr*.

Al-Rāzī, Muḥammad ibn 'Umar Fakhr al-Dīn, *Mafātīḥ al-Ghayb*.

Al-Ṣan'ānī, 'Abd al-Razzāq ibn Hammām, *al-Muṣannaf*.

Al-Suyūṭī, Jalāl al-Dīn 'Abd al-Raḥmān ibn Abī Bakr, *al-Durr al-Manthūr*.

Al-Ṭabarānī, Sulaymān ibn Aḥmad ibn Ayyūb, *al-Mu'jam al-Kabīr*.

Al-Ṭabarī, Muḥammad ibn Jarīr, *Jāmi' al-Bayān 'an Ta'wīl Āy al-Qur'ān*.

Al-Tirmidhī, Muḥammad ibn 'Īsā, *al-Sunan*.

Al-Yaḥṣubī, al-Qāḍī Abū al-Faḍl 'Iyaḍ, *al-Shifā bi Ta'rīf Ḥuqūq al-Muṣṭafā*.

Al-Zamakhsharī, Maḥmūd ibn Muḥammad ibn Aḥmad, *al-Kashshāf 'an Ḥaqā'iq Ghawāmiḍ al-Tanzīl*.

Al-Nīsābūrī, Muslim ibn al-Ḥajjāj, al-Ṣaḥīḥ.

[illegible] ad-Dīn al-Ḥasan ibn Muḥammad, [illegible]

[illegible]

[illegible]

Al-Qurṭubī, Muḥammad ibn Aḥmad, al-Jāmiʿ li-Aḥkām al-Qurʾān.

Al-Rāzī, ʿAbd al-Raḥmān ibn Abī Ḥātim, [illegible]

[illegible]

Al-Ṣanʿānī, ʿAbd al-Razzāq ibn Hammām, al-Muṣannaf.

Al-Suyūṭī, Jalāl al-Dīn ʿAbd al-Raḥmān ibn Abī Bakr, al-Durr al-Manthūr.

[illegible]

[illegible]

Al-Tirmidhī, Muḥammad ibn ʿĪsā, al-Sunan.

[illegible] al-Qāḍī Abū al-Faḍl [illegible]

Al-Zamakhsharī, Maḥmūd ibn Muḥammad ibn Aḥmad, al-Kashshāf [illegible]

Subject Index

Abbreviated Letters, 7-8

'Ād, 11, 115, 147, 149, 161-4, 233, 353, 355

Afterlife, 102, 128, 160, 168, 172, 179, 188, 197, 223, 254, 305-6, 313, 325, 328, 337, 339

Ammonites, 19

Angels, 41, 44-6, 87, 89, 98-101, 123, 130, 151, 162, 170-2, 178, 194, 200-1, 205-6, 244, 246-8, 257, 259-61, 275-6, 278, 283-4, 292-3, 341

Arabic Qur'ān, 69, 152-3, 181, 203, 249

Arabs, 3, 9, 52, 69, 146, 150, 153, 182, 209, 225, 246, 249-51, 270, 294

'Aṣr, 25-7, 126

Assyrian, 40

Awliyā', 201-2

barakah, 24

bayyināt, 108

Believers, 5, 8, 42, 62, 71, 82, 85, 92-3, 96, 99-101, 110, 113, 124-6, 150-1, 170-3, 177, 182, 189, 198, 205-6, 211-12, 214-15, 221, 230, 232-3, 236-9, 281, 285-6, 299, 302, 315, 321, 324, 345, 352, 358

Bible, 18, 35, 40, 110, 272

Biblical:
- narrative, 19
- passage, 18

Blasphemy, 56, 81, 200, 224

Chastisement, 10, 12, 18, 62, 64, 68, 73, 75, 79-80, 82-3, 87, 100, 115, 121, 123, 143, 163, 167, 169, 181, 187, 213, 220, 224, 228, 238-9, 268, 271, 281, 304, 308-9, 318-19, 343, 352-3, 355, 358, 360

Children of Israel, 124-5, 278, 300, 303-4, 312, 322-3, 345, 346

Christians, 9, 18, 40, 190, 209, 212, 247, 277, 280

Clear Signs, 108, 113, 116, 123, 136, 143, 271, 280, 328

Companions, 17, 49, 85, 93, 99, 121, 125, 148, 150, 167-8, 170-2, 197, 238, 259, 281, 297, 334, 358

Day:
- of Encounter, 104
- of Final Decision, 23, 307
- of Gathering, 203
- of Judgement, 41, 46, 68, 73, 85, 101-2, 105-6, 122, 124, 149, 150, 164-6, 169, 183, 185, 203, 206, 224, 281, 290, 307-8, 329-30, 337, 339
- of Reckoning, 12, 18, 93, 113, 301, 314, 340
- of Resurrection, 46, 62, 68, 72, 79, 83, 85, 101, 180, 190, 239, 290, 323, 329, 340

Deities, 54, 60, 64, 74-5, 78, 81, 85, 102, 119-20, 146, 185, 200, 202, 246, 258, 260, 262-3, 270, 277, 285-6, 289, 295, 315, 326, 340, 356

Devils, 30-1, 33-4, 47, 104, 149, 168, 171, 183

Dhā al-aydi, 13

al-Dhikr, 7, 132, 167

al-Dīn, 17, 27, 52-3, 112, 149, 169, 173, 210, 215

Divine:
- attributes, 24, 248, 258
- decree, 131
- dispensation, 167, 227, 313
- provenance of the Qur'ān, 147
- recompense, 24, 306, 337
- revelation, 203

Divinity, 44, 84, 103, 119-20, 139, 143, 149, 155, 178, 194, 306, 337

Doing good, 222, 325, 327

Error, 5, 43, 50, 60, 67-8, 76, 84, 95, 101, 116-17, 138-9, 141, 153, 155, 168, 183, 185, 187, 197, 203-4, 216, 218-19, 221, 238, 246, 251, 260, 263, 268, 281, 285, 294, 314, 326-7, 331, 336, 339, 342, 359

Establishing faith, 211, 213-15

Evil, 23-4, 35, 38-9, 41, 57-8, 68-9, 71, 79-80, 88, 97, 100-1, 118, 128, 167-8, 171, 173-4, 175, 180, 184, 228, 237, 250, 263, 268-9, 276, 282, 294, 305, 313, 321-2, 324, 327, 335, 350, 356

Evil-doers, 68, 184, 237, 282, 324

Falsehood, 93, 114, 139, 150, 170, 172, 175, 180-1, 202, 207, 213, 218-20, 227, 232, 235, 251-2, 261, 276, 282, 294, 324, 330, 343, 347

Final Judgement, 165

Fire, 23, 42, 45, 60, 63-4, 98, 119, 120-3, 138, 164, 167, 169-80, 204, 213, 252, 259, 299, 308, 332, 352, 359

Ghassāq, 41

God:
- act of creation, 160
- admonition, 67
- assistance, 207
- attribute of forgiveness, 56
- attributes, 161, 258, 284

– bestowal of bounties, 34, 80, 320
– blessings and favour, 124-5
– bounties, 97, 133, 168, 222
– cause, 25, 71, 236
– censure, 21
– chastisement, 12, 68, 80
– commands, 70-1, 82, 293
– creatures, 24, 54, 130, 133, 222, 246, 256
– decision, 207
– decree, 98
– decree of chastiment, 98
– design, 58
– directive, 130
– dispensation, 204
– dominion, 58-9, 185
– enemies, 164
– exhortation, 67
– favours, 29, 38, 59
– forgiveness, 30-1, 34, 155, 228
– glory, 85, 89
– glory and greatness, 85
– grip, 191
– guidance, 74, 95, 150, 207, 232, 238, 243, 313
– help and support, 133, 171, 232
– infinite glory, 86
– mercy, 96, 99, 201, 205, 251, 265, 266, 294, 310, 343
– message, 86, 97, 270, 339
– Messenger(s), 10, 29, 31, 71, 81, 94, 110-11, 113-14, 140, 288-90, 301
– most devout servant, 337, 344-5
– pardon, 13
– plan, 33, 82
– pleasure, 204
– power, 109, 130, 157
– prerogative, 77, 203
– Prophets, 102, 261
– protection, 207
– punishment, 12, 64, 96-7, 144, 184, 201, 213, 224, 230, 248, 268, 270, 324, 343, 355-6
– refuge, 207
– remembrance, 67

- reward, 53, 290
- servant, 70, 81
- Signs, 94, 97, 138, 179, 271, 316, 318, 356
- sonship, 55
- supremacy, 131, 133
- Throne, 11, 99
- unity, 178
- wrath, 101, 201, 230, 269

Godhead, 10, 57, 86, 102, 119, 194, 201, 275, 282, 340

Grand Assembly, 73, 101, 171-2, 330

Gratitude, 16, 59, 255, 312, 321

Guidance, 51, 53, 67, 74, 95, 108, 116, 124-5, 149-50, 152-4, 164, 181-2, 194, 197, 199-200, 202-4, 207, 210, 232, 238, 243, 246, 261-2, 268, 288-9, 294, 300, 313, 318, 320, 324, 327

Ḥadīth, 3, 26, 28, 31-2, 37, 52-3, 58, 132, 147, 243, 293, 333, 348
- *qudsī*, 58

ḥamīm, 107

Heaven and the earth, 159

Heavens, 10, 23, 43-4, 47, 56-7, 74, 77-8, 84-6, 118, 142, 158-61, 190, 194, 200, 208, 229, 241, 244, 246, 248, 252, 257, 283-4, 294, 306, 315, 320, 325, 329, 332, 338-40, 359

Hell, 5, 24, 41-2, 73, 83, 87, 98, 100-1, 121-3, 130, 138-9, 149, 164, 167-8, 246, 282, 309, 319
- Hellfire, 47, 99, 100, 122, 139, 213, 218, 239, 310, 331

Hereafter, 5, 24, 39, 42, 61, 63, 65-6, 68, 78, 94, 101, 103, 117-19, 127-9, 132, 151, 156, 163, 165, 171, 197, 202, 204, 206, 211, 221-3, 232, 234, 236, 244, 256, 267, 269, 281-5, 290, 299-300, 305-6, 311, 313, 319, 324-5, 327-8, 329, 331, 335, 339, 351-2

Hindus, 190

ḥiyal, 37

Hour, the, 76, 128, 137, 186, 220-1, 279-80, 284, 329, 331

Hypocrites, 167, 298

'ibādah, 52

Idolatry, 2, 9, 30, 40, 326, 356

īmān, 50, 82, 243

Inauspicious days, 162, 321

Intercession, 77, 107, 284-5, 319

'Ishā', 32, 126, 357

Islam's enemies, 172

Islamic:
- concept of intercession, 77
- law, 350
- state, 13

Israelite history, 28, 33, 110

Israelites, 18, 20, 110, 302

Jāhilīyah, 74, 82, 202, 220, 233, 261

Jews, 209
- Judaism, 18

Jihād, 25, 31, 225, 255-6, 336

Jinn, 30, 33-4, 58, 87, 104, 130, 146, 149, 167, 169, 284, 333, 336, 351, 355, 358-9

kasb, 68

Keepers of Hell, 123

khayr, 25

kufr, 59, 97
- *kuffār*, 54

Last Day, 46, 102, 106, 184-5, 191, 212-13, 221, 279-80, 298-9

Life to Come, 65

Maghrib, 25, 126

Magians, 9

Makkan unbelievers, 6, 8-10, 12, 43, 50, 74, 91, 93-4, 99, 140-1, 168, 173, 182-4, 220-1, 226-8, 238, 241, 244-5, 269, 279, 288-90, 299, 306, 312, 315, 334, 342, 346

Marriage, 18, 20, 21, 55, 349

Marxism, 157

Messengers, 5, 11-12, 29, 71, 87, 98, 101, 108-9, 123-5, 134, 138, 140, 143, 161-2, 181, 199, 204-5, 209-11, 246, 260, 264, 270, 277, 283, 289, 294, 337, 343-4, 347, 356, 360

Messengership, 211, 263-6, 285, 289, 337

Migration to Abyssinia, 1, 49

Miracles, 109-11, 140-2, 205, 271, 275, 278, 290, 301-2, 344-5

Monotheism, 5, 10, 12, 43-4, 50, 54, 69, 70-2, 94, 112, 117, 129, 133, 155, 160, 170, 177, 179, 194, 197, 200, 211, 311-12, 315, 324, 336

Next Life, 73, 168
- Next World, 107, 120

Oath , 36, 249, 260, 286, 292

Orientalists, 111

Paradise, 24, 40, 41, 73, 88, 100, 119, 122, 171-2, 204-5, 224, 281-2, 308-10, 348, 351

Patience, 12, 22, 50, 70, 125, 167, 175, 177, 312-13, 360

People of the Book, 19, 215

Piety, 70, 189, 255

Polytheism, 9, 40, 50, 54, 69, 74, 84, 101, 129, 155, 178, 197, 201, 223, 242, 247, 260, 263, 295-6, 315, 339, 340

Polytheistic communities, 13

Prayer, 13, 25-7, 34, 60, 92, 100, 126, 129-32, 136, 211-12, 214, 228, 233, 243, 255-7, 272, 288, 298-9, 336, 341, 357

Pride, 34, 94, 117, 126-7, 131, 178, 232, 247, 270, 318, 331, 346, 350, 352

Prophethood, 8, 12, 104, 147, 198, 252, 322, 334

Qur'ān:
- commentators, 17, 20, 25, 30-1, 155, 158, 188, 208, 275, 292, 297, 345
- message, 148-50, 188
- recital, 148

Rajīm, 46

Repentance, 16, 18, 82, 95-6, 144, 167, 227-8

Retribution, 74, 95-6, 98, 108, 184, 262, 268, 277, 297

Reward and punishment, 23

Revelation, 1-2, 11, 44, 49, 51, 91, 95, 104, 126, 128, 145, 148-50, 152, 155, 181, 187, 193-4, 198-200, 203, 205-6, 210, 225, 242-3, 245-6, 250-1, 277-8, 287-8, 292, 300, 311, 315, 333, 336, 338, 340, 342, 345-6, 357

Right way, 14, 16, 64, 74-5, 114, 162, 195, 244, 262, 268-9, 273, 327, 345-6, 357

Righteousness, 24, 62, 183, 281

rīḥ ṣarṣar, 163

rizq, 103

rūḥ, 104

rukū', 17

Saints, 54, 78, 107, 130, 284, 341

sajdah, 16-17, 45, 51, 145, 147, 155, 157-8, 160, 163, 165-7, 170, 179, 188, 190, 193, 245, 249, 316, 338, 345, 348, 355

Scriptures, 117, 125, 211-12, 218, 246-7, 250, 252, 260, 340, 346, 358

shukr, 59

Straight Way, 39, 66, 76, 101, 138, 195, 202-4, 216-18, 238-40, 253, 262-3, 269, 279-80, 294, 312, 331, 345, 347, 356, 358

Sunnah, 27, 66, 78, 270

Supplication, 33-5, 101, 130-2, 187, 200-1, 336, 340, 356

Sustenance, 59, 81, 103, 106, 119, 132, 134-5, 149, 153, 156-9, 186, 194, 263, 265, 294, 317, 322

ṭāghūt, 52, 63-4

Talmud, 30, 110

Thamūd, 11, 115, 147, 149, 161, 164

Torah, 30, 218, 346

Transgressors, 41

Trumpet, 86

Trust, 31, 36, 75, 120, 205, 207-8, 232-3

Unbelief, 8, 38, 58-60, 67, 71, 141, 201, 215, 242, 244, 267, 285, 312, 318, 342, 346

Vicegerency, 18, 205

Walī, 229, 319

Waḥy, 119, 200, 242-3

Wisdom, 14, 23-4, 51, 95, 124, 131, 133, 147, 157, 177, 200, 241, 250-1, 253-4, 280, 284, 288, 290, 293-5, 315-17, 321-2, 325, 338, 343

Woman, 18, 19, 20-1, 309, 345, 349-50

Worship, 3, 9, 39, 40, 50-4, 64, 74, 85, 130-1, 134-6, 215, 223, 246-7, 257-8, 260, 270, 277, 280, 283, 289, 294-5, 326, 331, 335, 341

Wrong-doer(s), 78, 80, 107, 124, 167, 205, 220, 224, 238, 239, 246, 268, 280, 313, 321, 322, 341, 343, 345, 347, 355

yanābī', 65

zakāh, 38, 155, 212, 214, 259

Ẓuhr, 126

Name Index

'Abd Allāh ibn 'Abbās, 2, 7, 16-17, 21, 28, 36, 75, 82, 155, 157, 165, 179, 225, 279, 293, 298, 300, 346, 349, 357
'Abd Allāh ibn 'Amr ibn al-'Āṣ, 92
'Abd Allāh ibn Mas'ūd, 132, 288, 298, 299, 357-8, 359
'Abd Allāh ibn 'Umar, 85, 122, 132, 179, 255, 259, 293, 298
'Abd al-Malik ibn Hishām, 3, 92, 335
'Abd al-Razzāq, 37
Abel Meholah, 40
Abraham, 38, 209-10, 242, 247, 262-3
Abū 'Abd al-Rahmān al-Sulamī, 179
Abū Bakr, 4, 21, 37, 92, 170, 176, 258-9, 293, 297, 326
Abū Bakr al-Jaṣṣās, 21, 36-7, 256, 258-9, 285, 326, 349
Abū al-Dardā', 13
Abū Dā'ūd, 16, 37, 82, 131, 255-6, 258, 348
Abū Ḥanīfah, 16-17, 36, 178, 259, 349
Abū Hurayrah, 31, 85, 131-2, 176, 348
Abū Jahl, 2
Abū Sa'īd al-Khudrī, 16, 132, 165, 299
Abū Sufyān, 2, 146, 288, 298, 370
Abū Ṭālib, 2-4, 9, 334
Abū Yūsuf, 36
Abyssinia, 1, 49, 231
Adam, 5-6, 45-7, 56, 94, 96, 110, 116-17, 149, 170, 188
Africa, 190, 231
Aḥmad ibn Ḥanbal, 2, 16, 27, 37, 85, 122, 131-2, 176, 185, 225, 255-6, 258, 298, 348, 358
'Alī, 27, 147, 165, 170, 179, 225, 256, 258, 297-8, 349
Ālūsī, 49, 78, 91, 112, 303
America, 190
Anas ibn Malik, 52, 131-2, 165, 170, 185
Arabia, 3, 9, 126, 162, 188-9, 215, 229, 257, 299, 305, 353-4
Arabic, 52, 63, 69, 148, 150, 152-3, 181-2, 201, 203, 208, 242, 249-50, 309, 319, 321, 347
Asia, 190
'Āṣ ibn Wā'il, 2
Aswad ibn al-Muṭṭalib, 2

Baghawī, 7
Bayhaqi, 225, 358
al-Bazzār, 165
Bukhārī, 13, 16-17, 31, 82, 85, 92, 122, 132, 167, 185, 225, 230, 233, 243, 298, 336, 346, 348

Ḍaḥḥāk, 7, 155, 225, 279, 293, 298, 346
David, 5, 12-22, 24, 29, 33-4
Dhū al-Kifl, 40

Egypt, 109, 112-13, 116, 122, 213, 248, 272, 274-5, 301-3, 371
Elijah, 40
Elisha, 40
Europe, 190

Fāṭimah, 225

Gabriel, 243, 293, 335
Goliath, 13

al-Ḥākim, 293
Hāmān, 109, 117-18
Ḥamzah, 145
Ḥasan al-Baṣrī, 22, 155, 167, 179, 225, 279, 293, 303, 346, 357
Heller, Bernhard, 111

Iblīs, 6, 45-7
Ibn 'Asākīr, 36
Ibn 'Aṭīyah, 163
Ibn Abī Ḥātim, 2-3, 75, 92, 131, 165, 298-9
Ibn Abī Shaybah, 2-3
Ibn al-'Arabī, 21, 293
Ibn Jarīr al-Ṭabarī, 82, 85, 165, 298-9, 326, 346
Ibn al-Jawzī, 27
Ibn al-Sā'ib, 155
Ibn Jubayr, 16, 21, 225, 279, 293, 357
Ibn Kathīr, 3, 82, 147, 293, 310, 346, 349
Ibn Mājah, 37, 85, 131-2, 348
Ibn Sa'd, 1, 4, 37, 225
Ibn Sīrīn, 179, 346
Ibn Taymīyah, 27
Ibn Zayd, 82, 91, 157, 225, 293, 346
Ibrāhīm al-Nakha'ī, 179, 298
'Ikrimah, 16, 155, 225, 279, 293, 346, 357
India, 190
Iraq, 9
Isaac, 39
Ishmael, 40, 213, 247, 263

Ja'far ibn Abī Ṭālib, 49
Jābir ibn 'Abd Allāh, 131, 147
Jābir ibn Zayd, 91
Jerusalem, 28, 33
Job, 34-8, 149
Jordan, 40
Joseph, 116, 213, 242, 287, 298, 302

Khadījah, 226, 334
Khaṭṭābī, 16, 17

Madīnah, 219, 345, 358, 359
Makkah, 1, 3-5, 11, 28, 49, 53, 81, 92, 124, 179, 193, 199, 203, 220, 225, 230, 248, 264, 269, 288-9, 299, 333, 344, 346, 355, 357-9
Mālik, 3, 52, 92, 132, 145, 170, 179, 185, 225, 279, 282, 293, 299, 335, 346
Mary, 247, 277, 279, 299
Masrūq, 21, 179, 297-8, 346
Moses, 20, 93, 108, 109, 110-14, 116, 118, 121, 124-5, 127, 162, 182-3, 209-10, 218, 242, 248, 270-6, 300-2, 346-7, 358
Mu'ādh ibn Jabal, 132
Muḥammad 'Alā' al-Dīn al-Ḥaṣkafī, 17
Muḥammad ibn al-Ḥasan, 36
Muḥammad ibn Isḥāq, 2, 145
Muḥammad ibn Ka'b al-Quraẓī, 145
Muḥammad Ṭāhir ibn 'Alī al-Hindī al-Fattanī, 27
Mujāhid, 16, 36, 82, 155, 225, 293, 298, 346, 357
Abū al-Mūsā Ash'arī, 165

Nasā'ī, 2, 16, 37, 85, 92, 131, 165, 170, 185, 255-7, 298, 336, 346
Naṣr ibn Aḥmad, 105
Nathan, 19
Nīsāpūr, 4, 22, 105
Nu'mān ibn Bashīr, 131

Palestine, 33, 40
Parvaiz, Ghulām Aḥmad, 157
Persia, 9, 182, 229
Pharaoh, 11, 91-3, 109-15, 117-18, 120-2, 124-5, 162, 248, 270-5, 290, 300-4, 306
Pharaoh's community, 92, 113-14, 117
Pharaoh's design, 111
Pharaoh's threat, 113
Prophet Hūd, 353
Prophet Muḥammad (peace be on him), 6, 8, 16, 22, 32, 47, 81, 93-4,

112-13, 124-5, 127, 148, 196-7, 199, 200, 209-10, 214, 219, 226, 247, 249-50, 256, 270, 275, 280, 292, 336, 357
Prophet Muḥammad's detractors, 22
Prophet Muḥammad's Ascension, 27-8
Prophet Muḥammad's Companions, 99, 238
Prophet Muḥammad's mission, 1-2, 4, 94, 168, 194, 251, 333
Prophet Job's story, 38
Prophet Moses's story, 108-9
Prophet Jesus, son of Mary, 247, 277, 279
Prophet Noah, 209
Prophet Solomon's supplication, 34

Al-Qāḍī Abū al-Faḍl 'Iyāḍ al-Yaḥṣubī, 27-8
Qatādah, 82, 155, 157, 179, 279, 293, 298, 303, 346
Quraysh, 1-5, 47, 52, 94, 124, 127, 145-7, 193-4, 225-6, 229, 232, 246, 251-2, 263, 266, 270, 275, 283, 287, 290, 298, 304, 306, 334, 347, 352, 353, 355
Qurṭubī, 21, 25, 27, 30, 179, 279, 298

Rāzī, 1, 4, 16, 31-2, 34, 145, 158-9, 308
Rehoboam, 33

Sa'īd ibn Jubayr, 16, 21, 225, 279, 293, 357
Sa'īd ibn al-Musayyab, 179
Sa'īd ibn Sa'd ibn 'Ubādah, 37
Salmān al-Fārsī, 131
Samaria, 40
Satan, 5, 35, 44, 46-7, 52, 151, 175-6, 267-8, 280
Sha'bī, 346
Shāfi'ī, 16-17, 36, 179
Shaybah, 2-3
Sinai Peninsula, 40
Solomon, 5, 18, 20-1, 24-34
Spain, 190
Suddī, 155, 157, 225, 279
Syria, 40

al-Ṭabarānī, 37, 225, 299
Ṭabarī, 2-3, 21, 82, 85, 131, 155, 157, 165, 167, 170, 188, 190, 208, 225, 256, 279, 288, 293, 298-300, 321, 326, 346, 349, 353, 357-9
Ṭirmidhī, 2, 16, 82, 131-2, 225, 255-6, 258, 298, 348, 358

'Umar, 1, 4, 85, 122, 132, 145, 159, 170, 179, 185, 255, 259, 293, 298
'Umar's acceptance of Islam, 1, 4, 145
Umayyah ibn Khalaf, 2
'Uqbah ibn Abī Mu'ayṭ, 2, 92
Uriah, 18-2
'Utbah ibn Rabī'ah, 2, 145-7, 264
'Uthmān, 170, 293, 349
'Uzzā, 81

Al-Yasa', 40
Yazīd al-Raqqāshī, 53
Yemen, 353

Zamakhsharī, 1, 4, 21, 31, 170, 274, 277, 286, 292, 321-2, 326
Zayd Ibn Ḥārithah, 293
Zufar, 36